CONNECTIONS

Second Edition
New Order and Content

a combined reader and rhetoric

Kerry L. Beckford

Donald C. Jones

D1412463

Kendall Hunt
publishing company

Cover image © Shutterstock, Inc.

www.kendallhunt.com
Send all inquiries to:
4050 Westmark Drive
Dubuque, IA 52004-1840

Copyright © 2015, 2017 by Kendall Hunt Publishing Company

PAK ISBN: 978-1-5249-3674-7

Text Alone ISBN: 978-1-5249-4313-4

All rights reserved. No part of this publication may be reproduced,
stored in a retrieval system, or transmitted, in any form or by any means,
electronic, mechanical, photocopying, recording, or otherwise,
without the prior written permission of the copyright owner.

Printed in the United States of America

TABLE OF CONTENTS

Thematic Chapters

PREFACE FOR INSTRUCTORS

The goals of this textbook are ambitious. This textbook aims to teach students to read insightfully, think critically, and write analytically about their cultures and themselves. To fulfill these goals, this book includes five instructional chapters and five thematic chapters. The thematic chapters involve students in challenging, yet accessible topics, but this textbook does not just expect students to comprehend the thematic chapters. Instead, the instructional chapters teach them how to engage with texts and write in response to readings so that more students will be able to fulfill these ambitious goals.

This combination of a rhetoric and a reader encourages students to make many connections. Students are encouraged to connect their current literacy skills to the best practices of reading and writing. They are urged to apply their new understanding of the reading process to their work in the thematic chapters. Students also are encouraged to connect the lessons on the writing process with their efforts on the short, post-reading questions and the longer, final assignments of the thematic chapters. There are many other connections for students to make, such as between the rhetorical instruction and their own developing arguments. In other words, the textbook's title was chosen with great care.

The instructional chapters teach college-level literacy explicitly. Each chapter begins by asking students to consider what they already know about reading, writing, rhetoric, or research. Then, as students engage in each chapter's instruction and application, they will expand their knowledge of these literacies. They are not taught that there is one "right" way to read or write; instead, students learn that they should vary these literacy processes to meet specific goals.

The thematic chapters promote the sustained inquiry of compelling issues. The themes range from family and race to energy and education. Each chapter presents students with diverse perspectives, represented by compelling written and visual texts. This array of perspectives invites students to render, explore, and analyze their thoughts, feelings, and beliefs on compelling issues.

The second edition maintains many other strengths of this textbook. For example, **the explicit instruction of critical thinking and writing conventions demystifies academic inquiry**. Three common forms of critical thinking are presented: the analysis of multiple perspectives, cultural influences, and historical trends. Some post-reading questions in the thematic chapters explicitly ask student to engage in these forms of critical thinking. Students also learn how and why they should follow such conventions as quoting and citing so they understand not only what to say about a text but also how to assert their insights.

NEW TO THE SECOND EDITION: A new strength of this edition is **the streamlined order**. The textbook has been reduced to five instructional and five thematic chapters. The first instructional chapter includes thematic content of literacy and technology that will both appeal to students and provide sample texts for new reading practices. However, as explained below, instructors can determine the sequencing of the instructional content and the thematic topics.

Another new strength is the **greater emphasis on application and transfer**. In Chapter 1, students are asked to read several texts on one theme as well as to consider their reading strategies for an array of cross-curricular readings that are drawn from Art History, Health Professions, Politics, and Literature.

Again, in Chapter 2, students are asked to analyze writing assignments from varied disciplines, such as Math, Psychology, and Education. Thus, students are trained to transfer knowledge from their first-year writing instruction to other college courses. In each thematic chapter, the second option of the final assignment asks student to apply their knowledge of rhetoric from Chapter 5 to one of the main readings. Thus, rhetorical analysis is practiced as well as taught.

More emphasis also is placed on source synthesis. The thematic chapters not only offer links to several other, related readings, but also new connections to relevant readings in other chapters have been added. The ability to synthesize various texts is crucial to students' college success.

The new thematic chapter on race and identity will stir student responses on important issues. The new Chapter 8 examines race and identity using an array of texts by Latino, Asian American, Native American, and African American writers and others of diverse ethnic and racial heritages. This chapter encourages students to explore, complicate, and refine their understandings of themselves and others.

These new strengths augment the central concept of this textbook: College-level reading and writing are demanding and multifaceted. However, with explicit instruction and repeated application, many students will be able to excel and even enjoy advanced literacy.

Instructional Chapters

The instructional chapters address the demands of college-level literacy. The subjects of these chapters include:

1. The Reading Process and Text Analysis
2. The Writing Process and Assignment Analysis
3. Process in Practice: Personal Narratives
4. Academic Honesty and Research Essays
5. Argument and Rhetoric

Each of the thematic chapters includes direct references to Chapters 1–5 so students are taught how to excel on the reading and writing tasks assigned. Thus, students will experience this textbook as an integrated whole; they will be able to connect the instructional chapters to the thematic content.

Reading Process: Students will learn many strategies of advanced literacy. Most college writing assignments depend on strong reading comprehension. This chapter includes revealing questions about student memories of learning to read and their most recent reading instruction. These memories will arouse the students' curiosity and prepare them to assess their current reading habits. Students then learn to engage in such active reading strategies as highlighting, annotating, and double-entry notes. These strategies will make students confident that they can analyze texts insightfully.

Writing Process: Students will learn *how* **to write well.** The writing process movement of Peter Elbow, Janet Emig, Donald Murray, and others is four decades old, but many students still have not learned its fundamental lesson of using a gradual, multifaceted method of writing. This chapter teaches students to engage in the invention, or prewriting, of ideas and phrases as an initial activity that precedes the drafting of a difficult text. This chapter also emphasizes the later parts of the writing process by treating revising and editing as two distinct and equally important steps. Students also will learn to vary their process according to their analysis of diverse writing assignments.

One problem at the start of the writing process movement was the excessive shift from a product orientation to a focus on process. Students, however, need to learn about the ends as well as the means of writing. They must consider the different conventions of various kinds of writing as well as why they sometimes differ. For instance, students are asked to consider why the first person is used in most narratives but rarely employed in a lab report. There are good reasons for these different conventions so students will be encouraged to consider this discursive variation.

Academic Honesty and Research Essays: Students are taught to appreciate the reasons for citation as well as the various forms of documentation. Rather than present rules, this chapter frames this issue as one of convention, a matter of accepted practices. Various kinds of plagiarism are explained, and the debates over intellectual property and paper mill purchases are presented. Using the concepts of communal dependence and individual assertion, the conventions of paraphrase, quotation, attribution, citation, and elaboration are explained further.

The research essay is presented as a synthesis of other reading and writing activities, not as an entirely separate and sometimes dreaded assignment. Through references to academic honesty and other instructional chapters, students are taught, for example, to read their research sources critically and to advance an argument persuasively. Students will learn to combine previous instruction and engage in a full range of research activities.

Argument and Rhetoric: Students will learn to appreciate and expand their persuasive powers. Starting with familiar examples, such as arguing over a weekend curfew, students will learn that rhetoric involves, as Aristotle stated, the discovery of the available means of persuasion. This chapter teaches students to recognize and employ the key concepts of rhetoric, such as the rhetorical triangle and the three rhetorical appeals. It also includes more contemporary concepts, such as Kenneth Burke's notion of identification, and these terms are taught through application to engaging examples.

The instructional chapters teach much more than "basic" skills. Each chapter relies on familiar examples and public issues to explain key concepts. These concepts are highlighted with bold lettering and are presented in a list for review at the end of each chapter. Every chapter also refers to several theorists so students learn that the academic study of reading, writing, and rhetoric has a long and rich tradition. As students become more capable readers, writers, and rhetoricians, they will be joining academic disciplines that date back to ancient Greece and are as current as today's bloggers.

The instructional chapters engage students in the construction of knowledge. Rather than talk *at* students, each chapter talks *with* students to scaffold their current knowledge into greater understanding. Addressing students as "you," these dialogic chapters make sophisticated concepts, theorists, and practices accessible to their intended audience. Knowledge, as John Dewey asserted, is not a brick; it cannot be handed to students. Genuine knowledge instead must be developed by learners engaged in instruction, application, and reflection, carefully guided by their teachers.

Thematic Chapters

The topics of the thematic chapters are diverse, engaging, and related. They include

1. Family Forms and Roles
2. Education and Outcomes
3. Race and Identity

4. Energy and Sustainability

5. Literacy and Technology

These chapters progress from concerns familiar to most students, like family and education, to other, more abstract ones, such as energy use and computer technologies. The later chapters will enhance student awareness of these seemingly less immediate but still pressing concerns.

Every thematic chapter has the same key features:

- **An engaging introduction**
- **A first freewrite on the students' initial beliefs**
- **A series of six historical and contemporary readings**
- **A headnote for each reading**
- **A set of eight post-reading questions**
- **Two visuals**
- **Two more freewriting possibilities**
- **Three final writing assignment sequences**
- **Additional reading suggestions**

The introduction and first freewrite of each chapter are designed to arouse student interest. The introduction can be used to promote an engaging class discussion of the two primary topics of each chapter. The twofold nature of each chapter means that they can be used in various ways; for example, in Chapter 6, students can focus on the legally accepted forms of American families today or the traditional roles of parents in these groups. The first freewrite is designed to elicit the initial beliefs of students on the chapter topic. These assumptions are not dismissed as derivative cultural reproductions or fixed as unalterable individual positions. Instead, they are treated as the starting points to be enriched, complicated, contradicted, and affirmed by the readings and the activities of each chapter.

The readings include historical, contemporary, and visual texts. The historical readings present other perspectives and help students gain some critical distance on their own viewpoints. The contemporary readings present multiple perspectives and immerse students in some of the ongoing debates of modern society. The visual texts reinforce the comprehension, analysis, and interpretation of the print texts in each chapter. These readings also range from literature and history to sociology and journalism so that students will encounter many of the texts they will be asked to read across the curriculum.

The headnotes and post-reading questions suggest interesting approaches to each reading selection. The headnotes include information about the author and the text's original publication so students can read rhetorically by considering speaker, audience, and message. The post-reading questions offer an array of approaches to each text. As explained in the first two chapters, the post-reading questions in every subsequent chapter progress from **Close Reading** questions to **Analytical Writing/Discussion** queries and then on to **Further Options**, which often suggest connections with other readings in the same or another chapter.

The post-reading questions teach college-level critical thinking. For each text, specific post-reading questions are identified as involving the analysis of multiple perspectives, cultural influences, and historical trends. Through this explicit instruction of critical thinking and its repeated practice, no student will be left behind to sink; instead, all are taught how to swim along the currents of academic inquiry.

The activities in each chapter can be used in various ways. For example, one instructor could use some of the **freewriting possibilities** to enrich the thematic exploration. These freewrites, however, are placed in the middle and at the end of each chapter so another professor could skip over them to create a quicker unit using several readings and a compelling visual or two. Again with the **post-reading questions**, an instructor could assign only one or two to discuss a text briefly, whereas another teacher could use several to create a pre-reading discussion, more thorough textual analysis, and a post-reading writing assignment.

Every thematic chapter ends with three final assignment sequences. There are two questions that require source synthesis to explore a problem or argue for a solution, and another question asks students to analyze the rhetoric of one or more readings. For example, a student can write about educational problems in Chapter 7, analyze the rhetoric of two readings on race in Chapter 8, or argue for a solution on energy in Chapter 9. The final assignments ask students to assert their now more informed opinions, and they are taught to develop their essays gradually. This process-oriented approach will enable more students to excel on their final essays.

Each chapter ends with the suggestion of additional readings. Both the instructional and the thematic chapters end with links to further readings online. These texts will enrich student understanding. The thematic chapters also end with the suggestion of several related readings found in other chapters. The additional readings can help students develop the depth of knowledge so they can write well.

Curriculum Design

As stated above, professors can determine the sequencing of the instructional content and the thematic topic(s). Some may start with an appealing thematic chapter, and others may combine that thematic content with Chapter 1 on reading. Some instructors may decide to begin with the writing process and personal narratives on specific subjects to lead into a thematic chapter.

A one-semester writing course can be devoted to one topic. Students can be asked to focus on one thematic chapter supplemented by the related readings in other chapters and the suggested reading links found at the chapter's end. This focus on one main topic would prepare students for the concentrated study in upper-level courses.

Another design twould be to link two of the thematic chapters in a one-semester course. Some chapters can be connected, such as when students examine family in Chapter 6, they can link Frederick Douglass' narrative to Chapter 8 on race. Or the effects of computers on literacy in Chapter 10 can be connected to Chapter 7 on education. These connections are encouraged by the related readings suggested from other chapters.

A sequence of two required writing courses can extend students' examination of a thematic topic. For example, in the first course, students can complete a final assignment on the nature of a problem, such as for education or energy in Chapters 7 and 9. Then, in a second course, their instruction can involve further reading on the theme plus Chapter 5 on rhetoric and Chapter 4 on research essays. The primary tasks of the second course can be a literature review and a research essay that makes an explicit argument for a specific solution. With this depth of knowledge, students will be more able to write well.

The instructional chapters can be tailored to meet the needs of a class or a particular subset of students. A professor can select from the five chapters to provide the most appropriate instruction for large or small groups of students. This tailoring of instruction can continue within these chapters because headings divide each one into several discrete segments. Then specific instruction, for example, on active reading strategies or invention methods can be provided from Chapters 1 and 2. Or, more advanced students can learn to evaluate online sources or employ the rhetorical appeals from Chapters 4 and 5.

Acknowledgments

We want to thank Kathy McCormick, Sherry Horton, Charles Lipka, and other colleagues who helped develop some of the central concepts of this textbook. We also are indebted to Donna L. Coffey, Michelle Huston, Kerri Provost, Sue Aliberti, Peter Elbow, Beth Richards, and Sally Terrell who supported our efforts and provided invaluable feedback. We benefited from the generous support of Angela Lampe, Sara McGovern, and Amanda Smith of Kendall Hunt.

Kerry L. Beckford
Tunxis Community College
Assistant Professor, English
M.F.A. Pine Manor College
Creative Nonfiction

Donald C. Jones
University of Hartford
Associate Professor, English
Ph.D. University of New Hampshire
Rhetoric and Writing

NOTE TO STUDENTS

This textbook is designed to build upon the many language and literacy skills you already have developed in school and at home. These abilities will vary among you and your classmates. Some students may be confident and capable readers and writers, in part, because the language practices in their homes approximate the academic discourses of college study. Other students may be less confident readers or writers, but they already are very adept at critical thinking. Still other students may have the rich linguistic skills of speaking another language and a heightened awareness of cultural differences. All of these diverse resources create a rich foundation for the students in a college writing course to continue their development. Using this textbook, you can develop further your critical reading, writing, and thinking skills—the abilities upon which so much of college success depends.

This textbook offers you both high expectations and clear explanations. Drawing upon your current knowledge and personal experiences, you will be expected to read challenging texts, write convincingly in various forms, and think critically about issues that are relevant to both your life and your studies. If you take a look at the table of contents, you will find that the themes of the reading chapters range from family, education, and race to sustainable energy and digital literacy.

The thematic chapters will immerse you in contemporary discussions of compelling topics. You will be invited to explore your initial opinion because each chapter begins with an engaging introduction and a first writing activity. Then the main readings will encourage you to expand, enrich, complicate, and even contradict your first thoughts and feelings. After each reading selection, you will find a set of questions that progress from close reading to analytical writing/discussion and on to further options. This progression is designed to elicit increasingly complex responses from you and your classmates. By reading some of the text selections and answering some of their post-reading questions, you will develop a more informed perspective.

At the end of each chapter, each final assignment sequence asks you to assert your deeper understanding insightfully and persuasively. However, as the word "sequence" suggests, you will be taught how to develop this final paper gradually. In other words, you will not be left in a sink-or-swim situation; instead, you will learn how to follow the currents of academic reading, writing, and thinking.

The final assignment sequences are just one of the many explanations provided so you will be able to fulfill the high expectations of this textbook. With the connections made from the thematic chapters to the instructional ones, you will learn how to excel at college-level literacies.

The five instructional chapters will teach you how to read critically, write insightfully, argue persuasively, cite properly, and much more. Each of these instructional chapters is divided into shorter segments with headings so you and your professor can tailor the use of this helpful information for your greatest benefit. The key concepts of each chapter are marked in bold and then listed at the end so you can review them. These chapters also refer to some of the key theorists because we want to show that you are becoming a member of an academic discipline as old as the study of rhetoric in ancient Greece and as current as the writing of today's bloggers.

Like this note, the instructional chapters defy the usual prohibition against addressing the reader as "you." The second-person pronoun is used so *you* will be engaged in a dialogue about reading or research, drawing upon your current beliefs on how to read closely or research effectively. These chapters are designed to talk *with* you rather than *at* you.

You are reading the final copy of many drafts, and this book is the result of our work with literally hundreds of students. Although we can't quote or acknowledge every one, we want to thank the countless students who have contributed to our teaching and to this effort. We hope you will enjoy using this textbook.

Kerry L. Beckford,
Tunxis Community College

Donald C. Jones,
University of Hartford

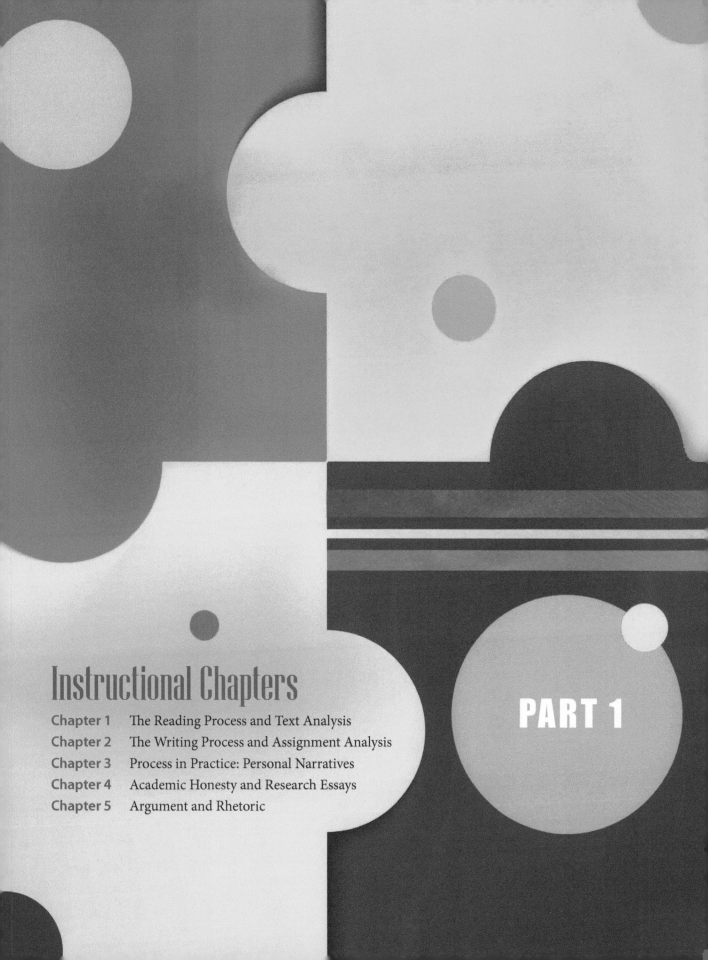

Instructional Chapters

PART 1

The Reading Process and Text Analysis

CHAPTER 1

If you have started to read this textbook, you are a capable reader. As a successful student, you can read many kinds of texts and for many different purposes. If you are like many of our students, each day you read such diverse texts as campus signs (Smith Hall), text messages (c u l8ter?), Facebook updates (studying 2nite), website info (Registration Schedule), textbook chapters *(Principles of Macroeconomics),* and literary texts *(The House on Mango Street).* If we pause to consider the sweep of history, we can add that two or three centuries ago, you would have been considered to be literate as long as you could recall a familiar text and write your name (see p. 17 on literacy standards across history).

Now, as we decipher many texts every day, we also read for different purposes. Although there may be as many reasons for reading as there are volumes in your college library, these purposes can be reduced to a few broad categories:

- Reading for **information/knowledge**
- Reading for **action/application**
- Reading for **analysis/interpretation**
- Reading for **enjoyment/pleasure**

Whether it's reading a campus sign or a favorite website, you probably never stop to consider how you read for information or enjoyment, you just do it. Sometimes, however, it is important to consider the process of reading. The easy process of reading a sign or a text message distinguishes this informational reading from the more challenging process of analyzing an academic text. We won't deny that analysis often requires more effort, and let us stress, more *deliberate* effort. Reading a textbook chapter to learn how to solve a problem (action) or reading a novel to analyze a character's motives (interpretation) makes us work harder and proceed more slowly. For most of us, harder and slower means less enjoyment. When you turn to these more difficult kinds of reading, you probably alter your process. You don't expect to comprehend quickly; instead you work harder by taking mental or written notes. If this effort becomes too hard and the pace too slow, our reading may bog down and then we later may claim, "I read it, but I don't remember much." Unfortunately, this claim usually leads to classroom frustration and perhaps course failure. Thus, examining how to read college-level texts will be crucial to your academic success.

Most professors believe that college students *should* be able to understand and interpret assigned readings. Yet, the very use of *should* reveals that not every student *can* fulfill these expectations. The purpose of this chapter is to help you close this gap between the ideal (*should*) and the actual (*can*). To make this chapter easier for you and your professor to use, we have added headings to create smaller sections. We will offer you many strategies, but we don't expect your reading process always will include each one. Instead, you will have to determine when a strategy will help you fulfill your purpose. By the end of this chapter, we want you to believe, if you do not already, that you are a capable reader, someone who can not only comprehend difficult texts but also can enjoy reading them.

Memories and Goals

Rather than start by telling you how you *should* be reading, let's consider how you actually read various texts. Please answer the following questions through writing and/or discussion:

- What is one of your most vivid memories of reading?
- What is one of your most memorable recollections of reading instruction?

Our own responses to the first question include a grade school book about a boy's adventures riding his horse out west and the comfort of reading a novel in a warm bed on a Saturday morning. You too may recall a favorite book or place to read. Or perhaps, you remember your sense of accomplishment when you could transform the marks on the page into spoken words and later when you were able to finish a long book, such as a Harry Potter novel. Most students have more difficulty answering the second question about reading instruction. They try to recall a reading lesson from elementary school.

The memorable responses to the first question and the vague recollections to the second reveal a problematic concept of reading itself. When students believe that they have not been taught to read since grade school, this belief suggests that reading only involves decoding letters like C-A-T and recognizing words like "cat." These skills, which are known as phonetic reading and sight reading, are two crucial lessons of early literacy instruction, but by high school and college, reading consists of much more than **letter decoding** and **word recognition**. What else do you think college students are expected to do when they are asked to read a textbook or a novel? What do you think we expect as you are reading this page?

- Decoding letters (**phonetic reading**)
- Recognizing words (**sight reading**)
- _____
- _____
- _____
- _____ ?

You may have used some slightly different phrases to assert some of the additional aspects of reading listed below, but it is important that you understand this list and can distinguish what is usually termed "basic" or "functional" literacy from "advanced" or "critical" literacy.

Functional Literacy	Advanced Literacy
Decoding letters	Comprehending meaning
Recognizing words	Applying information
	Interpreting ideas
	Analyzing an argument
	Connecting to other texts (synthesis)

To advance from basic literacy to critical literacy, a reader has to do more than decode letters and recognize words. The next step, as per a reading theorist named Louise Rosenblatt, is to learn to how to "perform" a text. Rosenblatt compares a text to a musical score:

> In the teaching of [reading], we are basically helping out students learn to perform in response to a text. In this respect we are perhaps closer to the [music] teacher . . . than we are to the teacher of history or botany. The reader [learns to] perform the poem or novel, as the violinist performs the sonata.

Let us stress that this performance will involve much more than decoding or even basic comprehension. When you are assigned a difficult, nonfiction text, such as a nonliterary essay or a textbook chapter, your professor probably will expect you to identify the main idea(s) and many supporting details. You may be able to identify the main idea quickly if the text has an explicit thesis statement. Or, you may have to work from some of the supporting details in order to determine what is the main idea. Beyond this summary, you probably will be expected to analyze a pattern in the reading, to interpret the significance of an implication, to connect one reading with another, and/or to apply some principles to a particular example. For more on tasks like summary, analysis, and synthesis, see pp. 34–37 in Chapter 2. You also may be asked to consider the intended effect on the reader (which is related to the main idea) or the writer's attitude to the topic (which is related to the supporting details and the author's phrasing). For more the relationship between a writer and the audience, see Chapter 5 on Rhetoric.

A Crucial Assumption

As explained below, there are many strategies for advanced literacy, but let us stress now they all depend on your assumptions about the process of reading. One of our students named Frank once summed up a problematic assumption about reading when he declared,

> I must not be a very good reader; I don't get the meaning all at once.

Frank did not lack the intelligence to read well; instead his assumption that reading involves **immediate and complete comprehension** prevented him from succeeding with difficult texts. Have you ever felt like Frank? What doesn't he understand about reading?

If we disagree with Frank and deny that reading always involves instantaneous, "all at once" comprehension, reading becomes a **gradual construction of meaning**. We can demonstrate this slower process by asking you to read a short article, which is related to Chapter 10 on literacy and technology. This reading describes young adults who have decided to live without computers and the Internet, and it originally was published as a newspaper article (*Boston Globe*, April 25, 2009).

YOUNG AND UNPLUGGED: DIGITAL NATIVES IN RETREAT

by Bella English

There's a television in Cara and Alan Kalf's Arlington living room, but it's stashed in a corner, its screen turned resolutely to the wall. It's used only for the occasional DVD—or as a favorite perch for the family cat.

As for music, the couple listens to record albums—remember those?—on a turntable or on one of the old jukeboxes Alan has restored. There's no Internet connection in the household. Cara has an iPod she uses only when traveling. She also has a cellphone: "But I don't always answer it. Sometimes I leave it in my coat pocket. I forget about it."

The couple aren't elderly Luddites terrified by technology. She's 27; he's 31. They are members of a small cohort: the young and unplugged. While their friends, relatives, and colleagues have every gadget known to mankind, the Kalfs have made a conscious decision not to blog, tweet, or instant message. They e-mail only when necessary. And they say they're better off without all that stuff.

According to the Pew Research Center's Internet & American Life Project, 96 percent of adults who work use the Internet, e-mail, or have a cellphone. Of workers and nonworkers alike, only 14 percent are "off the grid," with no online access or cellphone, and they tend to be older, low-income women. Nearly 40 percent of Americans use wireless mobile devices such as BlackBerrys. Almost a quarter of Americans use social networking sites such as Facebook.

Dr. Peter Whybrow, head of the Department of Psychiatric and Biobehavioral Sciences at UCLA's School of Medicine, says the preoccupation with high-tech tools is understandable. "By nature we are curious creatures and we love trinkets and novelties," he says. But the fast pace of technology has created a glut of gadgets—and a slight backlash.

"A small group of people are reacting to what is overload," Whybrow says. "They are fascinated by this initially… but after a while, they find it erodes time as opposed to saving time, and time is the only thing we've really got that is our own. If you become consumed by new technology and forget you are fundamentally creatures of the natural world, you do end up diminishing your life."

The Kalfs would agree with that. "We make it difficult for ourselves to access the Internet so we don't spend time just hanging out on it," says Cara, who teaches eighth-graders in Stoneham. Instead, they have more time for reading, for hobbies—and for each other.

"Worshiping at the church of the pixel comes at the expense of real-life experience," says Alan, who teaches biology at Lexington Christian Academy. His students are aghast at the fact that he doesn't watch TV. But by limiting their use of technology, they have freed up time for activities they love. She works on craft projects. He restores old jukeboxes, pinball machines, and furniture.

Not having Internet access can be inconvenient, but if they feel an urgent need for a computer, they go to her parents' house. They don't miss the sensory overload they had when they watched television and spent more time online. "It's not that I don't like doing these things," Alan says. "It's that I like them

From The Boston Globe, April 25, 2009, © 2009 Boston Media Partners. All rights reserved. Used by permission and protected by the Copyright Laws of the United States. The printing, copying, redistribution, or retransmission of this Content without express written permission is prohibited.

too much, and have a hard time setting limits. And then I feel frustrated at the end of the evening when I haven't accomplished or learned anything."

Instead, the couple listens to music and radio shows. They read a lot. They're involved in church activities. They cook from scratch and have friends over for dinner. They love board games. They play music: Cara the guitar, Alan piano, organ, and Dobro.

The Kalfs realize that few people their age limit their use of high-tech gadgets. "Sometimes friends think it's weird," Cara says. She recently told her brother-in-law that she was sure there were others like her and her husband. "Yeah, the Amish," he replied.

But there are a few others, and they're closer than Pennsylvania Dutch country. Anna Raassina and Stephen Seaward of Brookline have neither a television nor a microwave. Both 23, they gave up Facebook a couple of years ago. They don't IM. Because they're in college—senior philosophy majors at UMass-Boston—they must have computers, but once they finish, they plan to pack them away.

"I feel a little bit like a prisoner to it," Seaward says. "It's very useful—there's no denying that—but I think we also lose something. The more things become fast-paced, the less able we are to understand complex arguments, to concentrate on long artworks, like a symphony, or read a long novel."

As a demographic group, the couple would be considered "digital natives," or those in their mid-teens to mid-20s who have grown up in a highly technical, online world of video games, text messaging, websites, and social networking. But Seaward says his mother limited the time he spent using the Internet, watching television, and playing video games.

"I'm not a Luddite," he says. "I don't go off into the woods somewhere. I know how to do all this stuff." He had an iPod, but after it went through the washing machine in his pants pocket, he didn't replace it. He doesn't have a car; he takes the T. There's no microwave, he says, because "it doesn't do anything that my stove or oven don't do."

Rebecca Norman, 22, lives in an apartment with two other seniors at UMass-Amherst. They have no television. Norman sends texts only if it's urgent. She tried Facebook briefly but opted out. "I find the whole thing very voyeuristic," says Norman, who grew up in Newton. Instead, she writes letters—on stationery she makes—and uses the telephone to keep in touch. E-mail is reserved for academic or job-related missives.

Her friends wonder why she's not on Facebook. "They think I'm just trying to be a contrarian," she says, "but I tell them I'm not trying to make a statement. I just prefer not to have it in my life." She says she'd rather spend her spare time reading and working on art projects. Even her middle-age mother and her 80-year-old grandfather are on Facebook, as are her two sisters. But there's one advantage to not having it, she says: "My sisters have had to deal with whether or not to friend our mom."

Here's a sample of a student's messy, gradual construction of meaning from this article:

> *Ok, what am I supposed to be reading? It's a newspaper article so it shouldn't be too hard. It's about living without the Internet at home. Cara and Alan Kalf sound a little crazy to me. Especially when it says that 96% of American adults use the Internet, email, or cell phones. I wonder what percent of that number use computers at home as well as at work or school? It is true that Mom says she feels trapped by having to read work emails at home. Sometimes, I do waste too much time just surfing the web. I'm surprised that Alan admits that he likes tech "too much" versus too little like Kara. Alan is pulling back from computer use on purpose. Could Stephen Seaward be right that something is lost when we use computers so much? But is this article advocating that everyone should, or even could, go "unplugged?"*

As these thoughts reveal, reading a difficult text takes time; sometimes our minds may wander a bit, but once we understand one part and gain a sense of the overall purpose, these insights lead us on to more comprehension. As we understand or "see" some of the proverbial trees as well as the forest of a reading, we gradually construct meaning from the text. Through this gradual process, we learn, as Rosenblatt states, to "perform" a reading.

During this gradual construction of meaning, reading and writing no longer are opposite activities. We don't have to read once and then write in one draft. Instead, we can start to read, take a few mental notes or write down an idea, read on and understand more, write another idea . . . and on this process goes. As meaning is constructed, reading and writing become parallel and even complementary processes. Although we must admit, even some skilled readers may not be aware of, or be able to articulate, how they engage in these twin literacies so well. Yet again, if we do not identify and explain the strategies of reading explicitly, less skilled readers like Frank will feel that there is some secret to success, or, even worse, they just aren't smart enough to be skilled readers.

Some Effective Strategies

As a matter of convenience, we will provide some handy names for the following strategies, but the activities matter more than their labels. Many reading theorists and teachers like to refer to five fundamental strategies of comprehension as SQ3R. This acronym stands for Survey, Question, Read, Recall, and Review. However, to stress that reading involves all five of these strategies, we will refer to the third activity as Engage, and alter two other terms as well to clarify those strategies (Preview for Survey and Respond for Recall). When you are trying to read a difficult text for information, you can construct meaning gradually by

Previewing, Questioning, Engaging, Responding, and Reviewing

Let us stress that you do not always have to engage in every one of these strategies, and we will acknowledge that very skilled readers do not practice each one consciously. Like very prolific writers that brainstorm briefly and draft quickly, skilled readers employ some of these strategies intuitively while most of us have to learn to use them deliberately. All of them are the "secrets of success" that you can learn to use as needed.

Preview

Most of us preview a text in the most basic way; we flip from the first page to the last one to see how long is the reading. Previewing a reading (or surveying as it also is known) can involve a bit more than determining the number of pages. Before you settle down to read an assignment from front to back, try skimming over the text, noticing some of its most obvious features, such as the word "Unplugged" in Bella English's title or the short-paragraph format of this newspaper article. Most textbooks are designed for previewing so notice a reading's organization, such as the headings and sections. Ask yourself: what are the main sections, and what does the entire text seem to be about? Like a good student essay, most texts will assert a thesis in the first few paragraphs, and many academic articles begin with what is known as an abstract that summarizes the main points. You also should determine what kind of text you will be reading: is it primarily a narrative, an exposition, an argument, and so on? (For more on the various kinds of writing, see "What Tasks" in Chapter 2, pp. 34–37.) Previewing a challenging text is like watching another athlete or musician before you perform; you want to know what you will be facing.

Question

We often don't stop to question a text until we feel overwhelmed and then we ask, "What is this reading about?" or declare, "Why do I have to read this?" Both of these questions can help us avoid such frustration if we pose them *before* we start to read the entire text. If we assume that every aspect of the text has a purpose, we can ask and prepare to seek answers to questions like: Is "Unplugged" in English's article a deliberate reference to the MTV show with the same title? Does the later title phrase of "in Retreat" suggest a negative action? The headings or illustrations of a longer reading also can arouse our curiosity. We can ask what is the relationship between, say, the second and third heading or we can wonder if an image represents a major figure and if a chart depicts an important trend. Even if a text lacks headings or section breaks, we can wonder, how will this 10- or 20-page text be organized? You also should consider your professor as well as the text. Consider why does the professor want you to read this text, and what does he or she expect you to be able to do in response to the text? For example, if the professor wants you to learn new information so you can repeat it in class, you probably should read with a pen or a highlighter in hand. Yet, if the expectation is that you should be ready to interpret a reading, you can use more of the techniques for textual engagement presented below.

Engage

We decided to not refer to this part as the "Read" of SQ3R, because reading involves more than this strategy. We "engage" with a text as we start to read each sentence and paragraph carefully and closely. During this concentrated effort, our attention may wander so there are several techniques we can use. As you know, one option is to mark the text by **highlighting** or **underlining** main ideas. Another option to be even more active is **annotating** the text. These comments written in the margins can include an outline of key points, a comment on a pattern, an objection to an opinion, or a question for later consideration.

Here's an example of engaging with the first three paragraphs of English's article by using underlining and annotating:

There's a television in Cara and Alan Kalf's Arlington living room, but it's stashed in a corner, <u>its screen turned resolutely to the wall</u>. It's used only for the occasional DVD—or as a favorite perch for the family cat	*why to the wall?*
As for music, the couple listens to record albums— remember those?—on a turntable or on one of the old jukeboxes Alan has restored. <u>There's no Internet connection in the household.</u> Cara has an iPod she uses only when traveling. She also has a cellphone: "But I don't always answer it. Sometimes I leave it in my coat pocket. I forget about it."	*so they are against technology, again why?*

> *The couple <u>aren't elderly Luddites terrified by technol-</u>*   Who are the Luddites?
> <u>*ogy.*</u> *She's 27; he's 31. They are members of a small cohort:*
> *the young and unplugged. While their friends, relatives,*
> *and colleagues have every gadget known to mankind, <u>the</u>*
> <u>*Kalfs have made a conscious*</u> *not to blog, tweet, or instant*
> *message.*

> *They e-mail only when necessary. And <u>they say they're</u>*   Note - they believe they are better off
> <u>*better off*</u> *without all that stuff.*

Actively engaging with a text will help you avoid the problem of looking at a text but not being able to recall any details in class the next day. Instead you can use your underlining and annotations to make comments during a discussion.

After being told by most high school teachers NOT to write in your books, the benefit of buying or renting your college books is that you CAN annotate them. There's no gain in the resale value for keeping the pages clean because the buyback price usually doesn't depend on your markings. If you cannot annotate a text, such as for an assigned library reading, you can jot down the same comments on Post-it notes, in your notebook, or with your computer. It's easy to imagine that in the near future, most college students will engage with it. If you are given a digital copy of an assigned reading, you can write some annotations in your notebook or in the margin of the e-text using interactive software, such as Track Changes (under "Tools" of MS Word).

Unless we consider medieval manuscripts that lack word spacing and paragraph indenting, we tend to take the format of print texts for granted. We rarely stop to consider the benefits of the "white space" formatting to separate paragraphs and even letters. We also fail to notice that when we pick up a novel, we read each line from left to right and the page from top to bottom. However, when we engage with digital texts, we should consider its format as much as its content. Even more than a textbook or a newspaper, a digital text, such as a website, is organized spatially into discernable sections of meaning. The homepage of a website presents its main topics in a menu located at the top or in the left margin. The first block of text presents the key details, and the subsequent paragraphs are as concise as possible and separated by white space to focus attention and minimize eye-strain. Arrows to later pages or links to other sites indicate elaborations of meaning. Colors and images are other features of the format designed to attract attention and reinforce content. Thus, as we engage with websites and other digital texts, we again should notice the format as well as the content: What information is placed in the most prominent positions of top and left? What has first priority in the menu, and what is subordinated? What information is displayed prominently and highlighted with color, and what details are relegated to later pages or links?

Respond

Once you have completed a first-to-last page reading of a difficult text, you can continue your gradual construction of meaning by responding to the text through discussion, diagram/illustration, and double-entry notes. Through interactive programs, such as a class chat room, you can discuss a text with a classmate online before class, and some professors may require these electronic exchanges. Of course, you also can meet a classmate and ask, "Hey, what did you think of that reading?" Either form of **discussion** can help you determine what are some of the key details and the central premise of an assigned reading. For students who are visual learners, creating a **chart** or **diagram** of a reading or imagining an **illustration** (or two) for the main ideas will increase your comprehension of a difficult text.

Here's an example of diagramming from English on various reasons for deciding to go unplugged:

Cara Kalf	"Sometimes I leave it in my coat pocket. I forget about [my cellphone]."
Alan Kalf	"I like [high-tech] too much, and have a hard time setting limits."
Stephen Seaward	"I feel a little bit like a prisoner to it . . . I think we . . . lose something."
Rebecca Norman	"I find [Facebook] . . . voyeuristic . . . I just prefer not to have it in my life."

Double-entry notes are an even more active form of response. As their name suggests, the notes are "double" because you don't just copy down main ideas of a text. Instead, you take notes by writing out at least part of a key passage and then, in another column, you write a response to it. The very act of copying down a key passage—whether by typing or handwriting—makes you pay more attention to the author's words, and the second column is a space for you to write some of your thoughts. Ideally, your response should consist of more than a summary or a personal connection, although both are essential parts of comprehension. Your response can also include a question, a link to another part of the same text, or a placement of this reading in the larger context of your course. Here's one more example from English:

"Worshiping at the church of the pixel comes at the expense of real-life experience," says Alan, who teaches biology at Lexington Christian Academy. His students are aghast at the fact that he doesn't watch TV. But by limiting their use of technology, they have freed up time for activities they love. She works on craft projects. He restores old jukeboxes, pinball machines, and furniture.	*I know what he means by worshipping pixels and ignoring real life. My parents used to tell me to play outdoors, and now I sometimes wish I would talk to people face-to-face as much as I text them. But it's so hard for a teen to withdraw from social media and not feel left out. Yet if one were to exit the popularity game, couldn't one achieve much more as Cara and Alan do?*
Not having Internet access can be inconvenient, but if they feel an urgent need for a computer, they go to her parents' house. They don't miss the sensory overload they had when they watched television and spent more time online. "It's not that I don't like doing these things," Alan says. "It's that I like them too much, and have a hard time setting limits. And then I feel frustrated at the end of the evening when I haven't accomplished or learned anything."	*I guess it is a matter of setting limits and maybe the easiest limit to set is very little computer and Internet use. Yet wouldn't most people be "aghast" at that decision if you were to make it?! How much of our use of computers is based on personal choice or on peer pressure?*

The second-column response in double-entry notes does not have to be perfectly phrased; a teacher probably would notice the switching from "I" to "one" to "you" as the subject, but this rough writing can be revised later. However, in double-entry notes, you can use the quick phrasing of what is known as freewriting to develop good insights, to "write to learn" (for more on freewriting and writing to learn, see Chapter 2).

Review

As you finish reading a text, you can review by looking back over your marked text to reinforce your comprehension. You also can write a few comments at the end of the reading or in your notebook. This look back is similar to our reconsideration of any important event. You also may want to review a text before a class when you know a professor expects you to participate in a discussion or as you start to prepare to write a more formal assignment. Of course, if you turn to a previously read assignment and find marked pages and some notes, it will be much easier to say something "smart" and write insightfully.

Close Reading and Critical Thinking

By using effective reading strategies like annotations and double-entry notes, you will be practicing what is referred to as **close reading**. This insightful reading involves not only the comprehension of information but also other aspects of advanced literacy, such as analysis and synthesis. In the reading of fiction, close reading could involve analyzing the development of a character in a novel or connecting one poem to another by its imagery (synthesis). Close reading and **critical thinking** are terms that professors often use, but some students are never quite sure of their meanings. There are several ways to define and describe critical thinking, but we will rely on three common forms that are employed in many courses across the college curriculum: multiple perspectives, cultural influences, and historical trends.

Multiple Perspectives

The consideration of **multiple perspectives** asks you to distinguish several different viewpoints and examine what exact beliefs each perspective involves. This examination does not mean that you have to abandon your own perspective entirely, only that you seek to clarify and expand your initial position by being open, at least initially, to considering alternative viewpoints. For as the philosopher John Stuart Mill stated, "He who knows only his side of an argument knows little."

When faced with a question on multiple perspectives, it may be tempting to object: "How can I know what they were thinking?" and it is true that we sometimes cannot be certain about others' viewpoints. Yet, we often engage in just this kind of analysis, such as when we wonder, "What's up with her?" For instance, when a parent reacts with sudden anger or a friend is too subdued, we ask and often answer, "Where is he coming from?" Then we speculate not about a literal place but about his perspective, her viewpoint, someone's take on a situation. We engage in this kind of critical thinking not only in our daily lives but also in academic study. We try to interpret a literary character's assumptions or analyze a historical figure's motivations. We wonder, for example, does Huck Finn believe in racial inferiority as Twain's novel begins? Was the abolition of slavery Abraham Lincoln's primary motive for fighting the Civil War?

To consider various viewpoints, it may be helpful to create a chart such as the following one for "Young and Unplugged." The viewpoints of some people in English's article were charted back on p. 7 so can you now develop it further? See "Young and Unplugged" back on pp. 6–8.

	Multiple Perspectives on Using Digital Technologies	
Cara Kalf	"Sometimes I leave it in my coat pocket. I forget about [my cellphone]."	Cara simply doesn't care about high tech. She doesn't find it useful so she forgets about it.

Cara's brother-in-law	
Alan Kalf	"I like [high-tech] too much, and have a hard time setting limits."
96% of Americans	
Dr. Whybrow	
Stephen Seward	
Rebecca Norman	

What exactly does each person believe? It may be useful to rely on a quotation from the reading to help you determine each perspective, but you also should explain its significance. Then you will be able to understand and explain other viewpoints and answer "Where's he coming from?" and "What's up with her?" If you would like to read another account of a young adult making a deliberate decision to live with very little Internet connectivity, see "Here's Why I (Mostly) Skip the Internet" by Randi Stevenson in the online supplement for Chapter 1. Then you can consider how is Stevenson's perspective similar to and different from those presented in "Young and Unplugged."

Analysis based on multiple perspectives can involve different viewpoints within one reading (Cara Kalf and Stephen Seaward in "Young and Unplugged) as well as varied perspectives between two texts (Cara Kalf and Randi Stevenson in "Here's Why . . ."). Another form of this analysis can develop when writers differ about a literary interpretation or an academic issue. A noted educator named Gerald Graff explains that the differences in literary critics' interpretations of *The Adventures of Huckleberry Finn* helped him engage in his reading:

My interest was aroused . . . when our instructor mentioned that the critics disagreed over . . .the last part of the novel. . . [Some of my stumbling reactions] were not too far off from the thoughts of famous published critics. . . And having issues to watch out for made it possible [for me] not only to concentrate . . . [but also] to read with a sense of personal engagement..

In other words, a clash of perspectives, once recognized, can stimulate your reading; it can turn a dull process of decoding and basic comprehension into an engaging activity of analysis, of trying to determine if this interpretation is better than that one. To determine if one interpretation is better, one must return to the text to gather evidence for one's perspective as well as to notice counter-evidence that may require one to revise one's viewpoint.

Cultural Influences

As we examine other perspectives, we often start to wonder not only what someone else was thinking, but why did he or she have this viewpoint. We will refer to this consideration as the analysis of **cultural influences**, meaning what beliefs support a viewpoint. Again, you will be engaged in conjecture, but it is not just idle speculation because we can draw some reasonable inferences. For instance, most Americans like to emphasize their individuality, yet, the cultural influences on this viewpoint can be analyzed. Literary characters like Huck Finn, comic book heroes such as Superman, and famous Americans like Sojourner

Truth all stress the supposed uniqueness of our individual identities. Widespread cultural practices, such as every student being graded separately in most schools, also promote an individualistic concept of the self. In other words, our widespread belief in individualism, paradoxically, is promoted by many elements of American culture. As diagrammed below, many influences affect our development and help to shape our individual identities:

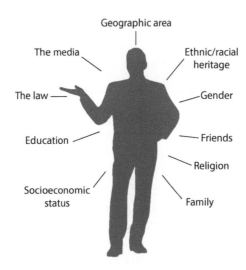

A famous theorist named Louis Althusser has explained an individual's relationship with society by stating that each person is "interpellated," is drawn into a culture. This process of interpellation begins when we are very young; long before we are aware that our attitudes about race, gender, wealth, pleasure, and so much more are being influenced by society. Yet, these cultural influences do not necessarily control every individual, making each person develop the exact same perspective. Instead, as another important thinker named Michel Foucault has theorized, the many influences of a culture are complex and sometimes even contradictory. We, therefore, have some freedom of choice from among these many influences.

In "Young and Unplugged," the writer, Bella English, examines the perspectives of Cara Kalf and others. To examine the influence of computers on our lives further, we can connect to another reading, and this synthesis will help us consider the effect computers can have on our lives. The following reading is an except from *Hamlet's Blackberry*, a book written by William Powers and published in 2010. As you read, try underlining to consider: According to Powers, how do computers affect us, and can we control any of these effects?

HAMLET'S BLACKBERRY

by William Powers

Today we're always just a few taps away from millions of other people, from endless information and stimulation. Family and friends, work and play, news and ideas—sometimes it seems everything we care about has moved to the digital room. So we spend our days there, living in this new ultra-connected way.

We've been at it for about a decade now, and it's been thrilling and rewarding in many ways. When the whole world is within easy reach, there's no end of things to see and do. Sometimes, it feels like a kind of a paradise.

However, there's a big asterisk to life in this amazing place. We've been doing our best to ignore it, but it won't go away. It comes down to this: We're all busier. Much, much busier. It's a lot of work managing all this connectedness. The e-mails, texts, and voicemails; the pokes, prods, and tweets; the alerts and comments; the links, tags, and posts; the photos and videos; the blogs and vlogs; the searches, downloads, uploads, files, and folders; feeds and filters; walls and widgets; tags and clouds; the usernames, passcodes, and access keys; pop-ups and banners; ringtones and vibrations. That's just a small sample of what we navigate each day in the room. By the time you read this, there will be completely new modes of connecting that are all the rage. Our tools are fertile, constantly multiplying.

As they do, so does our busyness. Little by little, our workdays grow more crowded. When you carry a mobile device, all things digital (and all people) are along for the ride. Home life is busier too. Much of what used to be called free time has been colonized by our myriad connective obligations, and so is no longer free.

It's easy to blame all this on the tools. Too easy. These tools are fantastically useful and enrich our lives in countless ways. Like all new technologies, they have flaws, but at bottom they can't make us busy until we make them busy first. We're the prime movers here. We're always connected because we're always connecting.

Beyond the sheer mental workload, our thoughts have acquired a new orientation. Of the two mental worlds everyone inhabits, the inner and the outer, the latter increasingly rules. The more connected we are, the more we depend on the world outside ourselves to tell us how to think and live. There's always been a conflict between the exterior, social self and the interior, private one. The struggle to reconcile them is central to the human experience, one of the great themes of philosophy, literature, and art. In our own lifetime, the balance has tilted decisively in one direction. We hear the voices of others, and are directed by those voices, rather than by our own. We don't turn inward as often or as easily as we used to.

In one sense, the digital sphere is all about differentiating oneself from others. Anyone with a computer can have a blog now, and the possibilities for self-expression are endless. However, this expression takes place entirely within the digital crowd, which frames and defines it. This makes us more reactive, our thinking contingent on others. To be hooked up to the crowd all day is a very particular way to go through life.

For a long time, there was an inclination to shrug all of this off as a mere transitional issue, a passing symptom of technological change. These are early days, we tell ourselves. Eventually, life will calm down and the inner self will revive. There's a basic wisdom in this hopeful view. It's never a good idea to buy into the dark fears of the techno-Cassandras,[1] who generally turn out to be wrong. Human beings are skillful at figuring out the best uses for new tools. However, it can take a while. The future is full of promise, but we have to focus on the present, how we're living, thinking, and feeling right now.

How well do you think Powers describes the influence of computer technologies on our lives? Why do you agree or disagree on his assertion of our ability to control this influence on our lives?

For more on Powers' *Hamlet Blackberry*, see the radio interview of the author in the additional sources for Chapter 1.

---

[1] In Greek mythology, Cassandra is a prophet of doom who predicted the downfall of her city during the Trojan War.

Excerpt from pp. 1–3 of Hamlet's Blackberry by William Powers . Copyright © 2010 by William Powers. Reprinted by permission of HarperCollins Publishers.

Historical Trends

Another common form of critical thinking is the analysis of **historical trends**. As the term suggests, this analysis examines how a perspective changes or remains the same over time. For example, some typical academic questions include Does Huck's perspective on Jim change as they journey down the Mississippi River? Or in *The Scarlet Letter*, does Hester remain steadfast in her love for the minister? During the Civil War, did President Lincoln ever waver in his conviction that our nation could not be divided? The analysis of historical trends is crucial to academic inquiry and much more because as a famous philosopher named George Santayana warned, "Those who cannot remember the past are condemned to repeat it."

English stipulates that Cara and Alan Kalf are not "Luddites terrified by technology," and to understand this reference to an anti-technology group in the early 1800s, read the following text. It is an excerpt from *Against Technology: From the Luddites to Neo-Luddism* by Steven E. Jones (published 2006).

THE LUDDITES

by Stephen E. Jones

The Luddites of 1811 to 1812 smashed machines. They did so in protest and to sabotage specific owners' looms and finishing shops. They did *not* voluntarily give up technologies of convenience or status, as do many neo-Luddites today. They rarely issued anything like philosophical statements. Mostly they wrote threatening letters and composed celebratory ballads. They picked up sledgehammers and other lowly tools as well as guns and other weapons, then marched through the darkness to sabotage the machines that promised increased productivity in their trades. They did so in order to make a point and to stop the use of the machines. Luddite direct action can be seen as taking from the relatively rich in order to give back (or keep) what was due to the workers (many of whom were poor). For doing this, the Luddites faced execution by hanging (and indeed some of them were hanged in the end) and they became legendary, their odd name eventually becoming a parable for antitechnology ideas and feelings as well as actions.

The name Luddite seems to have first been used in print in December 1811, in a newspaper account in the *Nottingham Review* about a group of protesting stocking-knitters in Nottinghamshire, who were presumably already calling themselves Luddites or at least naming themselves followers of Ned Ludd or General Ludd. Soon the term was also adopted to describe textile workers in Yorkshire and Lancashire, who began to organize themselves, to act in bands or secret groups, in order to take direct action against those they accused of violating the fair and customary practices of their trade, sometimes putting them out of work and generally profiting from changes in their social and economic conditions by deploying new kinds of machinery . . .

With their faces blackened or wearing masks like bandits, sometimes in women's clothing or other forms of disguise, and armed with sledgehammers, axes, pikes, and, on occasion, guns, the Luddites showed up at houses to seize arms (for further raids) or to destroy a machine-owner's property and goods. On occasion they harmed but more commonly merely threatened the owners or their families. Their signature act was to break "obnoxious," offending "frames"—kinds of knitting or cloth-finishing machines that, while efficient in terms of labor and costs, were making many of their jobs redundant and producing inferior cloth, thus harming their reputations and the reputation of their skilled trade as a whole. They

From Against Technology: From the Luddites to Neo-Luddism by Stephen E. Jones. Copyright © 2006 by Taylor and Francise Group LLC. Reprinted by permission. From Against Technology: From the Luddites to Neo-Luddism by Stephen E. Jones. Copyright © 2006 by Taylor and Francis Group LLC. Reprinted by permission.

were protecting their trade—which, more than a job, was a culture, an economy, and a group of coworkers, a labor "gang," their social identity in the community as well as a technique or set of practices.

Their actions, which became known as "ludding," spread during 1812, moving from the stocking knitters in Nottingham to skilled cloth-finishers (or croppers, those who cropped the nap of the cloth to make it smooth and ready to sell) in the West Riding of Yorkshire and then to other workers elsewhere in the North of England. An organized network may have been behind this expansion, or unconnected groups may have copied the example and name of the first Luddites. The net result was perceived as a movement or conspiracy, with only the degree of conscious organization in question. Luddism increased for a year or so, was squelched by government prosecutions and hangings, and then resurged briefly in 1816 to 1817.

To analyze the historical trend from the Luddites of 1811–17 to today's unplugged youth, answer the following question:

> How are the reasons for the technological resistance of the Luddittes similar to and different from the Cara Kalf and others in "Young and Unplugged?"

To examine historical trends further, you can learn more about the Amish who also are mentioned in English's article. When Cara Kalf states that there are others who reject technology, her brother-in-law joked, "Yeah, the Amish." See "The Amish" by Jamie Sharp in the additional sources for Chapter 1. Stephen Seaward makes another historical reference to Henry David Thoreau, when he asserts, "I don't go off into the woods somewhere." In *Walden*, Thoreau describes his mid-nineteenth century retreat away from society and into the woods near Walden Pond in Massachusetts.

In addition to synthesizing texts and trends across time, another way to analyze historical trends is to draw a timeline and locate several perspectives:

Resisting Technological Progress

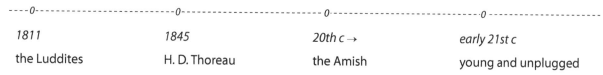

1811	1845	20th c →	early 21st c
the Luddites	H. D. Thoreau	the Amish	young and unplugged

Then, as suggested above, compare and contrast these perspectives: How have they changed and/or remain the same?

Historical Trends and Literacy Standards

For this chapter of reading, here is another quick example of analyzing historical trends. Two historians of literacy, Daniel Resnick and Lauren Resnick, explain that expectations for reading and writing were much lower. For example, in colonial America, the standard of literacy was much lower. If a colonist in New England could pronounce a biblical passage and/or sign his or her name, he or she was deemed to be literate. Using this minimal standard of literacy, approximately two-thirds of male colonists in New England were considered to be literate, yet, many women received very little literacy training and almost every African-American was denied instruction in seventeenth-century America. Thus, using even this low standard, no more than half of these colonists were considered to be literate. By the end of the nineteenth century, the standard of literacy had increased, but only 7% of Americans graduated from high school, so less than a third of the population met this higher measure of literacy. Today, our standard is not only much higher, but a much larger segment of our society is expected to not only comprehend but also interpret complex texts. By 2000, three-quarters of 18-year-olds graduated from high school, although their diplomas did not always guarantee full literacy. The No Child Left Behind Act of 2001 (NCLB) sets the goal of 100% fulfillment of high school literacy standards by 2014. Thus, if one looks back over history, our **literacy standards** have been a moving target and an ever-greater number has been expected to meet them. In this era of online texts, our twenty-first century standard of literacy has been raised even higher, for we are expected to be able to decipher visual texts as well. For instance, how does the following graph illustrate the history of literacy standards and their fulfillment?

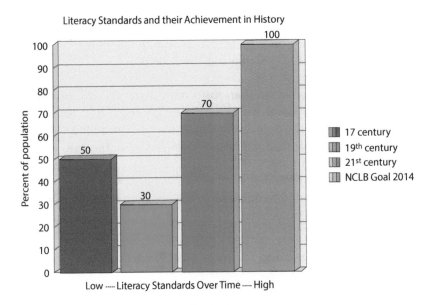

Some may doubt that it is possible for a nation to educate a great majority of its citizens to reach advanced literacy. Some scholars, such as Mike Rose, have conceded that educational and economic inequalities may make this lofty goal difficult to achieve, yet Rose also considers this ambition to be "an extraordinary social experiment: the attempt to provide education for all members of a vast pluralistic democracy." By coming to college, your classmates and you have become part of this great democratic experiment.

Varying Your Reading Process

You will be asked to complete many reading assignments in various college classes, and to be a more capable and confident, you will have to vary your reading process. Below are four sample readings, and how would you answer the following questions for each assigned text? Can you learn to practice **varied reading processes**?

- **Purpose:** Why do you think the professor assigned this reading? How will a student to be expected to respond to this reading: to show comprehension of information, be ready to apply information, and/or be able to analyze the main idea and details?

- **Difficulty:** How easy or hard will it be for a student to complete this reading?

- **Process:** What strategies will help a student complete this reading successfully? Should a student employ previewing, questioning, underlining, annotating, diagramming, double-entry note-taking, and/or reviewing?

Art History 100

When one starts to analyze a painting, one can consider the subject matter: what is being presented? Is this subject being presented in a representational or an abstract manner? Then some of the formal elements of its composition can be examined, such as shapes, lines, colors, perspective, and depth. Next, the context of the painting can be considered; where does this artwork fit into the artist's career, a historical era, and/or an artistic period? Sometimes, it is very helpful to examine one painting in relation to another. For example, how do two painters of the Renaissance period depict the Virgin Mary, or how do two abstract painters employ brushstrokes to create texture? Analyzing a painting will require you to collect various pieces of the proverbial puzzle of this artwork.

English 101

From Frederick Douglass' autobiography: I never saw my mother, to know her as such, more than four or five time in my life, and each of these times was very short in duration, and at night. She was hired by a Mr. Stewart, who lived about twelve miles from my home. She made her journeys to see me at night, travelling the whole distance on foot, after her performance of her day's work. She was a field hand, and a whipping is the penalty of not being in the field at sunrise. . . . I do not recollect of ever seeing my mother by the light of day. She was with me in the night. She would lie down with me, and get me to sleep, but long before I waked she was gone. (For more of this reading, see pp. 136–140 in Chapter 6).

Health Professions 110

To create medical terms, a suffix frequently is added to a root word. For example, the suffix *–itis* meaning inflamation is added to *gastro*, meaning to create the term *gastritis*—inflamation of the stomach. To alter the meaning, a different suffix can be used, such as *dynia* meaning pain to create the term *gastrodynia*—pain in the stomach. Here are three other examples of the formation of medical terms:

arthr (joint) + *itis* (inflamation) = *arthritis* (inflamation of a joint)

arthr (joint) + *centesis* (surgical puncture) = *arthrocentesis* (surgical pun

abdomino (abdomen) *centesis* (surgical puncture) = *abdominocentesis* (surgical puncture of the abdomen)

Politics 211

From David Orr's essay: It is said that we are entitled to hold whatever opinions we choose, but we are not entitled to whatever facts we wish. Whatever opinions you may have, there are four facts that will fundamentally shape the world in which you will live and work.

The first is the fact that we spend upwards of 95 percent of our time in houses, cars, malls, and offices. We are becoming an indoor species increasingly shut off from sky, land, forests, waters, and animals. Nature, as a result, is becoming more and more an abstraction to us. The problem is most severe for children who now spend up to eight hours each day before a television or computer screen and less and less time outdoors in nature. Author Richard Louv describes the results as "nature deficit disorder"—the loss of our sense of rootedness in place and connection to the natural world. (For more of this reading, see pp. 285–289 in Chapter 9).

We cannot claim that there is only one "right" answer for the best approach to each of these sample readings. However, a student who comes to his English class ready to only repeat the details of Douglass' autobiography (comprehension) probably will not excel that day, and a student who is prepared to use the principles of analyzing a painting (application) will do well in Art History 100.

Conclusion and Key Terms

As you learn to vary your reading process and employ different strategies in order to tackle diverse reading assignments, you will enjoy even more success in college. With our apologies to a well-known advertising campaign, we will assert,

> Annotating a reading—greater effort
>
> Responding to a text—better grades
>
> Enjoying your reading process—priceless!

It may seem that you usually are asked to read for academic purposes like comprehension and interpretation, but many of your professors also hope that you will read for action, such as applying a key concept to a new circumstance, and even for pleasure, like enjoying a challenging poem. Few of us enjoy our first encounter with a difficult poet like Emily Dickinson or a complex report on a technical problem, such as a flawed bridge design. However, by using some of the strategies for active and gradual comprehension, we hope you will be able to declare, in contrast to Frank's quotation above, that you "get it." You *will* have the ability to comprehend difficult texts, just as many of your professors think you *should*.

Before you finish with this chapter, here is a list of key terms; which ones can you explain easily, and which ones do you need to review?

Reading Purposes
    Information/knowledge
    Action/application
    Analysis/interpretation
    Enjoyment/pleasure

Functional literacy
    Decoding letters (phonetic reading)
    Word recognition (sight reading)

Advanced literacy
    Comprehending meaning
    Interpreting ideas
    Applying information
    Analyzing an argument
    Connecting to other texts and/or ideas (synthesis)

Immediate comprehension versus gradual comprehension

Reading strategies
    Preview
    Question
    Engage
        Highlighting
        Underlining
        Annotating
    Respond
        Discussion
        Diagram
        Illustration
        Double-entry notes
    Review

Close Reading

Critical Thinking
    Multiple Perspectives
    Cultural Influences
    Historical Trends

Literacy Standards

Varied Reading Processes

Additional Sources for Chapter 1

To deepen your understanding of the Chapter 1 topic of our digital lives, you can consult some of the following sources:

1. Similar to Bella English's article on "young and unplugged" adults, Randi Stevenson has defended her unusual choice to live with very few digital connections in "I'm a Millenial: Here's Why I (Mostly) Skip the Internet."

   http://digitaledition.chicagotribune.com/tribune/article_popover.aspx?guid=380cdace-53eb-4d71-8b8b-3e140f9c76bc

2. To learn more about William Powers' doubts about our digital lives, you may want to read (or hear) this radio interview with the author.

   http://www.npr.org/templates/story/story.php?storyId=128364111

3. To learn more about the complex approach to technology by the Amish, you may want to read an analysis written by Jamie Sharp, when he was a college student, in "The Amish: Technology Practice and Technological Change."

   http://archive.is/20130104171000/www.shawcreekgeneralstore.com/amish_article1.htm

4. For a positive and satirical perspective on Facebook, you may want to read "Why I Love Facebook" by Kurt Soller. This essay celebrates the many benefits of having many friends on this social network.

   http://www.newsweek.com/why-i-love-facebook-99205

5. For an analysis on why we find Facebook so engrossing, you may want to read "The Secret Psychology of Facebook" by Courtney Seiter.

   https://blog.bufferapp.com/psychology-of-facebook

6. For a vehement argument against Facebook, you may want to read "Why I Despise Facebook" by Tom Hodgkinson.

   https://www.1843magazine.com/content/ideas/robert-lane-greene/facebook

7. For a balanced analysis of the benefits and drawbacks of using Facebook, you may want to read "Facebook: Like?" by Robert Lane Greene.

   https://www.1843magazine.com/content/ideas/robert-lane-greene/facebook

8. For a surprising critique of the digital demands on our attention, you may want to check the site of "Time Well Spent" in which members of the digital industry call for change of their own practices.

   http://www.timewellspent.io

The Writing Process and Assignment Analysis

For most high school graduates, writing sometimes can be a relatively easy task. Most of us can write a "to-do" list, reply to an electronic message, or draft a five-paragraph essay without too much difficulty. However, at other times, most of us struggle to write well. We may struggle to complete the literary analyses, lab reports, and persuasive papers we are expected to write. As we try to explain, for instance, a literary character, we may find ourselves staring at a blank screen or crumpling sheet after sheet of half-started pages. Why is writing sometimes so easy yet at other times so difficult?

This is a crucial question for a college student to consider since you will be asked to write many assignments. One tempting answer to these difficulties is to doubt yourself as a writer: "I must not be very good, smart enough, a *real* writer ... " Yet these doubts can lead to a self-defeating cycle of apathy ("why try?"), procrastination ("not now") and failure ("oh no"), and then even more self-doubt. No one, however, should spend four years at college in this cycle of doubt, despair, and defeat.

To understand why writing sometimes is easy yet on other occasions so challenging, let's distinguish between two specific examples: texting an electronic reply and drafting a literary analysis. Beyond "easy" and "hard," what else do you think distinguishes these two kinds of writing? What differences can you add to the list below?

Texting a Reply	*Analyzing a Novel*
easy	*hard*

You probably added "fun" to one column, but does the enjoyable always have to be matched with easy? A crucial difference you may not have considered is that these two examples represent two very different processes of thinking and writing. Texting a friend is usually so easy because most likely you already know what you want to say (unless a difficult situation like a break-up is involved). Yet when it comes to analyzing a character in a novel, like Huck Finn's attitude toward Jim or Hester Prynne's love in *The Scarlet Letter*, we usually do not know what we want to say. Thus, we can add to our list an important distinction:

Texting a Reply	*Analyzing a Novel*
easy	*hard*
know what to say	*need to figure it out*

As we exchange text messages with a friend, such as in

"where r u?"

"goin 2 class"

"wanna have lunch"

"ya, at 12"

we don't stop to think (at least not for long) about what we want to say (except for that breakup again). This kind of writing goes straight from our thoughts and onto the screen—easy! We record what we are thinking, what we already know.

Analyzing Huck or Hester is—pardon the pun—another story; we usually do not know what we want to say. Is Huck a racist or not? Is Hester a fool for loving the minister? Such complicated questions involve much more than just recording what we think. If we try to write this literary analysis like we text a reply, we almost always will be doomed to frustration and failure. These problems develop because our first thoughts, phrases, and order are not ready to be our final draft. These difficulties, however, do not mean that a writer is destined to fail and just not smart enough. These problems instead reveal that some writing tasks require a different approach, another kind of writing process.

Let's consider how we would write the exception noted above: the break-up message. If someone is really heartless, he or she may text the first thought that comes to mind: "don't wanna see you; we're thru." Even with its rhyme, this probably isn't the best message to send. Most of us instead would practice what we want to say and how we would phrase it using our minds, our mouths, and our fingertips: "I need some space" (what a stupid cliché), "maybe we need a break" (better but too sudden), "spending every Saturday night together … " and on we would go. We would use writing to clarify our thinking, to see what we want to say. Unless we hit send immediately, writing lets us see our thoughts and imagine a reader's reactions. Or if we ask a friend about our not-yet-sent message, if we seek a peer response to a draft as described below, we can even learn how some readers might react and then revise as needed (for more on what is known as peer response, see p. 29 below).

Although completing a more difficult writing task requires greater effort, we can, in fact, use writing itself to make this assignment easier. As long as we do not assume that we already should know what we want to say, writing can become a useful tool rather than a frustrating struggle. This alternative approach to writing will require more writing, but it also will be more effective.

Texting a Reply	*Analyzing a Novel*
easy	*hard*
know what to say	*need to figure it out*
writing as recording one draft	*writing as thinking in several steps*

You probably have been taught about the **writing process**, but have you been convinced to really try it? To write a difficult paper, we can slow down the process and separate at least some of the steps we try to complete all at once in a first-*and*-final-no-time-to-revise-gotta-get-it-done draft. The steps of the writing process can be described as

- **Collect** ideas and phrases (invention)
- **Focus** on a main topic/idea

- **Order** the ideas (arrangement)
- **Draft** sentences and paragraphs
- **Revise** a draft
- **Edit** a final copy

Some writing theorists have used other terms to describe these steps of the writing process, such as prewriting, writing, and rewriting. Or back in elementary school, your teachers may have talked about a "sloppy copy." Our description is based on Donald Murray's theory, and as in chapter one, we will mention a few theorists because we want to show that these practical ideas are based on sound scholarship. To Murray's theory of the writing process, we have added two terms from ancient rhetoric: **invention** and **arrangement** (see Chapter 5 for more on rhetorical theory). Invention refers to the initial collection of ideas ("What the heck can I say about Huck and Jim?") and arrangement refers to the organization of those ideas once we have decided on a focus, a thesis ("As they travel down the Mississippi River, Huck slowly recognizes Jim's humanity.")

Although these six steps may seem like much more work than sitting down to "get it done," they actually make writing easier if you are trying to draft a challenging paper. To explain how more steps can be easier, let us add another writing theorist's analogy. Linda Flower has compared writing with juggling, and the trick to learning to juggle is to start with only one ball or two. Even when a skilled juggler is handling three balls or more, she really concentrates on only one or two at any time. Thus, it's easier for most of us to separate the writing process into several distinct steps, and focus on only one or two at a time. This alternative approach to writing reduces the number of steps we have to handle at one time so we can concentrate better and work more efficiently. You already may practice some of these steps, but we will explain each one and some related strategies below. We also will divide our explanations into several smaller segments, as marked by our headings, so this information will be easier to read and comprehend.

Three Initial Steps

As we start to write, we usually have to collect information, establish a focus, and create an order before we draft. Sometimes we complete these steps almost intuitively, and at other times, we must handle each one with a deliberate effort.

Collecting

To begin the gathering of ideas and phrases for subsequent drafting, we can try several strategies:

- **Brainstorm**—jot down a list of ideas as you think of them
- **Cluster**—diagram your initial ideas by linking some with lines
- **Freewrite**—think onto the page by writing quickly and imperfectly

What unites these varied strategies is their ease. We can let ourselves "blurt" out words while writing just as we often do while chatting, emailing, and texting. We can permit ourselves to collect ideas without worrying if our thoughts are perfect or our phrases are eloquent. As another writing theorist named Peter

Elbow explains, we don't need to heed our critical self yet; we let our creative self "talk" onto the page or screen. We can plan to return to these collected ideas later for critical judgment.

Focusing

Once we have collected some ideas, we have to find a focus, determine our purpose. Sometimes a **thesis** is assigned (Prove Huck is not…), but usually in college writing, you will have to determine your purpose on the subject given, your answer to the question posed. Although some of us shy away from controversy, a thesis has to make a deliberate claim, state an assertion someone else can reasonably disagree with (Huck is a racist when he…). Of course, not all writing begins with an explicit thesis (In this essay I will…). Some kinds of writing, such as a narrative, have a clear focus, but this purpose is not revealed immediately; instead it is shown throughout a narrative.

A reader of a narrative comes to this text with different expectations than the audience of a literary analysis or a lab report. To be successful, a writer will have to fulfill these expectations (or break them for a very deliberate reason) because as Donald Murray also explained, "Writers may write *for* themselves, but they do not write *to* themselves." Even most diarists or bloggers have an audience in mind as they write. Two more theorists, Patricia Bizzell and James Berlin, therefore, have insisted that writing is a social process as well as an individual one. In other words, as a writer completes these steps, this process is influenced by audience expectations and writing conventions; writing is an **individual *and* a social process**.

> *Writers may write* <u>*for*</u> *themselves, but they do not write* <u>*to*</u> *themselves.*

Ordering

To create an effective order, most writers have to shift from thinking about what they know to considering what a reader needs to learn if they are to understand our knowledge. Although a brainstorming list may spring quickly from our minds, we usually need to reorganize these thoughts if we are to communicate with others effectively. Some of the most common patterns for creating an effective order are

- **Chronological**: Present an event by following its time sequence
- **"In medias res"**: Follow the ancient pattern of beginning in the middle of the action, and then backtracking to the beginning before presenting the rest of the sequence
- **Problem to solution**: Explain a difficulty and then present a remedy
- **Cause and effect**: Describe a crucial factor and its result

Can you add any other organizational patterns? You may want to add two other common kinds of high school writing: pro/con and compare/contrast patterns.

Some kinds of writing, such as lab reports, already have a fixed order and for a good reason. This order allows another researcher to replicate an experiment exactly because science depends on the confirmation of experimental results. There are other, already established organizational patterns, such as the pro/con order, that help us produce satisfying results. Some writing tasks, however, do not have such fixed orders so it can be very beneficial to outline after a first draft has been completed. Most of us have been instructed to outline before we begin drafting, but outlining afterwards can help us judge and revise a first draft. But wait, we are getting ahead of ourselves; we need to discuss drafting next.

The Most Obvious Step

Drafting

As we draft, we try to turn our intentions into communication; we try to make our meaning clear enough to stand apart from ourselves. We try to reach a reader to whom we cannot explain face-to-face what we meant to say. To reach our audience, we turn our thoughts into phrases, sentences, and paragraphs. A handbook can help you transform ideas into written language on each of these levels, so let us offer some general advice. First, each of these levels represents a place to bog down and become frustrated with writing. Stumbling over word choice, also known as **diction**, can block even the best of writers (should I refer to Hester as *devoted* or *deluded* in her love?). Some decisions of diction can determine an entire analysis, but it usually is better to keep thinking and drafting even when the perfect word isn't at your fingertips. Let a less-than-perfect word suffice and mark it for later consideration and correction. The final draft of your paper, of course, must have grammatically correct and pattern-pleasing sentences. Again, your sentence structure, or **syntax**, may be less than perfect in a first draft. Bruce Ballenger, the author of several books on writing, argues that we sometimes have to write badly to write well. If you learned to write a "sloppy copy" in grade school, you probably know what he means. Perfection or even pretty good usually requires more than one attempt.

Paragraphs, as you know, are the building blocks of a paper. The old rule of thumb is that each paragraph should be organized around one main idea. Another way to consider paragraphing is to think about white space: those areas of a page or screen not filled with letters or images. A reader's eye and mind need white space to remind her or him to pause, complete one idea, and prepare for another one. The white space of an indentation as a new paragraph begins does so much for a reader with so little visually. It's easy to notice the importance of white space if you have ever tried to read a medieval manuscript. These texts usually lack paragraphs and sometimes even spaces between words. The modern equivalent would be a poorly designed web page jammed with information or even a page of a college student's paper that lacks any indentations. A paragraph longer than a page almost always can be and should be broken into two or more paragraphs.

To double-check our order, we can outline after a first or partial draft has been written. Number each paragraph of the draft and identify its topic. This additional effort again can help us write better; follow the outline in your mind. Does it seem sensible to start with 1, follow with 2, and then continue with 3, 4, and 5? Or would 4, 2, and then 3 be better? Once we realize that 1, 4, 2, and 3 is better, often 5, 6, and 7 will follow easily.

It's important to note that the writing process so far has been presented as though it were a fixed set of steps: first, collect; second, focus; third, order; fourth, draft. Although these fixed steps make it easier to explain the writing process, the reality of writing often involves more than marching up a set of steps once. Instead, we may, for example, create a draft and go back to check our order. Then a new order may lead to a sharper focus so more details may have to be collected, and on the complex process of writing will go. Although writing often is a messier process than these four fixed steps (plus revision and editing), we have to be able to separate these steps so we can handle the demands of a difficult task. Once we can distinguish these steps, we may be able to discern why we sometimes get stuck in the middle of the process. Most of us have become bogged

First Order	Better Order
1	1
2	4
3	2
4	3, 5, 6, 7

down, for instance, in the middle of completing a first draft. We are going along smoothly and suddenly we get stuck; we don't know how to start the next paragraph. We can keep drafting and drafting that next sentence, but we know that none of them are any good. Or our minds and fingertips may just stop, and we end up staring at a blank page or screen for too long. Yet if we understand the various steps, then we may realize that the best way to proceed is to go backward briefly. Perhaps we are stuck while drafting because our order is wrong or we haven't collected enough ideas for the next section. If we understand the separate steps of this process, we have a better chance of overcoming our moments of frustration. Once a first draft is complete, devoting some time to editing is essential, and a day or more for revision is even better.

Two Later Steps

Once we have drafted some complete sentences and organized paragraphs, we usually need to revise and edit.

Revising

Having the time to revise, to *really* revise, depends on starting the initial steps of the process long before the due date. It is tempting to assume that this extended process of writing takes too much time.

However, if you have ever spent three, four, or more hours working on a last-minute-gotta-get-it-done first *and* final draft, can you imagine distributing the same number of hours over several days? Starting early and collecting for 20 or 30 minutes, then seeking a focus for those ideas the next day can actually be a much more efficient and effective approach. Consider an athletic or musical ability that you excel at; did you learn to throw that ball or play that instrument all at once? Even now, do you practice separate parts of this ability for hours before you try to demonstrate your great proficiency to others? Why not approach writing just as you accomplish one of your talents?

Revision, like drafting, can occur on many levels, ranging from the entire draft to a single sentence or phrase. Some of the rhetorical concepts presented in Chapter 6 can aid you in your revision. For example, the rhetorical triangle can help you reconsider the draft overall: What is your purpose and for what audience?

All-Nighter	A Gradual Process
a struggle from	Monday: collect 30 min.
10 pm to 2 am on	Tues: focus and order 20 min.
Thursday night	Wed: draft 70 min. reorganize 10 min.
into Friday due 8 am =	Th: revise, edit, print, and proofread 80 min. =
4 hours	3 1/2 hours

The three rhetorical appeals can also help you "re-see" your draft. Have you established an effective relationship with your intended audience (ethos)? Have you arranged your ideas and evidence in a logical order (logos)? Have you evoked from your reader the emotions that match your purpose (pathos)? You also can revise on the smaller scale of a paragraph, sentence, or phrase. A good handbook will offer many helpful suggestions for revision, but it's also easy to be overwhelmed by so much advice.

Like athletes or musicians who keep track of their typical difficulties, most writers can revise better when they are aware of what kinds of improvements their writing usually needs. Teachers regularly identify weaknesses that require revision as they grade, but some students check their grade and turn toward their next assignment. Taking the time to look back at the comments on a graded paper, however, helps student writers improve their next efforts. Saying "Gee, I got a C" should not be a student's only reaction to a graded paper.

In addition to reviewing previous papers, **peer response** is another beneficial guide for revision. However, a response by another student must consist of more than superficial praise ("I really liked it") or dismissive critiques ("You lost me on page three; it wasn't very good"). Helpful peer response provides, just as its name suggests, a reader's reaction to a draft: where is the text effective (or not) and why? These responses are about meaning rather than grading or editing. Most of us need some training to become comfortable and competent with peer responding, but we can learn to use and even enjoy a trusted reader's reactions. This training can involve responding to anonymous sample texts, peer papers, and/or published writing as well as working in paired partners, small groups, and full class discussions.

Response guidelines are as varied as writing assignments, but here is a general response format that will fit almost any draft:

Strengths

Identify what phrases, sections, and/or features you find to be most effective and memorable. Be very specific, as in, "I can really imagine the scene on the top of page two when you used the phrase … " or "The analysis on page three is very good because …." Note the importance of explaining why as well as what.

Focus

Describe what you think is the purpose of the paper. In a sentence or two, answer: What do you think the writer is trying to accomplish?

Weaknesses

Admit when you, as a reader, were confused by some phrases or lost interest in certain sections. Again, be specific and concentrate on your reactions as a reader, for example, "By the bottom of page three, I wasn't sure if you still were trying to …. " You also can phrase these concerns as questions, such as "Can you tell me more why you felt this way?" Avoid statements that explicitly criticize the draft as in "The ending wasn't very good" because these judgmental assertions do not help a writer understand why a section is weak; concentrate on your reactions as a reader.

Editing

Notice a few minor editing problems and correct them, such as by adding a missing apostrophe or helping with a misspelled word. However, you are not responsible for making every edit or even identifying each one. Mark the first few, and then assert that "This draft needs a thorough editing. It started to be difficult for me to concentrate on your meaning because there are many errors involving ____ (spelling, punctuation, etc.)." As a sample of student writing, Aliza's narrative can be used to practice peer response (see pp. 53–54 in Chapter 3).

For more overtly persuasive writing, the following guidelines can help you assess the strengths and weaknesses of a draft:

Interest: How does the writer try to attract the attention of a reader who does not already agree with his or her viewpoint?

Thesis: What does the writer want to convince the reader to believe?

Supports: What evidence does the writer use to prove the validity of the thesis?

Objections: What counterarguments can be anticipated and answered?

Audience and Tone: Who is the writer trying to convince? To reach this intended audience (and not just those who already agree), what tone should be used? What tone will alienate an initially skeptical reader?

These response guidelines for persuasive writing can be practiced by responding to texts by professional writers, such as those in Chapters 6–10. Every page of this book has been reviewed by several preliminary readers, and we have made many revisions based on their responses.

When readers engage in peer response, the responders should almost always begin with positive comments, and this praise must be specific ("I thought p. 2 middle was very vivid because the details … " and "One of your best supports was … "). Then identify the focus or the thesis of the draft ("I think you are trying to … "). Thus far, the writer should listen more than reply to the response in order to demonstrate his receptiveness. Then as the response turns toward more problematic sections, a discussion should develop. The writer should not immediately resist the response ("You don't understand that … ") because then most responders will stop providing specific and sincere comments. If the writer listens well at first and signals her willingness to follow the responder, she later can start to imagine possible revisions ("Maybe I should say … " or "What if I explained next … ?"). As writers, we sometimes forget that what we meant to say is not always the same as what appears on the page for a reader; fortunately peer response can reveal this gap between intention and comprehension. As revisions are discussed, peer response becomes more constructive than critical so many writers learn to enjoy rather than fear reader feedback. These sessions ideally transform students concerned with deadlines and grades into writers concentrated on meaning and form.

Reader as Peer Responder	Writer of Draft-In-Progress
Start with positive comments.	Stay quiet and listen well.
Be specific and sincere.	Don't argue immediately.
Turn from strengths to weaknesses.	Keep accepting a reader's reactions.
Stress your reactions as a reader.	Start discussing possible revisions.
End with editing suggestions.	Assume the responsibility for editing the entire draft.

Editing

Like revision and response, editing is a later step in the writing process that can be completed best if the deadline is not looming ("It's due in six hours and I need some sleep!"). A frustrated student writing for a grade may find editing to be one last chore, but when expression, communication, and comprehension are the goals, editing can be a satisfying last step. It usually is easier to edit your own draft if you are aware of your frequent errors. Keep a list in your notebook or put a sticky note on your computer to remind yourself of your repeated errors. Then you can use the "Find" function to search for some of these errors, such as homonym misspellings like "then" and "than" that spell check will not detect. Spelling and grammar checks will reveal some editing problems so don't ignore the red and green squiggles of spelling and grammar checks, yet don't depend on them too much. Old-fashioned methods like consulting a print dictionary and reading a draft aloud can also help you complete the edits that a final draft deserves.

Timed Essays

We started this chapter by presenting the writing process with two extreme opposites: a quick text message and a gradually written assignment. Yet time, thought, and process clash in the messy middle of these two extremes, such as when you have to write an in-class, timed essay. Here's a typical essay question for an American history exam:

> Although slavery sometimes is considered to be the primary reason for the Civil War, what were several other significant causes of this conflict? In a well-organized essay, explain slavery as one of at least three causes of this war.

What would you do to answer this essay question? Consider both your thoughts as well as your actions: "To answer this question, I would .... "

Although the pressure of a timed essay may make you launch immediately into drafting the opening sentences of your essay, it usually is easier to condense but still follow the separate steps of the writing process. First, can you collect some ideas on the causes of the conflict? Through some quick thinking and/or brainstorming notes, you might consider, "Let's see, slavery and ... other causes? States rights and what else? Apart from slavery and states rights, another reason was economic tensions: Southern raw materials and Northern manufacturing. Anything else?" and on your thinking, brainstorming, and collecting might go. Then you could determine your focus ("I'll stress economic differences") and your order ("Start with slavery; I'll need some details like the Dred Scott decision. Then states rights and then end by emphasizing economic tensions.")

After a few minutes of this planning, it would be easy to start drafting if you knew the trick of turning the question into your introduction:

> *Slavery sometimes is considered the primary reason for the Civil War, but the issue of abolition was only one of several, sometimes related but not always connected causes. In addition to slavery, the controversies over states rights and economic policies transformed the once United States into a house divided.*

Then it would be time to pull the format of the five-paragraph essay out of your writer's toolbox. This format is not the only wrench you'll need for college writing, but it is a very useful one for timed essays. And if you are asked to explain four or five factors, just add another body paragraph or two. With these ideas already collected, it would be easier for you to plan coherent paragraphs (one cause per section-right?) and draft your answer. Don't forget to use a few topic sentences ("States rights also contributed to this conflict ... ") and explicit transitions ("The divisions created by the debate over states rights were exacerbated by other regional differences: economic priorities.").

To have enough time to emphasize these economic differences, you would have to monitor the 30 or 40 minutes allotted for this essay. After about 20 minutes, it would be time to turn to the third cause. You would have had to explain the first two causes quickly and avoided writing too much about one reason, slipping from focused analysis into rambling summary. Then to complete this essay, you would have to add an explicit conclusion, one that does not just repeat the introduction's ideas and phrases. Instead you would want to add a final thought without branching off into a new topic entirely. For example, you might end with

> *Slavery, states rights, and economic differences all led to the Civil War. The fact that historians may emphasize one cause over another demonstrates that they engage in interpretation as much as factual researching and reporting. The causes of this struggle are the subject of an endless debate.*

Ideally you would have a few minutes remaining as those final words are drafted. Although you probably could not revise much of this timed essay, you should proofread and edit so use the last few minutes to look for your typical errors. As with writing a homework assignment gradually over several days or more, it actually is more efficient to answer a timed essay by tackling each step separately: collect, focus, order, draft, edit (and possibly revise a little).

Completing a 40-minute, In-class Exam Essay

2–3 min.	Read the essay question more than once.
2–3 min.	Determine the essay's required form and features.
4–5 min.	Collect ideas and phrases for your answer.
2–3 min.	Organize your ideas into an effective order.
2–3 min.	Turn the main question into your introduction.
	Start drafting and avoid overwriting as you begin.
12–15	Monitor your time and develop each section adequately.
	Use paragraphs, topic sentences, and explicit transitions.
2–3 min.	End with an enriching conclusion.
4–5 min.	Review the draft, edit, and, if possible, revise as needed.

When faced with an exam essay, a short assignment, or a major paper, you can learn to control your writing process, and such control depends on your knowledge of the many steps of writing. Like a violinist who is aware of the angle of his bow or a hurdler who notices the extension of her first foot, most skilled writers understand and can articulate many aspects of their writing process or, we really should say, processes of writing. We want you to distinguish writing quickly about what you already know well and can phrase easily from writing when you still need to figure out your thoughts and word them carefully, which requires a more gradual process. Skilled writers, like any talented artist or athlete, know some shortcuts, but they also know when to use them *and* when not. Determining when to use a gradual process and when to combine, for example, collecting and drafting is not always easy. However, by looking back at successful writing as well as a less effective effort can help you control your process better for your next assignment.

Process Notes

To help you reflect on your writing process, you may be asked to write what are called "process notes." These notes can help you to not only look back at an effort but also to exert more control over your next effort. The following questions can help you reflect on your writing process; choose a few and write a page of **process notes**:

- *In what ways was your writing process for this assignment similar to or different from your usual writing practices in high school?*

- *How did you collect ideas? What strategies from brainstorming to premature drafting were productive or frustrating for you?*

- *How did you pick a topic and/or decide on your focus for an assigned topic?*

- *Why did you find it easy or hard to create an order for your reader to follow?*

- *What reader did you have in mind as you created this order?*

- *What expectations did you assume your intended reader had about your paper's content, order, and format?*

- *When was it easy or difficult for you to draft phrases, sentences, and paragraphs?*

- *When and why did you have to go back to an earlier step in the writing process?*

- *How did you revise your first draft?*

- *With more time and energy, what is another revision you would have liked to complete?*

- *If you engaged in peer response, what in particular was beneficial (or not)?*

- *What errors from a previous paper did you need to edit in this assignment? How did you edit this paper?*

Like a batter who makes an adjustment after missing a pitch or a artist who alters a technique, a writer should be able to vary the writing process to match the assignment. To sum up these lessons on the writing process, let us conclude: *The quick is not always the easiest, and the easy is not always the most effective. An effective writing process, however, is usually the most satisfying one.*

Assignment Analysis

To match your writing process with a particular assignment, the reflection we suggested at the end of the process actually should begin with analysis as soon as you receive a difficult assignment. When a student fails to recognize or can't fulfill the expected task of a writing assignment, the results usually are frustration ("What am I supposed to do?") and disappointment ("Why did I get a D?!"). It's important that you understand the range of writing you will be expected to complete at college and learn to ask several key questions about every writing assignment you receive.

When an assignment is given, almost every student will ask or wants to ask, "When is it due?" and "How long should it be?" However, there are several other equally important questions to ask about each assignment:

- What is the primary task?
- What sources should be used?
- What conventions should be followed?
- What specialized terms, if any, should be included?

Some students already consider these questions before they tackle an assignment; they have been taught to examine, for instance, the writing task(s) and been taught and to fulfill the conventions of academic writing. Some students, however, will have to make more of a transition from writing in high school to college so let's consider these four questions fully.

What Tasks

In high school, you probably wrote many five-paragraph essays, and **exposition** in general may have been emphasized. Yet this emphasis on exposition—explaining an event, a concept, or a text—can make the transition to college writing difficult for some students. They may not realize, at least initially, that many assignments involve other tasks, such as analysis and argument.

College writing assignments involve many tasks; in addition to exposition, the other kinds of assignments, also known as **modes of discourse**, include

- **Description**
- **Narration**
- **Analysis**
- **Comparison and Contrast**
- **Synthesis**
- **Argument**

Using your own words, how would you define each task? If a classmate were to ask you about a writing assignment, how would you explain the main task and distinguish it from other ones? For example, what would you say that analysis means? How does exposition differ from narration or argument?

Ideally, every writing assignment should use these exact terms to identify the task or tasks a student is expected to fulfill. Some professors, however, use other words and phrases to state their expectations; what do you think a professor expects if an assignment were to use the following phrases?

- Interpret the significance
- Recount an important event

- Summarize the main idea and several key points
- Defend your position
- Explain similarities and/or differences

The tasks implied by some of these phrases may seem obvious to you and your classmates; did most of your class assume that the first phrase requires analysis and the second involves narration? Yet does the third ("summarize") suggest exposition or analysis? The primary tasks of the last two probably seem to be argument ("defend") and compare/contrast ("similarities and/or differences"), but would you disagree with a classmate if he or she thought that both of those assignments also involve analysis?

"Analysis" is one of those words that we may try to take for granted. Yet some students awkwardly refer to "analyzation" so they probably are uncertain of what this task requires. What exactly should a college student do when analysis is assigned? The etymology of "analysis" suggests a "breaking into parts," and, to analyze an event or text, you have to distinguish some of the pieces of the whole. Yet what should you do next to avoid only explaining each part?

Analysis also involves discerning some pattern among those pieces. The analysis of a poem, for example, requires a reader to notice the rhyme pattern, the word choice, and the imagery. Then this interpretation could show how these parts work together to create a certain effect, such as a somber mood. The analysis of a historical event would require a similar identification, for instance, of several causes, and the demonstration of a cause–effect relationship. Usually, historical analysis also is tentative rather than absolute (e.g., *To what degree* do you think President Lincoln fought the Civil War in order to abolish slavery?). Thus, analysis involves not only the breaking down of the whole into parts and connecting some of the pieces into a significant pattern but also weighing one cause or trend against another (Lincoln's other reasons for war).

Although such analysis may seem to be difficult, it is something we do all the time, such as when we encounter an upset friend or an angry family member. We usually ask what is causing that emotion, we wonder if they are more troubled by this or that, and we weigh whether they will be calmed if we respond one way or another. A leading educator named Gerald Graff believes that most students have a "hidden intelligence," meaning they already know how to engage in complex intellectual tasks like analysis, but they may find it difficult to complete this task on an academic subject. When asked, for instance, to analyze an event, they lapse into summary. They repeat what happened instead of explaining why it happened.

The difference between summary and analysis will be crucial to your success in college writing. Let us be very clear that summary involves identifying the main ideas and some of the supporting details of a reading. Sometimes a professor will assign a summary of a difficult reading to encourage students to engage in close reading (see p. 12 of Chapter 1). The worst way to write a summary of a long and challenging text is to try to read and write simultaneously. This approach usually will lead you to include too many details from the start of the reading and too few from the ending. Another flaw will be that you probably will not distinguish between the main ideas and the supporting details; it's almost impossible to do so if you don't yet understand the entire reading. A better approach to writing a summary of a difficult reading is to use some of the techniques presented in Chapter 1. You can preview the entire text and notice, for example, the headings that organize a long reading into several sections. Next you can mark main ideas and annotate some supporting details as you read through the text. Finally, you can review the reading so you can discern both the proverbial "forest" of the main idea(s) and some of the "trees," meaning some of the supporting details. (For a more specific example of a summary assignment, see the rhetorical précis on p. 109 of Chapter 5.) Remember that a summary follows the ideas of the text; you should not add your opinions … unless you are being asked to analyze instead. Thus, let us repeat, it is vital that you determine the primary task of a writing assignment, or should we state the tasks of an assignment?

Although it's easier to discuss these tasks separately, most college writing assignments will involve more than one. Consider, for example, the basic lab report of many science courses. It usually contains:

- An introduction that states the problem
- A list that catalogs materials and equipment
- A procedure that presents each experimental step in correct order
- A results section that describes the outcomes, often with charts or graphs
- A discussion that interprets the significance of the results
- A conclusion that affirms or revises the original hypothesis and suggests further experimentation

Some lab reports also include a title page, an abstract, a reference list, and an appendix or two. The basic parts listed above involve a great deal of exposition, but what other tasks does this assignment require? When, for example, does the author of a lab report also have to engage in analysis and argument? The analysis presented in the discussion section leads to an argument that is summed up in the conclusion.

A lab report is only one example of many, usually quite complex, college writing assignments. Now we want you to pause and consider the various writing assignments of your college education. In your current college courses as well as your future study in a major, what different kinds of writing assignments do you think you will be assigned as you complete courses in the humanities (e.g., literature and philosophy), the social sciences (psychology and sociology), and the sciences (biology, chemistry, plus mathematics)? Over the next few years of your undergraduate education, your range of writing assignments may include but not be limited to the following:

- Personal narratives
- Expository essays
- Textual summaries
- Reading responses
- Literary analyses
- Poetry and fiction
- Creative nonfiction
- Opinion pieces
- Comparisons and contrasts
- Arguments
- Syntheses
- Research papers
- Lab reports
- Memos and proposals
- Websites and blogs
- Personal statements
- Application letters

Many of these assignments will involve not only various tasks but also diverse sources and conventions. However, before you read on, can you pause to consider the various kinds of papers you have been assigned to write this semester and/or last term? What tasks are suggested on your course syllabi and/or specific assignments?

What Sources and Which Conventions

As you reread an assignment, consider what **sources** you are expected to use. Many college writing assignments will require you to rely on one or more of the following sources:

- Personal experiences and/or observations
- Personal interviews and/or surveys
- Textbook and/or class notes
- Newspaper and/or magazine articles
- Scholarly articles and/or books
- Films and/or videos
- Blogs and/or websites

For more information on how to access some of these sources and evaluate their content, see Research Methods and Motives in the Further Resources Online, which accompany this textbook.

For some students, the difficulty of finding good sources is surpassed by their confusion over the diverse **conventions** of various writing assignments. It may seem to some students that one professor tells them to do this, but another instructor says to do that. There usually are some good reasons for these differences, but they need to be discussed explicitly. For example, let's examine a lab report in relation to a narrative: In what ways do the conventions of these two assignments differ? In what ways, if any, are they similar? In other words, how are you expected to write in each assignment?

At first, no writing tasks may seem to be more different than a narrative and a lab report. Don't English professors want flowery language while scientists value straightforward facts? Yet these assignments are not as different as they first appear. Each assignment has a main focus, includes detailed information, creates a cause-and-effect sequence, and leads readers to a final thought. Here is a list of some of their fundamental similarities as well as their apparent differences:

Narrative	Lab Report
Get the reader interested	State the problem and the hypothesis
Show with vivid details	List all materials
Create a compelling order	Present each step
Identify characters, including "I"	Avoid the first person "I"
Reveal the consequences of key actions	Discuss the results
Provide some greater meaning	Conclude on its significance

One of the most obvious contrasts between these two assignments is the subjective nature of a narrative and the objectivity of a lab report. In a narrative, "I" often is used to present sensory experiences, but in a lab report, the convention is to avoid the first person, so experimental details are presented using the passive voice. Rather than state "I weighed the item and found that it was 1.2 g," the writer of lab reports employs the passive voice to state, "The item was weighed, and its mass was 1.2 g." While a narrative includes sensory details like "the gorgeous sunshine warmed my hands," a lab report definitely would not mention "the pretty blue flame of the Bunsen burner"!

To understand the reasons for these differences in conventions, we must consider their results. A narrative allows the reader to imagine the writer's experience through vivid details, and the lab report is detailed yet detached because the experiment is supposed to be reimagined and even recreated by the readers. Anyone who follows the lab's procedure properly should reach the same results. Thus, the different conventions of a subjective narrative and a more objective lab report are a matter of rhetorical means and ends. Sometimes writers use different means, such as the first person "I" or not, to reach the same ends: reader comprehension, audience understanding.

What Terms and Why

Every academic discipline has its own specialized **terms**, its own jargon. For example, the average person would define a "line" as a mark from here to there; some are straight but others, wavy. Yet this word means much more when art students learn to study a painter's use of "line" or when math students are taught that in non-Euclidean geometry, parallel lines can cross. At college, a "line" can have several, very specialized meanings.

It's natural to resist these complicated terms and ask why can't we just use plain language and talk simply? Consider, however, whatever sport or hobby you enjoy. Why do baseball pitchers talk about two and four seamers? Or why do motorcyclists refer to "entering the apex" of a turn and quilters talk about "stitch in the ditch"? Every group has its own jargon, so what are some of the specialized terms of your major? In other words, what are some of the key terms and phrases your professors use in class and expect you to include in your speech and writing? Here are some quick examples from diverse disciplines:

- History: political legitimacy
- Philosophy: ontology
- Communication: relational processes
- Chemistry: covalent bonds
- Computer sciences: downward compatibility
- Economics: organizational behavior
- Music: cadence
- Engineering: structural dynamics
- Education: hidden curriculum

As students struggle with the use of terms like these, it is easy and tempting to dismiss them as words no one uses in the "real" world. Yet in the "real" world of professionals, many of these terms *are* used every day. These terms are central to your education, or as a writing theorist named Mike Rose states,

> You could almost define a university education as an initiation into a variety of powerful ongoing discussions … The more comfortable students become with this kind of influential talk, the more they will be included in further conversations, … which virtually defines them as members of an intellectual community.

As you learn to participate in these college-level discussions, it is crucial to consider: Do academics use these terms to impress students? Or do they use them, like motorcyclists and quilters who refer to "the apex" and "the ditch," as convenient labels for complex concepts?

The use and misuse of specialized terms depends upon **audience**. What happens when an expert uses a specialized term while addressing a general audience and yet while speaking with another expert? Depending on one's audience, jargon can be elitist and exclusionary or quick and convenient for bikers, quilters, and academics. To avoid the negative effects of jargon on a general audience, many writers rely on **embedded definitions** in their writing, such as when they refer to exposition, or explaining, in the same sentence. By slipping in, or embedding, quick definitions like "explaining" for exposition, a general reader can follow an expert's language. For students writing for professors, embedded definitions serve another important purpose: they demonstrate to the instructor that the student is not just mimicking the "big words" of **academic discourse** but is able to use them knowledgeably.

Five Sample Assignments

Below are five sample assignments for you to examine. Try analyzing their task(s), source(s), convention(s), and term(s):

Art History 100

When we visit the museum next week, your assignment is to write an analysis of a Renaissance, Romantic, or an Impressionist painting. In three, double-spaced pages, you should help your reader understand one particular painting. Start with the name of the painter, the title of the painting, and its date (if known). This basic information will be found on the label that accompanies the work, but you should not rely on the paragraphs that usually can be found on the label. Nor should you research the painting and repeat the opinions of an art historian. Instead you should examine the painting for yourself. Keeping the subject of the painting in mind, what is the overall expressive effect of the work? What formal and stylistic elements contribute to that effect? How does the physical display of the painting in the museum add to its impact on you? Thus, you should employ the analysis we have practiced by viewing slides in class.

Communications 101

Assignment One: Write a 2–4 pp. paper that describes your own public speaking strengths and weaknesses. Be honest about how you feel about public speaking (frank honesty will not affect your grade) and include a specific example from the past or your experience of speaking in front of the class today.

Education 102

Based on your recent school visits, what is the learning environment of this classroom? Remember you are not being asked to summarize the subject lessons of this class; instead you should examine its learning environment, which includes the teacher's actions, the students' reactions, and the physical space. This environment also involves the "hidden curriculum" as well as the explicit instructions of the teacher. In other words, what are students being taught about learning in this environment?

Math 105

This first paper is based on your experiences and your imaginative—be creative!

1. What was your most difficult math class in high school? What made it difficult for you?

2. Place that difficult class within your journey in mathematics: What are several key moments in your mathematical journey? For example, when did math seem easy to you? When was it fun? When was it frustrating or satisfying?

3. Based on this math journey, where are you now? If you were a person or animal in mathematics, who or what would you be and why? In other words, create a creative analogy for your current position in this journey.

Psychology 110

Find an article on parapsychology. Write a 2–3 pp. paper that presents the basic bibliographic info of the author, title, and source, and then summarize it in a paragraph. Refer to the author by his her last name in the summary. Add why do you think some people believe in this example of parapsychology, and finally, what do you think of this example (and why?)?

You may not be able to answer every question for each assignment, and some of your answers may differ from your classmates' responses. However, it is crucial that you consider more than the length and the due date of your next assignment.

Key Terms

Before you finish with this chapter, here is a list of the key terms of this chapter; which ones can you explain easily, and which ones do you need to review?

<u>Writing Process</u>

Collect/invention
    Brainstorm
    Cluster
    Freewrite

Focus
    Thesis

Order/Arrangement
    Chronological
    "in medias res"

      Problem to Solution
      Cause and Effect
      Pro/Con
      Compare/Contrast

Draft
      Diction
      Syntax

Revise
      Peer response

Edit

Process notes

<u>Assignment Analysis</u>

Tasks/modes of discourse
      Exposition/Summary
      Description
      Narration
      Analysis
      Comparison/Contrast
      Synthesis
      Argument

Sources

Conventions
      Rhetorical means and ends

Terms
      Audience
      Embedded definitions

Academic discourse

Additional Sources for Chapter 2

To deepen your understanding of the writing process and assignment analysis, you can consult some of the following sources:

1. For an inspiring essay on the writing process, you may want to read "A Way of Writing" by William Stafford. In this essay, Stafford emphasizes the freedom of starting to write.

   http://ualr.edu/rmburns/RB/staffort.html

2. For a much more business-oriented description of the writing process, you may want to read "The Composing Process of an Engineer" by Jack Selzer. In this article, Selzer both challenges and supports some of Stafford's observations on writing.

   http://english111writingasanengineercvk.weebly.com/uploads/9/0/4/5/9045635/selzer_composingasanengineer.pdf

3. For a study of the importance of writing for first-year students, you may want to read "Novice as Expert: Writing the Freshman Year" by Nancy Sommers and Laura Saltz. In this study of first-year writing students at Harvard University, the authors analyze the value of personal interest and critical analysis as students try to develop from novice to expert writers.

   http://www.bucknell.edu/Documents/WritingCenter/the%20novice%20as%20expert.pdf

4. For more guidance on analyzing writing assignments, you may want to consult the Online Writing Lab (OWL) of Purdue University. In addition to the general suggestions, see the further information on various assignments, such as arguments, proposals, and research papers.

   https://owl.english.purdue.edu/owl/resource/688/01/

5. For detailed instruction on punctuation, grammar, and proofreading, you may want to consult the Online Writing Lab (OWL) of Purdue University. See the tabs of each section.

   https://owl.english.purdue.edu/owl/section/1/6/

   https://owl.english.purdue.edu/owl/section/1/5/

   https://owl.english.purdue.edu/owl/resource/561/1/

Process in Practice: Personal Narratives

CHAPTER 3

In this chapter, we will ask you to practice the writing process (see Chapter 2) to write what can be termed a personal narrative, first-person essay, or nonfiction narrative. We will refer to this assignment as a personal narrative. You will be asked to write about a significant conflict in your life and present it as a story showing a sequence of events, actions, and words. In addition to presenting this sequence, this narrative also should include your thoughts, feelings, and insights because these impressions will add some significance to your tale. Then a reader will not only understand what happened in this conflict but why it is significant for you and others.

This twofold focus on yourself and others may seem difficult to develop. First, rather than avoid the first person, the writer of a personal essay must focus on the self. As Henry David Thoreau, the author of *Civil Disobedience* and *Walden*, explained

> In most books, the I, or first person is omitted … We commonly do not remember that it is after all, always the first person that is speaking. I should not talk so much about myself if there were anybody else whom I knew as well.

Yet second, even as a writer focuses on the self, he or she often must attend to the reader as well. As the poet bell hooks asserts,

> It is essential for any writer who wants to speak to a general audience … to write in a manner that welcomes any reader … Writers must trust that readers are ready to receive our words.

For more on the relationship between writers and readers, see Donald Murray's quotation on p. 26 of Chapter 2, plus Chapter 5 on rhetoric.

In this chapter, we will encourage you to focus on your experiences as well as keep your reader in mind and welcome this audience. The best of today's blogs demonstrate this combination of personal experience and public relevance. These digital texts are but the latest examples in the long tradition of personal narratives, which includes Michel Montaigne, Thoreau, and Virginia Woolf. More recently, writers such as James Baldwin, E. B. White, Alice Walker, Amy Tan, Richard Rodriquez, Annie Dillard, David Sedaris, and Mary Karr have explored the events, emotions, and expectations of their lives.

Genre and Convention

Before you start writing your own personal narrative, we want you to pause and consider the nature of this assignment (see pp. 33–37 on assignment analysis in Chapter 2). Most students learn to write five-paragraph essays before they come to college; you probably know the drill: an introduction, three body paragraphs, and a conclusion—right? Now let's consider what a reader will expect as she starts to read your draft; can you contrast a personal narrative with a five-paragraph essay? What are some of the expected features of each form of writing? How does "what a reader expects of each assignment" differ?

The following start of a personal narrative demonstrates why it is important to distinguish this assignment from a five-paragraph essay; a student began his first draft with an introduction like

> In the summer of my freshman year, I learned a valuable lesson. My soccer coach wanted me to play defense, but I had always been an offensive player who loved to score goals. My conflict taught me to be a better teammate.

This student states his focus exactly and sums up his conflict neatly, but as the opening of a personal narrative, this introduction tells a reader too much and too soon. This criticism initially confused this student writer because he had been taught to write precisely this kind of an introduction … for a five-paragraph essay.

When some students have discussed the differences between these assignments, their responses have included the following:

Personal Narrative	Five-Paragraph Essay
More flexible structure	Fixed structure
Engaging opening	Intro paragraph
Multiple paragraphs of various length	Three body paragraphs with topic sentences
Events presented	Ideas explained
Showing details	Supporting info
Order by chronology	Organize three topics
End with significance	Sum up main points

Of course, the students didn't always phrase these contrasts so precisely, but we have done so following the conventions of a textbook. Note in our example, how conventions help to determine what is expected and written. To sum up the differences between a narrative and a five-paragraph essay, we will assert that a personal narrative enables a reader to experience an event whereas a five-paragraph essay allows a reader to understand an idea. In other words, the first is more concrete and subjective, and the second is more abstract and objective. With this emphasis on the writer's thoughts, feelings, and actions, a personal narrative should include the first person, which most teachers forbid in a five-paragraph essay. This exclusion of "I" from this kind of essay matches its purposes, but so too does the use of the first person in a narrative essay. This reversal of the "rule" against "I" does not mean that your high school teacher or your current writing professor is wrong; instead it demonstrates that different writing tasks have different conventions (for more on tasks, see pp. 34–37 of Chapter 2).

A Personal Narrative

Here's the main assignment of this chapter:

> Write a narrative essay about a significant conflict in your life. This conflict can be a direct confrontation between you and a friend, a family member, or an authority figure, such as a teacher or a coach. It also could be a quieter, less obvious tension between you and others or within yourself. Remember that a personal narrative tries to make sense of these events so the conflict should not be one that is too recent or too painful for you to recall and later too difficult for you to examine critically. You also should be ready to share drafts of this narrative with at least a few classmates.

Your professor may give you a general topic for this assignment, one that matches the subject of one of the thematic chapters, such as family from Chapter 6 or education from Chapter 7. Then your personal experience of a significant conflict will lead you right into the views of others on this issue.

Below, we will provide a sequence of possible activities to guide you through the writing process, and these possibilities will address:

- Topic selection
- Detail collection
- Subject focus
- Tentative organization
- Preliminary drafting
- Draft revision
- Final editing

We also know that some students like to have a clear image of what it is expected before they are ready to proceed. Let us stress that this is just one example, and many other topics and variations of a personal narrative are possible. You will find two other sample narratives below, but let's get started with the following example.

DON'T CALL ME MARIA

by Judith Ortiz Cofer

As a child, Judith Ortiz Cofer grew up listening to the stories of her grandmother. As a writer, Ortiz Cofer tells her own tales of growing up and living in two sometimes clashing cultures: Puerto Rican and American. A prolific and acclaimed writer, she also examines the tensions between patriarchal oppression and female empowerment. Originally titled "The Myth of the Latin Woman," this narrative from 1993 appeared in a collection of essays called *The Latin Deli*.

From *The Latin Deli: Prose & Poetry* by Judith Ortiz Cofer. Copyright © 1993 by Judith Ortiz Cofer. Reprinted by permission of the University of Georgia Press.

On a bus trip to London from Oxford University, where I was earning some graduate credits one summer, a young man, obviously fresh from a pub, spotted me and as if struck by inspiration went down on his knees in the aisle. With both hands over his heart he broke into an Irish tenor's rendition of "Maria" from West Side Story. My politely amused fellow passengers gave his lovely voice the round of gentle applause it deserved. Though I was not quite as amused, I managed my version of an English smile: no show of teeth, no extreme contortions of the facial muscles—I was at this time of my life practicing reserve and cool. Oh, that British control, how I coveted it. But Maria had followed me to London, reminding me of a prime fact of my life: you can leave the Island, master the English language, and travel as far as you can, but if you are a Latina, especially one like me who so obviously belongs to Rita Moreno's gene pool, the Island travels with you.

This is sometimes a very good thing—it may win you that extra minute of someone's attention. But with some people, the same things can make you an island—not so much a tropical paradise as an Alcatraz, a place nobody wants to visits. As a Puerto Rican girl growing up in the United States and wanting like most children to "belong," I resented the stereotype that my Hispanic appearance called forth from many people I met.

Our family lived in a large urban center in New Jersey during the sixties, where life was designed as a microcosm of my parents' casas on the island. We spoke in Spanish, we ate Puerto Rican food bought at the bodega, and we practiced strict Catholicism complete with Saturday confession and Sunday mass at a church where our parents were accommodated into a one-hour Spanish mass slot, performed by a Chinese priest trained as a missionary in Latin America.

As a girl, I was kept under strict surveillance, since virtue and modesty were, by cultural equation, the same as family honor. As a teenager I was instructed on how to behave as a proper senorita. But it was a conflicting message girls got, since the Puerto Rican mothers also encouraged their daughters to look and act like women and to dress in clothes our Anglo friends and their mothers found too "mature" for our age. It was, and is, cultural, yet I often felt humiliated when I appeared at an American friend's party wearing a dress more suitable to a semiformal than to a playroom birthday celebration. At Puerto Rican festivities, neither the music nor the colors we wore could be too loud. I still experience a vague sense of letdown when I'm invited to a "party" and it turns out to be a marathon conversation in hushed tones rather than a fiesta with salsa, laughter, and dancing—the kind of celebration I remember from my childhood.

I remember Career Day in our high school, when teachers told us to come dressed as if for a job interview. It quickly became obvious that to the barrio girls, "dressing up" sometimes meant wearing ornate jewelry and clothing that would be more appropriate (by mainstream standards) for the company Christmas party than as daily office attire. That morning, I had agonized in front of my closet, trying to figure out what a "career girl" would wear because, essentially, except for Marlo Thomas on TV, I had no models on which to base my decision. I knew how to dress for Sunday mass, and I knew what dresses to wear for parties at my relatives' homes. Though I do not recall the precise details of my Career Day outfit, it must have been a composite of the above choices. But I remember a comment my friend (an Italian-American) made in later years that coalesced my impression of that day. She said that at the business school she was attending the Puerto Rican girls always stood out for wearing "everything at once." She meant, of course, too much jewelry, too many accessories. On that day at school, we were simply made the negative models by the nuns who were themselves not credible fashion experts to any of us. But it was painfully obvious to me that to the others, in their tailored skirts and silk blouses, we must have seemed "hopeless" and "vulgar." Though I now know that most adolescents feel out of step much of the time, I also know that for the Puerto Rican girls of my generation that sense was intensified. The way our teachers and classmates looked at us that day in school was just a taste of the culture clash that awaited us in the real world, where prospective employers and men on the street would often misinterpret our tight skirts and jingling bracelets as a come-on.

Mixed cultural signals have perpetuated certain stereotypes—for example, that of the Hispanic woman as the "Hot Tamale" or sexual firebrand. It is a one-dimensional view that the media have found easy to promote. In their special vocabulary, advertisers have designated "sizzling" and "smoldering" as the adjectives of choice for describing not only the foods but also the women of Latin America. From conversations in my house, I recall hearing about the harassment that Puerto Rican women endured in the factories where the "boss men" talked to them as if sexual innuendo was all they understood and, worse, often gave them the choice of submitting to advances or being fired.

It is custom, however, not chromosomes, that leads us to choose scarlet over pale pink. As young girls, we were influenced in our decisions about clothes and colors by the women—older sisters and mothers who had grown up on a tropical island where the natural environment was a riot of primary colors, where showing your skin was one way to keep cool as well as to look sexy. Most important of all, on the island, women perhaps felt freer to dress and move more provocatively, since, in most cases, they were protected by the traditions, mores, and laws of a Spanish/Catholic system of morality and machismo whose main rule was: *You may look at my sister, but if you touch her I will kill you.* The extended family and church structure could provide a young woman with a circle of safety in her small pueblo on the island; if a man "wronged" a girl, everyone would close in to save her family honor.

This is what I have gleaned from my discussions as an adult with older Puerto Rican women. They have told me about dressing in their best party clothes on Saturday nights and going to the town's plaza to promenade with their girlfriends in front of the boys they liked. The males were thus given the opportunity to admire the women and to express their admiration in the form of *piropos*: erotically charged street poems they composed on the spot. I have been subjected to a few piropos while visiting the Island, and they can be outrageous, although custom dictates that they never cross into obscenity. This ritual, as I understand it, also entails a show of indifference on the woman's part; if she is "decent," she must not acknowledge the man's impassioned words. So I do understand how things can be lost in translation. When a Puerto Rican girl dressed in her idea of what is attractive meets a man from the mainstream culture who has been trained to react to certain types of clothing as a sexual signal, a clash is likely to take place. The line I first heard based on this aspect of the myth happened when the boy who took me to my first formal dance leaned over to plant a sloppy overeager kiss painfully on my mouth, and when I didn't respond with sufficient passion, said in a resentful tone: "I thought you Latin girls were supposed to mature early"—my first instance of being thought of as a fruit or vegetable—I was supposed to *ripen*, not just grow into womanhood like other girls.

It is surprising to some of my professional friends that some people, including those who should know better, still put others "in their place." Though rarer, these incidents are still commonplace in my life. It happened to me most recently during a stay at a very classy metropolitan hotel favored by young professional couples for their weddings. Late one evening after the theater, as I walked toward my room with my new colleague (a woman with whom I was coordinating an arts program), a middle-aged man in a tuxedo, a young girl in satin and lace on his arm, stepped directly into our path. With his champagne glass extended toward me, he exclaimed, "Evita!"

Our way blocked, my companion and I listened as the man half-recited, half-bellowed, "Don't Cry for Me, Argentina." When he finished, the young girl said: "How about a round of applause for my daddy?" We complied, hoping this would bring the silly spectacle to a close. I was becoming aware that our little group was attracting the attention of the other guests. "Daddy" must have perceived this too, and he once more barred the way as we tried to walk past him. He began to shout a ditty to the tune of "La Bamba"—except the lyrics were about a girl named Maria whose exploits all rhymed with her name and gonorrhea. The girl kept saying, "Oh, Daddy" and looking at me with pleading eyes. She wanted me to laugh along with the others. My companion and I stood silently waiting for the man to end his offensive song. When he finished, I looked not at him but at his daughter. I advised her calmly never to ask her father what he had done in the army. Then I walked between them and to my room. My friend complimented me on my cool handling of the situation. I confessed to her that I really had wanted to push the jerk into the swimming pool. I knew that this same man—probably a corporate executive, well-educated, even worldly by most standards—would not have been likely to regale a white woman with a dirty song in public. He would perhaps have checked his impulse by assuming that she could be somebody's wife or mother, or at least *somebody* who might take offense. But to him, I was just an Evita or a Maria: merely a character in his cartoon-populated universe.

Because of my education and my proficiency with the English language, I have acquired many mechanisms for dealing with the anger I experience. This was not true for my parents, nor is it true for the many Latin women working at menial jobs who must put up with stereotypes about our ethnic group such as: "They make good domestics." This is another facet of the myth of the Latin woman in the United States. Its origin is simple to deduce. Work as domestics, waitressing, and factory jobs are all that's available to women with little English and few skills. The myth of the Hispanic menial has been sustained by the same media phenomenon that made "Mammy" from *Gone with the Wind* America's idea of the black woman for generations; Maria, the housemaid or counter girl, is now indelibly etched into the national psyche. The big and the little screens have presented us with the picture of the funny Hispanic maid, mispronouncing words and cooking up a spicy storm in a shiny California kitchen.

This media-engendered image of the Latina in the United States has been documented by feminist Hispanic scholars, who claim that such portrayals are partially responsible for the denial of opportunities for upward mobility among Latinas in the professions. I have a Chicana friend working on a Ph.D. in philosophy at a major university. She says her doctor still shakes his head in puzzled amazement at all the "big words" she uses. Since I do not wear my diplomas around my neck for all to see, I too have on occasion been sent to that "kitchen," where some think I obviously belong.

One such incident that has stayed with me, though I recognize it as a minor offense, happened on the day of my first public poetry reading. It took place in Miami in a boat-restaurant where we were having lunch before the event. I was nervous and excited as I walked in with my notebook in my hand. An older woman motioned me to her table. Thinking (foolish me) that she wanted me to autograph a copy of my brand new slender volume of verse, I went over. She ordered a cup of coffee from me, assuming that I was the waitress. Easy enough to mistake my poems for menus, I suppose. I know that it wasn't an intentional act of cruelty, yet of all the good things that happened that day, I remember that scene most clearly, because it reminded me of what I had to overcome before anyone would take me seriously. In retrospect I understand that my anger gave my reading fire, that I have almost always taken doubts in my abilities as a challenge—and that the result is, most times, a feeling of satisfaction at having won a convert when I see the cold, appraising eyes warm to my words, the body language change, the smile that indicates that I have opened some avenue for communication. That day, I read to that woman, and her lowered eyes told me that she was embarrassed at her little faux pas, and when I willed her to look up at me, it was my victory, and she graciously allowed me to punish her with my full attention. We shook hands at the end of the reading, and I never saw her again. She has probably forgotten the whole thing, but maybe not.

Yet I am one of the lucky ones. My parents made it possible for me to acquire a stronger footing in the mainstream culture by giving me the chance at an education. And books and art have saved me from the harsher forms of ethnic and racial prejudice that many of my Hispanic *compañeras* have had to endure. I travel a lot around the United States, reading from my books of poetry and my novel, and the reception I most often receive is one of positive interest by people who want to know more about my culture. There are, however, thousands of Latinas without the privilege of an education or the entrée into society that I have. For them life is a struggle against the misconceptions perpetuated by the myth of the Latina as whore, domestic or criminal. We cannot change this by legislating the way people look at us. The transformation, as I see it, has to occur at a much more individual level. My personal goal in my public life is to try to replace the old pervasive stereotypes and myths about Latinas with a much more interesting set of realities. Every time I give a reading, I hope the stories I tell, the dreams and fears I examine in my work, can achieve some universal truth which will get my audience past the particulars of my skin color, my accent, or my clothes.

I once wrote a poem in which I called us Latinas "God's brown daughters." This poem is really a prayer of sorts, offered upward, but also, through the human-to-human channel of art, outward. It is a prayer for communication, and for respect. In it, Latin women pray "in Spanish to an Anglo God/with a Jewish heritage," and they are "fervently hoping/that if not omnipotent, / at least He be bilingual."

Here are several questions for close reading and analysis of this text. For more on close reading and analysis, see Chapter 1. Several challenging questions are provided below so we do not expect a student will be asked to answer every one for homework. Instead, one of the pleasures of a good class discussion is for students to respond to a question or two and then develop expanded answers and insights through conversation and collaboration. By the end of the discussion, many aspects of a reading will have been examined.

Close Reading Questions

1. Why do you think Ortiz Cofer has (or has not) presented an engaging conflict?

2. What details are most (or least) compelling to you?

3. In addition to Ortiz Cofer herself, who would you identify as some of the other main participants in her conflict? How would you describe the perspectives of some of the participants, such as Ortiz Cofer's parents and her Anglo teachers? (Multiple Perspectives)

Analytical Writing/Discussion

4. How did the varied customs related to fashion create misunderstandings between Puerto-Rican girls like Ortiz Cofer and her Anglo classmates? What are some of the primary influences on your own fashion choices, and when, if ever, have they created a "cultural clash" for you? (Cultural Influences)

5. How do influences within Puerto-Rican culture both promote and protect a teenage female's sexuality? Why do you think some of your own cultural influences represent (or do not represent) a similar self-contradiction?

6. Ortiz Cofer both describes and disrupts some "pervasive stereotypes." To what degree do you think these stereotypes have been disrupted or continue today? (Historical Trends)

Topic Selection and Detail Collection

As you turn your attention back to your own personal narrative, please note that your conflict does not have to be sensational; you are not applying for a chair-throwing talk show or a headline-making reality television program. A conflict involves an opposition, but it does not always mean a loud argument or a physical confrontation. In the past, students have chosen to write about many diverse topics, ranging from athletic struggles, artistic fears, and authority confrontations to tragic losses, difficult choices, and disappointed ambitions.

As you develop this narrative, it will be shared with and discussed by at least a few of your classmates so don't pick a subject that you cannot imagine allowing another student to read about. There is a fine line between the personal and the private, and you and your instructor will have to determine where exactly that line lies.

You should choose your topic carefully because you will be devoting a few weeks to this chapter. Good topics depend on knowledge and interest. Avoid a topic in which you were not really involved in the conflict because you may not have enough knowledge to write well. Yet, you also should avoid a conflict in which you were a central figure if that event already is settled in your mind, for you soon will lose interest in it. Both knowledge and interest are essential.

As explained in Chapter 2, brainstorming, clustering, and freewriting can be used to generate an array of potential topics (see pp. 25 and 26). Once you have collected several topic possibilities, you will not be required to share all of these choices, but the topic you choose should not be too private to share with others. Use one or more of the following methods: brainstorming, clustering, and/or freewriting, generate at least four topics below:

Some Possible Topics

Once you have gathered some likely topics, pick at least two and try to collect what Donald Murray terms a "necessary abundance" of details. Using brainstorming or another invention method, gather as many details, phases, and connections as you can in several minutes. Be receptive to many ideas now, and only later should you try to judge them. These details will enable you to *show*, as the old adage goes, rather than to *tell* your audience about your conflict.

Topic One   *Topic Two*   *Topic Three*

Your professor may ask you to explain some of your topics and details to another classmate or two. Obviously, if you cannot discuss a topic for several minutes, you either need to develop it more or move on to another one. A likely topic is one that you feel you have enough to write about (knowledge) as well as a desire to understand the conflict better (interest).

Focus and Order

Once you have made a preliminary decision on your topic, you may want to sum it up in a sentence or two:

> *I think my conflict is about* _____, *and the primary*
> *conflict is between* _____ *and* _____ .

Some of you, however, may struggle to assert your focus so soon. If you have been able to collect a necessary abundance of details and your topic still interests you, keep going. Once you have worked on an order and drafted a few pages, your focus probably will be clarified. As we will explain below, sometimes we have to "write to learn" (see pp. 52 and 53). With your focus in mind, you may want to go back and collect more details, perhaps by focusing on your audience and their needs. Writing often involves a tension between a writer and a reader: What does the writer want to say? versus What can a reader understand? For example, is a conflict with a friend or teacher based on some previous moment of distrust? Or was a decision to leave a clique or quit a team influenced by an outsider? Try considering both what you want to say and what a reader needs to know to help you collect more details.

Since a narrative shows events rather than explains ideas, try imagining what we will call "scenes." These scenes resemble the panels of a graphic novel or the storyboard of a movie; they are frames filled with crucial details. What are three main scenes of your narrative? You can begin with the opening event or a central moment, then add two more.

Creating an Order

Scene One   *Scene Two*   *Scene Three*

Here's a sample of one student's scene planning. This student, Aliza Leavitt, decided to write about her conflict over her college choice, a struggle that she realized had been developing for several years.

Three Scenes:

Early Choices	College Visit	Application Process
Always knew what	Really loved it	Unbearable stress
I wanted to be yet	Advertising major	Rejection fears
It changed every year	Beautiful campus	Accepted at 6 of 7
Archeologist	College banner	Best birthday
Architect	over my bed	present yet !

Which details attract your attention as a reader? Which ones need to be developed more so you can understand them better? Do any seem unnecessary to you? What questions would you want to ask Aliza if she were one of your classmates? Next, your professor may ask you to apply some of these questions to your own scenes and/or to those of a classmate. Even as we are presenting a sequence that starts with topic selection, detail collection and a tentative order, you may want to return to these steps later on. Or, you may want to consider the order carefully only after you have started to draft. We do not intend our sequence to be a rigid progression that every student must follow exactly. Your topic choice, your writing habits, and your professor's suggestions will influence your process.

Drafting

Although we already have suggested a significant amount of writing, completing a draft may require more concentration for a more sustained period. This sustained concentration can be promoted or hindered by the time and place of writing. Many professional writers prefer to wake early to write; some reach for their favorite pen at a desk, whereas others settle with keyboard into a comfortable chair. Some students write late at night in a busy dorm room, while others need a quiet library corner at midday. Like so much of the process of writing, there is no single method that enables every writer to succeed. It, however, is important to choose a time and place that does not distract you from writing. For example, many writers like music as part of their drafting environment, yet as they settle into drafting, this music soon becomes "gray" background noise. Many songs may pass, but they go virtually unheard. Music and other elements of our writing environment, such as instant messaging, should be used to maintain our focus or take a planned break, but they should not disrupt the concentration needed to write well.

We already have mentioned that some students are able to write a first draft quickly and sometimes without engaging in much of the preliminary writing suggested above. These students usually have been turning their topics over in their minds, and they already have planned much of their writing, at least unconsciously. Other students, of course, are much less prepared to draft so here's an example of Aliza's early drafting:

> The last tour we went on before school started was to [University #1]. From the moment we got out of the car, I really loved it there. They had an advertising major, which many places did not, and that was something I was looking for. The school itself was beautiful, and I loved the atmosphere. It seemed like a perfect match for me, and it really could be the place I would end up spending my four years. For months after, a blue and gold banner hung over my bed.

The beginning of senior year came too quickly, and it wasn't long before we started sending out applications. The stress on all of us from parents, teachers, and guidance counselors was almost unbearable at times. Important deadlines were looming, and the dreaded thought of not getting into any schools was something my friends and I joked about all the time, but we were all secretly afraid of. Even though I knew where I wanted to go, I ended up applying to seven schools, just in case. After getting into six and being waitlisted at another, I had nothing to complain about. I got into my top 3 schools. I really only cared about one school though, and I happened to get that acceptance letter the day before my birthday. I was so excited to open the envelope and tell my mom as soon as she got home from work. She was so happy for me, and I thought that would be it.

As you probably suspect, Aliza's college search is far from over, and your reaction to this drafting demonstrates what we will term *peer response*. These reactions by other students involve more than editing suggestions, instead they are assertions of a reader's engagement with a text (or difficulty getting engaged). It is almost always better to begin responding to a draft by being positive: What do you think are some of the most effective, showing details that enable a reader to experience this event? Then shift from this specific praise to areas that may need some revision: Do any parts of this draft seem less effective to you and why? For instance, does Aliza sometimes lapse into telling her impressions rather than showing them for her reader? If there are any parts that you do not understand, can you state this problem as a question, as in "What did you mean when you said … ?" Based on your own, possibly similar, experiences with college decisions, what vivid details can you suggest to Aliza?

Revising

As explained in Chapter 2, the writing consists of several stages, and we often need to go back to a previous step so we can proceed forward. For example, to revise a draft, you may need to return to focus and ask yourself what is this draft really about? And what do you what a reader to learn? These two questions are distinct; the first addresses topic and the second is about message. For instance, as Aliza narrates her college search (topic), what does she want her readers to understand (message)?

Here is Aliza's complete draft. We have numbered the paragraphs for easier discussion of its strengths and possible revisions.

The Finish Line

1. *College is something that most people start dealing with in the middle of high school. However, in my case, I started thinking about college in middle school. The whole concept was so interesting to me. I don't know why, but maybe it is because I'm the oldest of four siblings. Like most oldest children, I thought it would be exciting to do something I had no experience with yet.*

2. *I've always known what I've wanted to be when I grew up, even though what I've wanted has changed a few times over the years. When I was younger, I wanted to be an archeologist (mainly because I had a really cool social studies teacher who did the same thing). A few years later, I decided that I wanted to be an architect, and after that phase, I finally settled on something I had always been interested in, business and advertising. I loved thinking about the future and what it would bring.*

3. I've never really had a "dream school" like some kids do. I didn't come from a line of Cornell or Harvard graduates, and there wasn't a particular school that I was expected to attend, so I was on my own to narrow the thousands of options down to one. Naturally, like my changing career interests, my top college picks changed as well.

4. The first college I visited was in 10th grade while on the way back from visiting relatives, and it was so exciting. Walking around the campus that day against the backdrop of the sparkling Hudson River was so different, and much better than being stuck in the same old high school hallways.... . It was a whole different world. We went to the bookstore after the tour, and I bought a sweatshirt and told my mom "this is where I'm going." At first, it was probably the excitement of it all, but this phrase became very familiar to her and seemed to pop up after every college tour that we would go on.

5. The last tour we went on before school started was to [University #1]. From the moment we got out of the car, I really loved it there. They had an advertising major, which many places did not, and that was something I was looking for. The school itself was beautiful, and I loved the atmosphere. It seemed like a perfect match for me, and it really could be the place I would end up spending my four years. For months after, a blue and gold banner hung over my bed in my room.

6. The beginning of senior year came too quickly, and it wasn't long before we started sending out applications. The stress from parents, teachers, and guidance counselors was almost unbearable at times. Important deadlines were looming, and the dreaded thought of not getting into any schools was something my friends and I joked about all the time, but we were all secretly afraid of. Even though I knew where I wanted to go, I ended up applying to seven schools, just in case. After getting into six and being waitlisted at another, I had nothing to complain about. I really only cared about one school though, and I happened to get that acceptance letter the day before my birthday. I was so excited to open the envelope and tell my mom as soon as she got home from work. She was so happy for me, and I thought that would be it.

7. The weeks came when it was time for the financial aid letters to be awarded. I'm not a genius, but my slightly above average grades in high school and good SAT scores managed to get me some scholarship money that I was so grateful for. Growing up with a single parent in a one-income household is something I knew would have an impact on college. The question was never if I could go at all, but how it would be made affordable. I knew that college came with a hefty price tag. The price of school is something that limits so many students' chances of going to college and getting an education. Looking back, I realize my good luck had to break some time, and the day came when the one place I wanted to go to didn't offer me nearly enough money in scholarships. We were all shocked, seeing as all of the other schools I had been accepted to, I would be able to attend financially. The full cost of [University #1] just wasn't feasible for my family.

8. Watching my mom go to a job everyday that she's never really loved, to provide the best for my sister and I, is something I'm so grateful for. She has always put us first and that means so much to me. There's always been a part of me that has wanted to work hard and make something of myself to thank her for all she's done. I guess that's one reason why college means so much to me.

9. It took a while to come to terms with the situation; I was so disappointed. Until then I thought getting in would be my biggest challenge. I always knew money would be a factor, but never a deciding one. Even though my mom never said no, it would have been personally hard for me to go, knowing what I would be leaving behind. I was left with a huge decision. I could go to this school, but in turn

put myself and my family into a huge amount of debt, or I could find another option. I knew that I really had no choice, but having my heart set on one thing for the good portion of a year was tough to get over.

10. *Over the next month I struggled with this decision; I knew what I had to do. So, the search started over again, which was a little strange as I was looking at the other colleges I had been accepted to. I spent a lot of time looking at my other options. We even went to a few more open houses to take one last look around.*

11. *I decided on [University #2]. I found out a lot of things I didn't know when I quickly filled out a free application one day in September (which is literally the only reason I'm here today). With one of the best business schools around, I realized there was nowhere else I should be. It's almost ironic that I ended up at a school I knew hardly anything about when applying and didn't go to the place I had invested so much of my time into. Even though [University #2] wasn't my first choice, looking back I can't believe I would have wanted to go anywhere else! Now the banner in my room is red and white, and I wouldn't have it any other way. Everything happens for a reason, as my mom likes to say. She's right.*

12. *Eventually, most conflicts come to a resolution. For me, it took a while, but I ended up realizing that I made the right decision. And while not all conflicts have happy endings, this one did, but that doesn't mean there weren't some bumps along the way. It's the way we deal with conflicts that determines how they turn out.*

13. *Once in a while, while I'm walking around campus, I think about what it would be like had I ended up at [University #1]. It's never for long, but the thoughts are still there. How would it be different? Would I be different? Would I be happy or happier than I am here? These thoughts don't stick around too long; I really am content with how things worked out in the end. Through it all, I've learned a lot about myself and how I handle difficult situations. I had always seen planning for college as a race and getting in as a finish line. I realize now that it's only just the beginning.*

Reading and reacting to the drafts of others can help you gain some perspective on your own writing. Your professor may ask you to engage in peer response to a classmate's draft so you may want to practice such helpful responding by reacting to Aliza's draft. Through freewriting and/or discussion, answer some of the following questions:

- What do you think are some of the more effective parts of Aliza's draft?

- Do you ever lose interest in her draft or have trouble understanding her conflict? If so, where and why is her draft problematic?

- In your own words, what do you think the writer wants you to understand about the college search process and possibly about life in general?

- Given this focus/message, how might Aliza revise her draft?

(For more on peer response, please see p. 29 in Chapter 2.)

As you revise, you also should keep in mind your professor's grading criteria. He or she may provide you with a grading rubric, and it can be very helpful to make sure that your expectations match those of your professor. It's so frustrating to be surprised by a low grade, and often when such a disappointment occurs, a student's assumptions about the assignment do not match a teacher's expectations (for more on assignment analysis, see pp. 33–37 in Chapter 2). To avoid this frustrating gap, you can try describing the traits of an excellent personal narrative from beginning to end. What would you say are some of the outstanding features of an "A" paper? What would a reader expect from the top of page one to the bottom of the final page?

The Features of Excellence in a Personal Narrative

p. 1   **p. 2**   **p. 3**   **p. 4**   **p. 5**

Please consult with your professor, but students in the past have asserted that these features include an engaging title and opening, a clear focus, showing details, fine phrases, an effective order, proper emphasis on main events, appropriate word choice, thoughtful reflection, a strong ending, and thorough editing. Of course, it is easier to name these features than to fulfill them, but it is even harder to fulfill expectations that have not been realized!

Here is the final draft by a published writer. You may find it helpful to examine the clarity of the focus, the quality of the details, the logic of the order, and other criteria of good writing so you then can revise your own draft better.

MOTORCYCLE TALK

by Thomas Simmons

As a child, Thomas Simmons learned to love motion and machines, and as an adult, he still rides a motorcycle and flies a small airplane. In the following narrative, he examines his relationship with his father through their shared interest in a motorcycle. This personal story is excerpted from his memoir from 1991 titled *The Unseen Shore, Memories of a Christian Science Childhood.*

From *The Unseen Shore: Memories of a Christian Science Childhood* by Thomas Simmons. Copyright © 1991 by Beacon Press. Reprinted by permission. From The Unseen Shore: Memories of a Christian Science Childhood by Thomas Simmons. Copyright © 1991 by Beacon Press. Reprinted by permission.

My father, who suffered from so many private griefs, was not an easy man to get along with, but in one respect he was magnificent: he was unfailing in his devotion to machines of almost any variety. When he chose to, he could talk to me at length on the virtues of, say, the 1966 Chevrolet four-barrel carburetor or the drawbacks of the Wankel rotary engine. Talking, however, was not his strongest suit: he was a man of action. As he liked to point out, talking would never make an engine run more smoothly.

On weekends sometimes, or on his rare summer days of vacation, he would encourage me in my first and last steps toward automotive literacy. He would allow me to stand beside him as he worked on the car, and when he needed a simple tool—a crescent wrench or needlenose pliers—I would be allowed to hand them to him. And when I was 12, he and my daring mother bought me a motorcycle.

It was a 50cc Benelli motocross bike—neither new, nor large, nor powerful, nor expensive. But it gave form and life to my imaginings. No longer did I have to confine myself wistfully to magazine photos of high-speed turns and hair-raising rides through rough country. I had the thing itself—the device that would make these experiences possible, at least to some degree.

And, although I did not know it at the time, I also had a new lexicon [set of terms]. The motorcycle was a compendium of gears and springs and sprockets and cylinder heads and piston rings, which between my father and me acquired the force of more affectionate words that we could never seem to use in each other's presence.

Almost immediately the Benelli became a meeting ground, a magnet for the two of us. We would come down to look at it—even if it was too late in the day for a good ride—and my father would simply check the tension of the chain, or examine the spark plug for carbon, or simply bounce the shock absorbers a few times as he talked. He'd tell me about compression ratios and ways of down-shifting smoothly through a turn; I'd tell him about my latest ride, when I leaped two small [mounds] or took a spill on a tight curve.

More rarely, he'd tell stories of his youth. His favorite, which he recounted in slightly different versions about four times a year, had to do with the go-kart he built from scrap parts in his father's basement during the Depression. It was by any account a masterful performance; he managed to pick up a small, broken gasoline engine for free, and tinkered with it until it came back to life. The wheels, steering gear, axles, chassis—all were scrounged for a few cents, or for free, from junkyards and vacant lots in and around Philadelphia.

Winter was in full swing when my father had his go-kart ready for a test-drive; snow lay thick on the ground. But he'd built the go-kart in his father's large basement, and given the weather he felt it made sense to make the trial run indoors. His engineering skills were topnotch. Assembled from orphan parts, the go-kart performed like a well-tuned race car. My father did what any good 13-year-old would have done: he got carried away. He laid on the power coming around the corner of the basement, lost control, and smashed head-on into the furnace. It was a great loss for him. The jagged wood and metal cut and bruised him; he had destroyed his brand-new car. Far worse was the damage to the furnace. In 1933 such damage was almost more than the family finances could sustain. Furious, my father's father called him names, upbraided him for his stupidity and irresponsibility, and made him feel worthless. Years later, as he would tell this story to me, my father would linger over those words—"stupid," "irresponsible"—as if the pain had never gone away.

In these moments he and I had a common stake in something. Though he might not know whether I was reading at the eighth-grade level or the twelfth-grade level—or whether my math scores lagged behind those of the rest of the class—he was delighted to see that I knew how to adjust a clutch cable or stop after a low-speed, controlled skid. These skills were a source of genuine adventure for me, and I came to life and he observed my progress.

But this was only part of our rapport with the motorcycle. My father found few occasions to be overtly tender with the family, but he could be tender with a machine. I began to notice this in the countless small adjustments he regularly made. His touch on the cranky carburetor settings for gas and air was gentle, even soothing; as least it seemed to soothe the motorcycle, which ran smoothly under his touch but not under mine.

I found that, from time to time, this tenderness buoyed me up in its wake. If my father was, in his dreams, a flat-track mechanic, then I was his driver: he owed me the best he could give me; that was his job. This dream of his bound us in a metaphor which, at its heart, was not so different from the straightforward love another child might have received from a more accessible father. I did not know this then, not exactly. But I knew, when we both hovered over the Benelli's cylinder head or gearbox, adjusting a cam or replacing a gasket, that he would not have worked on this machine for himself alone.

Yet there was a secret to our new language, a secret that only slowly revealed itself. What we shared through the motorcycle contradicted most of our other encounters in the family. It was almost as if we lived in another world when we came together over this machine, and for a time I hoped that world might be the new one, the ideal on the horizon. I was wrong. The bands of our words were strong, but too narrow to encompass the worlds rising before me.

Almost without knowing it I began to acquire other vocabularies—the tough, subtle speech of girls, the staccato syllables of independence, the wrenching words of love and emptiness. In this I began to leave him behind. He could not talk of these things with me. He remained with his engines, and long after I had ceased to ride it, he occasionally would open the gas jets, prime the carburetor, and take the motorcycle for a spin around the block.

But as it seems that nothing is ever wholly lost, this vocabulary of the garage and the flat-track speedway has a kind of potency, a place in the scheme of things. When, recently, I had dinner with my father, after not seeing him for nearly a year, we greeted each other with the awkwardness of child cousins: we hardly knew what to say. I had almost given up on the possibility of prolonged conversation until I happened to mention that my car needed a new clutch. Suddenly we were safe again, as we moved from the clutch to the valves on his souped-up VW and the four-barrel carburetor on the '66 Chevrolet Malibu, still pouring on the power after all these years. We had moved back to the language of our old country. And though one of us had journeyed far and almost forgotten the idioms, the rusty speech still held, for a time, the words of love.

Close Reading Questions

1. In what specific ways does the purchase of the motorcycle change the narrator's relationship with his father? What quotations from the text support your response? (Historical Trends)

2. What childhood story does the father repeat several times? Why do you think he would retell this tale?

3. What topics and terms bring the narrator and his father closer together? What topics and terms keep them separated? (Multiple Perspectives)

Analytical Writing/Discussion

4. Using both evidence from the text and speculation based on your own knowledge, how would you describe the father's viewpoint, and what do you think may have influenced his perspective? (Cultural Influences)

5. Over the years, how does the narrator's attitude toward his father's mechanical abilities change and/or remain the same? Similarly, how does his attitude toward his father's character change and/or remain the same? (Historical Trends—although only one specific reference to age is made, try drawing a timeline using such points as before the motorbike, its purchase at age 12, soon after its purchase, a few years later, and many years later.)

6. As you look back over the sample narratives that you have read in this chapter (by Ortiz Cofer, the student Aliza Leavitt, and/or Simmons), in what ways do you think these personal narratives are similar and different in their content and/or their style?

Before you turn to editing, you professor may ask you to analyze your personal narrative using the three forms of critical thinking presented in Chapter 1 (see pp. 12–17). This analysis is explained in the second part of this chapter found online.

Editing

Obviously, it is difficult to edit a paper at the same time one is drafting it or even when making majors revisions. A great benefit of using a gradual process is that one can concentrate on collecting ideas first, then on drafting, and after revising, concentrate on editing. There are, of course, many possible problems that may need your attention during editing, such as spelling, punctuation, and grammar. If one is trying to complete a draft at the last minute, editing may seem to be one last chore, but when one aims for reader comprehension, editing is an important and worthwhile final step. As explained in Chapter 2, it is easier to edit, if you have a list of your usual errors like their versus there, comma punctuation, and subject-verb agreement. Computer programs will indicate some of these problems, but they also may 'correct' a mis-spelled word into another one so re-reading your own draft is crucial. Reading your draft out loud may help you slow down and focus enough to discern spellcheck problems and other necessary corrections. Take the time to check a dictionary as well as a handbook with punctuation and grammar guidance so your draft receives the editing it deserves.

If your professor asked your class to all write on a general topic, you can develop significant issues on this subject from your personal experiences. Your professor may ask you to read the final drafts of several classmates and then answer the following questions:

- On the general topic, for example, of education, what kinds of conflicts did these narratives present?

- Do several of these personal narratives involve similar participants, such as frustrated teachers and reluctant students or a caring administrator and a student in need?

- What successes or problems are shown in these narratives? Are these issues also found in recent news reports?

If the topic of these narratives matches one of the thematic chapters (see Chapters 6–10), your professors may ask you to preview that chapter to anticipate the issues that will be raised in the series of readings. In other words, you can notice how much your writing corresponds with the concerns of more expert writers. Since some professors and their students may shift to a thematic chapter at this point, let us now present some additional sources on writing personal narratives.

Additional Sources for Chapter 3

To deepen your understanding of narrative writing, you can consult some of the following sources:

1. For a compelling argument on why first-year students should write personal narratives as well as analytical essays, you may want to read "Reflections on Academic Discourse" by Peter Elbow. This essay by a famous writing professor in 1991 continues to influence many writing teachers today.

   http://english1010information.pbworks.com/f/PeterElbow_Reflections+on+Academic+Discourse.pdf

2. For a different presentation of Elbow's argument for narrative writing (see above), you may want to watch this video version. This cartoon presentation shows the debate between those, like Elbow, who favor narrative writing assignments and those who oppose them, like David Bartholomae (see below).

   www.youtube.com/watch?v=me3jAbUaNGk

3. For a contrasting argument against assigning narrative writing rather (and in favor of analytical writing), you may want to read "Inventing the University" by David Bartholomae. In this influential essay, the author explains the intellectual position of an academic writer and the struggles of some students to reach this stance.

   http://wac.colostate.edu/jbw/v5n1/bartholomae.pdf

4. For an audio report (and its transcript) on the use narrative writing to help medical students become better doctors, you may want to learn about the Narrative Medicine Program at Columbia University. Led by Dr. Rita Charon, this program employs the power of stories so doctors and their patients understand illness and healing fully.

   http://www.npr.org/templates/story/story.php?storyId=1480863

5. For a specific example on the use of narratives in medical writing, you may want to read more on how nurses write narratives about their patients. See too the general description of a narrative essay, which also comes from the Online Writing Lab (OWL) of Purdue University.

   https://owl.english.purdue.edu/owl/resource/1012/02/
   https://owl.english.purdue.edu/owl/resource/685/04/

Another Option: Further Revision through Analysis

As explained above, your professor may shift from these narratives to a thematic chapter (6–10); however, you also may be asked to apply some of the forms of critical thinking, explained in Chapter 1, to your narrative. Then you will be able to revise your narrative further by analyzing your perspective on this conflict as well as examining the viewpoints of some other participants. Your final revision should present not only what happened but also to help a reader understand why this conflict occurred. Again, you will not be expected to complete this task all at once; instead you will be offered a sequence of several possibilities.

If you have read Aliza's draft of "The Finish Line" (see pp. 53–55), it will be easy for you to complete the first step of this assignment: the identification of the conflict's participants. Then this seemingly obvious question will lead to some complexity if you consider whether there are any other participants, including indirect ones, in Aliza's conflict as well as in your own narrative. Who else can you consider to be involved in Aliza's narrative?

Aliza's Narrative
Narrator
Her mom
_____ ?
_____ ?
_____ ?
_____ ?

As with your initial collecting of details, be receptive to many ideas now and save any hard judgments for later. When this question on participants is posed, there usually is a weighty pause, and then a student will suggest others are involved. However, this suggestion often is made with a tentative question (rather than a confident answer), such as "Couldn't you consider Aliza's teachers an important participant in her desire to attend college?" Then a line of many other participants quickly forms. Who else do you think can be considered, even indirectly, to be participants in these conflicts?

You probably have added for Aliza's conflict her teachers who discussed college preparation in their courses and her senior-year classmates who are stressed over their college choices. Let us emphasize that every idea you develop at this point does not have to be included in your revision; generating as many possibilities now will allow you to be more critical and insightful later on. Who else can you add to our list for Aliza? Then can you create a similar list of participants for your own narrative? Who are the most obvious participants as well as some indirect ones in your conflict?

Aliza's Narrative	Your Narrative
Narrator	_____ ?
Her mom	_____ ?
Teachers	_____ ?
Classmates	_____ ?
Guidance counselor	_____ ?
_____ ?	_____ ?

Multiple Perspectives

As explained in Chapter 1, the consideration of multiple perspectives asks you to distinguish several participants' viewpoints and examine what exact beliefs does each perspective involve. This examination does not mean that you have to abandon your own perspective entirely, only that you seek to clarify and expand your initial position by being open, at least initially, to alternative viewpoints (see pp. 12 and 13). Working from your list of participants, what do think were their viewpoints? Where do you think they were coming from? It may be helpful to create a chart as Aliza did below:

Participants	Perspectives
Aliza	I should go to the best college; what is the "right" school for me?
Her mother	a college education is important, my daughter will find her way
Classmates	we aren't geeks, but we study hard what if no one accepts me?
Guidance counselors	our top students go to good colleges: college acceptance = school success
Admission officers	we accept the best; our college = your career success

Your Conflict

Participants	Perspectives

Another more creative possibility is to explore someone's perspective by imagining a dialogue with another participant or an internal debate within one person. For example, what might a less academic-oriented friend say to Aliza as she worried about her college choice? Or what might be Aliza's own back-and-forth thoughts as she fretted over her financial aid problems?

Aliza:	
Other perspective:	
Aliza:	

… and so on

Let yourself have fun and even be funny in this dialogue, such as letting the final line in Aliza's dialogue come from her friend: "I can't believe you've had that blue banner over your bed since last year!" Sometimes when we allow our thoughts to flow, we can create fine phrases and strong insights.

Cultural Influences

As explained in Chapter 1 (see pp. 13–15), when we examine other perspectives, we often start to wonder not only what someone else was thinking, but why did he or she have that viewpoint. As we consider what beliefs support that perspective, we are engaged in an examination of cultural influences. Again, you will be engaged in conjecture, but it is not just idle speculation because we can draw some reasonable inferences. For instance, most Americans like to emphasize their individuality, yet this emphasis is supported by literary characters like Huck Finn, comic book heroes such as Superman, and famous Americans like Sojourner Truth. Widespread cultural practices like every student being graded separately in most schools also promote an individualistic concept of the self. In other words, our widespread belief in individualism paradoxically is promoted by many elements of American culture. Thus, many cultural influences affect our development and help to shape our individual identities. For example, on Aliza's topic of the college search process, what are some of the influences that may have affected her viewpoint? At most high schools, when you enter the guidance counselor's office, how is college choice portrayed? What else influences most students' desire to attend college? Do you think the alternative of a "gap year" of traveling or interning after high school is likely to become more popular?

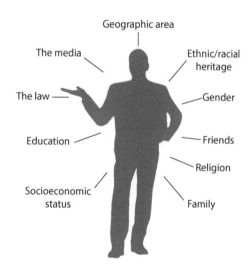

As with writing a compelling narrative, insightful analysis depends on specific details and vivid examples. For instance, as Aliza engaged in this analysis, at one point, she suddenly laughed with the insight that she had kept the last four years' copies of *The US News and World Report*'s special edition on "America's Best Colleges." Not only had she kept them, she also had stacked them on the nightstand next to her bed! How's that for a revealing specific of the cultural pressure on students to pick the "right school"?

You may want to create a messy brainstorm, a neat chart, or carefully phrased prose, but can you analyze some of the cultural influences on several perspectives in your conflict?

Participants	Perspectives	Cultural Influences

Here's part of what Aliza wrote about the cultural influences on her perspective:

> *When I first found out that I probably wouldn't be able to go to [my first choice], I was so disappointed. I thought that I would be missing out on my only opportunity to get a great education…. My mom was a lot more optimistic than I was at that time. She knew it wasn't the end of the world. I took [my financial aid problem] a lot harder than my mom because I had such a narrow perspective on it. I had set myself up [to find the "right school"]… . There were a lot of reasons, personal and cultural, that influenced my thoughts. I was really looking forward to getting out of high school and starting college. As much as I loved high school, I didn't cry on graduation day like some of my friends. I was excited to move on.*

> *I think that most students applying to colleges feel competitive with their friends (on some level). Many of my friends talked about going to schools in Texas, Michigan, California, and even Hawaii. All of their plans sounded so exciting, but I didn't want to be too far from home so I was limited to the New York and New England area … . I found some of the best colleges in the Northeast so I wouldn't be discouraged about not going far away; still, I was a bit jealous of my friends' choices… . The media plays up the idea of going to an Ivy League school. I think that's why so many students feel pressure to attend the "best" schools.*

Can you continue Aliza's analysis with some more specific examples on the cultural influences on college choice? Beyond the great example of *The US News and World Report* on top colleges, how else is finding the "right school" stressed in American culture?

Cultural Influences on College Choice
Parents' expectations
Competition with friends
US News on top colleges
_____?
_____?
_____?

Now, you also can examine the cultural influences that may have affected the participants in your narrative. Try answering the following questions:

- In your narrative, what is the most obvious conflict? AND what is the most significant conflict? (Note the answers to these two questions may or may not be the same.)

- Who are the direct participants in the most important conflict? Who are other indirect but possibly influential participants?

- At the time of the conflict, what was your perspective? How did it differ from at least one other perspective?

- Why was your viewpoint different from others? In other words, what beliefs, experiences, and cultural influences affected each perspective?

If you'd like to see a published author engaged in the examination of cultural influences, you can read or review "Don't Call Me Maria" by Judith Ortiz Cofer, which already was presented in this chapter. See pp. 45–49, and answer questions 2 and 3.

Historical Trends

As explained in Chapter 1, another form of critical thinking common to much of academic inquiry is the analysis of historical trends. As the term suggests, this analysis examines how a perspective changes or remains the same over time, in history. For example, does Huck's perspective on Jim change as they journey down the Mississippi River? Or during the Civil War, did President Lincoln ever waver in his conviction that our nation should not be divided? Understanding the continuity of today's perspectives with those of the past can reveal both the progress a person or a society has made and the problems that still persist.

One way to analyze historical trends is to draw a timeline and add several perspectives over time. Here's an example using Huck Finn's relationship with Jim:

Huck's Attitude toward Jim

-------o----------------------------o--------------------------------------o---------------------------o-------
at the start   *the raft trip begins*   *Huck lies for Jim*   *the ending*

Then, some of the changes and continuities in Huck's perspective can be analyzed.
When Aliza completed this analysis, she traced her evolving perspective:

-------o----------------------------o----------------o-------------------o--------------------------o-------
at age 14   *16*   *17*   *months later*   *now at 18*

at 14, already excited about college, knew I would go

at 16, started looking at specific colleges online, wanted to find the best one for me

at 17, after the campus visit, I knew it was the right school months later, so happy when I was accepted! Then when the disappointing letter on financial aid arrived, I felt panic and anger. After a few weeks, I knew I had to pick from my other good choices.

at 18, content at this college—how I study matters more than where I study.

Then she analyzed these changes more by writing:

Looking back, I think my thoughts and feelings have changed a lot. I had built up college choice to be such an important thing… . I went from being devastated [by the financial aid problem] to understanding that it wasn't the end of the world if I couldn't go there. Everything began to change when I [stopped] being so focused on the one negative aspect of my six choices. Not going [there] didn't mean that I would not succeed. It didn't mean that I would be miserable some-where else. I could get a really good education and have a good time at many of the places I had been accepted to … . My new perspective became much more similar to the way my mom was looking at things all along. She knew everything would be ok; she even wrote me an e-mail one day when I was struggling to narrow down my remaining options that said, "Don't worry, you WILL end up at a good school." I was making everything a lot more stressful than it had to be and she saw that. I was so disappointed at first because I had been so enthusiastic about going to [my top choice].

Using either your age or references to days and months, you too can analyze in historical trends, perhaps by first drawing a timeline describing the perspective at each point:

Participant's Name _____

---------------o-----------------------------o-----------------------------------o------------------------o-----------------o----------------

First Perspective:

Second:

.

.

Final Perspective:

You also can examine these perspectives and their changes or continuities over time by answering the following questions:

- What was your perspective or those of others before the conflict began?
- As your conflict developed, how did your perspective or those of others change or remain the same? At what point in time?
- Immediately after the conflict as well as long afterward, did these viewpoints shift? If so, from what to what, for whom, when, and why?
- Finally, now at this present time, what is your perspective or those of others?

For a published example of the analysis of historical trends, you can read or review "Motorcycle Talk" by Thomas Simmons, which already was presented in this chapter. See pp. 56–59, and answer questions 1 and 5.

Final Assignment: An Analytical Revision

As suggested by the examples of Aliza's analysis of her narrative, you probably will understand your conflict better, and perhaps differently, as you analyze its participants and their perspectives. This analysis will enable you, or even compel you, to revise your narrative. The final assignment of this option is for you to revise your narrative by adding some of your analysis:

> In a carefully drafted, revised, and edited final copy, narrate and analyze a significant conflict from your own life. You do not have to be a central figure of this conflict, but you should be a direct participant. In addition to presenting your perspective on this conflict, you also should examine the viewpoints of some of the other participants and analyze why some of these perspectives developed and differed.

Rather than just expect you to complete this revision, we will offer some suggestions on how to revise your draft.

Revision as Reseeing

Just as analysis often involves going back to collect more ideas, revision may require you to return to focus and order. Sometimes students realize that the focus of their narratives has changed. A classmate of Aliza named Heather, for example, realized that her similar conflict over college choice was actually about another related issue. During her analysis of her conflict, Heather realized that she saw New York City, where one college was located, as a center of boundless opportunities. Her mother, however, considered this city to be a place of many dangers, especially for a young woman far from home. Heather then revised her narrative by focusing on these differences in perspectives and explaining her mother's fears about allowing her daughter to attend college in New York.

The challenge of revision for Aliza and Heather was for each writer to combine the new insights of their analyses with the events of their original narratives. They had to revise, which literally means, when you consider its prefix of "re-", to see their previous drafts again and anew. Rather than just dump the explanatory insights at the end of their narratives, these students had to refocus and reorder their previous drafts.

Back in the section on focus, we asked you to answer

My conflict is about _____ *, and the primary conflict is between* _____ *and* _____ *.*

At that time, we conceded that you might not be able to answer this prompt fully, and we knew then but did not admit that for at least some students, your initial answer might change later. As you have been engaged in analysis, your focus may have changed as it did for Heather and your understanding of the conflict may have increased as for Aliza.

During this process of analysis and revision, what we as writing teachers find crucial and many students find exciting is the fact that you, as the narrative writer, still have the freedom and responsibility for revising your draft. Revision in this assignment does not mean completing only what the teacher tells you to do in order to get a better grade. Instead, like Heather, you will have to decide what you want to focus on in your revision. You will have to decide how you want to revise your narrative and what you want your reader to "see" in the new draft.

Checking Your Order and Emphasis

Even with a clearer focus in mind, it is not always easy to revise your narrative because you will have to decide not only where to add the insightful analysis but also where to condense and cut the previous draft. In the sometimes circular process of writing, this reorganization requires you to stand back and consider again the order and emphasis of your narrative. One way to create this critical distance on your narrative is to try outlining after drafting (see pp. 27–28 in Chapter 2 for more explanation). Most students are taught to outline before they draft, but many struggle to do so effectively. Some students, however, find that outlining *after* drafting can be very beneficial.

On a new page or screen, state the focus of your previous draft and then assert the planned focus of your revision, even if they are exactly the same. If they differ, then stating both will help you reconsider your previous draft. Next, number the paragraphs of the original narrative, and then outline what is the purpose of each one. What is each paragraph about?

Narrative Focus: _____
New Focus: _____

1. *Introductory scene*
2.
3.
4.
5.

Next you can freewrite and/or discuss with a classmate what you have learned from this analysis.

Revision Planning

Try answering some of the following questions to help you plan your revision:

- How has your understanding of the conflict been changed, enriched, or complicated?
- What parts of the previous draft will you use again?
- What parts need to be altered, expanded, condensed, or cut?
- What new scenes or details need to be added and where?
- Do you need to make any changes in order and where?
- To fulfill your "new" focus, how should your original paragraphs and new ideas be organized?

You already may have started to consider where to add some of the insights from your analysis, but to encourage yourself to make even more additions, try to layer onto your outline some of the information from your analysis. You may want to grab a different colored pen or use another font to add these analytical insights to your outline. Of course, using another pen or font is just another suggestion for you to try. Let us stress, you do not have to follow every recommendation we make. Our goal is for you to find a combination of strategies that work for you.

Here is a sample of this outlining after drafting based on Aliza's analysis:

	Narrative Outline	Revision Plans
1.	College choice intro	Revise final sentences
2–4	Different choices	
5.	Visit to university #1	Add high school emphasis on college
6.	Rejection fear yet accepted!	
7.	Financial aid problem	
8.	Mother's example	
9.	Difficult decision over debt	Explain more
		Add mother's perspective
		Add media stress on college
		Add my new perspective
10.	Struggle to choose	
11.	University #2 chosen	
12.	Retrospection on #1	
13–14.	Conclusion on the finish line	Change order and condense

Once you have planned your revision using some of these activities, you still have to actually write the revised draft, but your plan lets you concentrate on drafting.

Computers too make revision so much easier, especially if you have kept your narrative drafts and analyses in clearly labeled files. Now you can cut and paste from those files to create a revised copy. You also can do the same using the low-tech strategy of scissors and tape. Using the scissors, cut a clean copy of your original narrative apart into separate paragraphs and spread them out before you on a table. Next, cut apart sections of your analysis and literally tape them into place among the narrative paragraphs. Some students like the physical and spatial activity of this scissor and tape approach, while others can think and create more efficiently with the desktop cutting and pasting from several computer files. Again, you need to find the methods that work for you on this assignment.

Just as there are differences in the conventions of a narrative and a five-paragraph essay, you may find that the more informal phrasing used in your narratives differs from the more formal terms used in your analysis. Try to avoid any abrupt changes in the phrasing, the diction, of your revision. Then your new draft will seem like a coherent text and not some bumpy combination. To add the insights of analysis, try using some of the following phrases that will help you maintain the less formal, less academic tone of a personal narrative:

Multiple Perspectives -	He believed that …
	She didn't understand …
	Everyone in their group assumed …
Cultural Influences -	My friend probably was affected by …
	Her decision may have been influenced …
	It didn't help this conflict that he watched …
Historical Trends -	At that time, she felt …
	He later realized …
	Their attitude changed when …
	Looking back, I now understand …

To conclude your revision, you may want to rely on historical trends by explaining: What is your current perspective? As you look back, what do you now understand about this conflict and some of its participants? As you reflect on this conflict, how do you now react when you see others involved in a similar conflict?

Here is Aliza's revision that maintains many of her details and much of her original order. To aid discussion, we have numbered the paragraphs, presented her revisions in bold, and added comments on her revision.

Aliza's revision:

The Finish Line

1. College is something that most people start dealing with in the middle of high school. However, in my case, I started thinking about college in middle school. **My fascination with this idea played a big part in my life, or else I probably wouldn't have struggled as much as I did when deciding where to go to school.** [new phrasing in a condensed introduction]

2. I've always known what I've wanted to be when I grew up, even though what I've wanted has changed a few times over the years. When I was younger, I wanted to be an archeologist (mainly because I had a really cool social studies teacher who did the same thing). A few years later, I decided that I wanted to be an architect, and after that phase, I finally settled on something I had always been interested in, business and advertising. I loved thinking about the future and what it would bring.

3. I've never really had a "dream school" like some kids do. I didn't come from a line of Cornell or Harvard graduates, and there wasn't a particular school that I was expected to attend, so I was on my own to narrow the thousands of options down to one. Naturally, like my changing career interests, my top college picks changed as well.

4. The first college I visited was in 10th grade while on the way back from visiting relatives, and it was so exciting. Walking around the campus that day against the backdrop of the sparkling Hudson River was so different, and much better than being stuck in the same old high school

hallways.... [I thought] this was college and I was finally here. We went to the bookstore after the tour, and I bought a sweatshirt and told my mom "this is where I'm going". At first, it was probably the excitement of it all, but this phrase became very familiar to her, and seemed to pop up after every college tour that we would go on.

5. The last tour we went on before school started was at [University #1]. From the moment we got out of the car, I really loved it there. Compared to some of the other places we had visited, the campus was so open and beautiful. **Nestled quietly next to the mountains, I immediately loved the atmosphere and having visited right at the end of summer, everything was still green and full of life. Everyone just looked so happy.** They had the advertising major I was looking for, which many places did not. It seemed like a perfect match for me, and it really could be the place I would end up spending my next four years. For months after, a blue and gold banner hung over my bed in my room. [new showing details]

6. The beginning of senior year came too quickly, and it wasn't long before my friends, classmates and I started sending out applications. The stress from parents, teachers, and guidance counselors was almost unbearable at times. **Coming from one of the best public high schools in the area, our high school's reputation for education and college preparation could never be escaped. My guidance counselor once told us that by just going to our school, our applications would look better, which was something we found hard to believe. College was always made to be a pretty big deal, and planning for it wasn't just something that started at the end of junior year; it started right away. On our family information nights, we sat with our parents and listened to lectures about interviewing and how to write "the perfect college essay" from local admissions counselors. Last year marked the "highly anticipated" introduction of a new personalized college planning website that the school would be the first in the area to utilize (freshmen now are being strongly encouraged to explore this site). In the years I was in high school, a number of students from my graduating class and those older than me had been admitted to Harvard, Yale, Cornell, and Notre Dame. The guidance office used to have a big map with little push pins showing where all of our graduates were going. College was drilled into our heads from day one.** [cultural influences added]

7. Important deadlines were looming, and the dreaded thought of not getting into any schools was something my friends and I joked about all the time, but we were all secretly afraid of. **We had all seen the movie Accepted, where the characters decide to create their own college when nowhere else had accepted them, and as funny as the concept was, we promised ourselves not to end up in their position.** So, even though I knew where I wanted to go, I ended up applying to seven schools, just in case. After getting into six and being waitlisted at another, I had nothing to complain about. I really only cared about one school though, and I happened to get that acceptance letter the day before my birthday. I was so excited to open the envelope and tell my mom as soon as she got home from work. She was so happy for me, and I thought that would be it. [cultural influences added]

8. Then, the weeks came when it was time for the financial aid letters to arrive. I'm not a genius, but my slightly above average grades in high school and good SAT scores managed to get me some scholarship money that I was so grateful for. Growing up with a single parent in a one-income household is something I knew would have an impact on my college education. The question was never if I could go at all, but how it would be made affordable. I knew that college came with a hefty price tag. The price of school is something that limits so many students' chances of going to college and

getting an education. Looking back, I realize my good luck had to break some time, and the day came when the one place I wanted to go didn't offer me nearly enough money in scholarships. We were all shocked, seeing as all of the other schools I had been accepted to were very generous with their scholarship and aid money. The full cost of [University #1] just wasn't feasible for my family.

9. Watching my mom go to a job everyday that she's never really loved, to provide the best for my sister and I, is something I'm so grateful for. She has always put us first and that means so much to me. There's always been a part of me that has wanted to work hard and make something of myself to thank her for all she's done. I guess that's one reason why college means so much to me.

10. It took a while to come to terms with the situation; I was so disappointed. Until then I thought getting in would be my biggest challenge. I always knew money would be a factor, but never a deciding one. Even though my mom never said no, it would have been personally hard for me to go, knowing what financial difficulty I would be creating for her. **My younger sister will be starting college in a few years, which also factored into my situation.** I was left with a very difficult decision. I could go to this school, but in turn put myself and my family into a **huge debt**, or I could find another option. I knew that I really had no choice, but having my heart set on one thing for the good portion of a year was tough to get over. [slight changes in phrasing]

11. **For me, at that time, not going to [University #1] seemed like the end of the world. My view of the situation was so narrow that I didn't realize that I did have other options…. . My mom, on the other hand, had a different view on the whole situation. [Her] generation grew up in a different world than we are living in today. The world was moving at a much slower pace then. The amount of advertising wasn't nearly as substantial as it is now. In my mom's case, she wrote letters to a few colleges asking for catalogues, and then had to write another letter asking to set up a tour, months in advance. I, however, got my first college catalogue in the mail from a place hours away I had never heard of. I checked the box to be put on an extensive mailing list when I took the PSAT, something I later regretted. Only a week later I was receiving up to 50 emails a week from colleges trying to compete for my attention.**

12. **My mother reminded me that there also wasn't the amount of magazines, books and movies dedicated to "getting your kid into college." I am the self-admitted owner of the past four issues of** <u>U.S News & World Report's</u> **annual installment of America's Best Colleges. In fact, there are literally thousands of these types of books and magazines published each year, which says something about our society's view on the importance of a college education.**

13. **Since my mom wasn't the main target of all the pressure that is put on today's youth, she was able to see that not going to my first choice of school didn't mean I wouldn't succeed in life; I would be fine at any "good" college.** [cultural influences added]

14. Over the next month I struggled to pick another college; **I really did have other perfectly good options**, but I just didn't see that at the time. So, the search started over again, looking at the other colleges I had been accepted to, which was a little strange. **I had already decided on [University #1] in my mind and in doing so, I had ruled out the other places I had been accepted by finding their faults (which is the normal process). Now, I had to somehow go back and find the hidden qualities I had previously passed over. This was really difficult.** We even went to a few more open houses to take one last look around. [details added on historical trends]

15. Finally, I decided on [University #2]. I found out a lot of things I didn't know when I quickly filled out a free application one day in September (which is literally the only reason I'm here today).

With one of the best business schools around, I realized there was nowhere else I should be. It's almost ironic that I ended up at school I knew hardly anything about when applying and didn't go to the place I had invested so much of my time into. Even though [University #2] wasn't my first choice, looking back I can't believe I would have wanted to go anywhere else! Now the banner in my room is red and white, and I wouldn't have it any other way. [paragraph deleted]

16. Once in a while, while I'm walking around campus, I think about what it would be like had I ended up at [University #1]. It's never for long, but the thoughts are still there. How would it be different? Would I be different? Would I be happy or happier than I am here? These thoughts don't stick around too long; I really am content with how things worked out in the end. Looking back at it all, I realize now that getting a good education is more important, not where I study. I had always seen planning for college as a race and getting in as a finish line. I realize now that it's only just the beginning.

We have presented Aliza's revision with numbered paragraphs for easy reference. What parts of her revision seem stronger to you? Did you notice that she added a few more showing details about the campus in paragraph five? Do you think any more showing details could and should be added to paragraph five? Has she added the analysis to her original narrative smoothly? Does her analysis in paragraphs 6, 11, and 12 on the cultural influences that "drill" college choice into students seem effective to you? Does the contrasting perspective of her mother make the change in Aliza's perspective seem believable to you? Has she created enough vivid scenes or are more possible? What did you think of her ending? You may want to use Aliza's revision as a sample to practice peer response before you provide feedback for a classmate.

We chose Aliza's paper to serve as the primary sample of this chapter for three reasons. First, many first-year students have experienced a conflict over college choice. Second, Aliza's revision method of primarily adding to her original narrative makes her changes easy to understand. Third, her good effort can be improved even further, giving you the opportunity to suggest how the final draft could have become an even better paper. For instance, some students like Aliza's ending, but others object that it is a little too neat: "A finish line … just the beginning." Some readers also wish that Aliza had reflected even more on the issue of her conflict. Just as Ortiz Cofer considers stereotyping beyond her particular experiences, Aliza could have reflected more on the implications of the college pressures felt by most high school students. For instance, does the unrelenting pressure to be accepted by the "right school" place too much emphasis on getting good grades and not enough on learning itself in high school?

Editing the Final Draft

Donald Murray once quipped that a draft is never done, just due. With more time and energy, we often can keep working on a text, but a deadline must be met so the writing process must end. However, before that effort ceases, it is important to not only revise but also edit, and please note that these are two different activities.

Aliza's good revision can be edited further. Consider, for example, the problem in the following phrase from paragraph nine:

> … to provide the best for my sister and I

Although we sometimes may say "my sister *and I*" as the pronoun in a sentence like this one, this phrase should be written as "my sister and me." We can hear this correction if we focus on the pronoun choice

"I/me" by removing the other person and saying "provide the best for I" and "provide the best for me." Then the grammatically correct phrasing of "to provide the best for my sister and me" can be discerned.

Editing can be dismissed as nitpicking, but proper spelling, grammar, and punctuation actually make it easier for a reader to comprehend your writing. Consider two examples of a misplaced modifier in Aliza's revision. In paragraphs five and six, she states,

> Nestled quietly next to the mountains, I immediately loved the atmosphere and having visited right at the end of summer, everything was still green and full of life.

> Coming from one of the best public high schools in the area, our high school's reputation … could never be escaped.

Aliza does not mean to assert that she is "Nestled quietly next to the mountains," and she probably is referring to herself as someone "Coming from one of the best public high schools." These problems with a phrase modifying the subject of a sentence can be corrected easily to improve a reader's comprehension. The first example could be edited and improved to become:

> Compared to some of the other colleges we had visited, the campus seemed so open and beautiful. Several buildings were nestled quietly next to the mountains, and I immediately loved the setting. Since we visited at the end of summer, everything was still green and full of life.

Doesn't the elimination of the misplaced modifier and the other changes in sentence structure make this passage easier to read and understand? How would you correct the second example? Although it may be difficult to eliminate every editing problem, once you notice a repeated error, try focusing on it for a while. Perhaps you will notice and be able to improve a few more sentences, such as the following one from paragraph fifteen:

> With one of the best business schools around, I realized there was nowhere else I should be.

> With one of the best business schools around, this university feels like the right place for me.

Take the time to edit carefully, and a reader will be able to understand your writing better.

* * *

Just as we asked you to consider the traits of a strong narrative (see p. 56), the main expectations for this revision are as follows:

- A vivid, focused narrative
- The analysis of multiple perspectives
- A smoothly ordered and properly edited revision

In addition to presenting the general steps of the writing process from collecting to editing, we also have suggested some activities for writing a narrative in particular. For example, we have suggested that you plan several scenes and organize your draft. We also have presented three forms of analysis that are used frequently in academic inquiry: multiple perspectives, cultural influences, and historical trends. Your instructor may ask you to write what are termed "process notes" so you reflect on these assignments and become more aware of your writing process and college-level writing. For more on process notes, see p. 33 of Chapter 2.

In the two main parts of this assignment, our goals have been for you to learn to

- Practice the writing process more fully
- Pursue a topic based on your interest and knowledge
- Assume a writer's freedom of expression and responsibility for communication
- Fulfill the conventions of a particular genre
- Engage in the critical thinking of most college studies

This assignment emphasizes the writing process, and the subsequent thematic chapters (Chapters 10–14) involve reading as much as writing. For some students, it is better to focus on one of these related tasks first. Yet reading has been implicit, such as when you have been asked to comprehend and respond to the sample narratives by Aliza and others. Although you have been the primary source of the narrative and its analytical revision, you also have been encouraged to interact with others by discussing the published narratives and responding to each other's drafts. What seemed to be a personal conflict has been expanded and enriched by these interactions. On a more abstract level, you have been asked to place your conflict in a larger social context as you have considered reader expectations and examined cultural influences. Throughout this chapter and the rest of this book, we assume neither that an individual can ever be entirely free from all cultural influences nor that society always predetermines a person's thoughts, feelings, and actions. We instead assume that a back-and-forth, or dialectical, relationship exists between self and society. In other words, culture affects a person's perspective, but an individual also can have an impact on his or her viewpoint and those of others as well. In fact, a college education and its training in reading and writing in particular, can help you exert more control over your life and your society.

Academic Honesty and Research Essays

CHAPTER 4

Some things are easier said than done. This saying applies to many situations, and we believe that it holds true for both maintaining academic honesty and writing research essays. It definitely is easy for teachers to tell students to cite sources properly; when students rely on the writing of others, they should use quotation marks and cite the sources. And yet, if you skip ahead and thumb through this chapter, you'll find that there are many details to discuss, such as signal phrases, ellipses, elaborations, and the much more. Let us concede that there is even more than what we can list in the key terms at the end of this chapter. Maybe academic honesty is not so easy, especially when students are asked to write research essays. As we will explain, one of the challenges of writing a research essay is that the professor will no longer be asking students to rely primarily on their own thoughts and experiences or on readings provided by the instructor; instead, the professor is asking students to find good sources, to comprehend that material, to develop a thesis from the topic, to support that opinion, to make a persuasive argument to others, and to acknowledge their use of those sources through proper citation—whew! However, the good news is that all of those tasks have been explained in the chapters on reading, writing, and argument. In fact, we will present the research essay as the culmination of the literacy skills usually taught in first-year, college-level writing courses. In other words, you are already to tackle a research essay once you understand how to cite sources properly.

There are two reasons for you to learn to cite properly, and you already know the first one: to avoid any accusation of plagiarism and the academic penalties that may follow. The second reason may be less familiar to you: to take credit for your control over sources and for your own critical thinking. As we will explain below, proper citation allows a reader to discern when you are relying on sources and when you are asserting your own ideas in response to that research.

Academic Honesty and Its Conventions

As we discuss both the basics of how-to cite properly as well as the more abstract issues of why, we will be referring to the **conventions** of academic honesty rather than its rigid rules. By conventions, we mean expected actions, like what a family assumes everyone will do on a holiday such as Thanksgiving. Academic honesty is less a matter of what some authorities have determined is illegal—a rule not to be broken—and more a matter of what "we" usually do—a convention to be followed if you want to be seen as one of "us." The proper quoting and citing of sources show that you are ready and able to participate in an academic community. They are part of what every college student should know how to do, but sometimes these expectations are not explained sufficiently. As you'll see below, we will provide some supporting evidence of our own, identify our sources, and elaborate on our evidence. We will explain by *doing* and not just *saying*.

The Dreaded P-Word

By the time you reached college, you probably knew that **plagiarism** is an act of academic dishonesty because a writer fails to acknowledge his or her reliance on the writing of others. Yet, this basic understanding may not be enough to prevent problems for some students. Often, the devil is in the details, so let's consider some of the mistakes that can be made: what do you think are some of the various ways a student, deliberately or not, can commit plagiarism?

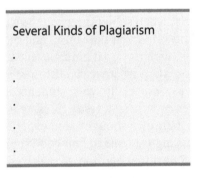

Several Kinds of Plagiarism

As we discuss four main examples below, we also will use them to explain the basics of how to cite properly. We won't claim that it is easy, but we do believe that it isn't that hard if one pays attention to the conventions and their reasons.

Deliberate Copying is usually an act of desperation. A student may have waited too long before beginning an assignment, and as the clock ticks past midnight, he may be tempted to grab the words of another for use in his paper. This example matches one of the etymologies of plagiarism: from Latin, *plagiarius*—a kidnapper. A plagiarist "kidnaps" the words of another for his own profit or engages in what is typically termed **intellectual theft**, meaning the stealing of another writer's ideas and/or phrases for one's own gain.

Imagine if a student, for instance, is writing about scientific inquiry, and she copies the following quotation by a writer named Kenneth Bruffee:

Plagiarism Example:

Scientists increase their discipline's knowledge by working from the results of experiments by others. Thus, for scientists, knowledge is an artifact created by a community of peers.

These sentences would raise the suspicions of many professors because the wording "an artifact created by … " is not a phrase that most students would use. Thus, deliberate copying usually is not very difficult for many professors to detect, and, even worse, it is easy for a student to avoid. In a minute or two, this student could have added the quotation marks and the citation needed for academic honesty to be maintained.

Copying Corrected:

Scientists increase their discipline's knowledge by working from the results of experiments by others. Thus, for scientists, "knowledge is an artifact created by a community of … peers" (Bruffee 642).

Even though the student has omitted the word "knowledgeable," this otherwise exact wording should be quoted and cited. The omission of a word (or several words) is shown by what is known as an **ellipsis** ("of … peers"), and the period follows the citation because the citation is a part of that sentence. Let us add that along with direct quotations, paraphrased info—when you restate ideas in your own wording—too should be cited.

Sloppy Notes and/or **Careless Drafting** can lead to less deliberate but still unacceptable plagiarism. When a student scribbles down notes without marking quotations or recording page numbers, this seemingly minor problem can cause a major one later on. For, as a student drafts a paper, she can't recall what information has been quoted or possibly even where it came from. As she drafts, this writer also may work so rapidly from her notes that she fails to distinguish her ideas and phrases from quoted language. Again, it does not require that much time to indicate when she is relying on another writer.

As we will explain below, the thesis for a research essay should address a debate found among your sources. A writer named Gerald Graff advises students to make their position within a debate explicit by using a phrase like: While most believe X, I will argue Y (55). Then, a student writer should indicate his reliance on other writers as he acknowledges the opposing viewpoint of others and provides evidence to support his thesis. For example, in *Clueless in Academe*, Graff supports his own perspective by relying on not one but two writers. He asserts,

> In *Lives on the Boundary* Mike Rose cites fellow compositionist David Bartholomae's suggestion that "when stuck, student writers should try the following machine: 'While most readers of ____ have said ____, a close and careful reading shows that ____.'"[1]

Graff uses a footnote instead of a parenthetical citation because he is using another citation system, and we will explain three different ones below. If Graff were to employ the MLA system, this citation would appear as "… shows that ____" (Bartholomae qtd. in Rose 189). Those familiar with MLA would read this citation as "Bartholomae is quoted by Rose on page 189 of his book."

It's also worth noting that Graff states that "Rose *cites* fellow compositionist" as he presents this quotation (italics added). Quoting and citing are so related that these two terms, though slightly different in meaning, can be used as interchangeable synonyms.

Cutting and Pasting is also known as "patchwork plagiarism." It happens when a student opens several sources, usually those online, and then as the name suggests, cuts and pastes several sentences from one writer with those of other writers. Like copying, this form of plagiarism is deliberate, and it too can be corrected by adding attributions and citations. Yet this correction is incomplete unless a student asserts her agreement, elaboration, skepticism, etc., *after* the citation and *before* the next signal phrase. For instance, if we continue our example based on Bruffee and Graff:

Cut and Paste/Patchwork:

Knowledge is an artifact created by a community of peers, yet this collaboration often involves arguing Y when most people think X.

This example demonstrates another etymological association of the word plagiarism: from the Latin *plaga* for "net," which is related to *plak*, meaning "to weave." A student engaged in cut and paste plagiarism is only weaving other writers' words together, but he risks being caught in a dishonest net of his own making! In the corrected version below, the student writer is controlling the source material rather than just repeating it. Notice the additional assertions by the student marked in bold.

Corrected Version:

Discussing a subject and employing the terms used by experts can help students develop a deeper understanding of their topic. Through such active study of a subject, students demonstrate that knowledge "is an artifact created by a community of knowledgeable peers" (Bruffee 646). **As he promotes this image of a collaborative community, Bruffee, however, fails to consider the degree to which academics add to a discussion by disagreeing with and rejecting outright the assertions made by their colleagues. For Gerald Graff asserts, academics often respond to each other by opposing what has been said.** In *Clueless in Academe,* Graff characterizes the typical academic discussion as "While most think X, I argue Y" (55).

Note too that the first time a writer is mentioned, his or her **full name** is provided, as in "Gerald Graff." In any subsequent references to this writer, only the **last name** is used.

Paper Mill Purchases may be the most dishonest form of plagiarism. Buying a complete paper from an Internet site, or "paper mill," cannot be explained away as an accident. It is an intentional act of dishonesty. Most sites, however, try to obscure these intentions. They offer papers for sale but add a disclaimer that these papers should be used only as a research aid. The disclaimers, however, usually appear in small print, and they often are contradicted by suggestions that students are not responsible for this academic dishonesty. Blame is shifted, as Kelly Ritter explains, to "professors for not creating new writing assignments, … [and universities for requiring] needless general education courses" (620). Once blame has been shifted away from plagiarizing students, it may be very tempting for some, as a paper mill site once urged, for students to "download your workload."

Once a paper is conceived as a commodity to be obtained so apparently pointless work can be avoided, the concept of plagiarism as intellectual theft becomes less clear. Ritter explains this confusion:

> Even when students understand that taking the intellectual and artistic property of others is *wrong*, they might not clearly understand why it is wrong when said product is for *sale* on the Internet. When students … see writing as a "product" designed to fulfill the distinct purpose in a college course, how far must those students leap to arrive at the conclusion that, like many other items in our culture offered online for sale, this product, too, can be bought? … [T]he consumer-minded student, unable to distinguish authorship from ownership, might wonder where is the "stealing" in this transaction. (615)

When a paper is purchased, the theft occurs not so much from its original writer, whose individual identity is erased on a seemingly authorless website, but through the misrepresentation of effort made when the paper is submitted for course credit. The fraudulent claim that the student has made the intellectual effort to produce this paper and earn course credit constitutes theft from the academic institution and, in essence, from the student's classmates who have made this effort.

With the long quotation from Ritter above, note the convention of using an **indented, block quotation** to present four or more lines of quoted material. These longer quotations are indented rather than indicated with quotation marks, and the parenthetical citation follows the period of the final sentence. There are, of course, many more conventions of proper citation; in fact, too many for us to present here. Fortunately, as listed in the Additional Sources at the end of this chapter, there are several very good websites to consult on the conventions of source quotation and citation.

Communal Dependence and Signal Phrases

For younger students, the question of why conventions like quotations and citations are used can be answered with "Because someone else said it first" and "You need to do it the right way." Yet, this is not an adequate explanation for most college students. A better answer is that academic writers quote and cite their sources in order to place their new ideas in the context of what is already known. By acknowledging this dependence, an academic anticipates and answers a skeptical reader's queries like "How do you know that?". Anticipating such skepticism, an academic writer places quotation marks around her reliance on the exact words by another writer. We already have quoted a leading theorist on the communal quality of academic knowledge: it "is an artifact created by a community of knowledgeable peers" (Bruffee 646). As just demonstrated, one easy way to indicate the source of a **quotation** is to place the author's last name and the page number in a **citation** at the end of the sentence. The period is placed after the parenthesis because the citation is part of that sentence. As you may realize, we are using the citation system of the Modern Language Association (also known by its acronym MLA), and this association includes those in the humanities, such as historians, philosophers, and literary critics. (Later, we will distinguish MLA citations from two other systems.)

As you probably know, **little known facts** and **paraphrased ideas** as well as exact quotations should be cited. Yet, this is another example of easier said than done. For instance, whether a fact is "little known" depends on the group of a writer. We assumed you were familiar with easier said than done so we didn't quote it, and what is considered common knowledge among majors in their senior year probably will be little known facts for most first-year students. Again with paraphrasing, changing a few words may not be enough. Just because information from another writer is not repeated word-for-word, a citation may not demonstrate clearly enough the extent of an academic's dependence on others. Consider the following example as a section of a student's paper:

> Sample Paraphrase: If students are to master the knowledge of a particular discipline, it is not enough for teachers to ask them to repeat this knowledge on a test. Teachers also need to engage students in discussions of this information and require them to utter the key terms of this discipline. For students can only think and know in the ways they can talk and write (Bruffee 642).

The citation clearly marks the information in the final sentence as paraphrased from Bruffee, yet in this example, where do you think the writer's dependence on this source begins? It's hard to tell, isn't it? In fact, the first and second sentences also are paraphrased ideas so a parenthetical citation isn't always enough to indicate fully a writer's reliance on a source. To clarify the extent to which a source has been used, an academic writer can employ what is known as **a signal phrase** or an **attribution**. As shown below, an attribution like According to Kenneth Bruffee, signals that a writer is relying on a source. Note too that when the author's last name is included in the signal phrase, the citation contains only the page number.

Example with Attribution Added (**in bold**):

"According to. . ." direct quote, graphicade

According to Kenneth Bruffee, if students are to master the knowledge of a particular discipline, it is not enough for teachers to ask them to repeat this knowledge on a test. Teachers also need to engage students in discussions of this information and require them to utter the key terms of this discipline. For students can only think and know in the ways they can talk and write (642).

Even if you had not heard of the term signal phrase before, you probably can add several more to our list:

Some Signal Phrases
According to Smith,
Muñoz explains,
As Waldman argues,
.
.
.

With an attribution to "signal" that the next information comes from another writer, the extent of this writer's reliance on a source is clear; it's marked from the signal phrase to the parenthetical citation. When an academic writer follows these conventions, he says, in essence, to others in his academic community: "Here's how I know this information," and this indication serves as more than a defensive gesture: "Look, I'm not making this up." These conventions also act as an implicit invitation for praise: "Wow, she has read so much." Thus, a writer can solicit a reader's admiration by acknowledging her dependence on others, but this dependence is not enough in itself to be an effective academic writer.

Citations and Individual Assertions

When an academic writer provides some quoted or paraphrased information, a reader may not understand how this information relates to his opinion. A writer, therefore, should explain its significance after the citation and not rush on to more cited material immediately. A reader may not be convinced if a writer only repeats what others have said on page after page until the required length has been reached. Consider this combination of the information cited from Bruffee above:

> According to Kenneth Bruffee, if students are to master the knowledge of a particular discipline, it is not enough for teachers to ask them to repeat this knowledge on a test. Teachers also need to engage students in discussions of this information and require them to utter the key terms of this discipline. For students can only think and know in the ways they can talk and write (642). Knowledge "is an artifact created by a community of knowledgeable peers" (Bruffee 646).

In this example, the student writer is showing her dependence on what others know without making her own assertion. The very conventions of academic honesty seem to have trapped this student, but knowing how to support, cite, and elaborate create the means for this writer's escape. The space for individual assertion also exists *after* a citation, as shown with the writing in bold below:

Example with Assertion Added (**in bold**):

According to Kenneth Bruffee, if students are to master the knowledge of a particular discipline, it is not enough for teachers to ask them to repeat this knowledge on a test. Teachers also need to engage students in discussions of this information and require them to utter the key terms of this discipline. For students can only think and know in the ways they can talk and write (642). **Sometimes students are able to get good grades for repeating information that they do not really understand. Discussing a subject and employing the terms used by experts can help students develop a deeper understanding. Through such active study of a subject, students demonstrate** that knowledge "is an artifact created by a community of knowledgeable peers" (Bruffee 646).

Just as an attribution signals to a reader "Here comes some cited info," the writing *after* a citation is read by other academics as "Okay, let's see what she is going to say about that writer's idea." The space *after* one citation and *before* the next attribution provides the room for the writer's own opinions, insights, interpretations, and arguments. Here's a continuation of the example from above; note the two sections **in bold**:

According to Kenneth Bruffee, if students are to master the knowledge of a particular discipline, it is not enough for teachers to ask them to repeat this knowledge on a test. Teachers also need to engage students in discussions of this information and require them to utter the key terms of this discipline. For students can only think and know in the ways they can talk and write (642). **Sometimes students are able to get good grades for repeating information that they do not really understand. Discussing a subject and employing the terms used by experts can help students develop a deeper understanding of their topic. Through such active study of a subject, students demonstrate** that knowledge "is an artifact created by a community of knowledgeable peers" (Bruffee 646). **As he promotes this image of a collaborative community, Bruffee, however, fails to consider the degree to which academics add to a discussion by disagreeing with and rejecting outright the assertions made by their colleagues.**

As suggested by this writer's critique of Bruffee's concept of a collaborative community, the interaction between writers is not always gentle cooperation. In addition to amiable agreement, an academic writer can contradict, limit, clarify, extend, or redirect what others already have stated. In fact, some scholars have characterized the primary academic response as one of opposition. Whether a writer follows or refutes cited info, each response to other writers serves the ultimate purpose of academic writing: acknowledging and then resolving a disagreement through communal dependence and individual assertion.

Attributions: Signaling More than a Source

An academic writer can keep repeating the same signal phrase throughout his paper: "Smith says ... " then "Muñoz says ... " and even later "Waldman says," but such repetition should be avoided on the grounds of sheer boredom. Yet, there is an even better reason to vary the signal phrases used. The wording of an attribution can signal not only a cited source, but also the kind of assertion that a writer will make after it. For example, what do you expect a writer's reaction to a quotation will be, based on these three different signal phrases?

Three Different Attributions
Smith states,
Smith assumes,
Smith claims,

From our longer list below, which ones might a writer use to suggest her support of the source material? To imply her doubt? Which ones do you frequently use? Which ones can you use to improve a reader's readiness for your individual assertions?

Acknowledges	**Emphasizes**
Advocates	Errs
Affirms	Explains
Argues	Insists
Asserts	Justifies
Believes	Laments
Claims	Pleads
Contends	Reports
Counters	Recommends
Demands	Rejects
Denies	States
Doubts	Urges

The phrasing of an attribution, like the conventions of quoting and citing, helps a writer persuade a reader. It is another rhetorical choice made by a writer. Plagiarism, as we have shown above, occurs when a writer exerts too little control over source information.

MLA and Other Citation Systems

Just as students can rationalize their use of paper mills as victimless purchases, they also can become cynical about proper citation when they are overwhelmed by the multiple systems ("MLA, APA, or Chicago! Why can't they all just agree on one way?"). This frustration, however, also offers a glimpse at why these different systems exist. Academics in various disciplines have some good reasons for not agreeing on one citation system; their assumptions about knowledge often inform what distinguishes their conventions from others.

As we have explained, the **Modern Language Association (MLA)**, system of citation places the author's last name and the page number (when available) in parentheses at the end of a sentence, as in (Smith 22). Unlike their colleagues in the humanities, many academics in the social sciences use the **American Psychological Association (APA)**, system of citation. Their convention differs from that of MLA because when a writer's name is not provided with a signal phrase, the parenthetical citation includes the publication date of the source followed by the page number, as in (Smith, 2007, p. 22). Note that in addition to including the date, the page is marked with p., and each item is separated by commas. APA differs from MLA because psychologists and others, such as sociologists, consider themselves to be social scientists. They want to indicate that they are using the most current information, as indicated by the publication date. In the humanities, it is much more acceptable for a literacy critic, for instance, to rely on a classic scholarly study published several decades ago. Like the great works of literature, this scholarship has "stood the test of time" so the date of its publication is not as important for someone in the humanities. Thus, the differences in the examples listed below suggest the different assumptions about scholarly knowledge held by academics in the humanities versus those in the social sciences.

MLA Parenthetical Citation	APA Parenthetical Citation
(Smith 22).	(Smith, 2007, p. 22).

These differences continue when a signal phrase is used; APA places the citation right after the writer's name, and a paraphrase of a general idea from the text does not include the exact page number.

MLA Parenthetical Citation

Smith argues that ... paraphrase (22).

APA Parenthetical Citation

Smith (2007) argues that ... paraphrase.

A third citation system, known as **Chicago**, relies on footnotes that are placed at the end of a sentence.

Chicago Footnotes

Smith argues that ... paraphrase.[1]

The fact that these citation systems are not rules, but conventions, is shown again by their gradual changes over time. For example, the most recent, eighth of MLA changed the formatting of what is known as a **works cited list**, which is provided at the end of a paper. For example, the place of publication is no longer listed for a book, and the presentation of the volume and the issue numbers of a journal have been simplified.

For both kinds of sources, this information enables a reader to check a writer's reliance on other authors. A reader, for example, may want to check the context of a quotation (so don't alter it!), learn other facts related to the data presented, and understand the cited author's argument better. A works cited page makes it easy for a reader to do so by listing each source and using the author's last name (when known). Here, for example, is the MLA works cited list for three sources used in this chapter:

Works Cited

Bruffee, Kenneth. "Collaborative Learning and the 'Conversation of Mankind.'" *College English* vol. 46, no. 7, 1984, pp. 635–52.

Graff, Gerald. *Clueless in Academe*. Yale, 2003.

Ritter, Kelly. "The Economics of Authorship: Online Paper Mills. Student Writers, and First-Year Composition." *College Composition and Communication* vol. 56, no. 4, 2005, pp. 601–31.

The first and third sources demonstrate the format for the works cited **documentation** of an article; the second, for a book. There are many other formatting conventions, such as the italicization of book titles and the quotation marks for an article title, so most academic writers keep a convenient site, such as easybib.com, on their desktop or the latest version of a handbook on their desk.

With repeated practice of proper citation, it's not hard for most academics to recall the general patterns of, say, MLA citation and documentation, but the listing of an authorless article found in an edited collection posted on the Web usually sends most to a how-to citation source. We have explained the reasons for the main conventions, but we will encourage you to consult a source on the particular details of diverse examples of citation and documentation. Like doing what a family expects on Thanksgiving, your use of the expected citation system indicates your readiness to participate in an academic community. On the night before a paper is due, these conventions may seem like one more thing you have to do, but when you submit the paper, your fulfillment of these expectations shows that you know how academics talk-the-talk. By carefully distinguishing cited source material from your own thinking, your use of signal phrases, citations, and elaborations allows a reader to appreciate you mastery of cited sources *and* critical thinking. Thus, as we mentioned at the start of this chapter, there are positive reasons (mastery) as well as negative ones (plagiarism) for learning how and why to cite properly. It's best to gradually learn to cite so you are ready to cite properly when you tackle a research essay in which your reliance on source material will be central to the success of your effort.

Research Essays: Putting it all Together

In Chapter 3, we presented personal narratives as a very good way of putting the writing process into practice. Now in the second half of this chapter, we will present research essays as the culmination of all of your efforts to become a better reader, writer, and thinker. However, we must admit that when a professor utters the word "research," a few students will groan, at least inwardly. If the word "paper" is added to this utterance, as in a "research paper," some of these groans will become audible. Let's take a step back from this assignment and consider just research.

In the last week, you probably have tried to check a fact or learn more about a subject. What information have you sought? How did you try to find it, and was this effort successful? Most students have little trouble answering these questions. They have checked a sports score or some news. They have sought the definition of a difficult term or details on a topic of interest. Although many students frequently seek information, some dread an academic "research" assignment—why? Through freewriting and/or class discussion, please consider this issue:

> **What images, feelings, and/or memories come to mind when you recall working on a research paper?**

When some students were asked to reflect on their experiences, they recalled:

Research means finding out what other people have said on an assigned topic until you have enough to fill up the required number of pages.

8:30 would turn into 10:30 then 12:30, then sleep. I would always get up at 4 a.m. to finish and there I was again, the same position, the same mess, the same procrastination, and the same frustration.

Yet, all of these recollections are not so negative; some students described research and writing research papers differently:

I chose to research the daily lives of Romans. While I usually don't like research papers, I liked this one because the topic was interesting to me. I really did want to learn more about it.

A smile usually comes to my face because I enjoy researching. Then I come to a place where I need a detail to back up what I believe, and I sort through the material to find the perfect fact or quotation. Slowly the paper starts to piece itself together from ideas I had never thought of until I researched my topic.

We believe that interest and commitment distinguish the second set of students from the first. Although curiosity may have "killed the cat," according to the old saying, it breathes life into research. This vitality continues as students become committed to their topics. These students have a point they want to prove and an audience they want to persuade. Of course, every research topic may not excite the interest of each student, but we will explain below some ways to get interested in a topic.

Some of the initial hesitation some students may feel toward a research paper may stem, in part, from their anxiety about the effort involved. Fortunately, this concern can be decreased by assuring you that you already possess many of the skills required and helping you understand the series of tasks to be completed. A research paper combines almost all of the reading and writing abilities presented in this textbook. If you have succeeded so far, there is no reason to doubt that you will have further success. As you will see, we will be referring to many of the abilities from previous chapters. For example, a research paper will involve active reading strategies, like annotating a text and taking double-entry notes. Along with that assurance of your abilities, we will outline many of the necessary tasks. However, we must acknowledge that you and/or your professor may choose to change the order of some of these efforts. Some students like to pose a precise question before they begin researching their topic, while others like to explore a topic widely before they narrow their focus. Such differences make it harder for us to present a detailed sequence. In the left column below, we have created an overview of our research advice, but we want to stress it is only one possible order. In the right column, we have suggested an alternative, and other variations exist.

One Sequence of Research	An Alternative Order
Exploring research topics	Exploring research topics
Finding search terms	Posing a research question
Seeking sources	Seeking sources

Posing a research question	Finding search terms
Engaging with your sources	Engaging with your sources
Evaluating your sources	Evaluating your sources
Asserting a tentative thesis	Conducting further research
Starting to draft	Introducing & asserting a thesis
Conducting further research	Drafting
Finalizing your thesis	Concluding
Introducing and concluding	Revising before the deadline
Revising before the deadline	Editing the almost final draft
Editing the almost final draft	

Which sequence would you rather follow and why? What, if any, further changes would you like to make? Along with insisting that more than one order may be possible, we will suggest that you may want to read this section on research essays gradually, such as by using the headings to follow a sequence that will be most effective for you. In other words, you should, as explained back in Chapter 1, preview this section. We have to follow some order in this chapter, so let's start with how you can get interested in a topic, whether it is chosen or assigned.

Getting Interested

Using the theme of the education chapter, let's imagine being assigned a terrible topic. How would you react if you were assigned the following topic:

High School Desks

At first, this seems like an impossible topic. What could be interesting about desks? And yet, if you stop to think about what seems to be a hopelessly dull topic, can you get involved with it, at least as a possible topic for another student? How can this subject become an interesting one?

In the past, students have suggested some intriguing possibilities; these suggestions include the changing sizes and designs of desks, the development of left-handed ones, their patterns of arrangement and what that reveals about teaching methods, the annual budget for desk repair and replacement in a large school district, various attempts to make desks graffiti-proof, and perhaps the most original idea: the total weight of chewing gum placed under desktops each year, and what that amount suggests about student apathy! We promise that we will not assign any of those topics here or in the education chapter, but they demonstrate that **interest** can turn even what seems to be a dull topic into an intriguing issue for research.

The forms of critical thinking and persuasive reasoning presented in this textbook offer other ways to get interested in a topic:

Multiple Perspectives: Each reading chapter suggests several debates on its theme, and each debate depends, of course, on the differences among various viewpoints. You can become interested in a topic by asking: What do other people believe about this subject? What do they think is true or right? For example, in Chapter 6, we show that there are different perspectives on what should or should not be considered to be an American family today. Also, what are the proper roles of mothers and/or fathers in these families?

Or back in the first chapter, we presented the unusual viewpoint of young adults who have decided to forego modern computer technologies, such as social networks like Facebook. Trying to understand why someone holds a particular belief can not only arouse your interest but also lead you to the next approach.

Historical Trends: Asking how a current opinion relates to past viewpoints can pique our interest. For instance, the current claim in education that every student should meet certain standards of learning (and be tested until they reach that mark) becomes even more debatable when you learn that, in 1893, educators were wondering if school standards and methods should be "differentiated" for various kinds of students (see Chapter 7). This historical trend could lead to a research question like: For what reasons and in what ways should student be tracked (or not) by their academic abilities?

Cultural Influences: Wondering what other beliefs support a specific viewpoint can make a topic come alive. For example, defenders of digital literacy are quick to point out that those who doubt the benefits of computer technology are not the first skeptics to do so. In fact, we tend to fear the latest technology as it affects literacy, such as when government officials feared the printing press and when teachers worried that erasers on pencils would ruin students' handwriting. Yet, when skeptics of technology doubt the benefits of computers on literacy, they run into another cultural influence: our assumption that progress is always good (see Chapter 10). These cultural influences could lead to a research question like: What steps must be taken so the benefits of computers outweigh their drawbacks for literacy?

We have offered a few examples from some of the thematic chapters. Can you now develop some other research topics? You can focus on what intrigues you or what topics might interest some of your classmates:

	Multiple Perspectives	Historical Trends	Cultural Influences
Ch. 1 Technology			
Ch. 6 Family			
Ch. 7 Education			
Ch. 8 Race			
Ch. 9 Energy			
Ch. 10 Literacy			

Some of the rhetorical concepts in Chapter 5 on Argument can also help you become more interested in a topic.

Inductive Reasoning: Starting with specific examples can lead you to a broader question. For example, in Chapter 10, Nicholas Bilton quotes several studies that show that computer technologies are harming our minds and more (see pp. 325–329). Then one can start to wonder: What are the negative effects of computers? Are they really harmful?

Deductive Reasoning: Beginning with a general principle on a topic can also lead you to an engaging issue. For instance, from Chapter 6 on education, most of us would agree with the general principle that every child in America deserves an equal chance to be educated. The system of mastery testing so "no child is left behind" is based on this principle, but is annual testing the best way to promote greater academic achievement by every group of students?

Let's continue with the topic of education and consider the three kinds of arguments (see pp. 111–112 in Chapter 5).

Arguments over Blame, Values, and Action: If some students are not learning enough, should their teachers or their parents be blamed (a forensic argument over blame)? Or should we try to place more emphasis on academic achievement than on athletic victories (an epideictic argument on values)? Or should teachers use passive teaching methods, like lecturing, less and instead employ active ones more (a deliberative argument over actions)?

Becoming Committed

Along with getting interested in a topic, **becoming committed** to your subject will help you sustain your research efforts. To test your commitment to a topic, try completing the following statement through writing and/or discussion:

> On the topic of _____, I want to learn more
> about _____.

If you repeat only the same words in the second blank, you may not have enough interest in this research. Or, if what you want to learn heads off in many different directions, your commitment may be spread too thin.

A second test for your research topic is to consider the consequences of your effort.

Again, try completing the following assertion through writing and/or discussion:

> What I hope to learn on this topic will be significant
> to _____ (whom?) because _____ (why?).

If you can't yet answer these questions, it doesn't mean that your research won't succeed. However, you will have to tackle these rhetorical questions of audience (whom?) and purpose (why?) at a later time. Let us stress that your commitment to your topic does not have to be totally fixed at this time; it probably will change as your research progresses. Yet, the fact remains: your research must be supported by your interest and your commitment. If you ultimately don't care about your topic, who will?

Search Terms

As you begin to seek sources, the success of this effort will depend on the search terms you use. You probably have experienced the frustration of the following story. A student decided to research the trend of interracial marriages in relation to the Chapter 10 on American families. He wanted to learn more about the increasing number of such marriages as well as the difficulties and the successes of these families. He typed "interracial marriages" into a recommended database (Academic Search Premier). Then the dreaded message appeared: "No items match this search request." How, he wondered, can this be? No sources on interracial marriages; that's impossible!

Search engines and databases look for exactly what they are told to seek, so a researcher sometimes must experiment with various search terms. It turned out that when the frustrated student tried searching for "marriage and race," he found exactly the sources he had been seeking. Since so much depends on your **search terms**, it's a good idea to keep a list of the various terms you use.

You can also avoid some of this experimentation by consulting the **Library of Congress Subject Headings (LCSH)**. These subject headings, meaning search terms, were established so all American libraries use the same terms to organize sources. You'll find them on the back of the title page of any book, and many databases rely on them as well. Checking the LCSH in your library or online can eliminate the frustration of a fruitless search. One good source, such as a book, may reveal the best search terms for your topic. A reference librarian will also help you, so don't hesitate to ask them for help with your search terms or any other aspect of your research.

Another key component of search terms is the use of words like AND, OR plus quotation marks. These words are known as **Boolean operators**; they are named after George Boole who created this system to "operate" searches. As you can imagine, combining two terms with AND means that both terms must be subjects in a source, but OR means that either term will lead to a source. Search terms in quotation marks mean that sources must have that exact phrase.

The sooner you gain control over your search terms, the sooner you can start reading widely on your topic.

Seeking Sources and Reading Widely

As you become committed to a specific research topic, you can learn more about this interest by **reading widely** on it using various kinds of sources. At the start of this chapter, we asked you to consider how you checked a fact or sought some information. Now can you consider:

What are some of the different kinds of sources you can use for your research?

There, of course, is a rich array of sources you can consult.

We can rely on popular **search engines**, such as Google, bing, and Ask.com, but keep in mind that the sponsor links or matches that appear at the top of the search results are paid placements. Just like tempting foods placed at the end of supermarket aisles, these "sponsored" results have been placed there by companies that have paid a fee for their prominence. There also are general but more **scholarly databases**, such as Academic Search Premier, JStor, and Lexis Nexis. These databases do not have paid placements, and they offer more authoritative, expert sources. There also are particular databases for almost every academic discipline. Various colleges and universities subscribe to certain academic databases so you may need to ask your professor which ones are best for your research (and this is especially true for research in upper-level courses).

Other online sources include blogs and Wikipedia entries. Both, however, are the subject of some debate. Some blogs offer expert opinions, while others are less informed, so a reader has to have some knowledge on a subject in order to discriminate between the two (see more on source evaluation below). Various Wikipedia articles vary in their quality as well: the best ones include rich resources linked in supporting notes while the worst ones make some professors forbid their use. Again, it is wise to ask your professor about appropriate sources for your assignment.

Let's not forget print sources, such as books, journals, magazines, and newspapers. When you are looking through the stacks for one promising book, one pleasant surprise may be that you will find an even better source on the same shelf. Newspapers and magazines can be first, very beneficial sources because they often provide overviews and identify experts. Academic journal articles, which usually appear in print as well as online, are written by scholars so they will lead you to current debates and key terms on your topic. You may not be ready to read a journal article during your first foray into research on an unfamiliar subject, but your wide reading should include them a little later on. Why?

One last point: the presence on the Internet of full-text sources that originally were published as print sources obscures the traditional bias for hard copy sources over online ones. Now entire books and scholarly articles can be found online. Where a source is found matters less than our evaluation of its credibility, which we will address below. Many researchers, but not all, still find it easier to comprehend difficult texts by reading printed copies. It is not that we cannot comprehend online texts, but our habits of skim reading Facebook and other website pages may be too quick for our desire to understand and annotate texts.

Here is a list of some of the different kinds of sources we can consult as we begin to read widely. By habit, we may be drawn to some kinds more than others, but which sources do you think are most likely to provide the best information? Consider your current research topic (or a recent one), and make a conscious choice: With which sources should (or did) you start, and which ones should (or did) you consult later?

- Books
- Magazines
- Newspapers
- Dictionaries
- Encyclopedias
- Academic journals
- Reference guides
- Government documents
- Blogs
- Websites
- Wikipedia

Posing a Primary Research Question

At some point, you will probably want to and/or be asked to pose a precise research question. As we explained above, some students will be ready to pose this query as soon as they are interested in a topic, but others will want to wait. Our initial phrase of "At some point ... " has been chosen very carefully, but let us explain posing a research question now.

Most college-level research assignments will ask you to do more than summarize several sources on a topic. Rather than this research report, you will be asked to assert a thesis and support it using evidence from your research. This paper is more of an argument, and it requires a researcher to select and synthesize information from several sources. To distinguish this kind of research-based writing, we will refer to it as a research essay (versus a research report).

Your **research question** will help you focus your search for information, yet, its exact answer will be determined in the future. This question should not be phrased as a simple yes or no query or suggest only a report that summarizes information on a topic. To demonstrate these kinds of questions, let us continue with more examples from the familiar subject of education. Which questions suggest the developed argument of an essay, a yes/no response, or the broad summary of a report?

Some sample research questions

1. Does participation in high school athletics affect a student's academic achievement?
2. How can high school students be motivated to learn more?
3. What are the best ways to reduce bullying in high schools?

All of these topics could be developed into informative and persuasive research essays, but as each question is phrased above, we think that the third question most obviously suggests a thesis-driven, opinionated essay. The phrase "best ways" indicates more than a report on several approaches to this problem; this research essay will debate which one is most effective.

On the basis of its phrasing, the first question implies a broad yes/no response, and the second one suggests a report on several methods of motivation without much judgment among them. However, all is not lost because both questions can be revised into better ones. For example, the first one can be rewritten as

> *#1* Revised: What are the most effective programs to increase academic achievement by high school athletes?

Again, "at some point" you may want to pose several smaller, more specific questions for your research efforts. For instance, if a student wanted to research the best ways to reduce school bullying, what are ten specific questions that would have to be researched and answered?

Primary research question: What is the most effective way to reduce bullying in schools today?

Ten secondary questions:

1.

2.

3.

4.

5.

6.

7.

8.

9.

10.

Of course, ten is an arbitrary total; we could have requested seven or twelve, but if you can only pose two or three specific questions to guide your research further, you probably should read and think about your topic more.

Some of the first questions we can imagine posing are

- What percentage of public high school students feel they have been bullied?
- What types of students are targeted most frequently for harassment?
- How many cases of bullying are reported each year now versus 10, 20, and 30 years ago?

Those are our first reactions, and what questions can you add? Then which ones do you think can be answered with relative ease and using what kind of sources? If you cannot generate a list of ten or more specific questions on your topic, you may need to reconsider the focus of your research. To sum up your efforts so far, your professor may ask you, or you may choose to write a research plan, which can include your topic, your interest, your primary and secondary research questions, and some likely sources.

Engaging with Your Sources

Once you pose several secondary research questions, you can shift from leafing through your likely sources to **engaging** with them more actively. As you start to **annotate sources** and **take notes**, you may find it helpful to keep your reason for research in mind. Try writing your primary research question on the first page of your notes from a source or on a sticky note attached to your computer monitor. This reminder may help you avoid straying too far from your topic. Of course, in some cases, you may choose to change your topic, perhaps in consultation with your professor.

We will also suggest that you should record the publishing information for a source as you start taking notes. For a book, record the author(s), title, place of publication, publisher, and copyright. For most shorter texts, note the author, title, source title, date, and page numbers (plus volume and issue numbers for some magazines or journal articles). For websites, record the author(s) if known, the title, the URL address, and the date accessed (in case the site is altered). It is much easier to gather this information as your research begins rather than at the end of your writing process. Thus, a page of notes, whether typed or handwritten, can start with the following information:

> Primary question: What programs have proven to be most effective at bullying in high schools, and why are they effective?

> Source Info: "Anti-bullying policies target staff in schools." *American School Board Journal*, June 2010, Vol. 197 Issue 6, p.12.

> p. 12: As of 2010, forty-one states have laws against bullying in schools. Some districts in Iowa and California are passing laws that are explicitly against bullying by teachers and other staff members.

> My reaction: I'm surprised that in 2010, every state did not have laws against students -bullying their peers. I never would have thought that a law against teachers bullying others would be necessary, but it seems like a good idea. It stops a few bad ones and makes all teachers set a good example for students.

> p. 12: In Broward County, Florida, students are encouraged to report bullying in several ways, such as in person, by phone, via e-mail, or in a text message. This encouragement led to a 4% increase in reports.

As shown in our example, it's also better to record specific page numbers with your notes. Ideally, this information addresses not only your broad primary question but also some secondary questions. Of course, if you are starting to take notes on a less familiar topic, your notes may not be so precise. These notes are a step beyond the annotations explained in Chapter 1 on Reading (see pp. 3–22), and it's only one more step to create **double-entry notes** also described in Chapter 1. Double-entry notes combine important information from a source with your immediate reaction to these facts, figures, and details (see p. 11). With these responses, you are prepared to add an assertion after some cited information so that you can make the research information to support your thesis.

Evaluating Your Sources

After you have taken notes from a few sources, you probably will be able to tell that one source is not only better for your research but also seems to be more accurate, more authoritative. To avoid information that seems too biased or unreliable, you can **evaluate your sources**. This evaluation may sound difficult, for how can a student judge the published writing of an expert? Yet, we often do something very similar when we meet a new person. We ask ourselves, "Can I trust him?" and "Is her opinion biased?" We can ask similar questions about any research source.

Questions for Source Evaluation

- How well does the author demonstrate his or her expertise by citing other sources?

- Is the information current or out of date?

- Does the author include opposing viewpoints? Does the author include the strongest or weakest version of this opposition?

- How thoroughly does the author respond to opposing views?

- As the author engages in a public debate and/or a scholarly discussion, is she or he mentioned or cited by others, which suggests her or his expertise?

- Where was the author's work published?

- Was this work reviewed by others before it was published?

- Who is the intended audience of this publication?

- Is this publication source primarily interested in spreading knowledge or earning some gain?

You and/or your professor may want to add other questions to this list. It is important for you to evaluate your sources because your readers will be evaluating you; they will be judging your ethos, your character as the writer of a research essay (for more on ethos, see Chapter 5, p. 106).

Asserting a Tentative Thesis

When we asked you to make a commitment to your topic, you stated what you wanted to learn and why you thought this topic was significant. You may not have been able to answer each of those questions perfectly, but it was important that you advanced beyond only announcing your topic. If you haven't already done so, it is an appropriate time for you to develop your opinion further in a **tentative thesis**, and it may be easier to do so by engaging in freewriting or discussion. Rather than surrounding yourself with your notes and sources immediately, try responding to the following prompts more informally, as if someone asked you what you are thinking about your topic before class started:

What have you started to believe about your topic?

What do you want others to understand about this issue?

In a casual conversation, we rarely discuss what everyone already believes (what's the point?); instead we talk about what is debatable. In a research essay too, you should add your opinion to the published sources by agreeing with some writers but disagreeing with others. For example, in Chapter 9, the readings differ as they defend and criticize the reliance on oil for energy in the United States. Why do you consider the dependence on oil for energy a minor issue or a major problem?

Once you have a sense of the position you want to assert, the next challenge is to sum it up in a few succinct sentences. The phrasing of this thesis is important because it provides both you and your audience with a sense of the purpose of your essay. Consider this example based on the readings of the chapter on cities and suburbs:

> Since the early 1900s, the United States has depended on oil as its primary source of energy. The twin problems of excessive consumption and environmental damage, however, mean that our country must turn to cleaner and more sustainable sources of energy.

Don't worry; your thesis is just a tentative one so you can modify it later on.

One good way to get feedback on your thesis is to share it with several classmates. This can be done through e-mail, a discussion board, or the whiteboard in your classroom. Create a list of several theses, and label them with numbers instead of students' names. Then ask everyone to identify some of the stronger theses by their numbers and explain why they seem so strong: What purpose does each one assert? Who might disagree and why? How might the writer try to answer that disagreement?

Next, turn to some of the weaker theses and identify them by number. Rather than discuss what is wrong with each one ("Number 2 is weak because … "), focus on how each one can be improved ("Number 8 can be improved by creating a more debatable purpose like … ").

Once you have developed a strong, though still tentative, thesis, you probably will be ready to start drafting at least some of your essay.

Starting to Draft

As you turn from taking notes to **drafting your paper**, it will be important to keep your audience in mind: you are trying to convince a reader who does not already agree with you. Chapter 6 on Argument has many suggestions on how to reach an uncertain audience or even an opposing one. Let us repeat one suggestion on **organizing your draft**: you can follow the classic advice on the arrangement of the three rhetorical appeals. In your opening paragraphs, appeal by your ethos, your character as a writer, and a researcher. Then, turn to logos and provide logical supports for your position. Don't be afraid to acknowledge some of the sound objections that others might raise, and qualify your argument by admitting, for example, that in some cases your position may have to be modified. Finally, don't forget to appeal by pathos, meaning to the audience's emotions. Make sure they understand why your opinion is important, such as by showing what effect it will have on the lives of particular people. Let us stress that this is only one of many possible ways to arrange your argument; the key is to have some clear reasons for the order of your research essay.

If you are not just trying to fill up the required number of pages of a research report, you should be able to explain that your essay starts here, goes on to this, and proceeds to that … because … Working with your professor, you can decide whether you will outline your essay before, during, or after drafting. However, at some point, you should check the order of your draft and be able to explain it to yourself and others.

As you are drafting, you should also practice the conventions of **academic honesty**. As explained in this chapter, you should cite the sources used for quotations, paraphrases, and little-known information. Yet your essay should not consist solely of cited material; you should also help a reader understand the meaning and appreciate the purpose of cited material, such as by using signal phrases and interpretative elaborations. As explained in Chapter 1, double-entry notes make it especially easy to add elaborations on cited information (see p. 11).

Let us add an unusual simile to explain your relationship with your readers: they are like special guests at a gathering on your topic. At this gathering, you would not just meet them at the door and tell them to talk to your sources; instead you would lead these special guests to this source and introduce them, then introduce them to that source in order to create a compelling and pleasing evening for this audience.

Although it may seem like a hassle to start citing sources while you are drafting, it is even harder to go back and add citations later to an almost final draft. Even worse is trying to correct citation problems once the issue of academic honesty has been raised; when citing, sooner is better.

Conducting Further Research

If you start drafting after you have asserted a tentative thesis, one benefit is that you will often develop a feeling for where your research is strong and where you still need to learn more. This further research can lead you to the authoritative citations within an already good source, to **specialized academic databases**, and into **government documents** (as mentioned above on sources). It also may lead you to engage in some firsthand research, such as by conducting a survey, an interview, or an observation.

Have you ever started to answer a **survey** and quit before you finished? Let that experience inform the design of your own survey. It should not require too much time, and the questions should be relatively easy to answer. For example, you may want to ask several multiple-choice or 1- to 5-scale questions and then add a longer response question or two. Survey questions should also use neutral phrases, rather than steer the respondent toward one answer. To seek a widespread and representative array of respondents, you can distribute and collect your surveys in person or rely on an online survey instrument, such as those available at surveymonkey.com.

A good **interview** depends on the expertise of the person questioned. Yet, with all of the experts on a college campus and/or available online, it is not difficult to find a good subject. As with a survey, your questions should not reveal your own bias. Instead, you want to elicit this person's knowledge through probing but inviting queries. The actual interview can be conducted in person, by phone, or electronically. An e-mail interview has the advantage of providing a written record of the exchange, yet the subtleties of voice tone and physical gestures are lost. A phone or face-to-face interview provides those benefits, but you will have to use a tape or video recorder to create a record of the interview. Such recordings can be made only with the explicit consent of the interview subject.

The same consent must be secured for an **observation**, such as by visiting a school for research on an education-related topic. Again, the observer has to be careful to minimize the influence of his or her perspective, such as a researcher focusing on only the flaws of a class based on lecture or discussion. As with a good interview, the researcher has to have a focus prepared but must also be flexible enough to follow a surprising response when it is made.

After any one of these three forms of firsthand research, it is helpful to reflect upon the results as soon as possible, such as by freewriting on their significance. These results can be reinforced through further research to check if others have made similar findings in published research. As your own expertise grows, you will be ready to engage in further research using more specialized and authoritative sources.

Finalizing Your Thesis

As you draft and research further, you may find that you want to alter your initial thesis. Such revisions usually reveal the strengths of your research. As you understand a topic better, you will be more able to confront the complexities of your topic. You now may want to include some qualification of your argument or be ready to preview your main points in your thesis. Yet, as you **finalize your thesis**, you probably should check the development of your argument as well. Do your order and emphasis still match your thesis?

Introducing and Concluding

Do we dare refer to "At some point … " again? Some writers can't imagine starting a draft without creating an introduction first. Others prefer to jump into the middle of a draft and write. Regardless of your preference, you will want to concentrate on your introduction at some point because, like most first impressions, your audience's reaction to your opening will be important.

This **introduction** should lead your readers to your thesis and prepare them to follow your argument. Below, we have started a list of several options for an introduction. What other possibilities can you add?

> **Introduction Options**
>
> – A personal experience
> – An illustrative anecdote
> – A case study
> – A revealing fact or figure
> – A complicated example
> – A provocative question
> – A compelling scene
> – A general principle
> – A "big picture" description
> –
> –

If you can impress your audience with your experience, knowledge, and/or insight, you will have succeeded in the crucial appeal by the writer's character, by ethos (see Chapter 5, p. 106). Then they will be more receptive to the rest of your essay.

Although it may seem to defy common sense, a good way to write one effective introduction is to draft two or more. Working with more than one approach will make you more conscious and critical of the first impression each one makes. Once you have drafted two or more introductions, you can ask a peer to read each one and explain why this or that is preferred. This explanation may lead you to additional revisions of one, the combination of two, or the use of another later in your essay. Even students who already have one good introduction often find that this doubling of their initial effort improves some aspect of their draft. Try it!

Ideally, an effective **conclusion** yields the final conviction of your readers. They finish feeling that "She's so right" or "I agree with him." However, repeating all of the ideas of your essay may not be the best approach. Reminding a reader of a main point or two is fine, but you don't have to rehash your entire essay. Here is another list of options. What other possibilities can you add?

Conclusion Options
– Explain the significance of your viewpoint
– Describe the impact of other choices
– Return to the essay's title or an introductory idea
– Extend the thesis in a what-is-next step
– End with a compelling quotation and explain its relevance
–
–
–

As explained above, many persuasive conclusions appeal to our emotions more than our logic. This final appeal to pathos can make an audience not only understand but also eager to act on an issue.

Revising before the Due Date

In Chapter 1 on the writing process, we encouraged you to start early enough so you will have time to **revise**, to *really* revise. We explained that revision can occur on many levels, such as from paragraph order to sentence structure. To revise your research essay, you should also check your use of source information. Have you cited all quotations, paraphrases, and little-known facts? Have you offered some attributions to help guide a reader's understanding of this cited information? Have you varied the phrasing of those signal phrases? Have you elaborated on much of this information? Have you avoided large sections filled with only source material or very little source material?

It may be easier to ask a peer or tutor to help you review your draft with such questions in mind. Your professor may provide you with some review questions (or ask you to help create them).

Here is a general list of **peer review questions** that can be adapted to your particular research assignment:

Some Questions for Draft Review

- Do the title and the introduction get the intended audience interested in this essay? Why or why not? If not, what title and introduction could be used to interest a reader?

- Does the opening give the reader a clear sense of the thesis and not just of the topic? Is the thesis debatable, meaning who can disagree and on what? If necessary, how can the thesis be improved?

- After the thesis, does the writer provide general information that an unfamiliar reader may need to understand the topic? Does the writer seem to know some of the key terms and crucial distinctions of this issue?

- What are two of the strongest research sections of this draft? Why is each section effective, especially in relation to the essay's thesis?

- What is one section that seems to be less effective? For example, does the writer seem to be just filling a page with facts? How can this section be improved?

- Does the draft seem to follow a smooth and logical order? What is the general order, meaning from this to that, then on to what and so on?

- Does the writer use diverse sources, and where are they combined, meaning synthesized, well? Or, where might more of this synthesis be done?

- Does the writer anticipate and answer possible objections?

- What research, if any, is still needed?

- Does the paper end well? Why is or isn't the conclusion effective?

- Is the research presented properly with citations for direct quotations, paraphrased information, unique phrases, and little-known facts?

- Does any section seem to need a citation so the writer will not be accused of plagiarism?

- How well does the writer elaborate after cited information?

- Does the final list of sources include only sources actually cited? Are they presented in the proper format?

- Has the final draft been proofread for editing errors?

Editing the Almost-Final Draft

If you are not drafting desperately hours before your deadline, the day before the deadline ideally should be reserved for revising *and then* editing. In Chapter 2, we suggested that you should edit an almost-final draft by keeping a list of your **common errors** in mind (see p. 30). You may also want to remind yourself of the exact conventions of the **citation system** you are employing and double-check your fulfillment of these conventions (see pp. 37 and 38). Again, your professor may provide you with editing and citing guidelines; give yourself the time to fulfill them.

As you may already know or will experience soon, there is great satisfaction in researching and writing a strong essay on a topic to which you are committed. Then, you too will feel the satisfaction of the student we quoted at the start of this section: "A smile usually comes to my face.... I sort through the material to find the perfect fact or quotation. Slowly, the paper starts to piece itself together from ideas I had never thought of until I researched my topic."

Key Terms

Before you finish with this chapter, here is a list of the key concepts; which ones can you explain easily and which ones do you need to review?

Academic honesty
Plagiarism
     Intellectual theft
     Deliberate copying
     Sloppy notes and careless drafting

Cutting and pasting/
 Patchwork plagiarism
 Paper-mill purchases

Communal dependence
Individual assertion
Conventions
 Quotations
 Paraphrased ideas
 Little-known facts
 Citation
 Signal phrase or attribution
  Full name/last name
 Ellipsis
 Indented, block quotations
 Documentation/work cited list
 Citation systems
  Modern Language Association
  American Psychological Association
  Chicago

Research topics
 Getting interested
 Becoming committed
Search terms
 Library of Congress Subject Headings
 Boolean operators
Seeking sources
 Search engines
 Scholarly databases
Posing a research question
 Research essay versus research report
 Primary and secondary questions
Engaging with your sources
 Annotating
 Taking notes
 Double-entry notes
Evaluating your sources
Asserting a tentative thesis
Starting to draft
 Organizing your essay
 Practicing academic honesty
Conducting further research
 Specialized academic databases
 Government documents

Additional Sources for Chapter 4

To deepen your understanding of academic honesty and research essays, you can consult some of the following sources:

1. For a strong argument on why plagiarism is significant problem that must be confronted, you may want to read "Reflections of the Cultural Climate of Plagiarism" by Matthew Willen.

   https://www.aacu.org/publications-research/periodicals/reflections-cultural-climate-plagiarism

2. For a complicated view on plagiarism as students are surrounded by online content, you many want to read "Plagiarism Lines Blur for Students in Digital Age" by Trip Gabriel.

   http://www.nytimes.com/2010/08/02/education/02cheat.html

3. For a scholarly analysis of student attitudes toward plagiarism and the particular problem of online paper mills, you may want to read "The Economics of Authorship" by Kelly Ritter.

   http://writing2.richmond.edu/training/383/383restricted/ritter.pdf

4. For advice on how students can enjoy writing a research essay, you may want to read "Writing as an Exploration: Rethinking the Research Paper" by Hermann Bailey.

   http://journals.library.wisc.edu/index.php/wej/article/viewFile/538/579

5. For more instruction on research essays, you may want to consult various sections of the Online Writing Lab (OWL) of Purdue University:

   https://owl.english.purdue.edu/owl/resource/658/01/

   https://owl.english.purdue.edu/owl/resource/747/01/

   https://owl.english.purdue.edu/owl/resource/560/18/

6. For assistance with citation formats, you may want to use what are known as citations generators, but please note that these free sites will lead you on to paid services:

   http://www.easybib.com

   http://www.citethisforme.com/us/citation-generator/mla

   http://www.citationmachine.net/mla/cite-a-website/manual

Argument and Rhetoric

CHAPTER 5

Rhetoric dates back to ancient Greece, making many of its concepts more than two millennia old. It's tempting to dismiss a theory so ancient: How can rhetoric, meaning the art of persuasion, still be relevant? Yet, many aspects of the human condition have not changed that much over the last twenty-or-so centuries. We still find ourselves disagreeing with others, wanting to win an argument, or needing to persuade another person. On a daily basis, we encounter others or find ourselves engaged in these angry clashes, such as when a roommate complains about a noisy alarm clock, classmates disagree during a discussion, or a student decides to end an online friendship. These disputes may be brief, but they often end with more anger than agreement: "You'd better turn off that alarm … ," "That's a ridiculous statement … " and "You're off my list; leave me alone." Our challenge continues to be, as it has been for centuries: Can we learn to use rhetoric well? In this chapter, we will use some familiar experiences to explain how we can understand and create arguments better in our daily lives as well as in college reading and writing assignments.

Argument is a fundamental form of college-level reading and writing. Much of high school instruction involves reading an explanation of an event in a textbook and writing an exposition of a concept, but college reading and writing often involve arguments. For instance, college students often are asked to not only explain an event or a concept but also argue why *this* analysis or interpretation is better than *that* one.

Let's start with an argument that you probably can easily imagine; you may have engaged in this kind of argument recently: a teenager and a parent differing over a weekend curfew. In one version of this argument, the teen and the parent recognize their differences ("Be home by 11." then "How about 1?") and start to trade accusations ("You never let me … " and "Don't be childish … "). This argument usually ends with a door slammed, a party missed, or a curfew violated. This version matches the concept of argument that many of us have when we are asked to imagine one: a verbal battle between two or more people. It's easy for us to slip into a combative argument as the media surrounds us with aggressive disputes. Guests on daytime television insult each other, sports radio callers rip into a coach, and politicians trade charges during a debate. As Gerald Graff asserts, the very word "argument … conjures up an image … of acrimonious warfare." As we argue, we usually "make enemies … yet rarely change each other's minds."

Two theorists named George Lakoff and Mark Johnson have analyzed the development of these warlike arguments. When a difference of viewpoints is recognized, we exaggerate these differences so those who disagree with us become our "enemies." Then we characterize them as jerks, idiots, and other words not fit for print in a textbook, so they *have* to be defeated. The war must be won; there can be no compromise. If a rule has to be bent a bit, well so be it. If this were the only kind of argument possible, we'd have to end this chapter right now because we all know how to conduct these martial arguments.

Fortunately, our example of a curfew dispute can result in another kind of argument. Can you imagine a more positive version? One that doesn't end with loud voices and a door slammed?

<u>Weekend Curfew</u>

<u>A Teen</u>   <u>A Parent</u>

Of course, many positive variations are possible, but here's one. Once the difference in time is recognized ("Do I have to be home by 11 or 1?"), each person could acknowledge the other's position. The teen could acknowledge the parent's concern that driving late at night can be more dangerous, and the parent could recognize the teen's desire for greater independence. As the parent and teen acknowledge each other's position instead of exaggerating their differences, a more positive outcome becomes much more likely. The teen can overcome the parent's fears by admitting, "I know that late-night driving can be more dangerous, but you know I'm a good driver." The parent can acknowledge and even appeal to the teen's independence: "I know you want to spend time with your friends before you head off to college, but can you help me avoid worrying about you so much?" These recognitions of the other's concerns could create a better outcome, though a little compromise by both may be necessary: "Okay, I'll leave the party before midnight, and I'll call you if I'll be home later than midnight." Although it sometimes is very satisfying to crush the other side in an argument, this compromise not only makes both sides feel more content, it also makes them more likely to seek a more productive resolution when the next argument arises. The positive result of this curfew argument also suggests the original meaning of argument. In Latin, "argumentum" means "to make clear," not name calling or chair throwing. As we argue, we can try to make our positions clear to others and ourselves. Then everyone can decide better what positions we will and will not alter in order to resolve some difference of opinion.

The theories of rhetoric, which date back to the Greeks, can help us "make clear" the best ways to resolve an argument. As the Athenians of ancient Greece tried to establish their fledgling democracy, they argued over who should be considered a citizen and what is the best kind of leader. Aristotle and others like Gorgias tried to understand and teach the most effective methods of argumentation by developing theories of rhetoric. Aristotle defined **rhetoric** as "the discovery of the available means of persuasion." By using the best of these possible methods, the ancient Greeks tried to resolve their societal differences through oral arguments instead of physical aggression. Ever since, we have been disagreeing at home, at work, in classrooms, and in government, but rhetoric can teach us how to make the most persuasive arguments so anger, regret, and violence can be avoided.

The Rhetorical Triangle

We will use our example of a curfew conflict to demonstrate the first and most fundamental concept of their ancient theories: the **rhetorical triangle**.

Speaker/Writer — Message/Purpose — Audience/Reader

When a **speaker** considers his **audience** as well as his **message**, it prevents an impulsive assertion of his position ("I wanna stay out late."). This attention to audience makes a speaker balance what she wants to say with how it will be heard ("Yes, driving at midnight can be dangerous, but … "). The Greeks had names for these "Yes" and "but" strategies: **concession** and **refutation**. Most teens are very good at refuting a parent's argument, but some do not precede this counterargument with a concession, by admitting that the parent may have a valid point. Such a concession usually will gain some goodwill from the parent that, in turn, may make this elder more likely to listen to the teen's response (" … but you know I'm a safe driver."). Of course, the parent may offer his or her own concession and refutation ("Yes, I know you're a good driver, but it's other drivers out late at night that scare me."). Now, at least both parties have agreed on what is the real issue: How great are the dangers of other drivers late at night? You probably can imagine how this argument might continue: The parent wants to protect the child, and the teenager counters that a parent can't always be protective, the child has to go forth into the world.

Next, if some of the principles of effective argumentation are used, the results may be less divisive and more satisfying. These principles may even help some of you stay out later next summer.

Three Appeals

Our example of the curfew conflict also demonstrates three other crucial concepts of rhetoric. You probably can imagine listening to this verbal dispute so let us represent it in writing with the ALL CAP SHOUTING of text messaging. Can you hear a teen shouting, "BUT MOM you don't need to WORRY"? This impulsive assertion also could be expressed as "Mom, I know you worry, but … " This difference of expression involves not only what is said but also how it is said, and the latter reveals the role of a speaker's character in an argument. The ancient Greeks referred to the influence of a speaker's character as **ethos**, and it is one of what they called the three rhetorical appeals. The other two appeals are by reason, logic—**logos and** feelings, emotions—**pathos and**. As with the rhetorical triangle, the Greeks liked to think in threes, in triads, and the three appeals can be listed as

1. Ethos—the appeal by character

2. Logos—the appeal by reason

3. Pathos—the appeal by emotion

Let us explain each one briefly.

Ethos

Former President Ronald Reagan is the epitome of this appeal. Both his supporters and his critics called him the "Teflon President" because nothing negative ever seemed to stick to him. Many voters liked his character so much that they easily accepted his arguments ("Tear down that wall") and they ignored his mistakes (the Iran-Contra scandal). President Reagan is a perfect example of Aristotle's explanation of ethos: "Persuasion is achieved by the speaker's personal character, when the speech is so spoken as to make us think him credible. We believe good men more fully and readily than others."

A modern theorist named Kenneth Burke coined the term **identification** to explain the appeal by character further; he asserted, "You persuade a man only insofar as you can talk his language by speech, gesture, ton[e], … [and] attitude, *identifying* your ways with his" (italics added). Consider, for example, a teen in the curfew argument who concedes, "I know you worry Mom, but I'd like to spend some time with my friends before college" versus one who exclaims, "You never let me … " The second speaker already has lost this argument because that comment shows the very immaturity that the parent fears will endanger the teen. In contrast, the first speaker presents the poise that the parent hopes will keep the child safe.

One last point about ethos and identification: Despite the old saying "When in Rome do as the Romans do," a speaker's character does not have to match that of the audience exactly. In fact, we cringe when a parent tries to talk and dress like a teen or when a student mirrors the middle-age manner of an older teacher. Ethos only requires that the audience connects with a speaker's language and demeanor so she is considered likeable and credible. Then the audience is more ready, as Aristotle explained, to believe the appeals made by pathos and logos.

Logos

As we already have explained, techniques, like concession and refutation, can create a series of logical premises that can bring an audience to a desired conclusion. These series can proceed from specific examples to general principles or follow the reverse pattern. Perhaps you already know the names of these patterns from a writing or a philosophy course. **Inductive reasoning** presents several specific examples to prove a general principle, such as when someone argues that he knows three people who were in car accidents as they were texting while driving so he concludes that texting behind the wheel is dangerous. **Deductive reasoning**, on the other hand, begins with a general principle like drivers should avoid unnecessary risks and applies it to a specific example, such as texting while driving, in order to conclude that drivers should not text behind the wheel. "complete"? Can you complete these two examples of inductive and deductive reasoning?

Inductive Reasoning	Deductive Reasoning
Single example:	General principle:
Another specific example:	Particular case:
Conclusion:	Conclusion:

The Greeks created names for these two patterns of logic as well as two more specific forms of deductive reasoning that we still use today: syllogism and enthymeme.

A **syllogism** is a three-step, logical series built on what we can explain informally as an "if this and if that, then … " pattern. You probably know this famous example of a syllogism:

A Famous Syllogism

1. All men are mortal.

2. Socrates is a man.

3. Socrates is mortal.

Another way to understand a syllogism is to imagine a listener's reactions: "All men are mortal"—that's true, "Socrates is man"—okay, so "Socrates is mortal"—who could deny that conclusion?! Yet, syllogisms sometimes seem a bit too obvious, a little too drawn out for an audience to stay interested in the reasoning.

An **enthymeme** reduces the three steps of a syllogism (1. if this, and 2. if that, then 3. conclusion) to only two. It provides a premise and depends upon the audience to supply the next step so the desired conclusion will be reached. The two-step process of an enthymeme can be diagrammed as

An Enthymeme's Two-Step Logic

1. If this (and an audience knows that)

2. Then the conclusion is. . .

In another Shakespearean play, *The Merchant of Venice*, the protagonist creates a memorable enthymeme that reduces the three-step syllogism on Socrates's mortality to a two-step argument for the humanity of a Jewish character named Shylock. In a climatic scene, Shylock protests his poor treatment by others when he exclaims, "If you cut a Jew, does he not bleed?" Through this enthymeme, Shylock makes the following appeal through deductive reasoning:

Shakespeare's Enthymeme

1. If wounded people suffer and bleed (Shylock will bleed when cut)

2. Then Shylock is as human as his tormentors

Enthymemes, of course, are only effective if the audience can supply the second premise. However, when they do, they will reach the conclusion sought by the speaker based on what seems to be on their own logic. Then an audience is more convinced because they are involved in, and not just following, an argument's reasoning process.

One possible flaw in the use of enthymemes is when an argument appeals only to those who already agree with the speaker. Consider, for example, those on both sides of the abortion debate. As they refer to "a woman's choice" or "the right to life," each side expects the audience to assume that the rights of the mother or the fetus are paramount so the desired conclusion on abortion as being right or wrong is reached. Of course, those who do not already agree could respond that some choices aren't good or a mother's life matters too. The abortion issue has become so contentious because some on both sides engage in what is known as **preaching to the choir**. Appealing to those with the same views as yours is a great campaign strategy to mobilize one's supporters, but it is a much less effective strategy when one must convince others and create a consensus.

Another potential problem in logical appeals is that we sometimes argue, as another theorist named Stephen Toulmin asserts, backward, meaning we develop our arguments in reverse. Rather than start with the facts of a dispute, we often start with the outcome we want to reach and then gather the evidence to support that result. Toulmin, therefore, calls the desired outcome of an argument the **claim** for which one gathers **evidence** or what he termed the data. However, if we only collect the facts that support our position, we end up making one-sided arguments that can be countered easily. Toulmin, therefore, urged that as we develop an argument, we should anticipate possible counterarguments or rebuttals, to our claim. This **rebuttal** may force us to modify, to qualify our claim, such as by making an absolute claim into a conditional one: "Yes, it's not always the case, but I still will argue that it usually is true that ... " It's easy to imagine an advocate of male superiority making such a **qualification,** or modification of one's claim, after the physical strength of top female athletes has been raised as a rebuttal to his original claim of absolute male dominance.

Pathos

This appeal depends on the emotions aroused in the audience. Like President Reagan, Barack Obama was elected because he stirred feelings of optimism in voters. Like Reagan's slogan of "It's morning in America," Obama emphasized change and hope to an electorate ready for both. He made Americans feel confident and capable. Pathos depends less on the emotions shown by the speaker and more on the feelings evoked from the audience.

Perhaps, the best way to demonstrate this distinction between the emotions of speaker and audience is through a counterexample. When a teen exclaims, "But MOM, you NEVER let me ... " the outrage of the speaker may not be matched by a similar feeling of unfairness in a parent. Instead, it's liable to provoke anger from a listener upset by the teen's self-centered demands. The mistake of confusing a speaker's emotions with those of an audience is a common one. We even have phrases ready to catch this error; we turn to another listener and reject this "sob story" or ask a speaker if he isn't "laying it on a bit too thick?"

Sometimes, the most effective emotional appeal is made by an understated assertion. Rather than model feelings for an audience, a subdued speaker can create the conditions for the desired emotional reaction of the audience. In Shakespeare's play *Julius Caesar*, you may recall Mark Antony's famous speech in which he asserts that he has come "to bury Caesar, not to praise him." Then in a solemn voice, he catalogs many of this murdered leader's best traits. The grief he has brought to "bury" this fallen leader provokes exactly the anger he wants from the crowd. This emotion turns the crowd against Brutus and the other conspirators, just as Antony intended. When it comes to pathos, sometimes less feeling expressed by the speaker can create more emotion for the audience.

To test your knowledge of these appeals, here are three more statements by a parent in the curfew conflict. What appeal do you think is primarily being used in each one? Ethos, pathos, or logos?

- "It's a fact that there are many more fatal car accidents after midnight."
- "I'd never forgive myself if you were hurt in a late night crash."
- "I've been driving for thirty years, and I've seen too many teens make stupid driving mistakes."

We think these three statements rely primarily on logos in the first, pathos in the second, and ethos in the third. Of course, these appeals sometimes overlap so you could argue that the second involves the speaker's character, or ethos, as well as pathos.

Since ethos is based on the speaker, pathos with audience, and logos with message, we can sum up our explanation of the three appeals be layering them onto the rhetorical triangle:

Thus, a persuasive speaker tries to project a credible ethos, which makes the audience more receptive to the logic of her message and the emotions the speaker wants to arouse in the audience. As suggested above, Aristotle believed that the most effective order of an argument is to start with the speaker's ethos, develop the logic of the message, and then end with the desired emotions of the audience:

Ethos first, Logos next, and Pathos last

A Rhetorical Précis

In each of the thematic chapters (Chapters 6–10), one option for the final assignment is to write a lengthy rhetorical analysis of the arguments made in at least two readings (see, for example, p. 168 in Ch. 6). To practice for the longer rhetorical analysis, your professor may assign a shorter analysis known as a rhetorical précis. This assignment consists of four sentences in an exact order with some specific phrasing required. For this assignment, you should answer the following questions:

1. What is the title of the text and who is the author? What is the thesis/main claim of the argument? You should answer these questions in a precise sentence, such as by using the following format: In _____ (title in italics), _____ (full name of author) argues that _____ (main claim). Be sure to use a strong verb like argues, asserts, denies, demonstrates, refutes, etc.

2. How does the author support the thesis? In a single sentence, provide an overview of the evidence provided and possibly, its organization.

3. Given the thesis stated in question 1, what is the author's purpose? In a sentence, assert the purpose of the argument and then elaborate with the phrase "in order to." Here's a sample of this format: _____ 's (author's last name) purpose is to _____ in order to _____ (elaborate on the effect on the audience).

4. Who is the intended audience of this argument, and what kind of relationship does the author try to establish with the audience? Consider the language, information, and/or the original publication site of the author's argument to identify the audience in the fourth and final sentence.

For more explanation of a rhetorical précis, see #3 of the Additional Sources of Chapter 5 (see p. 121).

Three Kinds of Argument

The ancient Greeks, and Aristotle in particular, loved to categorize; we already have suggested that there are several ways to categorize various kinds of arguments. We have distinguished between positive and unproductive arguments as well as between aggressive arguments (win–lose) and conflict compromises (win–win). In what other ways do you think various kinds of arguments can be classified?

Kinds of Arguments

One other way to categorize arguments is to consider arguing over facts, over causes, and over effects ("Is it true that … .?", "Why did this happen … ?", and "What will the result be if … ?"). Of course, these three kinds of argument overlap because, for example, an argument over causes involves the results, the effects.

Despite Aristotle's love for categories and his desire to create absolute classifications, the three kinds of arguments from ancient rhetoric are not airtight categories. Yet, these classic categories are easy to recall and use, and they will help you focus and develop an argument. Even better, during the heat of an argument, these categories will encourage you to anticipate and counter the arguments made by others. Thus, they will help you discover, as Aristotle's definition of rhetoric states, the available means of persuasion.

The Greeks created a three-part classification of arguments based on time and topic. For Aristotle and other ancients, the three kinds of argument are **forensic** arguments focused on the past and on the topics of blame and guilt, **epideictic** arguments focused on the present and the topic of values, and **deliberative** arguments focused on the future and the topic of actions.

Three Kinds of Argument	Time	Topic
Forensic	Past	Blame/guilt
Epideictic	Present	Values
Deliberative	Future	Best action

Some theorists also refer to epideictic arguments (pronounced ep-i-DAKE-tic) as **demonstrative** ones because a speaker demonstrates his or her values.

Let's use an argument more significant than a curfew conflict to illustrate these categories, yet it is an issue related to those parent-teen clashes: the legal drinking age. How would you develop an argument over this issue using each one of these three kinds?

Three Arguments over the Drinking Age	Time	Topic
Forensic		
Epideictic		
Deliberative		

A forensic argument over this issue would focus on the past and blame, such as who is responsible for teen drinking and driving accidents: the alcohol companies that promote their products in advertisements aimed at young adults, those who sell alcohol to underage drinkers, or those teens who drink and drive.

An epideictic, or demonstrative, argument would focus on the present and values, such as should we care more about keeping kids safe or teaching teens to be mature? Epideictic arguments over values tend to be framed as absolute ones with no gray area; we **either** care about children's safety *or* teens' maturation.

To break through this either/or dispute, one can shift to a deliberative argument. Then, in a future-oriented argument, one could approach this contentious issue by arguing over the best action, such as *when* should teens have legal access to alcohol so they can avoid tragedies and learn to drink responsibly. This shift from present values to future actions would involve an argument, such as on whether or not the legal drinking age should be lowered back to 18 or perhaps 19.

The shift to a deliberative argument makes a resolution that both sides can accept more likely. The future action could be to enact, as with teen driving licenses in many states, some sort of graduated access policy. This deliberative argument could be for gradual access to alcohol. Then, for instance, this access could be developed gradually, such as

- At age 17, teens legally could consume alcohol in their parent's home.

- At 18 or 19, teens could purchase alcohol in a bar and restaurant (where others are liable for serving to excess so they would prevent it).

- At 20 or 21, teens could purchase alcohol for private use.

This deliberative argument will hinge on gradually promoting teens' independence while maintaining adult supervision. Thus, deliberative arguments often end in compromise. In contrast, epideictic arguments often produce no-win stalemates, and forensic arguments yield win–lose outcomes.

To test your understanding of these three kinds of arguments, here are three more assertions about the issue of teen drinking. What kind of argument do you think each one primarily represents: forensic, epideictic, or deliberative?

- We need to improve teen alcohol education by eliminating the scare tactics.

- Seat belts and air bags, not the drinking age of 21, have caused the decrease in teen deaths in car accidents over the last decade.

- If parents really love their children, they will keep their teens away from alcohol.

We think these three examples primarily consist of a future-oriented deliberative argument in the first statement, a past-focused forensic one in the second, and a present-oriented epideictic argument over values in the third. However, as with the three appeals, these categories are not absolute. They are not like three bins set apart so items can be sorted into them easily. The third example, for instance can be considered a deliberative argument if you emphasize the future action ("keep ... teens") over the present values ("really love"). This emphasis, however, will alter the rest of the argument made ("How can we best keep teens ... ?" versus "Do parents love their teens enough to ... ?"). Despite the ambiguity of some arguments, these categories can help you determine what is your focus and how to develop your argument.

Here's one last way to help you distinguish the three classic kinds of arguments: consider where they frequently occur.

Three Kinds	Time	Topic	Setting
Forensic	Past	Blame/guilt	Courtrooms
Epideictic	Present	Values	Campaigns
Deliberative	Future	Best action	Government

As the last column of our chart now shows, forensic arguments often occur in legal courtrooms ("Did he do it?"), epideictic ones dominate political campaigns (pro-life or pro-choice?), and deliberative arguments usually are stressed in our legislative government (school reform?).

Just as the location of an argument corresponds with the kind of argument made, so too does the kind of argument often match the result. For instance, a forensic argument over guilt almost always ends with a win/lose result. An epideictic argument over values usually results in a divisive debate in which some values are deemed right and others, wrong. A deliberative argument over an action can lead to more compromises, especially when each side feels pressured to address an urgent problem ("We can't just keep arguing; we have to do something."). Thus, it often is important to decide in advance what kind of argument you want to have; it may well determine much of the outcome.

Two Other Approaches to Argument

Stasis Theory

Although the ancient Greeks developed many of the fundamental concepts and theories of rhetoric, many others have continued to develop its principles. For example, the Romans refined a form of forensic argument known as stasis theory, which courtroom lawyers to this day still practice. A modern version of this theory provides a sequence of four questions with which to argue almost any courtroom case:

1. **What happened? (Argument of fact)**
2. **What is the nature of this event? (Argument of definition)**
3. **What is the quality of this event? (Argument of evaluation)**
4. **What is the best response to this event? (Argument of recommendation)**

Let's shift from our earlier example of a curfew conflict to a potentially even more divisive event at a school: a physical confrontation between a teacher and a student. If a principal had to address this confrontation, this administrator—or perhaps a lawyer for the school district—could use the four questions of stasis theory in order to understand this event and decide how to react better.

The first question asked would be an **argument of fact: What happened?** Who was the first person to physically confront the other person? How did the physical actions then escalate? Who grabbed, punched, or tackled whom? Who suffered what physical injuries?

Whoever seems to deserve more blame in this conflict is likely to shift from this factual argument to the next question. This person's ultimate goal in a forensic argument would be to show that although he/she may have initiated the physical aggression, this person does not deserve the final blame for this fight.

Thus, if the teacher or student must admit that he/she grabbed the shirt of the other person or threw the first punch of this confrontation, the next question would be about the nature of those actions.

The second question concerns whether or not, for instance, the teacher grabbing the shirt of a belligerent student should be categorized as an act of physical aggression that every school district forbids. The teacher or the lawyer representing him or her would ask, **"What is the nature of this event?"** This **argument of definition** focuses on whether or not this seemingly aggressive gesture instead was a protective gesture. Was the teacher trying to ensure his/her own safety, or perhaps the teacher grabbed the student's shirt in order to draw this student from another who seemed ready to fight. In this circumstance, the nature of the teacher's action is transformed from an unprofessional act of aggression to a responsible gesture of protection: exactly what a teacher should do for a student.

If the student believes that the teacher did not act to protect the student or even for self-protection, this next question would be over **"What is the quality of this event?"** This **argument of evaluation** might examine exactly how the teacher grabbed the student's shirt. The student or a lawyer then would try to evaluate that grasp by arguing that the teacher took the front of the student's shirt into two fists, lifted the shirt's collar up to the student's chin, and knocked the student backward. Thus, this intimidating grasp was not a protective gesture but an aggressive one. The quality of this action, of course, would help to determine whether the teacher's initial action should be defined as an appropriate response or unprofessional aggression.

Once the quality of the teacher's and/or the student's physical actions have been judged, the final question creates an **argument of recommendation** over "What is the best response to this event?" With this question, a forensic argument shifts to a deliberative one. Once a hearing or trial reaches a conclusion about blame, the issue of punishment must be faced. If this case reached a courtroom, a judge or jury would have to decide, for instance, whether the teacher should be fined, fired, decertified, and/or imprisoned or if the student should be suspended, expelled, prosecuted, and/or incarcerated. The findings from the first three questions on blame would result in some sort of recommendation.

Here are two more events for you to apply the stasis theory. Imagine a parent comes home to find two preteen children and a broken plate or window. Or imagine that the stockholders of a company learn from the business's lavish-spending president that bankruptcy must be declared. How might the parent and children or the stockholders and the company president argue according to stasis theory?

Fact: What happened? _____

Definition: What is its nature? _____

Evaluation: What is its quality? _____

Recommendation: What is the best response? _____

As these two examples and the teacher–student fight suggest, a stasis argument usually ends with a win–lose result. The next approach to argument is designed to deliberately promote a win–win outcome through a less combative process.

Rogerian Argument

Developed by psychologist Carl Rogers, this alternative style of argument can help people resolve their differences so that both sides are satisfied with the outcome. A Rogerian argument involves two or more people that differ in their opinions, but their positions cannot be as fixed as those in a forensic argument. This alternative begins by seeking areas of agreement between the two sides. The first question to be posed is not "How do we differ?" but **"What common ground, if any, exists between our positions?"**

Consider, for an example, the ongoing controversy over gun control in America. Two individuals or groups may differ because one believes that Americans have an absolute right to bear arms while the other believes that the possession of weapons by citizens must be regulated to ensure more public safety. It's easy to imagine a divisive debate over this issue with lines like:

A Divisive Debate over Gun Control

"Citizens have the right to bear arms."
"No, guns kept at home are too dangerous."
"But hunting is an American tradition."
"Who needs a machine gun?!"
"Guns don't kill; people DO!"

This argument could continue with the voices becoming louder and angrier as positions are "defended" and opponents are "attacked." The Rogerian alternative is designed to avoid such antagonism among adversaries.

A Rogerian argument over gun control would begin, as stated above, by seeking areas of agreement rather than "squaring off" in fixed positions. The participants would ask "What do *all* of us believe?" and **"Is there any common ground between our positions?"** Through discussion, both sides could realize they want people to be kept safe.

A Rogerian Argument over Gun Control

Common Ground

"Although we may differ in our means, our ends are the same. We want people to be safe. We want innocent citizens to be protected from harm."

After the two sides recognize their differences, the first step, as shown above, is to seek some basic, shared belief.

The second step is for each side to explore the other position through sincere questions. These inquiries serve as an invitation for elaboration: **"Can you tell me more about your belief?"** The intent of these questions must be in the spirit of learning more about the other position, not setting a trap for the other side. How might each side on gun control encourage the other one to explain more? Consider these questions posed by the speaker indicated:

Elaboration Questions

Pro-gun person: "What types of guns do you think the average citizen should not be allowed to purchase?"

"How stringent do you think gun permit regulations should be?"

Anti-gun person: "How should a homeowner handle a weapon when he is trying to stop an intruder?"
"What are the best ways to store weapons in a home?"

These questions are intended to allow the other side to elaborate on their perspective, yet they also may lead both sides to confront the complexities of the topic.

Next, a participant in a Rogerian argument should repeat the opposing viewpoint in a respectful manner. This response should demonstrate that one has listened with understanding and empathy. These responses are intended to build trust rather than tension between the two sides. Imagine, for example, if the participants in an argument over gun control were to comment:

Listening and Restating

Pro-gun person: "I hear you saying that it is tragic when a distraught person grabs a gun, and in a moment of anger or despair, this person kills a loved one. Even worse are the cases of children playing with an unlocked gun and accidentally shooting someone."

Anti-gun person: "The news often has terrible reports of home invasions. When a homeowner can retrieve a weapon from the locked storage that you mentioned and protect the family and values, it's a much better outcome than a robbery and other horrible crimes."

These comments may have to continue for a while to make the two sides willing to step back from their initial divisions ("Who needs … ?" and "Guns don't kill … ").

The final step of a Rogerian argument comes when the two sides realize that some sort of complex and usually imperfect solution is possible. The gun-control controversy, for example, has led to more restrictions on gun purchases as well as more freedom to carry a concealed weapon.

Complex Solutions

We agree that stricter laws should keep guns out of the hands of criminals but citizens should have the right to own carefully stored weapons.

Cynics may find it hard to believe that Rogerian arguments can accomplish much, yet these steps have helped to solve labor disputes and perhaps even a few curfew conflicts in America. They also have helped to bring peace to Northern Ireland and South Africa. The main steps of Rogerian theory are as follows:

1. Recognize differences but be willing to alter one's initial position.
2. Seek common ground with the other side.
3. Explore the opposing viewpoint through sincere questions.
4. Practice listening with empathy and restate the other opinion accurately.
5. Pursue new, complex, and often imperfect solutions.

Let's return to the conflict over the teacher and the student who engaged in some kind of physical confrontation. Rather than seek the win–lose outcome of stasis theory, let's shift from the courtroom setting of a forensic argument to the office of a mediator trying to prevent a lawsuit. How do you think this mediator could foster a Rogerian argument on this issue? What would the teacher and the student each have to do differently in order for a win–win resolution to be achieved?

Student–Teacher Conflict
Recognize differences
Seek common ground
Ask exploratory questions
Listen well and restate
Pursue complex solutions

A Few More Rhetorical Concepts

Here are some other important concepts of rhetoric, which will be organized by the five parts of what is known as the rhetorical **canon**.

The Roman rhetorician Cicero summed up the process of creating an effective argument, and his theory of the canon includes

Invention: determining what are the available means of persuasion

Arrangement: creating the order of the persuasive evidence and appeals

Style: using the appropriate language to reach an audience

Memory: using one's knowledge of rhetoric to speak persuasively

Delivery: presenting an oral or a written argument effectively

Although Cicero described rhetoric as "A good man speaking well," neither this definition nor Aristotle's definition fully addresses the issue of ethics in argumentation. During **invention**, a speaker or writer develops many possible ways to argue for one's opinion. However, just because part of an argument is "available," should it be used? For example, should a candidate use an embarrassing detail from his opponent's past, such as a drunken driving arrest at age 22, to discredit him or her? Aristotle's definition of ethos again provides little guidance, for he explains the appeal by character as "Persuasion is achieved by the speaker's personal character, when the speech is so spoken as to *make us think him credible*. We believe good men more fully and readily than others" (italics added). On the one hand, Aristotle seems to insist that a speaker should be a "good man," but on the other, he acknowledges that ethos is a matter of appearance: "to make us think him credible." Thus, ethos and ethics are not necessarily the same.

Like Murray's concept of ordering during the writing process (see p. 26 in Ch. 2), **arrangement** refers to the most effective organization of an argument. Aristotle believed that most arguments should follow a general pattern of the rhetorical appeals organized as

Ethos first, Logos next, and Pathos last

Of course, a writer's credibility and likeability depend on subject knowledge and audience emotions so ethos can never be separate entirely from logos and pathos. Aristotle, however, insisted that a speaker's initial concern must be to appeal by ethos.

The ancients urged speakers to be clear, vivid, and appropriate in their language. They also developed many word patterns to create a **style** that would help sway an audience. There are many more figures than we can present, but here are three of the most common ones:

Antithesis

This phrasing places two ideas side-by-side. In a divisive argument, you can use this figure to assert, "You're either with us or you're against us." During the Vietnam War, those who opposed the protestors used antithesis to argue "America, Love It or Leave It."

Chiasmus

This figure (pronounced kee-AZZ-muss) reverses the first phrase to assert a compelling second phrase. The most famous example probably is President Kennedy's declaration: "Ask not what your country can do for you, but what you can do for your country." Perhaps you have seen another example on a birthday card for an older person: "Rather than counting the years, make the years count."

Synecdoche

This phrasing (pronounced si-NEK-do-ke) uses a part to represent the whole. For instance, Homer announces the return of the hero's ship by referring to Odysseus's sails reaching port.

The fourth part of Cicero's canon, **memory**, seems like the hardest one to transfer from speaking to writing. It seems to us to refer to a speaker's ability to recall a prepared argument, but for the ancients, this concept meant much more than our current sense of memorizing. Memory meant a storehouse, a treasure house of rhetorical knowledge. Skilled orators would travel mentally through this treasure house each day so they could "visit" any room of their rhetorical knowledge when they needed to do so. For example, rhetoricians have developed a set of reasoning errors that they should avoid and will expose when others commit one of these **logical fallacies**. Here are ten of the most common examples of this faulty logic:

Logical Fallacies

Ad Hominen Attack

This fallacy occurs when the advocate of an opposing view is criticized. The person, rather than the opinion, becomes the focus of this attack, such as when a political debate shifts from a policy argument to the denigration of "free-spending Democrats" and narrow-minded Republicans."

Bandwagon Appeal

This flaw replaces reason with popularity, and then one asserts, "But everyone else is … " Of course, the quick counterargument is "If everybody else is jumping off a bridge … ?"

Circular Logic

This fallacy confuses a claim and its evidence. Then only one point ends up being repeated, as in "She's too good for him because he's not nice (or smart) enough." This argument fails to explain why nice (or smart) is equivalent to good. Instead, the speaker assumes that this criteria is obvious so he or she "begs the question," meaning in this case, the central question of what makes a good match is never addressed.

Correlation versus Causation

This logic assumes that because two events occur, the first must be the reason for the second. For example, proponents of music education sometimes argue that because many music students earn good grades, the study of music must make children smarter. This causal argument fails to consider that smart children may be more likely to be interested in music. Correlation does not prove causation.

Distracted Logic

This flaw introduces irrelevant information into an argument. If we can continue our "good enough" dating example from above, it's easy to imagine someone adding, "Yea, and he's not even a member of our group." Yet whether or not he belongs to a social circle has no relevance to this argument. Such distraction is also known as a "red herring" from the old fox-hunting trick of dragging a dead fish across a path to deflect the dogs from their prey and keep the hunt going longer.

Either/Or Fallacy

This argument pits two extreme opposites against each other and denies that any middle ground is possible. In the abortion debate, each side can assert, "we value life and you don't." This dichotomy, however, fails to recognize that instead of just one life, at least two lives are involved in this difficult issue.

Hasty Generalization

This fallacy makes a general claim from insufficient evidence. Prejudice depends on this misuse of inductive reasoning, for it claims that since a few members of a group display some flaw, then every member has this defect. For instance, "My friend's son just lost his third cell phone; children today are so careless."

Non Sequitur

This is another flaw based on a faulty connection between claim and evidence. Political ads often show candidates with their families, but there is not necessarily any relationship between being a caring parent and an effective leader. The English translation of this term is "it does not follow."

Slippery Slope

This fallacy involves a dubious cause-and-effect relationship. It assumes that from a debatable position, next something bad will happen, and the worst will follow: for example, in an argument over controversial books: "If we let children read this novel, they will have immoral thoughts, and then they will act in immoral ways." Those who make such assertions fail to consider that such books can be taught as cautionary tales against undesirable actions.

Straw Man Argument

This flaw creates a caricature of an opposing viewpoint. From our gun-control example, those against all restrictions could characterize their opposition as "those naïve liberals who want only the bad guys to have weapons." Once the opposition has been built conveniently out of straw, they are easy to knock down. This fallacy, however, leaves the actual position of the other side still standing and the argument unresolved.

By storing these logical fallacies and many other rhetorical concepts in your memory, you will be able to argue and react to arguments made by others more effectively.

For speech, the **delivery** of an argument involves voice tone and volume as well as facial expressions and physical gestures. In writing, Cicero's fifth and final canon involves letters, words, sentence patterns, and so much, more including the visual presentation of information, such as through font choices, margins, spacing, bullets, white space, and images.

Key Terms

Before you finish with this chapter, here is a list of the key concepts; which ones can you explain easily, and which ones do you need to review?

Rhetoric
    Aristotle's definition and ethics

The rhetorical triangle
    Speaker/writer
    Message/purpose
    Audience/reader

Three rhetorical appeals
    Ethos
        Identification
    Logos
        Premise
        Evidence
        Concession
        Refutation
        Rebuttal
        Qualification
        Inductive reasoning
        Deductive reasoning
        Syllogism
        Enthymeme
        Preaching to the choir
    Pathos

Rhetorical Précis

Three kinds of argument
    Forensic
    Epideictic/demonstrative
    Deliberative

Two more kinds of argument
    Stasis theory
        Argument of fact
        Argument of definition
        Argument of evaluation
        Argument of recommendation
    Rogerian argument
        Common ground
        Elaboration questions
        Listening and restating
        Complex solutions

Canon
    Invention
    Arrangement
    Style
        Antithesis
        Chiasmus
        Synecdoche
    Memory
    Logical fallacies
        Ad hominen attack
        Bandwagon appeal
        Circular logic
        Correlation vs. causation
        Distracted logic/red herring
        Either/or—dichotomy
        Hasty generalization
        Non sequitur
        Slippery slope
        Straw man argument
    Delivery

Additional Sources for Chapter 5

To deepen your understanding of argument and rhetoric, you can consult some of the following sources:

1. As the author of *Thank You for Arguing*, Jay Heinrichs has argued that rhetoric is a valuable tool that everyone should learn, including his own children when they want to argue with their father. For an engaging argument in favor of rhetoric, you may want to read the following by Heinrichs.

   http://inpraiseofargument.squarespace.com/teach-a-kid-to-argue

2. For more on the persuasive power of rhetoric and the three rhetorical appeals, you may want to watch the following videos. In "What is Rhetoric?" and "The Most Powerful Persuasion Tool," Christina Fox of ArgueLab (in association with Jay Heinrichs) explains the power of persuasion and the importance of character/ethos.

   https://www.youtube.com/watch?v=SumctzBDJ9Y

   https://www.youtube.com/watch?time_continue=60&v=EEJJFRotbSs

3. For more information on a rhetorical précis, you may want to read the following explanation, which includes a detailed example.

   http://oregonstate.edu/instruct/phl201/modules/rhetorical-precis/sample/peirce_sample_precis_click.html

4. For more on the rhetorical triangle, which can be expanded into the six-part rhetorical situation, you may want to consult the Online Writing Lab (OWL) of Purdue University. Then each part of the rhetorical situation is explained further.

   https://owl.english.purdue.edu/owl/resource/625/1/

   https://owl.english.purdue.edu/owl/resource/625/02/

5. For a good overview of rhetoric, especially its role in avoiding violent conflict, you may want to consult the following site. Note the opening paragraphs on rhetoric as an alternative to physical struggle and the necessary attitudes and actions of those engaged in a debate.

   https://web.cn.edu/kwheeler/resource_rhet.html#persuasive_anchor

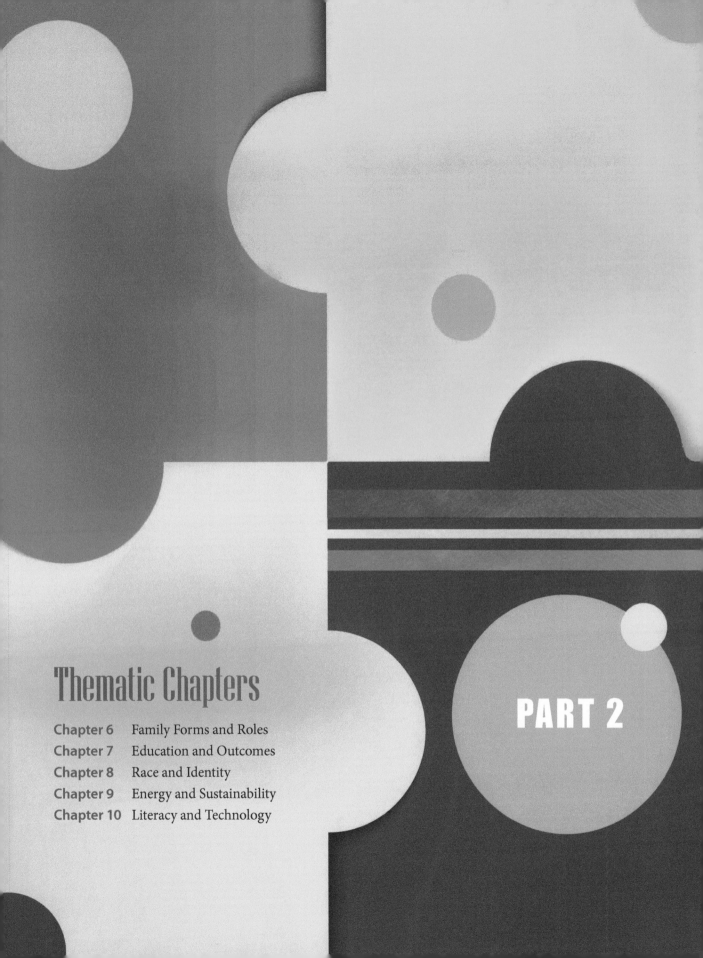

Thematic Chapters

PART 2

Family Forms and Roles

[The word] family has an especially significant social history ….In none of the pre-seventeenth century senses, can we find the distinctive modern sense of a small group confined to immediate blood relations …. Yet it is clear that between the seventeenth and nineteenth centuries the sense of the small kin-group, usually living in one house, came to be dominant.

—*Raymond Williams (1977)*

Middle-class and working-class families alike developed a belief that married women should not work outside the home. The special responsibility of men for breadwinning made sense in the early nineteenth century …. It followed from the demands of physical strength and dealing with strangers in the new industrial setting.

—*Peter Stearns (1977)*

The very nature of white institutions works against the black extended family as it attempts to fulfill its collective responsibilities and functions within the context of Afro-American values. [Imagine] what black college freshmen go through trying to explain the income of their multiple extended family parents … to college financial aid officers.

—*Joseph White (1984)*

If the decade of the 1950s was the "heyday" of the nuclear family, it was also a historical aberration. The social stability of the 1950s was less the result of that decade's family forms or values than its unique socioeconomic and political climate.

—*Stephanie Coontz (1995)*

Introduction

Many of us take family for granted; it's the group of people with whom we have lived and grown up—right? Family seems like such an obvious subject that it deserves little attention and even less academic study. Yet most colleges and universities offer courses that focus on the family from diverse angles: the history of family structures, the communication styles of effective parents, and the genetic inheritance of terminal illnesses. Over the last three centuries, the form and function of families have changed so greatly in the United States that many contemporary families would seem very strange to past generations, just as their family structures would strike many of us as unusual today.

Colonial families, for example, often consisted not only of parents and children, but also of other relatives, <u>indentured</u> servants, apprentices, and journeymen. Most of the members of colonial families lived in the same dwelling, and they regularly ate their meals together. These families were less defined by blood relationships and more by household membership; in fact, the word family was a synonym for household in the English spoken during the sixteenth and seventeenth centuries. Because the male head of this household and his assistants often worked and lived in the same dwelling, there was little distinction between a father's economic and domestic roles. He frequently treated his children like workers and his helpers like children. Apprentices, for example, had to promise not only to work for their master but also to obey his commands concerning their conduct. Would you want to live in a family under these conditions? What might be some of the advantages or disadvantages over your family life today?

Since colonial times, the size of US families has steadily decreased. In 1790, most families had seven or more members living in one house. By 1890, less than half of all families were as large, and many had only three members. The definition of family, however, had changed as well; servants and apprentices were no longer considered family members. By 1970, three-quarters of all US families had three members or fewer in the same household. Multiple factors account for this: Grandparents frequently no longer lived with their adult children; some couples chose to have fewer children or none at all; many divorces created single-parent families; and young adult children moved into their own households at an earlier age, often before marriage. By 2000, the number of people in American households had reached the lowest average ever—fewer than three people. More than a quarter of all Americans lived alone at the start of the twenty-first century.

With these differences in numbers, there also have been more complex changes in the roles of family members. For example, while we take for granted that most mothers naturally want to bond with their babies soon after birth, this was not always the case. In colonial times, when many babies did not survive birth or did not live beyond age two, mothers delayed forming emotional bonds with their babies because their survival was too uncertain. Only since the late nineteenth century, with its significant decrease in infant mortality, have mothers been expected to nurture their infants emotionally soon after birth.

The role of fathers has also changed. When the United States was primarily an agrarian society, fathers worked on farms with their wives and children. With the industrialization and urbanization of the United States in the nineteenth century, the location of men's work moved from home workshops and farm fields to factories and offices. As the primary economic providers of their families, fathers had to labor long hours while separated from their wives and children.

As these historic changes suggest, multiple and often conflicting perspectives now exist on what is a family, and what is the expected role of each member. Every reading in this chapter provides a snapshot of a perspective in what is a much larger family album. This chapter is not intended to be a definitive history of the family in the United States. It instead is designed to make you question your own assumptions and those of others about what a family is, has been, and will be. This chapter encourages you to ask and answer these questions about the family's form and function by requiring you to consider your beliefs in relation to readings that offer past and present perspectives.

The three historical readings present three different genres: analysis, autobiography, and fiction, which represent the array of texts you will be asked to read at college. This first reading by the historian Tamara Hareven may surprise you as you learn how different some families were two centuries ago. Then the literary works by Frederick Douglass and Mary Wilkins Freeman reveal some of the nineteenth-century efforts to change family and society. In the two contemporary readings, diverse family issues are examined, such as gender roles, child discipline, cross-racial adoptions, and single mothers. Each of these issues is subject to an ongoing debate, which you will be asked to join.

These texts, along with the reading questions, freewriting activities, and visual elements of this chapter, are designed to develop the reading and writing abilities required for academic study. After each reading, you will find a set of questions that are divided into Close Reading Questions, Analytical Writing/Discussion, and Further Options. Some questions involve the same investigation of multiple perspectives, cultural influences, and historical trends that were introduced in Chapter 1. Answering some and discussing more of the post-reading questions will better prepare you to complete the final assignments options. These final writing assignments will ask you to assert your own, more informed perspective on the American family. This chapter asks: **What do you think should be the accepted form(s) of the family and the proper role(s) of each member?**

Freewrite 1: Initial Impressions

Before you turn to the first reading, your professor may ask you to develop some images and ideas of your own through freewriting and/or discussion. (For more on freewriting, see p. 25 of Chapter 2.)

Images: The modern British poet Christopher Isherwood compared himself to a camera as he began to collect ideas for his poetry. He wrote, "I am a camera with its shutter open, quite passive, recording, not thinking … Some day all of this will have to be developed carefully, fixed [and] printed." Like Isherwood, can you open your mind's shutter, your creative camera, to capture several images of your family? Rather than creating a posed group portrait with everyone standing still, shoulder to shoulder, saying "cheese," try to get some "candid" shots that create some realistic images of your family life. Freewrite one or two descriptive images that record a moment of your family members in action and that reveal their roles within your family.

Analysis: Through further writing and/or discussion, analyze the significance of your descriptive images by answering one or more of the following questions:

- Whom did you include or exclude in your images? Why?

- What is the expected role of each member of your family?

- How do these roles match those expected by society in general? How do they differ?

- What internal and external forces can pull this family together and push it apart?

- How would you define the contemporary American family? What is a family?

THE NINETEENTH-CENTURY RETREAT: FAMILY AND HOME

by Tamara K. Hareven

During the nineteenth century, urbanization and industrialization fundamentally changed the lives and homes of American families, such as the colonial family described in the introduction to this chapter. This relocation of many families from rural to urban and then to suburban areas, as well as

Hareven, Tamara K., "The Home and the Family in Historical Perspective." *Social Research* 58:1 (1991), 254–262, 264–265, 267–273, 275–276, 279–282, 284–285. The New School for Social Research. Reprinted with permission of Johns Hopkins University Press.

the transfer of many jobs from farms to factories, altered the roles of husbands and wives. Tamara Hareven traced this history of the family in such books as *Family Time and Industrial Time* (1982) and *Families, History and Social Change* (1999). This article was originally published in 1991.

The concept of the home as the family's haven and domestic retreat emerged only about one hundred fifty years ago, and was, initially, limited to the urban middle classes. In order to understand the development of the home as the family's abode, as a reality and as an ideal, it is necessary to examine the relationship between household, family, and home as they changed over time.

First, the ideal Western family of the past, in which three generations co-resided harmoniously in the same household, has been proven to be a myth. It is part of what William Goode referred to as the classic ideal of "Western nostalgia."[1] Actually, historians of the family have identified the persistence of a nuclear household structure in Western Europe since the sixteenth century, and in the United States since the times of settlement. More recently, historians have found that a nuclear household structure has predominated in England and Italy since the twelfth century.

The persistence of a nuclear household pattern in Western society has significant implications for our understanding of the role of the home and its emergence as a way of life and a symbolic concept. Membership in a nuclear household rested on the principle of residential separation of the generations. Marriage meant the establishment of a separate household by the new couple, even if the older generation was living nearby. In rural society, aging parents often lived on the same land with their married children, but still in separate households. This commitment to the separate residence of the family of origin and the family of procreation should not be misconstrued as a commitment to privacy. Contrary to prevailing myths, preindustrial households rarely included relatives other than the members of the nuclear family, but they often contained unrelated individuals whose presence in the household reflected the various special functions that the family held.[2]

In preindustrial society, there was a significant difference between the family's domicile—the household—and the home as it became idealized later in Western European and American society. In addition to serving as the family's place of residence and the focus for the family's various domestic activities, such as eating, sleeping, and child rearing, the household was the site of a multiplicity of activities. It served as the site of production, as a welfare agency and correctional institution, as an educational institution, and as a place for religious worship. Rather than catering strictly to the needs of the family, the household served the entire community, by taking in dependent members who were not related to the family and by helping maintain the social order.

Accordingly, household membership was not restricted to individuals related by ties of blood and marriage. The household also contained unrelated individuals, such as servants, apprentices, boarders and lodgers, and "unfortunates" from the community, such as orphans, the elderly, the sick and infirm, delinquents, and mentally ill who were placed with families by the local authorities. Even though extended kin were not present in the household as a general pattern, household membership was sufficiently flexible to accommodate extended kin at certain points over the family's cycle, especially when aging parents were too frail to live by themselves and needed to coreside with their children ....

---

[1]William Goode, *World Revolutions and Family Patterns* (New York: Free Press, 1963), p. 6.
[2]John Demos, *A Little Commonwealth: Family Life in Plymouth Colony* (New York: Oxford University Press, 1970); Peter Laslett, "Characteristics of the Western Family Over Time," in Peter Laslett, ed., *Family Life and Illicit Love in Former Generations* (Cambridge: Cambridge University Press, 1977).

Sociability versus Privacy

The family in preindustrial society was characterized by sociability rather than privacy. As Philippe Aries has emphasized, by contrast to the conception of the home in contemporary society as a private retreat from the outside world, in preindustrial society the family conducted its work and public affairs inside the household. Households were teeming with various activities, and family members, even couples, could hardly retreat into privacy within the crowded household space. The head of the household's various business associates and other individuals actively involved in the family's economic or social activities were often present in the household. Aries provides a vivid description of life in the "big house" in preindustrial France and England. As long as family life was characterized by sociability, the household did not serve strictly as the family's private retreat. Rather, the family's public and private activities were inseparable, and the family's domestic life was often conducted with strangers present …..[3] Spaces within the "big house" were not differentiated into family space and public space. No rooms were specifically designated as bedrooms. Beds stood in public areas of the house, and family members slept behind curtains while social activities including outsiders were going on in other parts of the same room. Similarly, in colonial America, bedchambers were not separate or private. Individuals and couples had to share beds with relatives or with unrelated individuals. Colonial American court records, especially those dealing with divorce, abound in various such graphic descriptions, all confirming the lack of privacy that families and unrelated individuals experienced when residing together ….

The concept of the home as a private retreat first emerged in the lives of bourgeois families in eighteenth-century France and England, and in the United States among urban, middle-class families in the early part of the nineteenth century. Its development was closely linked to the new ideals of domesticity and privacy that were associated with the characteristics of the modern family—a family that was child-centered, private, and in which the roles of husband and wife were segregated into public and domestic spheres, respectively. The husband was expected to be the main breadwinner and worker outside the home and the wife a full-time housekeeper and mother. This new separation of domestic and public spheres led to the rearrangement of the family's work and living patterns within the home. While earlier, all family members, including children, worked together, or participated in various activities, even if they did not work, in the new setting the world of work became separate from family activities.[4] Family time became restricted primarily to the home, and leisure became an important aspect of domestic life. Reading, embroidering, viewing art, and listening to music had become important pastimes in the home.

Following the removal of the workplace from the home as a result of urbanization and industrialization, the household was recast as the family's private retreat, and home emerged as a new concept and existence. Eventually, other agencies took over the functions that had been earlier concentrated in the family. Factories and business places took over the work and production functions of the family, schools took over the family's formal educational functions, and asylums and correctional institutions took over the family's functions of welfare and social control. The separation of the workplace from the household and the transfer of various other functions and activities of the family to outside institutions resulted in the emergence of the home as a specialized site for the family's consumption, child rearing, and private life. The display of the family's domestic lifestyle through the architectural style of the home and its

---

[3]Philippe Aries, *Centuries of Childhood: A Social History of Family Life*, trans. R. Baldick (New York: Vintage Books, 1962).

[4]Barbara Welter, "The Cult of True Womanhood 1820–1860," *American Quarterly* 18 (1966): 151–174; Mary Ryan, *Cradle of the Middle Class: The Family in Oneida County, New York 1790–1865* (New York: Cambridge University Press, 1981); Carl Degler, *At Odds: Women and the Family in America from the Revolution to the Present* (New York: Oxford University Press, 1980).

furnishings and appointments became of extreme importance in the self-characterization of the urban middle-class family in Western Europe and in the United States ....[5]

In the private home that emerged in the middle of the nineteenth century, household membership had become restricted to the nuclear family, except for servants. Unlike in earlier periods, apprentices, boarders or lodgers, and dependent community members virtually disappeared from middle-class households. Even the role and social origins of servants changed in relation to the new functions of the home and the family. In preindustrial households, the servants were "lifecycle" servants—young people who were sent to serve in other people's households for educational purposes as much as for service. Such exchanges usually occurred within the same community. On the other hand, servants in nineteenth-century families were usually migrants or immigrants to the city, whose main function was to work in middle-class or upper-class households. For the majority of young women servants, domestic service was still restricted to a life-cycle stage but was now clearly defined as a form of employment rather than as a temporary residence for purposes of socialization.

The Domestic Role of Middle-Class Women

In this new domestic regime, it became inappropriate for middle-class women to work outside the home. "Our men are sufficiently moneymaking. Let us keep our women and children from the contagion as long as possible," wrote in 1832 one of the main advocates and advisers on the cult of domesticity, Sara Josepha Hale, editor of *Godey's Lady's Book* in 1832. Women's main responsibility and all their energies now had to focus on the home and the family, and especially on children. Homemaking became an occupation in itself, one that demanded physical and material resources, planning, and the persistent following of changing fashions. As one writer in mid-century put it, a house "is not only the home center, the retreat, and shelter for all the family, it is also the workshop for the mother. It is not only where she is to live, to love, but where she is to care and labor. Her hours, days, weeks, months, and years are spent within its bounds; until she becomes an enthroned fixture, more indispensable than the house itself." Homemaking was idealized as part of the cult of domesticity, and was accorded special social status. The complicated tasks of home management required specific advice in how-to-do-it manuals and etiquette books.[6]

Women were expected to be the perfect designers, executors, and custodians of the new domestic retreat. Housework and cooking became, therefore, extremely significant for the maintenance of the perfect home, which, in turn, was viewed by reformers as indispensable for the nation's prosperity and survival. Even the most trivial tasks were considered to be of utmost importance. "It is within your power to create a domestic haven in the lowliest cottage," wrote Daniel Wise. Various magazines, especially *Godey's Lady's Book*, as well as numerous cookbooks and advice books, provided guidance aimed at enabling housewives to achieve perfection in their domestic tasks ....[7]

---

[5]Michelle Perrot, *A History of Private Life, vol. 4, From the Fires of the Revolution to the Great War*, trans. Arthur Goldhammer (Cambridge: Harvard University Press, 1990); Dolores Hayden, *The Great Domestic Revolution: A History of Feminist Designs for American Homes, Neighborhoods and Cities* (Cambridge: MIT Press, 1981).

[6]On domestic-advice literature, see: Welter, "Cult of Domesticity"; Kathryn Kish Sklar, *Catherine Beecher: A Study of Domesticity* (New Haven: Yale University Press, 1973). For domestic-advice literature of the first half of the nineteenth century, see Lydia Sigourney, *The Western Home and Other Poems* (Philadelphia: Parry & McMillan, 1854); *Godey's Lady's Book* (Philadelphia, 1840–60); Lydia Maria Child, *The Mother's Book* (Boston, 1831); Ann Kuhn, *The Mother's Role in Childhood Education: New England Concepts, 1830–1860* (New Haven: Yale University Press, 1947): 35.

[7]Daniel Wise, *Bridal Greetings: A Marriage Gift* (New York, 1850), p. 84; quoted in Kirk Jeffrey, "The Family as a Utopian Retreat from the City: The Nineteenth Century Contribution," *Soundings: An Interdisciplinary Journal 55* (Spring 1972): 35.

A variety of new appliances and gadgets made their way into the home from the middle of the nineteenth century on. These inventions became important not only as labor-saving devices but as status symbols of the efficient, well-ordered home. Initially, the most important invention was the cooking stove, which replaced open-hearth cooking. The stove revolutionized cuisine, and opened up a new range of possibilities in the simultaneous preparation of a variety of dishes on the top of the stove, rather than the one-pot meals cooked in the hearth. In addition, a whole slew of gadgets and implements, such as apple corers and slicers, vacuum cleaners, laundry strainers, and other devices appeared on the market and made their way into the middle-class home. Ruth Schwartz Cowan claims that these new appliances, rather than saving housewives' time, actually caused "more work for mother," because they provided the opportunity for more complex preparations which required increased time and labor investment on the women's part, and a decrease in the involvement of men in household work ....[8]

New Designs for Family Life

The new specialization in the functions of the home and the family also necessitated corresponding architectural designs. Architects joined the trend by busily developing blueprints for new styles of homes that were to accommodate the new domestic lifestyle. The domestic architecture that emerged in the United States in the middle of the nineteenth century, featuring Gothic revival cottages, Italianate villas, and bracketed cottages that were published in builders' guides between 1840 and 1860, translated the domestic ideal into architecture in several ways: These cottages were aimed at segregating the home from the outside world, thus securing privacy for the family. Within the home, spaces were organized in a manner that separated the family's private activities from the public ones such as receiving guests. The parlor became a central space for the family's social activities and entertainment. The kitchen, which had been previously outside, was brought inside, alas, into the basement or the back of the house. Nevertheless, the kitchen became an important component of the home. The parlor was decorated by the family's heirlooms, portraits, lace and embroidery, shadow boxes, and artwork ....

In his analysis of the new spaces designed in the domestic architecture which emerged in the middle of the nineteenth century, Clifford Clark concluded that "the design of the second floor, with its emphasis on creating a separate space for each member of the family ... implies that the family was not an organic unit but rather was made up of separate, unique individuals who each had a specific role to play ...." Interaction within the family, like the public interaction with guests, was to take place primarily in specifically designated areas—the dining room, porch, and back parlor (family room). In these areas, family interaction became organized around certain rituals—meals, musical events, and games. Clark concluded that the design of the house implied that "the family was an organization which was not an end in itself, but rather a vehicle for promoting the development of each of its members."[9] The new domestic style required two types of privacy: privacy of the family from the community, and privacy of family members from each other within the home.

While the ideal middle-class domestic home is linked in the contemporary popular image with suburbs, as suggested above, initially the ideals of domesticity were played out in the city. The new middle-class

---

[8]Ruth Schwartz Cowan, *More Work for Mother* (New York: Basic Books, 1983).

[9]Clifford Edward Clark, Jr., "Domestic Architecture as an Index: The Romantic Revival and the Cult of Domesticity in America, 1840–1870," *Journal of Interdisciplinary History 7* (Summer 1976): 33–56. Andrew Jackson Downing, *Cottage Residences: A Series of Designs for Rural Cottages and Villas* (New York, 1842); *Godey's Lady's Book* published a series of revival designs, see George L. Hersey, "Godey's Choice," *Society of Architectural Historians Journal 17* (1959); see also Clifford Edward Clark, Jr., *The American Family Home* (Chapel Hill: University of North Carolina Press, 1986).

home was designed as a response to urbanization as a retreat from the world of work and from the hustle-bustle of urban life. At the same time, it depended on urban services, conveniences, and public activities in order to achieve domestic refinement … But as the nineteenth century progressed, the ideals and lifestyle of domesticity were transferred to the suburbs and became identified with suburban living ….

The development of domesticity as a suburban phenomenon, which flourished in the late nineteenth century, according to Margaret Marsh, was a response to the masculine domestic ideal, which by that point in time emphasized the virtues of a suburban retreat from the pressures of city life: "The new domestic ideal centered firmly in the suburbs, represented family pride, family identity and togetherness in face of an urban society that promised individual achievement, anonymity and excitement." By the eve of World War II, she claims, "a new suburban domestic ideal had materialized—an ideal that both reorganized domesticity to make it independent of the notion of separate masculine and feminine spheres and one which redefined the suburbs to emphasize 'place' more than the ownership of property."[10] As urban life became more bewildering, because of a high concentration of immigrants and poverty, domestic life in the suburbs had become idealized as an escape from the city.

The new domesticity in the suburbs led to the isolation of women and children from urban life, and eventually to the entrapment of women in suburban domestic lifestyles … Philippe Aries introduced this question when he lamented the loss of the "big house" and the isolation of the modern family in its domestic retreat: The modern family … cuts itself off from the world and opposes to society the isolated groups of parents and children. All the energy of the group is expended in helping the children to rise in the world, individually and without any collective ambition, the children rather than the family.[11]

The suburban form of domesticity had become entrenched in American society and predominated until the 1960s, despite various challenges by feminist reformers, especially Charlotte Perkins Gilman, who advocated the establishment of urban residential hotels with communal dining rooms for families so that working women would be free of housekeeping chores. Gilman expected that these apartment hotels would enable women to pursue professional careers along with motherhood without being confined to child-rearing and domesticity …. For people who preferred suburban life, Gilman also recommended a suburban counterpart to the apartment hotel, which involved the grouping of several residential houses, all kitchenless but interconnected by covered walkways with a central eating house.[12]

Beyond the Middle Class

When discussing these trends, it is important to remember that the separation of the home from the outside world occurred initially in the lives of a small segment of the population, namely, the urban middle classes. In rural families, and in urban working-class families, the home was viewed less as a specialized retreat, and was open to a multiplicity of functions and activities as it had been in preindustrial society. Significantly, at the very time when middle-class women were being discouraged from pursuing gainful employment, working-class women and children were being recruited as the primary labor force of the industrial revolution. Even after working-class families began to emulate middle-class domestic lifestyles and furnishings, they continued to use the household space in a more diversified and complex way than the middle class. In rural families, the household continued to serve as the site of production

---

[10]Margaret Marsh, "From Separation to Togetherness: The Social Construction of Domestic Space in American Suburbs, 1840–1915," *Journal of American History* 76 (1989): 506–527.

[11]Philippe Aries, *Centuries of Childhood*, p. 404.

[12]Charlotte Perkins Gilman, *Women and Economics*; quoted in Hayden, *Grand Domestic Revolution*, p. 189.

in agriculture as well as in domestic industries. Family members worked side by side in related tasks, and there continued to be little separation between domestic life and work life ....

In working-class homes, there was little separation between domestic life and work life. The world of work spilled over into the household. In the major cities, "homework," such as garment finishing, engaged all family members in the household. Under such circumstances, the space in the home was used creatively, and was arranged and rearranged to fit the various functions of the family as they came up. At supper time, bundles of garments or other sewing materials were removed from the table so that family members could eat their supper. Beds for lodgers or boarders, or for children were opened up in the hallway or in the kitchen in the evening and were folded back again in the morning ....

Families that had attained higher standards of living made a special effort to have a parlor or its semblance. "In one three-room house, where there were seven children, a room which had in it a folding bed, a wardrobe, the carriage where the baby slept in the daytime, and the sewing machine, was referred to with pride as the 'front room,' a phrase with a significance quite beyond its suggestion of locality." Residents invested much money and energy in making the front room the center of family life. "Here in the evening the family gathers about the soft coal or gas grate, while the mother sews and one of the older children plays to the father. Such 'front rooms' are the scenes of those simple festivities which enliven existence in this town." The family scenes and activities described here represent on a more modest scale the activities of middle-class families in the parlor or in the family room. In the four-room houses, the family ate in the kitchen ....[13]

Even in the poorest tenements in New York's West Side, residents made a special effort to appoint and decorate their shabby and crowded dwellings. Mary White Ovington, one of the founders of the National Association for the Advancement of Colored People, was impressed by the efforts of black families to decorate a "home," sometimes with "cheap pictures, photographs, cards, vases, little ornaments," that the women, many of whom had been engaged in domestic service, received from their employers. These items, which their employers were happily rid of, nevertheless gave "an air of home likeness to the place." Ovington, who had visited many tenements of this kind, was moved by their residents' hospitality and homelike atmosphere:

> The Negroes' homes are often sadly cluttered, but they are rarely bare and ugly. With this love of pretty things goes a desire to live with something of form in the arrangement of the rooms and in the ordering of the meals. When breakfast or dinner comes you will almost always find the table set. I have been surprised to find in the most modest homes that the meal carried with it the air of a social function; the mother would use many dishes though she must take the time from her laundry work to wash them.[14]

Similarly, the poor Jewish home in which writer Alfred Kazin grew up in Brownsville, New York, left a lasting impression on his subsequent life. In that home the kitchen was the center of family life, and the various objects within became an unforgettable source of his identity:

> The kitchen held our lives together. My mother worked in it all day long, we ate in it almost all meals except the Passover seder, I did my homework and first writing at the kitchen table, and in winter I often had a bed made up for me on three kitchen chairs near the stove ... A

---

[13]Margaret F. Byington, *Homestead: The Households of a Mill Town* [1910] (Pittsburgh: University of Pittsburgh Press, 1974): 55–56.

[14]Mary White Ovington, "The Negro Home in New York," *Charities* 15 (October 7, 1905): 25–26.

large electric bulb hung down the center of the kitchen at the end of a chain that had been hooked into the ceiling; the old gas ring and key still jutted out of the wall like antlers. In the corner next to the toilet was the sink at which we washed, and the square tub in which my mother did our clothes. Above it, tacked to the shelf on which were pleasantly ranged square, blue-bordered white sugar and spice jars, hung calendars from the Public National Bank on Pitkin Avenue and the Minsker Progressive Branch of the Workman's Circle; receipts for the payment of insurance premiums, and household bills on a spindle; two little boxes engraved with Hebrew letters. One of these was for the poor, the other to buy back the Land of Israel.[15]

In their effort to impress American ideals of domesticity on immigrants, social reformers left nothing to chance. A 1909 textbook for teaching English to foreigners incorporated a lesson about the ideal home:

This is the family, in the sitting-room.

The family is made up of the father, the mother, and the children.

That is the father who is reading.

The father is the husband.

That is the mother who is sewing.

The father and mother are the parents.

The sister is playing the piano.

The brother is standing beside her.

The family makes the home.[16]

Despite the differences between the middle class and the working class and between native born and various ethnics in the family's use of the home, as the twentieth century progressed, the significance of "home" in American society cut across all classes. For working-class as well as for immigrant families, heading one's own household was identified with autonomy. Establishment of a separate household by a newly formed family, as well as the maintenance of household headship in the later years of life, were sacred values and markers of autonomy in American society ....

Conclusion

In this brief examination of the emergence of the home as the family's domestic abode in reality and in ideal in Western society, I have tried to emphasize that in the past the family's place of residence—the household—did not always carry the symbolic meaning of "home"; that, indeed, home was the invention of the middle class and was closely related to the emergence of the family as a private, emotional entity. By contrast to the middle class, working-class families continued to maintain greater flexibility and diversity in the use of their domestic space and ways of life. By the twentieth century the ideals of "home" had assumed powerful meaning in the domestic life of working-class families as well. Middle-class styles of consumption and furnishing permeated working-class families .... Working-class and immigrant

---

[15]Alfred Kazin, *A Walker in the City* (New York: Harcourt, Brace & World, 1951), 65–66.
[16]Sara R. O'Brien, *English for Foreigners* (Boston, 1909), p. 55.

families responded to these influences selectively: they adopted those aspects that suited their needs and their budgets, and blended them into their traditional culture, which they retained.

The privacy of the home and the family have become central concerns in Western civilization. Some historians, like Christopher Lasch, have claimed that the family's private haven has been invaded excessively by modern bureaucracies and by the helping professions. Others, like Philippe Ariès and Richard Sennett, have emphasized the negative consequences of the family's retreat into domesticity and privacy, and its repressive impact on the individual. The first major critics of middle-class domesticity, however, were the women themselves, who had to carry out the high domestic ideals defined for them by the advocates of domesticity in the nineteenth century. Women responded to the pressures to create and maintain an ideal home in isolation from the rest of the world by taking the ideals of domesticity into the larger society, and by investing their energies in various reform movements and purity crusades.

Close Reading Questions

1. According to Hareven, American families have not always been the way you probably have assumed. What was the structure and purpose of the family before the nineteenth century?

2. Early in the nineteenth century, middle-class homes originally existed primarily in cities. For what reasons did urban middle-class homes later migrate to the suburbs? Then how did urban and rural working-class homes compare to these suburban, middle-class homes? (Cultural Influences)

3. Why does Hareven assert that suburban living led to "the entrapment of women"? Why do you agree or disagree with her assertion?

Analytical Writing/Discussion

4. After the Industrial Revolution, the household became "the family's private retreat." What changes in the design of homes promoted this greater privacy for family members? What do you think were the benefits and drawbacks of these forms of privacy in the home? (Multiple Perspectives)

5. How did the "cult of domesticity" for nineteenth-century women increase the division of labor by gender in families? Using the example of a family you know well, to what degree do you think that these divided family roles for men and women still exist today? (Historical Trends)

6. The emergence of household appliances in the mid-nineteenth-century home became "status symbols of the efficient, well-ordered home." Using references to this text, to what degree do you think these devices simplified or complicated the household labor of mothers? Using references to the modern family, why do you think this trend of household appliances and labor has continued or changed?

Further Options

7. Hareven explains that as the nineteenth family changed, so too did the architectural design of middle-class homes. Considering the now popular open floor plans that combine the kitchen, dining room, and living room in one large space, what do you think this design suggests about families today?

8. Hareven discusses concepts of family, home, and household that might seem antiquated to a twenty-first-century reader. Using methods discussed in Chapter 1 on Reading, such as double-entry journaling or highlighting, make note of the concepts that even now apply to American families, homes, and households. Why do you think some of those concepts have not changed in over a century?

FIGURE 6.1 An image of a nineteenth-century American family: Captain William T. Shorey and family, Oakland, CA, 1898. In the following reading, note how Frederick Douglass employs nineteenth-century assumptions about family to oppose slavery.

Source: Courtesy of National Park Service

FAMILIES ENSLAVED

by Frederick Douglass

As an escaped slave, Frederick Douglass joined the abolitionist movement and quickly became one of the leading figures of this antislavery movement. To oppose those who claimed that enslaved Africans in the United States were intellectually and morally inferior, Douglass wrote eloquent speeches and essays to prove his own rationality and slavery's brutality. He, however, had to elicit sympathy as much as horror from his primarily Northern, "white" audience. This reading is excerpted from Douglass' first autobiography, *The Narrative of the Life and Times of Frederick Douglass,* which was published in 1845.

I was born in Tuckahoe, near Hillsborough, and about twelve miles from Easton, in Talbot county, Maryland. I have no accurate knowledge of my age, never having seen any authentic record containing it. By far, the larger part of the slaves know as little of their age as horses know of theirs, and it is the wish of most masters within my knowledge to keep their slaves thus ignorant. I do not remember to have ever met a slave who could tell of his birthday. They seldom come nearer to it than planting-time, harvest-time, cherry-time, spring-time, or fall-time. A want of information concerning my own was a source of unhappiness to me even during childhood. The white children could tell their ages. I could not tell why I ought to be deprived of the same privilege. I was not allowed to make any inquiries of my master concerning it. He deemed all such inquiries on the part of a slave improper and impertinent, and evidence of a restless spirit. The nearest estimate I can give makes me now between twenty-seven and twenty-eight years of age. I come to this, from hearing my master say, some time during 1835, I was about seventeen years old.

My mother was named Harriet Bailey. She was the daughter of Isaac and Betsey Bailey, both colored, and quite dark. My mother was of a darker complexion than either my grandmother or grandfather.

My father was a white man. He was admitted to be such by all I ever heard speak of my parentage. The opinion was also whispered that my master was my father; but of the correctness of this opinion, I know nothing; the means of knowing was withheld from me. My mother and I were separated when I was but an infant—before I knew her as my mother. It is a common custom, in the part of Maryland from which I ran away, to part children from their mothers at a very early age. Frequently, before the child has reached its twelfth month, its mother is taken from it, and hired out on some farm a considerable distance off, and the child is placed under the care of an old woman, too old for field labor. For what this separation is done, I do not know, unless it be to hinder the development of the child's affection toward its mother, and to blunt and destroy the natural affection of the mother for the child. This is the inevitable result.

I never saw my mother, to know her as such, more than four or five times in my life; and each of these times was very short in duration, and at night. She was hired by a Mr. Stewart, who lived about twelve miles from my home. She made her journeys to see me in the night, travelling the whole distance on foot, after the performance of her day's work. She was a field hand, and a whipping is the penalty of not being in the field at sunrise, unless a slave has special permission from his or her master to the contrary—a permission which they seldom get, and one that gives to him that gives it the proud name of being a kind master. I do not recollect of ever seeing my mother by the light of day. She was with me in the night. She would lie down with me, and get me to sleep, but long before I waked she was gone. Very little communication ever took place between us. Death soon ended what little we could have while she lived, and with it her hardships and suffering. She died when I was about seven years old, on one of my master's farms, near Lee's Mill. I was not allowed to be present during her illness, at her death, or burial. She was gone long before I knew anything about it. Never having enjoyed, to any considerable extent, her soothing presence, her tender and watchful care, I received the tidings of her death with much the same emotions I should have probably felt at the death of a stranger.

Called thus suddenly away, she left me without the slightest intimation of who my father was. The whisper that my master was my father, may or may not be true; and, true or false, it is of but little consequence to my purpose whilst the fact remains, in all its glaring odiousness, that slaveholders have ordained, and by law established, that the children of slave women shall in all cases follow the condition of their mothers; and this is done too obviously to administer to their own lusts, and make a gratification of their wicked desires profitable as well as pleasurable; for by this cunning arrangement, the slaveholder, in cases not a few, sustains to his slaves the double relation of master and father.

I know of such cases; and it is worthy of remark that such slaves invariably suffer greater hardships, and have more to contend with, than others. They are, in the first place, a constant offence to their mistress. She is ever disposed to find fault with them; they can seldom do anything to please her; she is never better pleased than when she sees them under the lash, especially when she suspects her husband of showing to his mulatto children favors which he withholds from his black slaves. The master is frequently compelled to sell this class of his slaves, out of deference to the feelings of his white wife; and, cruel as the deed may strike any one to be, for a man to sell his own children to human flesh-mongers, it is often the dictate of humanity for him to do so; for, unless he does this, he must not only whip them himself, but must stand by and see one white son tie up his brother, of but few shades darker complexion than himself, and ply the gory lash to his naked back; and if he lisp one word of disapproval, it is set down to his parental partiality, and only makes a bad matter worse, both for himself and the slave whom he would protect and defend.

Every year brings with it multitudes of this class of slaves. It was doubtless in consequence of a knowledge of this fact, that one great statesman of the south predicted the downfall of slavery by the inevitable laws of population. Whether this prophecy is ever fulfilled or not, it is nevertheless plain that a very different-looking class of people are springing up at the south, and are now held in slavery, from those originally brought to this country from Africa; and if their increase will do no other good, it will do away the force of the argument, that God cursed Ham, and therefore American slavery is right. If the lineal descendants of Ham are alone to be scripturally enslaved, it is certain that slavery at the south must soon become unscriptural; for thousands are ushered into the world, annually, who, like myself, owe their existence to white fathers, and those fathers most frequently their own masters.

I have had two masters. My first master's name was Anthony. I do not remember his first name. He was generally called Captain Anthony—a title which, I presume, he acquired by sailing a craft on the Chesapeake Bay. He was not considered a rich slaveholder. He owned two or three farms, and about thirty slaves. His farms and slaves were under the care of an overseer. The overseer's name was Plummer. Mr. Plummer was a miserable drunkard, a profane swearer, and a savage monster. He always went armed with a cowskin and a heavy cudgel. I have known him to cut and slash the women's heads so horribly, that even master would be enraged at his cruelty, and would threaten to whip him if he did not mind himself. Master, however, was not a humane slaveholder. It required extraordinary barbarity on the part of an overseer to affect him. He was a cruel man, hardened by a long life of slaveholding. He would at times seem to take great pleasure in whipping a slave. I have often been awakened at the dawn of day by the most heart-rending shrieks of an own aunt of mine, whom he used to tie up to a joist, and whip upon her naked back till she was literally covered with blood. No words, no tears, no prayers, from his gory victim, seemed to move his iron heart from its bloody purpose. The louder she screamed, the harder he whipped; and where the blood ran fastest, there he whipped longest. He would whip her to make her scream, and whip her to make her hush; and not until overcome by fatigue, would he cease to swing the blood-clotted cowskin. I remember the first time I ever witnessed this horrible exhibition. I was quite a child, but I well remember it. I never shall forget it whilst I remember anything. It was the first of a long series of such outrages, of which I was doomed to be a witness and a participant. It struck me with awful force. It was the blood-stained gate, the entrance to the hell of slavery, through which I was about to pass. It was a most terrible spectacle. I wish I could commit to paper the feelings with which I beheld it ....

As to my own treatment while I lived on Colonel Lloyd's plantation, it was very similar to that of the other slave children. I was not old enough to work in the field, and there being little else than field work to do, I had a great deal of leisure time. The most I had to do was to drive up the cows at evening, keep the fowls out of the garden, keep the front yard clean, and run of errands ....

I was seldom whipped by my old master, and suffered little from anything else than hunger and cold. I suffered much from hunger, but much more from cold. In hottest summer and coldest winter, I was kept almost naked—no shoes, no stockings, no jacket, no trousers, nothing on but a coarse tow linen shirt, reaching only to my knees. I had no bed. I must have perished with cold, but that, the coldest nights, I used to steal a bag which was used for carrying corn to the mill. I would crawl into this bag, and there sleep on the cold, damp, clay floor, with my head in and feet out. My feet have been so cracked with the frost, that the pen with which I am writing might be laid in the gashes.

We were not regularly allowanced. Our food was coarse corn meal boiled. This was called mush. It was put into a large wooden tray or trough, and set down upon the ground. The children were then called, like so many pigs, and like so many pigs they would come and devour the mush; some with oyster-shells, others with pieces of shingle, some with naked hands, and none with spoons. He that ate fastest got most; he that was strongest secured the best place; and few left the trough satisfied.

I was probably between seven and eight years old when I left Colonel Lloyd's plantation. I left it with joy …. The ties that ordinarily bind children to their homes were all suspended in my case. I found no severe trial in my departure. My home was charmless; it was not home to me; on parting from it, I could not feel that I was leaving anything which I could have enjoyed by staying. My mother was dead, my grandmother lived far off, so that I seldom saw her. I had two sisters and one brother that lived in the same house with me; but the early separation of us from our mother had well nigh blotted the fact of our relationship from our memories. I looked for home elsewhere, and was confident of finding none which I should relish less than the one which I was leaving. If, however, I found in my new home hardship, hunger, whipping, and nakedness, I had the consolation that I should not have escaped any one of them by staying.

Close Reading Questions

1. According to Douglass, when an African American slave has been fathered by a "white" master, what are some of the terrible effects on many members of this family?

2. How does Douglass argue that the Biblical defense of slavery was becoming obsolete in the nineteenth century? (Historical Trends)

3. Douglass calls attention to his own literacy when he refers to "the pen with which I am writing" later as an adult. With specific references to the text, what do you consider to be some of Douglass's most eloquent descriptions? What effect do they have on you and why?

Analytical Writing/Discussion

4. As Douglass describes the horrors of slavery, he portrays some situations in very graphic detail. With what details do you think he convinced his nineteenth-century Northern readers of the horrors of slavery, and what details do you think might have overwhelmed some of them? (Multiple Perspectives)

5. Douglass portrays himself as a child denied basic knowledge and material comforts that most Americans now take for granted. What effects do you think Douglass's description of these deprivations might have had on his diverse readers, including those who opposed slavery as well as those who supported it?

6. Many eighteenth- and nineteenth-century defenders of slavery referred to this ownership of one person by another as the "benign institution," one that helped rather than harmed Africans by supposedly civilizing them. Based on your knowledge of the nineteen-century ideal of the family from reading Hareven's "Retreat," how do you think Douglass uses his readers' beliefs about family—the desired relationships between mothers, fathers, and children—to challenge the allegedly "benign institution" of slavery? (Cultural Influences)

Further Options

7. As explained in Chapter 5 on Argument, a speaker or writer almost always tries to appeal to some of the values of the audience he or she is trying to persuade. Given your assumptions about Northern "white" Americans in the nineteenth century who read Douglass' autobiography, what values does Douglass portray to establish a bond with his audience?

8. Some literary scholars have worried that as Douglass wrote his autobiography, he became "enslaved" to the values of the readers he wanted to reach. For instance, a leading scholar of African American literature named Houston Baker has voiced his concern that "Determined to move beyond subservient status, cut off from alternatives …. Douglass adopted a system of symbols that seemed to promise him an unbounded freedom." Why do you think that such assimilation can result in the destruction of an identity as much as the enrichment of one's sense of self?

THE REVOLT OF "MOTHER"

by Mary Wilkins Freeman

Mary Wilkins Freeman was a prolific writer of thirteen novels and many more short stories. She struggled to support her family as her husband provided less and less. Once when her writing was praised by a critic, she modestly replied, "[I] wrote my little stories about the types [of people] I knew." In this short story published in 1891, Freeman demonstrates her knowledge of a hard-working nineteenth-century farm family through her use of a regional dialect and her portrayal of the complex relationship between "Father" and "Mother." This relationship changes, along with the names used to refer to these two characters, over the course of this story. Freeman received little acclaim as a writer during her lifetime, but contemporary critics have hailed her as much more than the author of "little stories."

"Father!"

"What is it?"

"What are them men diggin' over there in the field for?"

There was a sudden dropping and enlarging of the lower part of the old man's face, as if some heavy weight had settled therein; he shut his mouth tight and went on harnessing the great bay mare. He hustled the collar on to her neck with a jerk.

"Father!"

The old man slapped the saddle upon the mare's back.

"Look here, father, I want to know what them men are diggin' over in the field for, an' I'm goin' to know."

"I wish you'd go into the house, mother, an' 'tend to your own affairs," the old man said then. He ran his words together, and his speech was almost as inarticulate as a growl.

But the woman understood; it was her most native tongue. "I ain't goin' into the house till you tell me what them men are doin' over there in the field," said she.

Then she stood waiting. She was a small woman, short and straight-waisted like a child in her brown cotton gown. Her forehead was mild and benevolent between the smooth curves of gray hair; there were meek downward lines about her nose and mouth; but her eyes, fixed upon the old man, looked as if the meekness had been the result of her own will, never of the will of another.

They were in the barn, standing before the wide open doors. The spring air, full of the smell of growing grass and unseen blossoms, came in their faces. The deep yard in front was littered with farm wagons and piles of wood; on the edges, close to the fence and the house, the grass was a vivid green, and there were some dandelions.

The old man glanced doggedly at his wife as he tightened the last buckles on the harness. She looked as immovable to him as one of the rocks in his pasture-land, bound to the earth with generations of blackberry vines. He slapped the reins over the horse and started forth from the barn.

"Father!" said she.

The old man pulled up. "What is it?"

"I want to know what them men are diggin' over there in that field for."

"They're diggin' a cellar, I s'pose, if you've got to know."

"A cellar for what?"

"A barn."

"A barn? You ain't goin' to build a barn over there where we was goin' to have a house, father?"

The old man said not another word. He hurried the horse into the farm wagon and clattered out of the yard, jouncing as sturdily on his seat as a boy.

The woman stood a moment looking after him, then she went out of the barn across a corner of the yard to the house. The house, standing at right angles with the great barn and a long reach of sheds and out-buildings, was infinitesimal compared with them. It was scarcely as commodious for people as the little boxes under the barn eaves were for doves.

A pretty girl's face, pink and delicate as a flower, was looking out of one of the house windows. She was watching three men who were digging over in the field which bounded the yard near the road line. She turned quietly when the woman entered.

"What are they digging for, mother?" said she. "Did he tell you?"

"They're diggin' for—a cellar for a new barn."

"Oh, mother, he ain't going to build another barn?"

"That's what he says."

A boy stood before the kitchen glass combing his hair. He combed slowly and painstakingly, arranging his brown hair in a smooth hillock over his forehead. He did not seem to pay any attention to the conversation.

"Sammy, did you know father was going to build a new barn?" asked the girl.

The boy combed assiduously.

"Sammy!"

He turned and showed a face like his father's under his smooth crest of hair. "Yes, I s'pose I did," he said, reluctantly.

"How long have you known it?" asked his mother.

"'Bout three months, I guess."

"Why didn't you tell of it?"

"Didn't think 'twould do no good."

"I don't see what father wants another barn for," said the girl, in her sweet, slow voice. She turned again to the window and stared out at the digging men in the field. Her tender, sweet face was full of a gentle distress. Her forehead was as bald and innocent as a baby's, with the light hair strained back from it in a row of curl-papers. She was quite large, but her soft curves did not look as if they covered muscles.

Her mother looked sternly at the boy. "Is he goin' to buy more cows?" said she.

The boy did not reply; he was tying his shoes.

"Sammy, I want you to tell me if he's goin' to buy more cows."

"I s'pose he is."

"How many?"

"Four, I guess."

The girl went to the sink and began to wash the dishes that were piled up there. Her mother came promptly out of the pantry and shoved her aside. "You wipe 'em," said she; "I'll wash. There's a good many this mornin'."

The mother plunged her hands vigorously into the water, the girl wiped the plates slowly and dreamily. "Mother," said she, "don't you think it's too bad father's going to build that new barn, much as we need a decent house to live in?"

Her mother scrubbed a dish fiercely. "You ain't found out yet we're women-folks, Nanny Penn," said she. "You ain't seen enough of men-folks yet to. One of these days you'll find it out, an' then you'll know that we know only what men-folks think we do, so far as any use of it goes, an' how we'd ought to reckon men-folks in with Providence an' not complain of what they do any more than we do of the weather."

"I don't care; I don't believe George is anything like that, anyhow," said Nanny. Her delicate face flushed pink, her lips pouted softly, as if she were going to cry.

"You wait an' see. I guess George Eastman ain't no better than other men. You hadn't ought to judge father, though. He can't help it, 'cause he don't look at things jest the way we do. An' we've been pretty comfortable here, after all. The roof don't leak—ain't never but once—that's one thing. Father's kept it shingled right up."

"I do wish we had a parlor."

"I guess it won't hurt George Eastman any to come to see you in a nice clean kitchen. I guess a good many girls don't have as good a place as this. Nobody's ever heard me complain."

"I ain't complained either, mother."

"Well, I don't think you'd better, a good father an' a good home as you've got. S'pose your father made you go out an' work for your livin'? Lots of girls have to that ain't no stronger an' better able to than you be."

Sarah Penn washed the frying pan with a conclusive air. She scrubbed the outside of it as faithfully as the inside. She was a masterly keeper of her box of a house. Her one living-room never seemed to have in it any of the dust which the friction of life with inanimate matter produces. She swept, and there seemed to be no dirt to go before the broom; she cleaned, and one could see no difference. She was like an artist so perfect that he has apparently no art. Today she got out a mixing bowl and a board and rolled some pies, and there was no more flour upon her than upon her daughter who was doing finer work. Nanny was to be married in the fall, and she was sewing on some white cambric and embroidery. She sewed industriously while her mother cooked, her soft milk-white hands and wrists showed whiter than her delicate work.

"We must have the stove moved out in the shed before long," said Mrs. Penn. "Talk about not havin' things, it's been a real blessin' to be able to put a stove up in that shed in hot weather. Father did one good thing when he fixed that stovepipe out there."

Sarah Penn's face as she rolled her pies had that expression of meek vigor which might have characterized one of the New Testament saints. She was making mince pies. Her husband, Adoniram Penn, liked them better than any other kind. She baked twice a week. Adoniram often liked a piece of pie between meals. She hurried this morning. It had been later than usual when she began, and she wanted to have a pie baked for dinner. However deep a resentment she might be forced to hold against her husband, she would never fail in sedulous attention to his wants.

Nobility of character manifests itself at loopholes when it is not provided with large doors. Sarah Penn's showed itself today in flaky dishes of pastry. So she made the pies faithfully, while across the table she could see, when she glanced up from her work, the sight that rankled in her patient and steadfast soul—the digging of the cellar of the new barn in the place where Adoniram forty years ago had promised her their new house should stand.

The pies were done for dinner. Adoniram and Sammy were home a few minutes after twelve o'clock. The dinner was eaten with serious haste. There was never much conversation at the table in the Penn family. Adoniram asked a blessing, and they ate promptly, then rose up and went about their work.

Sammy went back to school, taking soft sly lopes out of the yard like a rabbit. He wanted a game of marbles before school and feared his father would give him some chores to do. Adoniram hastened to the door and called after him, but he was out of sight.

"I don't see what you let him go for, mother," said he. "I wanted him to help me unload that wood."

Adoniram went to work out in the yard unloading wood from the wagon. Sarah put away the dinner dishes, while Nanny took down her curl-papers and changed her dress. She was going down to the store to buy some more embroidery and thread.

When Nanny was gone, Mrs. Penn went to the door. "Father!" she called.

"Well, what is it!"

"I want to see you jest a minute, father."

"I can't leave this wood nohow. I've got to git it unloaded an' go for a load of gravel afore two o'clock. Sammy had ought to helped me. You hadn't ought to let him go to school so early."

"I want to see you jest a minute."

"I tell ye I can't, nohow, mother."

"Father, you come here." Sarah Penn stood in the door like a queen; she held her head as if it bore a crown; there was the patience which makes authority royal in her voice. Adoniram went.

Mrs. Penn led the way into the kitchen and pointed to a chair. "Sit down, father," said she; "I've got somethin' I want to say to you."

He sat down heavily; his face was quite stolid, but he looked at her with restive eyes. "Well, what is it, mother?"

"I want to know what you're buildin' that new barn for, father?"

"I ain't got nothin' to say about it."

"It can't be you think you need another barn?"

"I tell ye I ain't got nothin' to say about it, mother; an' ain't goin' to say nothin.'"

"Be you goin' to buy more cows?"

Adoniram did not reply; he shut his mouth tight.

"I know you be, as well as I want to. Now, father, look here"—Sarah Penn had not sat down; she stood before her husband in the humble fashion of a Scripture woman—"I'm goin' to talk real plain to you; I never have sence I married you, but I'm goin' to now. I ain't never complained, an' I ain't goin' to complain now, but I'm goin' to talk plain. You see this room here, father; you look at it well. You see there ain't no carpet on the floor, an' you see the paper is all dirty, an' droppin' off the walls. We ain't had no new paper on it for ten years, an' then I put it on myself, an' it didn't cost but ninepence a roll. You see this room, father; it's all the one I've had to work in an' eat in an' sit in sence we was married. There ain't another woman in the whole town whose husband ain't got half the means you have but what's got better. It's all the room Nanny's got to have her company in; an' there ain't one of her mates but what's got better, an' their fathers not so able as hers is. It's all the room she'll have to be married in. What would you have thought, father, if we had had our weddin' in a room no better than this? I was married in my mother's parlor with a carpet on the floor, an' stuffed furniture, an' a mahogany card-table. An' this is all the room my daughter will have to be married in. Look here, father!"

Sarah Penn went across the room as though it were a tragic stage. She flung open a door and disclosed a tiny bedroom, only large enough for a bed and bureau, with a path between. "There, father," said she— "there's all the room I've had to sleep in forty years. All my children were born there—the two that died, an' the two that's livin'. I was sick with a fever there."

She stepped to another door and opened it. It led into the small, ill-lighted pantry. "Here," said she, "is all the buttery I've got—every place I've got for my dishes, to set away my victuals in, an' to keep my milk-pans in. Father. I've been takin' care of the milk of six cows in this place, an' now you're goin' to build a new barn, an' keep more cows, an' give me more to do in it."

She threw open another door. A narrow crooked flight of stairs wound upward from it. "There, father," said she, "I want you to look at the stairs that go up to them two unfinished chambers that are all the places our son an' daughter have had to sleep in all their lives. There ain't a prettier girl in town nor a more ladylike one than Nanny, an' that's the place she has to sleep in. It ain't so good as your horse's stall; it ain't so warm an' tight."

Sarah Penn went back and stood before her husband. "Now, father," said she, "I want to know if you think you're doin' right an' accordin' to what you profess. Here, when we was married, forty years ago, you promised me faithful that we should have a new house built in that lot over in the field before the year was out. You said you had money enough, an' you wouldn't ask me to live in no such place as this. It is forty years now, an' you've been makin' more money, an' I've been savin' of it for you ever since, an' you ain't built no house yet. You've built sheds an' cow-houses an' one new barn, an' now you're goin' to build another. Father, I want to know if you think it's right. You're lodgin' your dumb beasts better than you are your own flesh an' blood. I want to know if you think it's right."

"I ain't got nothin' to say."

"You can't say nothin' without ownin' it ain't right, father. An' there's another thing—I ain't complained; I've got along forty years, an' I s'pose I should forty more, if it wa'n't for that—if we don't have another house. Nanny she can't live with us after she's married. She'll have to go somewheres else to live away from us, an' it don't seem as if I could have it so, noways, father. She wa'n't ever strong. She's got considerable color, but there wa'n't ever any backbone to her. I've always took the heft of everything off her, an' she ain't fit to keep house an' do everything herself. She'll be all worn out inside of a year. Think of her doin' all the washin' an' ironin' an' bakin' with them soft white hands an' arms, an' sweepin'! I can't have it so, noways, father."

Mrs. Penn's face was burning; her mild eyes gleamed. She had pleaded her little cause like a Webster; she had ranged from severity to pathos; but her opponent employed that obstinate silence which makes eloquence futile with mocking echoes. Adoniram arose clumsily.

"Father, ain't you got nothin' to say?" said Mrs. Penn.

"I've got to go off after that load of gravel. I can't stan' here talkin' all day."

"Father, won't you think it over, an' have a house built there instead of a barn?"

"I ain't got nothin' to say."

Adoniram shuffled out ....

Nanny came home with her embroidery and sat down with her needlework. She had taken down her curl-papers, and there was a soft roll of fair hair like an aureole over her forehead; her face was as delicately fine and clear as porcelain. Suddenly she looked up, and the tender red flamed all over her face and neck. "Mother," said she.

"What say?"

"I've been thinking—I don't see how we're goin' to have any—wedding in this room. I'd be ashamed to have his folks come if we didn't have anybody else."

"Mebbe we can have some new paper before then; I can put it on. I guess you won't have no call to be ashamed of your belongin's."

"We might have the wedding in the new barn," said Nanny, with gentle pettishness. "Why, mother, what makes you look so?"

Mrs. Penn had started and was staring at her with a curious expression. She turned again to her work and spread out a pattern carefully on the cloth. "Nothin'," said she.

Presently Adoniram clattered out of the yard in his two-wheeled dump cart, standing as proudly upright as a Roman charioteer. Mrs. Penn opened the door and stood there a minute looking out ....

The barn was all completed ready for use by the third week in July. Adoniram had planned to move his stock in on Wednesday; on Tuesday he received a letter which changed his plans. He came in with it early in the morning. "Sammy's been to the post office," said he, "an' I've got a letter from Hiram." Hiram was Mrs. Penn's brother, who lived in Vermont.

"Well," said Mrs. Penn, "what does he say about the folks?"

"I guess they're all right. He says he thinks if I come up country right off there's a chance to buy jest the kind of a horse I want." He stared reflectively out of the window at the new barn.

Mrs. Penn was making pies. She went on clapping the rolling-pin into the crust, although she was very pale, and her heart beat loudly.

"I dun' know but what I'd better go," said Adoniram. "I hate to go off jest now, right in the midst of hayin', but the ten-acre lot's cut, an' I guess Rufus an' the others can git along without me three or four days. I can't get a horse round here to suit me, nohow, an' I've got to have another for all that wood-haulin' in the fall. I told Hiram to watch out, an' if he got wind of a good horse to let me know. I guess I'd better go."

"I'll get out your clean shirt an' collar," said Mrs. Penn calmly.

She laid out Adoniram's Sunday suit and his clean clothes on the bed in the little bedroom. She got his shaving-water and razor ready. At last she buttoned on his collar and fastened his black cravat.

Adoniram never wore his collar and cravat except on extra occasions. He held his head high, with a rasped dignity. When he was all ready, with his coat and hat brushed and a lunch of pie and cheese in a paper bag, he hesitated on the threshold of the door. He looked at his wife, and his manner was defiantly apologetic. "If them cows come today, Sammy can drive 'em into the new barn," said he; "an' when they bring the hay up, they can pitch it in there."

"Well," replied Mrs. Penn.

Adoniram set his shaven face ahead and started. When he had cleared the doorstep, he turned and looked back with a kind of nervous solemnity. "I shall be back by Saturday if nothin' happens," said he.

"Do be careful, father," returned his wife.

She stood in the door with Nanny at her elbow and watched him out of sight. Her eyes had a strange, doubtful expression in them; her peaceful forehead was contracted. She went in, and about her baking again. Nanny sat sewing. Her wedding day was drawing nearer, and she was getting pale and thin with her steady sewing. Her mother kept glancing at her.

"Have you got that pain in your side this mornin'?" she asked.

"A little."

Mrs. Penn's face, as she worked, changed, her perplexed forehead smoothed, her eyes were steady, her lips firmly set. She formed a maxim for herself, although incoherently with her unlettered thoughts. "Unsolicited opportunities are the guideposts of the Lord to the new roads of life," she repeated in effect, and she made up her mind to her course of action.

"S'posin' I had wrote to Hiram," she muttered once, when she was in the pantry—"s'posin' I had wrote, an' asked him if he knew of any horse? But I didn't, an' father's goin' wa'n't none of my doin'. It looks like a providence." Her voice rang out quite loud at the last.

"What you talkin' about, mother?" called Nanny.

"Nothin'."

Mrs. Penn hurried her baking; at eleven o'clock it was all done. The load of hay from the west field came slowly down the cart track and drew up at the new barn. Mrs. Penn ran out. "Stop!" she screamed—"stop!"

The men stopped and looked; Sammy upreared from the top of the load and stared at his mother.

"Stop!" she cried out again. "Don't you put the hay in that barn; put it in the old one."

"Why, he said to put it in here," returned one of the hay-makers, wonderingly. He was a young man, a neighbor's son, whom Adoniram hired by the year to help on the farm.

"Don't you put the hay in the new barn; there's room enough in the old one, ain't there?" said Mrs. Penn.

"Room enough," returned the hired man, in his thick, rustic tones. "Didn't need the new barn, nohow, far as room's concerned. Well, I s'pose he changed his mind." He took hold of the horses' bridles.

Mrs. Penn went back to the house. Soon the kitchen windows were darkened, and a fragrance like warm honey came into the room.

Nanny laid down her work. "I thought father wanted them to put the hay into the new barn?" she said, wonderingly.

"It's all right," replied her mother.

Sammy slid down from the load of hay and came in to see if dinner was ready.

"I ain't goin' to get a regular dinner today, as long as father's gone," said his mother. "I've let the fire go out. You can have some bread an' milk an' pie. I thought we could get along." She set out some bowls of milk, some bread, and a pie on the kitchen table. "You'd better eat your dinner now," said she. "You might jest as well get through with it. I want you to help me afterward."

Nanny and Sammy stared at each other. There was something strange in their mother's manner. Mrs. Penn did not eat anything herself. She went into the pantry, and they heard her moving dishes while they ate. Presently she came out with a pile of plates. She got the clothes basket out of the shed and packed them in it. Nanny and Sammy watched. She brought out cups and saucers and put them in with the plates.

"What you goin' to do, mother?" inquired Nanny, in a timid voice. A sense of something unusual made her tremble, as if it were a ghost. Sammy rolled his eyes over his pie.

"You'll see." . . .

At five o'clock in the afternoon, the little house in which the Penns had lived for forty years had emptied itself into the new barn.

Every builder builds somewhat for unknown purposes and is in a measure a prophet. The architect of Adoniram Penn's barn, while he designed it for the comfort of four-footed animals, had planned better than he knew for the comfort of humans. Sarah Penn saw at a glance its possibilities. These great box-stalls, with quilts hung before them, would make better bedrooms than the one she had occupied for forty years, and there was a tight carriage-room. The harness-room, with its chimney and shelves, would make a kitchen of her dreams. The great middle space would make a parlor, by and by, fit for a palace. Upstairs there was as much room as down. With partitions and windows, what a house would there be! Sarah looked at the row of stanchions before the allotted space for cows and reflected that she would have her front entry there.

At six o'clock the stove was up in the harness-room, the kettle was boiling, and the table set for tea. It looked almost as home-like as the abandoned house across the yard had ever done. The young hired man milked, and Sarah directed him calmly to bring the milk to the new barn. He came gaping, dropping little blots of foam from the brimming pails on the grass. Before the next morning, he had spread the story of Adoniram Penn's wife moving into the new barn all over the little village. Men assembled in the store and talked it over, women with shawls over their heads scuttled into each other's houses before their work was done. Any deviation from the ordinary course of life in this quiet town was enough to stop all progress in it. Everybody paused to look at the staid, independent figure on the side track. There was a difference of opinion with regard to her. Some held her to be insane; some, of a lawless and rebellious spirit.

Friday, the minister went to see her. It was in the forenoon, and she was at the barn door shelling peas for dinner. She looked up and returned his salutation with dignity, then she went on with her work. She did not invite him in. The saintly expression of her face remained fixed, but there was an angry flush over it.

The minister stood awkwardly before her and talked. She handled the peas as if they were bullets. At last she looked up, and her eyes showed the spirit that her meek front had covered for a lifetime.

"There ain't no use talkin', Mr. Hersey," said she. "I've thought it all over an' over, an' I believe I'm doin' what's right. I've made it the subject of prayer, an' it's betwixt me an' the Lord an' Adoniram. There ain't no call for nobody else to worry about it."

"Well, of course, if you have brought it to the Lord in prayer and feel satisfied that you are doing right, Mrs. Penn," said the minister, helplessly. His thin gray-bearded face was pathetic. He was a sickly man; his youthful confidence had cooled; he had to scourge himself up to some of his pastoral duties as relentlessly as a Catholic ascetic, and then he was prostrated by the smart.

"I think it's right jest as much as I think it was right for our forefathers to come over from the old country 'cause they didn't have what belonged to 'em," said Mrs. Penn. She arose. The barn threshold might have been Plymouth Rock from her bearing. "I don't doubt you mean well, Mr. Hersey," said she, "but there are things people hadn't ought to interfere with. I've been a member of the church for over forty years. I've got my own mind an' my own feet, an' I'm goin' to think my own thoughts an' go my own ways, an' nobody but the Lord is goin' to dictate to me unless I've a mind to have him. Won't you come in an' set down? How is Mis' Hersey?"

"She is well, I thank you," replied the minister. He added some more perplexed apologetic remarks; then he retreated.

Towards sunset on Saturday, when Adoniram was expected home, there was a knot of men in the road near the new barn. The hired man had milked, but he still hung around the premises. Sarah Penn had supper all ready. There were brown bread and baked beans and a custard pie; it was the supper Adoniram loved on a Saturday night. She had a clean calico, and she bore herself imperturbably. Nanny and Sammy kept close at her heels. Their eyes were large, and Nanny was full of nervous tremors. Still there was to them more pleasant excitement than anything else. An inborn confidence in their mother over their father asserted itself.

Sammy looked out of the harness-room window. "There he is," he announced, in an awed whisper. He and Nanny peeped around the casing. Mrs. Penn kept on about her work. The children watched Adoniram leave the new horse standing in the drive while he went to the house door. It was fastened. Then he went around to the shed. That door was seldom locked, even when the family was away. The thought of how her father would be confronted by the cow flashed upon Nanny. There was a hysterical sob in her throat. Adoniram emerged from the shed and stood looking about in a dazed fashion. His lips moved; he was saying something, but they could not hear what it was. The hired man was peeping around a corner of the old barn, but nobody saw him.

Adoniram took the new horse by the bridle and led him across the yard to the new barn. Nanny and Sammy slunk close to their mother. The barn doors rolled back, and there stood Adoniram, with the long mild face of the great Canadian farm horse looking over his shoulder.

Nanny kept behind her mother, but Sammy stepped suddenly forward and stood in front of her.

Adoniram stared at the group. "What on airth you all down here for?" said he. "What's the matter over to the house?"

"We've come here to live, father," said Sammy. His shrill voice quavered out bravely.

"What"—Adoniram sniffed—"what is it smells like cookin'?" said he. He stepped forward and looked in the open door of the harness-room. Then he turned to his wife. His old bristling face was pale and frightened. "What on airth does this mean, mother?" he gasped.

"You come in here, father," said Sarah. She led the way into the harness-room and shut the door. "Now, father," said she, "you needn't be scared. I ain't crazy. There ain't nothin' to be upset over. But we've come here to live, an' we're goin' to live here. We've got jest as good a right here as new horses an' cows. The house wa'n't fit for us to live in any longer, an' I made up my mind I wa'n't goin' to stay there. I've done my duty by you forty years, an' I'm goin' to do it now; but I'm goin' to live here. You've got to put in some windows and partitions, an' you'll have to buy some furniture."

"Why, mother!" the old man gasped.

"You'd better take your coat off an' get washed—there's the washbasin—an' then we'll have supper."

"Why, mother!"

Sammy went past the window, leading the new horse to the old barn. The old man saw him and shook his head speechlessly. He tried to take off his coat, but his arms seemed to lack the power. His wife helped him. She poured some water into the tin basin and put in a piece of soap. She got the comb and brush and smoothed his thin gray hair after he had washed. Then she put the beans, hot bread, and tea on the table. Sammy came in, and the family drew up. Adoniram sat looking dazedly at his plate, and they waited.

"Ain't you goin' to ask a blessin', father?" said Sarah.

And the old man bent his head and mumbled.

All through the meal he stopped eating at intervals and stared furtively at his wife, but he ate well. The home food tasted good to him, and his old frame was too sturdily healthy to be affected by his mind. But after supper he went out and sat down on the step of the smaller door at the right of the barn, through which he had meant his Jerseys to pass in stately file, but which Sarah designed for her front house door, and he leaned his head on his hands.

After the supper dishes were cleared away and the milk-pans washed, Sarah went out to him. The twilight was deepening. There was a clear green glow in the sky. Before them stretched the smooth level of field; in the distance was a cluster of haystacks like the huts of a village; the air was very cool and calm and sweet. The landscape might have been an ideal one of peace.

Sarah bent over and touched her husband on one of his thin, sinewy shoulders. "Father!"

The old man's shoulders heaved: he was weeping.

"Why, don't do so, father," said Sarah.

"I'll—put up the—partitions, an'—everything you—want, mother."

Sarah put her apron up to her face; she was overcome by her own triumph.

Adoniram was like a fortress whose walls had no active resistance and went down the instant the right besieging tools were used. "Why, mother," he said, hoarsely, "I hadn't no idee you was so set on't as all this comes to."

Close Reading Questions

1. As you read, notice when and how each family member learns of Adoniram Penn's decision to build a new barn. What do you think each member's knowledge of the new barn suggests about his or her position in this family?

2. Throughout this story, Sarah Penn and her husband Adoniram each repeat several phrases as they converse. What is a phrase each one of these married characters repeats, and what do you think these phrases reveal about each person and their marriage?

3. Note the various reactions by Sarah's neighbors to her decision to move. What do you think the responses of the hired man, the minister, and other townspeople reveal about their expectations for nineteenth-century fathers and mothers?

Analytical Writing/Discussion

4. As Sarah discusses men's knowledge and later Hiram's letter, she refers to "Providence," the biblical belief in divine aid for certain individuals. Using these references to Providence, what do you think is Sarah's attitude toward male authority and her decision to move? (Cultural Influences)

5. Both the title and the opening scene of the story refer to "mother." Only later does the story refer to the main character and her husband by their married names: Mrs. and Mr. Penn and then by their first names: Sarah and Adoniram. Using specific references to both Freeman's story and the expected roles in nineteenth-century families, what do you think this progression of names suggests?

6. As twenty-first-century readers of Freeman's story, many of us may be tempted to read this story as an absolute rebellion by a wife against her husband. However, when Adoniram returns, Sarah has prepared one of his favorite meals. Considering the words and deeds of each family member, what are some of the different ways to interpret the final scene, and how can you defend the interpretation you prefer? (Multiple Perspectives)

Further Options

7. As Hareven explains in "The Nineteenth-Century Retreat" (see pp. 127–136), sons and daughters usually were raised to fulfill very different family roles in this era. In what ways are Nanny and Sammy being raised to become the traditional mothers and fathers of nineteenth-century families? Then, using specific references to the text, why do you think each child will or will not fulfill these gender-specific family roles? (Historical Trends)

8. As a relatively long short story, "The Revolt" has many detailed and sometimes ambiguous scenes. Using the double-entry notes described in Chapter 1 on Reading, select three or four of the key passages of this story, and explain each one to a classmate.

Freewrite 2: Past and Present

As this chapter's readings shift from historical texts to more recent ones, your professor may ask you to pause and connect your own family to some of the historical trends that may have shaped your family's form and its members' roles.

Using one or more of the images of your own family from Freewrite 1, can you now place that family scene(s) in the context of the nineteenth century? In what ways and to what degree does your family conform to or diverge from the typical family of nineteenth-century America?

Once you have completed this freewrite, you may want to expand this rough writing into a more formal paper with some direct quotations from some of the historical texts by Hareven, Douglass, and Freeman. The synthesis of sources is key aspect of academic writing.

PARENTING 101: CONSERVATIVE CHRISTIANS ON CHILDREARING

by John P. Bartkowski and Christopher Ellison

In 1979, a new conservative Christian group emerged as a powerful social and political force in the United States. Known as the Moral Majority, this conservative Christian group opposed abortion and homosexuality in favor of the "traditional" family. This advocacy group demonstrated its political muscle when it helped the 1980 Republican candidate, Ronald Reagan, defeat the incumbent, President Jimmy Carter. Although other conservative Christian groups like Focus on the Family have since eclipsed the Moral Majority, their views on family structure and child rearing continue to influence many Americans. In the following text, two sociologists contrast the child-raising practices of conservative Protestants with those of "mainstream" parents. Written by and for academics, this abridged article from 1995 draws sharp contrasts.

Contemporary conflicts over the American family have attracted widespread popular commentary and academic research (Thorne and Yalom 1982; Berger and Berger 1983; Dornbusch and Strober 1988; Stacey 1990; Faludi 1991; Hunter 1991). To date, however, these and other social scientists have constructed the "battle over the family" almost exclusively in terms of debates regarding gender roles. Indeed, many have dismissed other dimensions of this conflict, including conflicts over parenting issues, asserting that they are insignificant and obfuscatory. For instance, Cohen and Katzenstein (1988) put the matter bluntly: "The debate [over the family] is fundamentally about the places in society of men and women. The discourse about what is good for children is *simply not so polarized . . .*," (p. 25, emphasis added).

While we readily grant the importance of ongoing debates over gender roles, we also believe that disagreements over parent–child relations are much more fundamental and significant than previous discussions have recognized. A sharply polemical literature on parenting surfaced within conservative Protestant circles in the 1970s, extolling the virtues of "traditional" parenting techniques and challenging the views of mainstream experts. Since that time, sales of popular literature on "Christian" (generally conservative Protestant) parenting have mushroomed, and the core themes of this parenting ideology have been widely circulated via broadcast media and organizations devoted to family issues, such as "Focus on the Family." Conservative Protestant writers and commentators have clearly emerged as the leading spokespersons for "traditional" hierarchical child-rearing practices.

By John P. Bartkowski and Christopher Ellison, "Divergent Models of Childrearing in Popular Manuals: Conservative Protestants Vs. the Mainstream Experts," in *Sociology of Religion*, Volume 56, Number 1 (Spring 1995) Pages 21–34. By permission of Oxford University Press.

Our study explores this conservative Protestant parenting ideology in greater detail. We argue that the parenting ideas embraced by many conservative Protestant writers are legitimated via two related theological tenets ….Our analysis suggests that conservative Protestant parenting specialists part company with their mainstream counterparts in four key areas: (1) long-term parenting goals; (2) the structure of parent–child relations; (3) the definition of parental roles; and (4) strategies of child discipline and punishment ….

For mainstream and conservative Protestant specialists alike, we have focused primarily on the writings of the most prominent, best-selling child-rearing experts, as determined via sales figures and interviews with publishers' representatives ….Because we are primarily interested in the differences between conservative Protestant and mainstream parenting ideologies, our discussion necessarily downplays the inevitable heterogeneity within these camps …. Our goal is to distinguish the common parenting prescriptions and shared presuppositions of conservative Protestant writers from those of mainstream experts …

Divergent Models of Parenting: Long-Term Goals

What constitutes successful parenting? Mainstream and conservative Protestant advice manuals emphasize strikingly different outcomes. Almost without exception, leading mainstream writers focus on "healthy" personality development and social competence. Most mainstream parenting manuals underscore the importance of helping children develop desirable personality profiles: self-esteem, self-confidence, self-discipline, creativity, and intellectual curiosity. According to Lawrence Balter, the parent must be careful to foster "mastery, self-respect, and hopefulness … [based on] a loving relationship in which empathy and support are the central motifs" (1989:36). Although it is recognized that parents must elicit compliance from youngsters in various settings, they are strongly urged to refrain from employing any child-rearing or disciplinary techniques that might undermine the development of these personality traits in their children.

… Many mainstream parenting specialists [also] stress the importance of teaching empathy and verbal communication skills. For instance, Balter (1989:85–6) suggests that teaching empathy to toddlers reduces parent–child conflicts, allows the child to become more considerate of the needs and desires of others, and promotes self-control and self-discipline. LeShan (1985:106–08) recommends that parents should teach their children to interpret the moods and actions of others effectively, because this will foster greater tolerance of human frailty. Taken together, the interrelated social skills of empathy and communication help children to create a common understanding between two interacting individuals—the very definition of a "healthy" relationship.

Although most conservative Protestant specialists grant the value of "healthy" personalities and social competence, these traits are not seen as the most important outcomes of successful parenting. Instead, conservative Protestant writers emphasize that to succeed in adult roles, children must be trained to embrace the divinely-ordained principles of authority and hierarchy. This emphasis on authority is vital because of the view that children are born with sinful natures, prone to challenge authority in all forms. Conservative Protestants contend that a child who is not taught to submit to familial authority (1) will not develop a respect for [superior] figures outside the family (e.g., teachers, employers, guardians), and (2) will be unable to exercise rightful authority when assuming a [superior] role in human relationships (e.g., as a father, parent, or employer).

Moreover, the kind of authority training advocated by conservative Protestant writers is also believed to convey a crucial spiritual lesson to children. According to these writers, Christian parents are responsible for leading their children toward righteousness and salvation. Given their belief that human nature is fundamentally sinful, conservative Protestants maintain that training children to submit their selfish desires to the will of God, the creator and supreme authority of the universe, is central to this project of salvation. In short, conservative Protestant parents are warned that abrogating their divinely ordained parenting responsibilities—i.e., failing to command respect from their child—may substantially decrease the likelihood that the developing youngster will be inclined to "humble" him/herself before the divine authority of God.

Parent-Child Relationships

Both mainstream and conservative Protestant parenting specialists strive for [consistency] between the structure of family life and the social order. Mainstream experts tend to view the family as a dynamic entity that changes in both form and content to mirror normative and organizational shifts in the broader society. In particular, many mainstream specialists believe that all human institutions—including the family—should be guided by democratic and egalitarian principles. Consequently, the dominant discourse in much of the mainstream literature centers on the "rights" and "interests" of family members. Most mainstream parenting manuals suggest that conflicts within the family should be resolved through negotiation and that ideal solutions to these conflicts are solutions that maximize the joint satisfaction of the conflicting parties ....

In sharp contrast to the prevailing mainstream perspectives on the structure of parent–child relations, conservative Protestants view the family as an organic whole, rather than a compilation of potentially conflicting "rights" and "interests." Conservative Protestants assert the moral superiority of one "timeless," divinely ordained blueprint for parent–child relations, a model based on (and legitimated by) the biblical principles of authority and hierarchy that are articulated within contemporary literalist communities.

Not surprisingly, conservative Protestant parenting writers have reacted with alarm and hostility to calls for democracy within the family. Families, in their view, are characterized by specific sets of [superior] and subordinate roles. Conservative commentators cite an array of passages from Old and New Testament sources underscoring the respective obligations of children and parents. Conservative Protestant writers frequently stress the imperative of intergenerational hierarchy within the family. They repeatedly exhort children to honor and obey parental authority, and they call attention to Old Testament writings that threaten disobedient children with familial and societal ostracism and even death. These conservative religious commentators also emphasize that parents are held strictly accountable for any deviations from biblical parenting guidelines ....

Popular notions of children's "rights" especially rankle these conservative religious writers. As Dobson puts it, "I find no place in the Bible where our little ones are installed as co-discussants at a conference table, deciding what they will and will not accept from the older generation" (1978:170). Yet some religious writers appropriate the language of "rights" and "interests" in the service of conservative parenting ideals, countering that religious Scripture accords children the right to receive love, protection, religious training, and responsible leadership from their parents. These writers commonly contend that children, regardless of what they may say, actually want and expect these benefits from their parents and that these crucial children's rights are undermined by the egalitarian impulses of mainstream experts.

Further, conservative religious writers believe that popular democratic and egalitarian family models also have undesirable spiritual consequences. Virtually all of the Christian parenting specialists reviewed for this study claim that children develop their initial images of God based on the behavior of parents. This belief makes the preservation of hierarchical parent–child relations crucial. Those adults who opt for egalitarian households are denounced by conservative Protestant parenting specialists for abrogating their divinely ordained parental responsibilities and for sabotaging their youngsters' respect for parental, institutional, and (ultimately) divine authority.

Parental Roles

Perhaps the most common image of the ideal parent in mainstream parenting literature is that of the proactive tactician or manager. This ideal parent is knowledgeable about child development issues and consequently holds "reasonable" expectations of the child, consonant with the child's developmental stage. In addition, the ideal parent remains sensitive to the feelings of the child and permits him/her considerable latitude for the expression of these feelings. The mainstream literature emphasizes the importance of manipulating the child's environment in order (1) to minimize the potential for conflict between parents and child or between siblings, and (2) to facilitate the safe exploration of the physical and social world, thus building his/her self-esteem and self-confidence. The parent is advised to encourage desired behavior through love, praise, and various forms of positive reinforcement (hence the hackneyed phrase "catch 'em when they're doing good"). According to mainstream experts, competent parents plan lessons and games to communicate values and promote desired behavior, and they find ways to engage children in their own training whenever possible. Finally, the parent-as-tactician organizes household life in ways that maximize "win-win" situations among family members, instilling egalitarian values while carefully reconciling the needs and interests of various parties ....

Although parenting advice has generally been directed toward mothers, on the assumption that they have primary responsibility for child care, mainstream experts have increasingly promoted ungendered parenting roles. It seems that a growing number of mainstream parenting manuals acknowledge that child rearing should be understood as a partnership between equals ....Some reason that these youngsters are better equipped to participate fully and successfully in a society experiencing slow but steady progress toward gender equality in the workplace, political arena, and other institutions. Like their mainstream counterparts, many conservative Protestant family experts urge parents to become knowledgeable about child rearing. However ... Christian parents are encouraged to consult what is believed to be the most reliable parenting manual, the Bible. The lessons to be learned from Scripture apparently differ notably from the information conveyed by mainstream parenting experts.

While some conservative Protestant specialists occasionally acknowledge the value of parental cleverness, empathy, and communication .... Conservative Protestants are repeatedly advised to demonstrate firm leadership. Because children are perceived to be naturally sinful and rebellious, according to these specialists, the Christian parent should "shape the will," training the child to submit to authority figures. Parents are told to expect conflict and respond decisively, often with physical force, to the youngster's inevitable expressions of willful defiance. Dobson maintains that parents who shrink from this challenge will be hard-pressed to elicit obedience from their children thereafter.

Finally, unlike mainstream experts, conservative Protestant writers generally do not approve of ungendered parental roles .... They argue that the de-gendering of parental roles undermines the authority of the Bible as the word of God, because some scriptural passages place the father as the divinely ordained head and protector of the family The absence of a clear, biblically inspired gender hierarchy within the household is thought to undermine the child's ability to learn submission to authority .... Some worry that ungendered parental roles will erode the allegiance of youngsters to more traditional gender roles, thus exacerbating what they see as a societal devaluation of masculinity.

Discipline and Punishment

Central to the ongoing debate over parent–child relations are the sharp disagreements over appropriate strategies of discipline and punishment. Mainstream specialists overwhelmingly oppose the use of physical discipline. In place of corporal punishment, mainstream specialists advocate setting firm guidelines accompanied by various pragmatic disciplinary techniques, including combinations of positive reinforcement, logical consequences and/or natural consequences, time-outs, and empathetic communication and reasoning. Specialists who endorse these myriad strategies argue that they promote the internalization of moral judgment and self-discipline.... Harsh forms of punishment, including corporal punishment, are believed to inhibit parent–child communication and produce counterproductive degrees of guilt and aggression in youngsters.

In contrast to their mainstream counterparts, conservative Protestant parenting specialists strongly endorse the use of corporal punishment, albeit under specific conditions. In general, they recommend that physical punishment should be administered regularly: (1) on occasions of willful defiance to parental authority, (2) promptly after the defiant act, (3) with the use of a "rod," specifically designated for the purpose of physical chastisement, and (4) only to preadolescents.

Most conservative Protestant specialists support the use of corporal punishment for a variety of reasons. First, they believe that chastisement is commanded by Scripture. Indeed, they interpret some passages as indicating that chastisement is a sign of parental love and caring. Thus, in addition to serving as a behavioral corrective, corporal punishment is believed to promote youthful security by communicating both a deep concern for the child's welfare and an unswerving commitment to biblical principles.

Further, because children initially understand God in terms of parental images, conservative Protestants suggest that children will infer God's view of them based on the treatment they receive from their parents. These writers are quick to point out that parents should teach their children by example that God is loving, merciful, and forgiving. At the same time, however, because God's punishment of sin is understood as both inevitable and consistent, they also believe that parental discipline should embody these characteristics as well. Given such convictions, conservative Protestants argue that the experience of a loving physical discipline helps the child to develop an appropriate, accurate image of God and underscores the importance of obedience to His authority. Thus, corporal punishment is believed to demonstrate to the young child that deviation from biblical principles will provoke consistent and inevitable reproof from authorities in this life and from God in the next ....

Conclusion

...We began this study by noting that most previous analyses of the "battle over the family" have centered on the issue of gender roles and have given short shrift to debates over parenting. In contrast, we have argued that conflicts over parent–child relations should be viewed as a significant part of this contemporary cultural conflict ....

A number of recent books by conservative luminaries suggest that various "threats" to the welfare of American children—ranging from drugs and "cults" to public school counseling programs—are emerging as potent themes in the current and future campaigns of New Christian Right groups. Thus, it is vitally important that sociologists of religion and the family explore these developments, and the ideologies that legitimate them, with care.

References

Balter, L. (with A. Shreve). 1989. *Who's in control: Dr. Balter's guide to discipline without combat*. New York, NY: Poseidon Press.

Berger, B., and P. L. Berger. 1983. *The war over the family*. Garden City, NY: Anchor Press/Doubleday.

Cohen, H. 1980. *Equal rights for children*. Totowa, NJ: Littlefield, Adams. and Co.

Cohen, S., and M. F. Katzenstein. 1988. The war over the family is not over the family. In *Feminism, children, and the new families*, eds. S. M. Dornbusch and M. Strober, 25–46. New York, NY: Guilford Press.

Dobson, J. 1978. *The strong-willed child: Birth through adolescence*. Wheaton, IL: Living Books/Tyndale House.

Dornbusch, S., and M. Strober, eds. 1988. *Feminism, children, and the new families*. New York, NY: Guilford Press.

Faludi, S. 1991. *Backlash: The undeclared war against American women*. New York, NY: Basic Books.

Hunter, J. D. 1991. *Evangelicalism: The coming generation*. Chicago, IL: University of Chicago Press.

LeShan, E. 1985. *When your child drives you crazy*. New York, NY: St. Martin's Press.

Stacey, J. 1990. *Brave new families*. New York, NY: Basic Books.

Thorne, B., and M. Yalom, eds. 1982. *Rethinking the family: Some feminist questions*. New York, NY: Longman.

Wald, K. D., D. E. Owen, and S. S. Hill. 1989. Habits of the mind? The problem of authority in the New Christian Right. In *Religion and behavior in the United States*, ed. T. G. Jelen, 93–108. New York, NY: Praeger.

Close Reading Questions

1. Why do the authors of this sociological study believe the focus of family research should be expanded and to what new topic?

2. According to the authors, upon what biblical beliefs do the child-rearing practices of most conservative Protestants depend?

3. Although the authors want to focus on more than the gender-specific roles of parents, in what ways do the expected gender roles of parents differ between conservative Protestants and "mainstream" families? (Multiple Perspectives)

Analytical Writing/Discussion

4. According to the authors, how do conservative Protestants' assumptions about hierarchical authority and human nature lead them to beliefs about the goals of parenting and relationships with children that diverge from "mainstream" views? (Cultural Influences)

5. If some of the child-rearing practices of conservative Protestants seem outdated to you, then in what historical period do you think these practices might belong? Why might these practices seem sensible to many Americans during this period? (Historical Trends)

6. Bartkowski and Ellison refer to parenting manuals by leading authors to create a sharp contrast between "mainstream" and conservative Protestant families. Using examples from your own childhood and/or families you know well, to what degree does your personal knowledge confirm, contradict, or complicate the researchers' conclusions about the differences between these two types of families?

Further Options

7. The noted philosopher J. S. Mill once asserted that one who knows only his or her side of an argument knows little. What do you think he meant by this assertion, and can you apply it to the example of conservative Protestant and mainstream practices of child punishment? Using specific references to this text, can you explain why the "side" with which you do not agree believes its punishment practices are sensible and beneficial?

8. In Chapter 2 on Writing Assignments, the issue of the elaborate language of academic discourse is raised (see pp. 23–42). Why do you think these sociologists use language like "establish a paradigm for social relationships that is generalized to other spheres, especially the family"? Why, in general, do you think that academics usually employ complicated language in their scholarly writing?

FINDING FAMILIES FOR AFRICAN AMERICAN CHILDREN: THE CHALLENGES OF TRANSRACIAL ADOPTION

by Susan Smith, Ruth McRoy, Madelyn Freundlich, and Joe Kroll
of The Evan B. Donaldson Adoption Institute

According to the US Department of Health and Human Services, nearly 500,000 children were in the foster care system in 2007. That same year, only 51,000 children left the public foster care system to join adoptive homes. The issue of race plays a salient role in the adoption process: African American children spend longer in foster care than other children and are adopted at lower rates than children of other races. In an effort to encourage the adoption of children of color, the Multiethnic Placement Act of 1994 prevents discrimination in the placement of children of color (with the exception of Native American children). The following policy paper, published by The Evan B. Donaldson Adoption Institute in 2008, examines the laws that affect the transracial adoption of African American children and the extent to which adoption across racial boundaries affects children and parents.

When children cannot grow up in their families of origin, adoption can provide new parents who can love and guide them through childhood and into adulthood. The benefits of adoption are well recognized; at the same time, it also can present complexities for children and their adoptive families that are not typically found in families of origin—issues related to separation and loss, belonging, and identity. Children may come to adoption from social, economic, and racial and cultural backgrounds that differ from those of their new parents. For many children who are adopted from a different racial or ethnic background and/or from countries other than the United States, these differences can be visibly evident.

Transracial adoption is generally defined as occurring when a child's race/ethnicity is different than that of both parents when a couple adopts or that of a single parent when only one adopts. Transracial adoption—which primarily involves White parents adopting children of color—has been the subject of discourse and debate for decades. In books, articles, and professional discussions for much of the past 50 years, it frequently has been portrayed in a polarizing manner, as either "good" or "bad" for children. The most intense discussion has centered on the placement of African American children with White parents. All sides lay claim to the "best interest of the child," with very different concepts of what that means.

In practice, transracial adoption is not inherently good or bad but, rather, is a practice that benefits some children who may not otherwise have families to raise them. At the same time, this practice clearly adds an

From *Finding Families for African American Children: The Role of Race & Law in Adoption From Foster Care* (May 2008) by Evan B. Donaldson Adoption Institute. Copyright © 2008 by The Donaldson Adoption Institute. Reprinted by permission.

additional layer of complexity to the issues dealt with by adoptive families. White parents adopting children of other racial or ethnic groups can provide excellent nurturance, but they need to address their sons' and daughters' racial/ethnic identity issues to fully meet their needs as they develop. Children's racial and ethnic needs and issues include the implications of the physical difference between children and parents, especially in relation to handling the reactions of others; the children's gaining understanding of and comfort with their own race/ethnicity; learning social skills to interact comfortably with peers; and learning coping skills to deal with discrimination. Adoption practitioners and policymakers therefore need to address some difficult questions relating to transracial adoption in order to best serve children and families.

The Historical Role of Race in African American Adoptions

Throughout most of the nineteenth century and beyond, transracial adoption in the United States rarely occurred and, as a result of racism institutionalized in law, it was illegal in many states. During this time, adoption was largely arranged informally and, to the extent that efforts were made to "match" children with adoptive families, religion was the most important criterion. By the mid-twentieth century, adoption had become the province of professional social workers, who assumed the responsibility for placing children. They utilized a wide range of criteria that were considered vital to a proper "match" in a social environment that required children and adoptive parents to share as many traits as possible, from physical appearance (including race) to religious and cultural background to potential talents. Within the context of the country's highly segregated social environment during the 1950s and 1960s—including antimiscegenation laws that prohibited interracial marriage—transracial adoption was rare (Freundlich, 2000).

Although there were a few transracial placements as early as the 1940s, the practice began in earnest in the 1960s as a result of two significant developments. First, the civil rights movement significantly altered societal views of racial relationships; as integration was embraced as an ideal in the 1960s, interest in transracial adoption began to grow. At the same time, changes occurred in the demographic profile of children available for adoption; that is, the number of healthy Caucasian infants relinquished for adoption began to decline as a result of changing attitudes about single parenting, the legalization of abortion, and the increased use of contraceptives. White couples continued to want to adopt, so a growing number began to seek biracial or minority infants. Adoption agencies, including some private ones that had previously discouraged the relinquishment of children of color, began to accept them for adoptive placement planning (Day, 1979), and they started being placed with White families.

From a historical perspective, racial matching has been the predominant practice. In 1958, the Adoption Standards of the Child Welfare League of America (CWLA), a national association of public and private child welfare agencies, suggested that in most cases, children with the same racial characteristics as their new parents would more easily be incorporated into the family. In the 1950s and into the 1960s, formal adoptions primarily involved the placement of White infants with White families. Stringent criteria were used to qualify parents seeking to adopt a healthy White infant, considered the "ideal adoptable child." If White couples did not qualify for such an infant (often as a result of parental age or number of children already in the home), some agencies considered the family for a "child with special needs," typically one who was Black, of mixed race, older, or with emotional, behavioral, or health issues (McRoy, 1989).

In 1968, the CWLA revised its Adoption Standards and incorporated transracial adoptions. The new standards stated that "in most communities, there are families who have the capacity to adopt a child whose racial background is different from their own. Such couples should be encouraged to consider such a child" (CWLA, 1968, p. 34). With greater acceptance of transracial adoptions, their numbers began to grow. By 1971, the number of transracially adopted Black children reportedly reached 2,574 (Simon & Altstein, 1987).

In 1972, as a result of concerns about the growing number of Black children being placed with White families, the National Association of Black Social Workers (NABSW) issued a position statement opposing transracial adoption. The NABSW stated that Black children "belong physically and psychologically and culturally in Black families where they receive the total sense of themselves and develop a sound projection of their future" (NABSW, 1972, pp. 2–3). African American leaders also expressed concern about limited efforts to recruit Black families to adopt these children. Despite the fact that Black children historically had been cared for within their families and communities and informally adopted at significant rates, agencies—which were primarily and often exclusively staffed by White caseworkers—seldom recruited from African American communities (Duncan, 2005). Concerns grew that many White workers "knew little about stable African American families or their potential as resources for the children" (Duncan, 2005, p. 2), and they assumed such families were either not available or were not interested in adopting (Sullivan, 1994).

The Impact of Transracial Adoption on Children of Color

Although he was not adopted, Barack Obama's struggle to come to terms with racial identity issues without close relationships with Black caring adults mirrors the emotional struggles of many transracially adopted individuals—though these experiences obviously vary. In describing his experience, he wrote:

> Away from my mother, away from my grandparents, I was engaged in a fitful interior struggle. I was trying to raise myself to be a black man in America, and beyond the given of my appearance, no one around me seemed to know exactly what that meant. (Obama, 2004, p. 76)

Many transracially adopted individuals become highly competent in matters of race and successfully negotiate challenges regarding their racial identity and their place in the cultures of both their adoptive and birth families. Others deal with moderate difficulties that they are able to resolve as they achieve the developmental tasks of adolescence and adulthood. Yet others experience strong feelings of marginality and difficulties in self-acceptance that persist through childhood and into their later lives.

Transracially adopted children face challenges in coping with being "different." Coming to terms with a sense of difference is challenging for many adopted children in various areas of their lives and is compounded by transracial adoption. Research has not specifically addressed issues of color differences for Black children adopted from foster care, but the recent findings of a study of intercountry transracially adopted children (Juffer, 2006) shed light on transracially adopted children's perceptions. For example, based on parent reports, many of these children—particularly those with dark skin color—expressed the wish to be White....

Some studies have found transracially adopted children struggle more with acceptance and comfort with their physical appearance than do children placed in-race (Andujo, 1988; Kim, 1995). Although some children leave this feeling behind, many transracial adoptees continue to have a sense of difference into adulthood. Brooks and Barth (1999) studied 25-year-old adoptees and reported that about half of African American and Asian transracial adoptees expressed discomfort about their ethno-racial appearance. Feigelman (2000) found that appearance discomfort was linked with higher levels of adjustment difficulties in transracially adopted young adults.

Research and reports from transracially adopted adults indicate that the sense of physical difference is more intense for children of color growing up in homogeneous White communities. One Black man who grew up with White parents in a small Minnesota town described his pervasive feelings of difference while growing up: "I always felt like I had this 'A' on my forehead, this adoptee, that people could see from a far distance that I was different" (Clemetson & Nixon, 2006, p. A18). Feigelman (2000) found transracial adoptees—adopted in the early 1970s—who were raised in heavily White communities were twice as likely as adoptees living in racially mixed areas to feel discomfort with their appearance (51 percent versus 25 percent). Feigelman summarized his findings as follows:

> One of the study's most striking findings showed that transracial adoptive parents' decisions on where to live had a substantial impact upon their children's adjustments. Transracial adoptive parents residing in predominately White communities tended to have adoptees who experienced more discomfort about their appearance than those who lived in integrated settings. Adoptees feeling more discomfort, in turn, were more likely to have adjustment difficulties. (p. 180)

Transracially adopted children often struggle to fit in—within their own families, their social environments, and their cultures of origin .... In a study by de Haymes and Simon (2003), transracially adopted youth described their struggles to "fit in" and their beliefs about the importance of addressing this issue:

> If we lived in a different neighborhood, I'd feel more comfortable. People wouldn't ask so many questions or call me names. I feel a little more comfortable around people who are my color because I know they won't call me names. (p. 261)

Reports from transracial adoptees at times describe struggles to feel a sense of belonging within their cultures of origin. A transracially adopted African American man interviewed for a *New York Times* story said he always felt awkward around other Blacks because he did not understand their culture, trends in fashion or music, activities (such as playing the dozens), or the Black oral tradition of dueling insults (Clemetson & Nixon, 2006). Having grown up in a small town in Minnesota, few people around him could help him develop an understanding of Black culture. Others who grew up in similar situations have reported that it was not until they went to college that they began to cultivate relationships with persons of their own race. John Raible (1990), a transracial adoptee, described his struggle:

> I got to know other middle-class black students as real people who were not that different from me. I began to appreciate the variety of ways of being black .... Yet all was not smooth sailing, by any means. I felt nervous and anxious around my new black friends and peers. I was self-conscious about sounding or acting 'too white.' I felt scrutinized for having white girlfriends, and continued to fret over being rejected and not being taken seriously as an equal .... When my parents would come to visit, I was self-conscious about being seen with them. I worried about being seen too often, or in the 'wrong' places, with my white friends. I was very aware of feeling caught between two cultures, of having to tread the line between two worlds.

Raible's experience illustrates the marginal man phenomenon experienced by those who are, to a large extent, caught between two cultures.

Transracially adopted children may struggle to develop a positive racial/ethnic identity. Racial/ethnic identity, a component of personal identity, develops over the course of childhood, adolescence, and early adulthood. It is linked to some extent with a child's cognitive abilities and developmental stage. Generally, by age 4, children are aware of physical racial differences, and, by age 9, they can see themselves through the eyes of others and understand the consequences of a particular racial group membership, including prejudice (Lee & Quintana, 2005). This process has particularly important implications for African American children for whom racial/ethnic identity is salient and closely tied to self-esteem (Phinney, 1991).

Research has focused on various constructs related to the ethnic/racial identity of transracially adopted persons, including self-identification, attitudes toward one's own group, a sense of belonging to a given group, a reference group orientation, and racial preferences. McRoy and colleagues conducted one of the few early studies that included measures of both self-esteem and racial identity for same-race and transracially adopted children (McRoy et al., 1982). Although the researchers found no significant differences between transracially and in-racially adopted children on self-esteem, they found transracially adopted children scored lower on racial identity measures than their in-race counterparts. They further found that the manner in which White parents addressed race was linked with the extent to which their children acknowledged racial differences. Black children had a greater sense of racial pride when their parents acknowledged racial identity, moved to integrated neighborhoods, and provided African American role models. Black children whose White parents minimized the importance of racial identity were reluctant to identify themselves racially. Eighty percent of the transracially adopted Black children had been told that "they were not like other Blacks" (McRoy et al., 1984, p. 38). Andujo (1988) found similar results in her study of 60 Mexican American children placed with Hispanic and White families ....

Three critical areas of cultural competence for transracial adoptive parenting have been identified in professional literature: racial awareness, multicultural planning, and survival skills (Vonk, 2001). The following summary discusses each area and draws on comments from transracial adoptive parents and children asked about their service needs (de Haymes & Simon, 2003):

Racial awareness: This is defined as self-awareness of one's own experiences and attitudes regarding race and difference; awareness of the roles that race, ethnicity, and culture play in children's development; and understanding of the importance of these issues in fostering a child's positive identity development.

> Transracial adoption will change your life forever .... You are not the same person you were when you adopted a child transracially. I'm not just a white, middle-class mother anymore, but the mother of two Black children. I've changed. (p. 262)

> Racism is subtle and not always overt. White families need to be tuned into the pressures that a Black child experiences. The agencies need to have classes by people who are knowledgeable in this area. They need to know about racism and how it manifests itself. It can be subtle exclusion. We had to take our son out of the preschool because he was always the one assumed to be the cause of trouble. (p. 268)

Multicultural planning: Through this process, families create ways for children to learn about their racial/ethnic groups and access relationships and experiences that afford children opportunities for positive identity development.

> Some of the biggest challenges have involved getting access to her culture, her heritage, and her people. (p. 260)

> I would advise a family who wanted to adopt transracially to find out what the neighborhood is like where they are going to live and to see what kinds of kids are there. Talk to the neighbors about racial issues first. Make sure that people will not treat the kids as outcasts, but like normal children, which is what we are. (p. 260)

Survival skills: Recognizing that children of color need specific skills in a society in which racism continues to exist, professionals prepare parents to help their children and themselves cope successfully with racial prejudice and discrimination. ("Survival skills" is a term used in the literature to refer to coping skills for overcoming discrimination.)

> As far as transracial, it is a huge responsibility, because America is extremely racist. Some parents say, 'I'm not out to change the world.' That is so naïve. You are out to change the world for your child. It's not just going to be nice. You don't want to pass it over when your child gets called a racist name, and give a sugar coating to it by saying something like 'All children get called names.' Some people [who adopted transracially] say things like 'Some children get called names because they wear glasses.' That's a whole different issue than racism (p. 263).

In some cases, both Black and White parents may express interest in adopting a specific African American child. In selecting the most appropriate family, it is essential to assess each one's strengths and abilities to meet the child's needs. Just as the assessment must address the family's ability to address any specific physical health, emotional, behavioral, or developmental issue, it must also address the family's ability to meet the child's racial/ethnic identity and socialization needs. The assessment also must take into consideration how the child will fit in with other children in the family, the parents' preferences and expectations, and their willingness to support the child in maintaining appropriate relationships with birth siblings and other family members.

Color Consciousness—Not "Color Blindness"—Adoption Policy

Race is a factor in adoption decisions. Although it should definitely not be the primary or sole basis for choosing an adoptive family, it cannot be dismissed as irrelevant to a child's healthy development and adjustment. Whether adopted by Black or White parents, children's best interests are served by ongoing connections to their racial heritage. The CWLA's *Standards of Excellence for Adoption* (2000) state that all children deserve to be raised in families that respect their cultural heritage: "Assessing and preparing a child for a transracial/transcultural adoption should recognize the importance of culture and race to the child and his or her experiences and identification. The adoptive family selected should demonstrate an awareness of and sensitivity to the cultural resources that may be needed after placement."

When parents adopt transracially, they and their children are not well served when they do not receive preparation and training that promote racial awareness and assist them with multicultural planning and the development of survival and coping skills. Families lose critical opportunities to gauge their own preparedness to adopt transracially and to develop the awareness and skills essential to meeting their children's racial/ethnic identity and socialization needs. Failing to provide families with this preparation and training is contrary to sound and ethical social work practices and contrary to the best interests of children.

References

Andujo, E. (1988). Ethnic identity of transracially adopted Hispanic adolescents. *Social Work, 33*, 531–535.

Brooks, D., & Barth, R.P. (1999). Adult transracial and inracial adoptees: Effects of race, gender, adoptive family structure, and placement history on adjustment outcomes. *American Journal of Orthopsychiatry, 69*, 87–99.

Child Welfare League of America (1968). *Standards of Excellence for Adoption Services.* Washington, DC: Author.

Child Welfare League of America (2000). *Standards of Excellence for Adoption Services*. Washington, DC: Author.

Clemetson, L., & Nixon, R. (August 17, 2006). Breaking through adoption's racial barriers. *New York Times*.

Convention on Protection of Children & Co-operation in Respect of Intercountry Adoption. (1993). Available online at: http://hcch.e-vision.nl/index_en.php?act=conventions.text&cid=69.

Day, D. (1979). *The adoption of Black children*. Lexington, MA: Heath and Company.

De Haymes, M. V., & Simon, S. (2003). Transracial adoption: Families identify issues and needed support services. *Child Welfare, 82*(2), 251–272.

Duncan, S. (2005). Black adoption myths & realities. *Adoptalk* (Summer), North American Council on Adoptable Children, 1–5.

Feigelman, W. (2000). Adjustments of transracially and inracially adopted young adults. *Child and Adolescent Social Work Journal, 17*, 165–183.

Freundlich, M. (2000). Adoption and ethics, Volume I: *The role of race, culture, and national origin in adoption*. Washington, DC: Child Welfare League of America and Evan B. Donaldson Adoption Institute. Available online at: http://www.holtintl.org/pdfs/Survey2.pdf.

Juffer, F. (2006). Children's awareness of adoption and their problem behavior in families with 7-year-old internationally adopted children. *Adoption Quarterly, 9*(2/3), 1–22.

Kim, W. J. (1995). International adoption: A case review of Korean children. *Child Psychiatry and Human Development, 25*(3), 141–154.

Lee, D., & Quintana, S. (2005). Benefits of cultural exposure and development of Korean perspective-taking ability for transracially adopted Korean children. *Cultural Diversity and Ethnic Minority Psychology, 11*(2), 130–143.

McRoy, R. G. (1989). An organizational dilemma: The case of transracial adoptions. *Journal of Applied Behavioral Science, 25* (2) 145–160.

McRoy, R., Zurcher, L. A., Lauderdale, M. L., & Anderson, R. M. (1982). Self-esteem and racial identity in transracial adoption. *Social Work, 27*, 522–526.

McRoy, R. G., Zurcher, L. A., Lauderdale, M. L., & Anderson, R. L. (1984). The identity of transracial adoptees. *Social Casework, 65*, 34–39.

National Association of Black Social Workers. (1972, April). Position statement on transracial adoptions. Presented at the National Association of Black Social Workers Conference, Nashville, TN.

Obama, B. (2004). *Dreams from my father*. New York: Three Rivers Press.

Phinney, J. S. (1991). Ethnic identity and self-esteem: A review and integration. *Hispanic Journal of Behavioral Sciences, 13*(2), 193–208.

Raible, J. (1990). The significance of racial identity in transracially adopted young adults. Available online at: http://www.nysccc.org/T-Rarts/Articles/Raible/RacialSignigicance.html. (accessed August 16, 2007)

Simon, R. J., & Altstein, H. (1987). *Transracial adoptees and their families: A study of identity and commitment*. New York: Praeger.

Sullivan, A. (1994). On transracial adoption. *Children's Voice, 3*(3), 4–6.

Vonk, M .E. (2001). Cultural competence for transracial adoptive parents. *Social Work, 46*(3), 246–254.

Close Reading Questions

1. According to the Donaldson report, what events helped to cause a rise in transracial a doptions?

2. According to the report, what are the three reasons that transracial adoptees struggle to identify with their adoptive parents?

3. Why does the Donaldson report suggest that white parents who want to adopt children of color should pay particular attention to "racial awareness, multicultural planning, and survival skills?"

Analytical Writing/Discussion

4. By the 1950s, social workers were largely responsible for placing children with adoptive parents. To what extent do you think those placements were affected by existing values about race, religion, and socioeconomic status? (Cultural Influences)

5. The voices of transracial adoptees add a personal note to the Donaldson report. Making specific references to the quotations from transracial adoptees, what do you think are some of the most significant challenges they face as children and young adults?

6. Given the rise in the number of African-American children available for adoption, why do you think the position of the National Association of Black Social Workers (NABSW) is or is not still legitimate? What is the implication for children if the NABSW stance is outdated? (Historical Trends)

Further Options

7. Using some of the methods described in Chapter 5 on Argument, how persuasive do you find some of the positions about transracial adoption made by researchers and professional organizations versus those of adoptees and their parents? What makes the positions persuasive or how do you think they could be improved? (Multiple Perspectives)

8. The Child Welfare League of America asserts, "All children deserve to be raised in families that respect their cultural heritage." Using the consensus building techniques of a Rogerian argument explained in Chapter 5 on Rhetoric (see pp. 113–114), what common ground do you think can be created on respecting the cultural heritage of transracial adoptees?

WHAT MAKES A FAMILY?

by Vanessa de la Torre

Published in the *Hartford Courant* on Nov. 21, 2014, this news report presents a recent controversy over family, housing, and zoning. As the capital city of Connecticut, Hartford (like most cities and towns) has multiple zoning areas with different kinds of housing and occupancy allowed in each area. In this reading, love, law, and biology intersect, sometimes in conflict and other times in agreement. This debate reflects the historical trends of American families as well as their contemporary variety.

A neighborhood [squabble] on one of the city's wealthiest residential streets has triggered a cease-and-desist order, fervent appeals and debate over what constitutes a family.

The controversy centers on 68 Scarborough St., a nine-bedroom brick mansion shared by eight adults and three children—an arrangement among longtime friends who share monthly expenses, chores and legal ownership of the stately home, said Julia Rosenblatt, who lives there with her husband and two kids.

The residents bought the nearly 6,000-square-foot house for $453,000 in August, although only two of the owners are listed on the mortgage and city property record. They take turns cooking dinner, have

Copyright © 2008. Hartford Courant. Reprinted with Permission.

pooled money into one bank account and entertained themselves last week with a family talent show because, Rosenblatt said, "Thursday, we intentionally came together as a family."

But a coalition of neighbors, while conceding that the occupants of 68 Scarborough "are nice people," have argued that the nontraditional household violates the neighborhood's zoning for single-family homes. Living in the house are two couples with children, a couple with no children and two individuals.

About three weeks ago, 68 Scarborough was hit with a cease-and-desist order from the city after zoning officials determined that the setup "doesn't meet the definition of a family," said Thomas Deller, the city's director of development services, which oversees zoning code enforcement. The city's code defines members of a family as those related by blood, marriage, civil union or legal adoption.

It was unclear Thursday whether the owners eventually would be forced to vacate the home or sell it. Rosenblatt said they have appealed the order to the Hartford Zoning Board of Appeals.

"Now it's just the waiting game," said Joshua Blanchfield, Rosenblatt's husband and a teacher at a [magnet school] in Hartford. If the residents at 68 Scarborough lose their appeal, "they need to conform to city zoning," Deller said. He added that they also have the right to sue, and "that's something they'll have to decide."

"We don't know yet what all of our steps are; we're just trying to figure this out," said Rosenblatt, a cofounder of [a local] theater company. "It's quite unnerving and upsetting. ... What is scarier than talking about losing your own home?"

The West End Civic Association convened a committee meeting Wednesday night to hear arguments from both sides. Dozens showed up to back the 68 Scarborough residents, a group that includes Blanchfield and another Hartford public school teacher, a professor at Capital Community College, employees for Charter Oak Cultural Center and the Wheeler Clinic, and a stay-at-home dad.

Rather than a fight over one mansion, neighbors who oppose the arrangement have framed their case as a broader stand against any challenges to Scarborough's single-family zoning that could chip away at the quiet character of the affluent, estate-lined street.

The University of Connecticut Foundation, Wadsworth Atheneum and [a Hartford] charter school group each own property on Scarborough. Neighbors opposed [the charter group's] now-defunct plans to use the former Hartford Medical Society building for a school.

The 68 Scarborough owners "seem like a nice group of people," said John Gale, chairman of the West End association's planning and zoning committee. On the other hand, he said, he also sympathizes with the concern that a "Pandora's box" might open without a strict interpretation of single-family homes.

In a statement to the West End Civic Association, which may decide to issue a recommendation to the city, the neighbors compared the use of a single dwelling by multiple families to "an apartment building, or a rooming house, or a fraternity house." The letter was endorsed by the residents of 16 homes on Scarborough Street and a couple who lives on neighboring Asylum Ave.

"Regrettably, over the years ... people have attempted to change properties away from single-family housing," the letter stated. "We have learned that we cannot ignore violations that will set a precedent and provide a legal standard to allow multiple other properties to be changed on the same basis."

One notable Scarborough Street resident who did not sign the letter was Hartford City Council President Shawn Wooden, who said he has not taken a public position on the controversy.

The city may have to reconcile what Blanchfield described as "contradictory" language in its zoning regulations. One section calls for a maximum density of 3.6 families per acre in Scarborough's R-8 zoning district, although it's not clear that the rule applies to single-family lots. The mansion at 68 Scarborough, built in 1921, sits on two acres.

"The house is gigantic," said Brendan Mahoney, a friend of the owners. "I've had dinner there and everybody was home….. The house was designed to have that many people in it."

So far, the owners have spent about $20,000 to upgrade the plumbing—there are six bathrooms—and the electrical system to bring the home up to code, Blanchfield said. They have a household bank account to share the cost of groceries, utilities and mortgage payments, and have also gotten used to the emotional support.

"Even just coming home at the end of the day, from a rough day," Rosenblatt said. "Because there's so many more people to help out, and to be good to each other, it just feels a lot less lonely than I think it might otherwise be." Next week, the children are planning a night of charades, she said. "We're not trying to change the zoning law," she said. "We're trying to change the definition of a family."

To learn more about this controversy and its outcome, see the Additional Sources for Chapter 6 (see pp. 170 and 171).

Close Reading Questions

1. Who are the members of the group living together at 68 Scarborough St.? What is your initial reaction to this group (surprise, doubt, support, etc.) and why?

2. In what ways is this group like or unlike families you know?

3. What are some of the most significant consequences of the zoning decision for the residents of 68 Scarborough St. and for their neighbors?

Analytical Writing/Discussion

4. What inconsistencies in the zoning regulations seem to both permit and forbid the household at 68 Scarborough St.? (Multiple Perspectives)

5. The definition of family can emphasize the form of this group (i.e., "those related by blood") or its function (i.e., how member love and care for one another). Why do you think the legal definition of a family should emphasize the form or the function of this group? (Cultural Influences)?

6. Please read the related opinion essays that are available in the additional sources of this chapter ten. Which opinion essay do you think offers the most persuasive defense the residents of 68 Scarborough St. and why? Which one do you think provides the most convincing opposition and why? Quote from two of these supplemental sources and explain your reaction to their pro/con arguments.

Further Options

7. How does the example of the preindustrial family living a "big house" that Hareven describes in "The Nineteenth Century Retreat" (see pp. 127–136) support the definition of family sought by Julia Rosenblatt and others in her home? Why do you think this earlier concept of family is or is not relevant to the current controversy over the residency of 68 Scarborough St.? (Historical Trends)

8. The outcome of this controversy is explained in one of the additional sources of this chapter. For what reasons was this resolution reached, and why do you agree or disagree with this outcome?

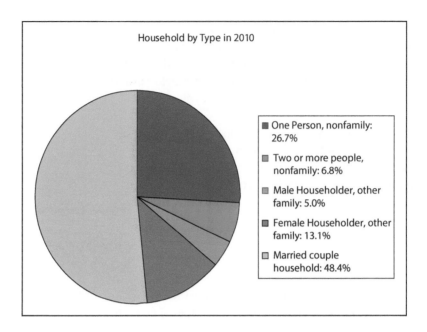

FIGURE 6.2 The percentage of various kinds of households based on 2010 US Census data. How can this information be used to support arguments for or against diverse family forms?

Freewrite 3: Televised Families

Although we do not always recognize the impact of television on our thinking, consider the influence of this media on your family's form and its members' roles. Brainstorm a list of as many television shows featuring families as you can recall. Include older shows as well as recent ones, dramas as well as comedies.

Then use freewriting and/or discussion to answer at least one of the following questions:

- How do you think the depiction of the family on television has changed from the 1950s to today?
- How similar is your own family to the most idealistic and/or the most realistic family shows?
- How have these television shows influenced, if at all, your assumptions about your own family?

Once you have completed this freewrite, you may want to expand this rough writing into a more formal paper by answering one of the questions below:

- To what degree do you think the depiction of family on television has reflected or guided the actual changes of families in American society?
- In addition to television, what are some other cultural influences on your perspective on American families?

Final Assignment 1: Defining the Family Form

For legal reasons, such as marriage, adoption, insurance, and taxation, the term "family" must be defined explicitly. For example, Douglass describes the enslavement of any child whose mother was a slave in nineteenth-century Southern families, and the Donaldson report examines the complexities of transracial adoptions in the twenty-first century. Thus, any attempt to define family must take into account these larger social contexts as well as the ability of various kinds of family forms to care for their members.

Essay Question

Given the great diversity of family forms today, how do you think "family" should be defined legally? Your definition of family must take into account the ability of various kinds of families to care for their members as well as the consequences of legal inclusion or exclusion of various families.

Write a formal and extended essay to answer this question. Be sure to include specific references and direct quotations from several readings in this chapter (see Chapter 4 on Academic Honesty on quoting and citing properly). Be sure to not only support your informed perspective but also anticipate and answer the possible objections of those who do not already agree with you. Your task is to assert your opinion and persuade others to consider it carefully.

Freewrite 4: Assignment Analysis

Before you start to answer this complex question, analyze its parts. Reread the question above and underline several phrases that represent key parts of the larger answer you will be developing. Then pick two or three of these phrases and freewrite your immediate impressions: What do you think right now? Then, pause to look for connections, contradictions, and omissions within your first response: What else do you want to discuss, what else do you want to add, and/or what order of your ideas is developing? Finally, consider the audience of your essay: Who does not agree with you already, and why might they disagree?

Reading Review

Once you have sketched some of your initial ideas, review some of the readings to find specific details and persuasive evidence to support, enrich, and possibly complicate your response. Here are some readings and post-reading questions that you may want to consider:

1. Freewrite 1
2. Hareven, Close Reading Question 1
3. Hareven, Close Reading Question 3
4. Figure 6.1
5. Douglass, Analytical Writing Question 6
6. Bartkowski and Ellison, Close Reading Question 3
7. Bartkowski and Ellison, Analytical Writing Question 6
8. Donaldson Report, Analytical Writing Question 5

Feel free to include other readings and post-reading questions. You also may want to review the suggestions for writing persuasively in Chapter 5 on Argument as well as to practice the peer response described in Chapter 2 on the Writing Process.

Final Assignment 2: Rhetorical Analysis

For two readings of this chapter (or possibly using one of the additional readings suggested below), compare and/or contrast their arguments. As explained in Chapter 5, this rhetorical analysis will answer the following questions:

- Based on the rhetorical triangle, what is the message of this text? What does the publication source suggest about the audience of this text? How do you think these readers will react to this message and why? Finally, who is the writer, and how might the author affect the audience's response to the text? (See pp. 104–105 of Chapter 5.)

- How does the writer try to use each of the three rhetorical appeals: ethos, logos, and pathos, and when are they used effectively or not? (See pp. 105–109 of Chapter 5).

- Your professor may ask you to consider also the kind of argument being made, meaning a forensic, epideictic, or deliberative argument (see pp. 110–112 of Chapter 5). What kind of argument is being made, and how does it affect the audience's reaction to this persuasion?

- Finally, through comparing and contrasting the arguments of these two readings, what can you conclude about their power to persuade their intended audiences (and possibly additional readers)?

Your task is to help your readers to understand these two arguments and their efforts to persuade their audiences.

Final Assignment 3: Describing Parental Roles

In "The Revolt of 'Mother,'" Mary Wilkins Freeman questions the nineteenth-century concept of a mother as Sarah Penn challenges some of her husband's family decisions (see pp. 140–150). In "Parenting 101," Bartkowski and Ellison present the conservative advocacy of two-parent families with a mother and a father (see pp. 150–156). Thus, the roles of parents have been and will continue to be the subject of considerable debate.

Essay Question

Given the controversies over married, divorced, single, and homosexual parents, who do you think is capable (or not) of fathering and mothering a child well? Your description of parental roles should include both what is ideal and what is realistic in America today.

Write a formal and extended essay to answer this question. Be sure to include specific references and direct quotations from several readings in this chapter (see Chapter 4 on Academic Honesty on quoting and citing properly). Be sure to not only support your informed perspective but also anticipate and answer the possible objections of those who do not already agree with you. Your task is to assert your opinion and persuade others to consider it carefully.

Freewrite 5: Assignment Analysis

Before you start to answer this complex question, analyze its parts. Reread the question above and underline several phrases that represent key parts of the larger answer you will be developing. Then pick two or three of these phrases and freewrite your immediate impressions: What do you think right now? Then, pause to look for connections, contradictions, and omissions within your first response: What else do you want to discuss, what else do you want to add, and/or what order of your ideas is developing? Finally, consider the audience of your essay: Who does not agree with you already, and why might they disagree?

Reading Review

Once you have sketched some of your initial ideas, review some of the readings to find specific details and persuasive evidence to support, enrich, and possibly complicate your response. Here are some readings and post-reading questions that you may want to consider:

1. Hareven, Analytical Writing Question 5
2. Freeman, Analytical Writing Question 5
3. Freeman, Analytical Writing Question 6
4. Freewrite 2
5. Bartkowski and Ellison, Close Reading Question 3
6. Donaldson report, Close Reading Question 3
7. Figure 6.2
8. de la Torre, Analytical Writing Question 5

Feel free to include other readings and post-reading questions. You also may want to review the suggestions for writing persuasively in Chapter 5 on Argument as well as to practice the peer response described in Chapter 2 on the Writing Process.

Readings on Family in Other Chapters

For two additional readings on education, you may want to read the following texts:

1. "Motorcycle Talk" by Thomas Simmons in Chapter 3 (see pp. 56–59)
2. "In Search of Our Mothers' Gardens" by Alice Walker in Chapter 8 (see pp. 216–222)

Additional Sources for Chapter 6

To deepen your understanding of American families and strengthen your final assignment for Chapter 6, you can consult some of the following sources:

1. To learn more about the designs of American homes since the nineteenth century (as analyzed by Hareven in this chapter), you may want to read (or listen to) "Behind the Ever-Expanding American Trend House" by Margot Adler. This report on National Public Radio analyzes the continuing trend by many Americans to desire larger homes to match the form and the function of their families. You also may want to read "Overstuffed: Clutter, Consumption . . ." by Michael De Groote. This news reports presents a study of the cluttered homes of Americans today.

   http://www.npr.org/templates/story/story.php?storyId=5525283

   http://www.deseretnews.com/article/865564019/Overstuffed-Clutter-consumption-and-the-study-that-shows-how-possessions-shapes-us.html

2. For more on the development of American families in the last two centuries, you may want to read "The American Family" by Stephanie Coontz. As a leading family historian, Coontz may surprise you on what you think you know about families today and what you think their future will be.

   http://www.stephaniecoontz.com/articles/article10.htm

3. To learn more about conservative perspectives on the American family and this issue in society, you may want to read two controversial texts. The first is titled "20 Years Later, It Turns Out Dan Quayle Was Right about Murphy Brown and Unmarried Moms." In 2012, a *Washington Post* reporter named Isabel Sawhill revisited the debate over family values and declared that "Dan Quayle was right." She was referring to former Vice President Dan Quayle's speech during the 1992 election that ignited the political debate over the forms and values of American families. See the links for both readings below:

   http://www.washingtonpost.com/opinions/20-years-later-it-turns-out-dan-quayle-was-right-about-murphy-brown-and-unmarried-moms/2012/05/25/gJQAsNCJqU_story.html

   http://www.vicepresidentdanquayle.com/speeches_StandingFirm_CCC_1.html

4. For multiple perspectives on the American family, you may want to read "The Changing American Family" by Natalie Angier. This 2013 report in the *New York Times* chronicles many kinds of families and how they function today.

   http://www.nytimes.com/2013/11/26/health/families.html?pagewanted=all&_r=0

5. For diverse opinions on the family and zoning controversy created by the household living together at 68 Scarborough Street in Hartford, CT, you may want to read "Scarborough Street: Testing the Zone." These five opinion essays present an array of viewpoints on family definition and zoning regulations. Then in a later report, the outcome of this controversy was reported in "Scarborough 11 To Stay."

http://www.courant.com/opinion/op-ed/hc-scarborough-street-controversy-1130-20141128-story.html#page=1

http://www.courant.com/community/hartford/hc-hartford-scarborough11-withdrawal-1028-20161027-story.html

6. For two recent perspectives in support of "traditional" marriages and families, you may want to read the following two news articles by Ruth Graham and Jonah Goldberg, respectively.

   https://www.bostonglobe.com/ideas/2015/04/25/scholarly-kiss-for-wedded-bliss/INyenlyr0FIuWzaJDuFWGK/story.html

   http://www.latimes.com/opinion/op-ed/la-oe-1027-goldberg-family-structure-20151027-column.html

7. For an example of how cultural influences, such as the media and government institutions, affect our perceptions of American families, you may want to read "Cheerios, Gay Marriage and the Supreme Court" by Leonard Pitts Jr. This newspaper essay refers to television ads for Cheerios cereal so links to two ads are included below:

   http://www.tmsfeatures.com/columns/political/independent/leonard-pitts/Leonard-Pitts-Jr-columnist.html?articleURL=http://rss.tmsfeatures.com/websvc-bin/rss_story_read.cgi?resid=201410071800TMS_____LPITTS___ctnwl-a_20141008

   Gracie ad:

   http://www.youtube.com/watch?v=pbWeH9cztHw

   Raphaelle ad:

   http://www.youtube.com/watch?v=QvHGKSqBVjs

8. In a landmark decision in 2015, the Supreme Court legalized gay marriage in every state, and one key factor in this decision was the effect on the children on gay parents who previously could not marry in thirteen states. To learn more about this ruling, you may want to read this report from the Huffington Post.

   http://www.huffingtonpost.com/2015/06/26/supreme-court-gay-marriage_n_7470036.html

Education and Outcomes

CHAPTER 7

Schooles. It being one chiefe project of that old deluder Sathan, to keepe men from knowledge of the Scriptures … [it is] ordered by this Courte and Authority thereof, that euery Towneshipp within this Jurissdiction, after the Lord hath increased them to the number of fifty householders, shall then forthwith appoint one within theire Towne to teach all such children as shall resorte to him, to read and write.

—*Connecticut General Court (1650)*

[Education is the great equalizer of the condition of men—the balance wheel of the social machinery.

—*Horace Mann (1848)*

In the field of public education, the doctrine of "separate but equal" has no place. Separate educational facilities are inherently unequal. Therefore, we hold that the plaintiffs and others similarly situated … are, by reason of the segregation complained of, deprived of the equal protection of the laws guaranteed by the Fourteenth Amendment.

—*US Supreme Court (Brown v. Board of Education, 1954)*

Thanks to No Child Left Behind, AYP's [Annual Yearly Progress] have replaced the ABC's as the most important letters in many schools.

—*Stan Karp (2004)*

Introduction

In colonial America, education was recognized as vital to society. For example, in 1650, the colony in Connecticut decided that every town with more than 50 households should establish schools to teach children to read and write because it is the "chief project of that old deluder Satan to keep men and women from knowledge of the Scripture." Thus, the goal of education was to promote faith through literacy.

A century later, the aim of education was less religious and more secular, such as when Benjamin Franklin in 1749 asserted that education is "the foundation of the happiness" of individual and communities. Students should learn "those things that are likely to be most useful" in the "professions for which they are intended." The outcomes expected for various students, however, varied greatly. In more prosperous families, sons were educated to be lawyers, doctors, and clergymen, while daughters were taught to be refined wives and good mothers. And this was not the only difference in educational outcomes. Children in less privileged families received very little formal education and instead were trained for trades, such as boys becoming carpenters or blacksmiths and girls becoming servants or seamstresses. In 1848, Horace Mann hoped that education would be "the great equalizer" in American society, but to the contrary, schools often have hindered rather than promoted equal opportunity in a country created as an egalitarian democracy.

As late as the 1890s, less than 7% of American adolescents attended high school, while most teenage children already were working in fields and factories. Fast-forward 60 years, and those fortunate enough to attend public high schools still were educated according to their expected social roles: males to be civic and economic leaders, and females to be the nurturers of offices and families. Such gender differences were not the only educational inequality that had to be confronted in the 1950s. The 1954 Supreme Court decision of *Brown v. Board of Education* rejected the racial segregation of students in what supposedly had been "separate but equal" schools. This desegregation of public schools, however, was met with public protests and violent acts in many communities, such as Little Rock, Alabama in 1956–1958 and Boston, Massachusetts in 1975–1977. Despite the dreams of Horace Mann in 1848 and later of Martin Luther King in the 1960s, equal access to education has not yet been achieved in many cities and towns.

Many public schools in urban areas, with large populations of minority and/or disadvantaged students, provide inadequate education, and some are labeled as nothing more than drop-out factories. Rural schools, with their small classes, serve as a model for some, but they struggle to meet state standards for enhanced curriculum, like Advanced Placement classes, and educational facilities, such as labs and libraries. Suburban schools, populated primarily by more affluent students, are assumed by many to offer the best education. Some educators, therefore, refer to college aptitude exams, like the SAT and ACT, as little more than zip code tests: where students live determines the likely results.

The persistent inequalities in education—based on race, gender, and class—have led to the increased involvement of the federal government in local schools. In addition to the 1954 *Brown* decision, the federal government has intervened to address economic disparities (the Elementary and Secondary Education Act [ESEA] of 1965), sexual discrimination (Title IX in 1972), and physical and mental disabilities (All Handicapped Children Act of 1975). This federal involvement culminated with the No Child Left Behind (NCLB) Act of 2001, seeking greater accountability in public education. The emphasis on NCLB mastery tests in many schools, however, has stripped enjoyment from education for many students and their teachers. Teaching to the test unfortunately has not eliminated the achievement gap between privileged and nonprivileged students.

The three historical readings of this chapter are all relatively recent ones. The oldest ones date back to 1938 and 1984, as John Dewey and Theodore Sizer criticize traditional education, and in another, Deborah Meier encourages a return to small school districts and less federal control of education. In the contemporary readings, each author asserts the need for school reform, but they differ, for instance, on the value of mastery tests that probably dominated your own education in grades K–12.

These texts, along with the reading questions, freewriting activities, and visual elements of this chapter, are designed to develop the reading and writing abilities required for academic study. After each reading, you will find a set of questions that are divided into Close Reading Questions, Analytical Writing/ Discussion, and Further Options. Some questions involve the same investigation of multiple perspectives, cultural influences, and historical trends that were introduced in Chapters 1 or 2. Answering some and discussing more of the postreading questions will better prepare you to complete the final assignments options. These final writing assignments will ask you to assert your own, more informed perspective on education, equality, and outcomes. This chapter asks: **What do you think should** of education?

Freewrite 1: Initial Impressions

Describe in detail a specific scene, either one from your actual memory or a co on several recollections that represents a significant aspect of your high school education. Imagine your pen is a video camcorder and collect impressions of the setting, the characters, the actions and inactivity, and the sounds and the silences. What are your dominant thoughts and feelings toward your high school learning? What scene best represents these feelings? Where were you? What was (and was not) happening? (For more on freewriting, see p. 25 of Chapter 2.)

WHAT HIGH SCHOOL IS

by Theodore Sizer

Theodore Sizer is one of America's leading educational reformers. As the author of *Horace's Compromise: The Dilemma of the American High School* (1984) and *Horace's School: Redesigning the American High School* (1992), he has examined the goals and methods of American high schools. As chair of the Coalition of Essential Schools, Sizer has helped individual schools engage in self-examination and enact many reforms. In this reading, excerpted from *Horace's Compromise* (1984), Sizer uses an imagined student named Mark to depict the daily realities of a public high school. (For more on previewing and annotating a text, see pp. 8–12 of Chapter 1.)

Mark, sixteen, and a genial eleventh-grader, rides a bus to Franklin High School, arriving at 7:25. It is Assembly Day, so the schedule is adapted to allow for a meeting of the entire school. He hangs out with his friends, first outside school then inside, by his locker. He carries a pile of textbooks and notebooks; in all, it weighs eight and a half pounds.

From 7:30 to 8:19, with nineteen other students, he is in Room 304 for English class. The Shakespeare play being read this year for eleventh grade is *Romeo and Juliet*. The teacher, Ms. Viola, has various students in turn take parts and read out loud. Periodically, she interrupts the (usually halting) recitations to ask whether the thread of the conversation in the play is clear. Mark is entertained by the stumbling readings of some of his classmates. He hopes he will not be asked to be Romeo, particularly if his current steady, Sally, is Juliet. There is a good deal of giggling in class, and much attention is paid to who may be called on next. Ms. Viola reminds the class of a test on this part of the play to be given next week.

The bell rings at 8:19. Mark goes to the boys' room, where he sees a classmate who he thinks is a wimp but who constantly tries to be a buddy. Mark avoids the leech by rushing off. On the way, he notices two

"What High School Is" from *Horace's Compromise* by Theodore R. Sizer. Copyright © 1984 by Theodore R. Sizer. Reprinted by permission of Houghton Mifflin Harcourt Publishing Company. All rights reserved.

...gaged in some sort of transaction, probably over marijuana. He pays them no attention. 8:24. ...ing class. The rows of desks that embrace the big office are almost filled before the bell. Mark is uncom-...rtable here: typing class is girl country. The teacher constantly threatens what is to Mark a humiliating female future: "Your employer won't like these erasures." The minutes during the period are spent copying a letter from a handbook onto business stationary. Mark struggles to keep from looking at his work; the teacher wants him to watch only the material from which he is copying. Mark is frustrated, uncomfort-able, and scared he will never complete his letter by the class's end, which would be embarrassing.

Nine-tenths of the students present at school that day are assembled in the auditorium by the 9:18 bell. The dilatory tenth still stumble in, running down the aisles. Annoyed class deans try to get the mob settled. The curtains part; the program is a concert by a student rock group. Their electronic gear flashes under the lights, and the five boys and one girl in the group work hard at being casual. Their movements on stage are studiously at three-quarter time, and they chat with one another as though the tumultuous screaming of their classmates were totally inaudible. The girl balances on a stool; the boys crank up the music. It is very soft rock, the sanitized lyrics surely cleared with the assistant principal. The girl sings, holding the mike close to her mouth, but can scarcely be heard. Her light voice is tentative, and the lyrics indecipherable. The guitars, amplified, are tuneful, however, and the drums are played with energy.

The students around Mark—all juniors, since they are seated by class—alternately slouch in their upholstered, hinged seats, talking to one another, or sit forward, leaning on the chair backs in front of them, watching the band. A boy near Mark shouts noisily at the microphone-fondling singer, "Bite it … ohhh," but quickly subsides. A teacher walks down the aisle. Songs continue, to great applause. Assembly is over at 9:46, two minutes early.

9:53 and biology class. Mark was at a different high school last year and did not take this course as a tenth-grader. He is in it now, and all but one of his classmates are a year younger than he. He sits on the side, not taking part in the chatter that goes on after the bell. At 9:57, the public address system goes on, with the announcements of the day. After a few words from the principal ("Here's today's cheers and jeers …" with a cheer for the winning basketball team and a jeer for the spectators who made a ruckus at the gymnasium), the task is taken over by the officers of ASB (Associated Student Bodies). There is an appeal for "bat bunnies." Carnations are for sale by the Girls' League. Miss Indian American is coming. Students are auctioning off their services (background catcalls are heard) to earn money for the prom. Nominees are needed for the ballot for the school bachelor and bachelorette. The announcements end with a "thought of the day. When you throw a little mud, you lose ground."

At 10:04 the biology class finally turns to science. The teacher, Mr. Robbins, has placed one of the several labeled laboratory specimens—some are pinned in frames, others swim in formaldehyde—on each of the classroom's eight laboratory tables. The three or so students whose chairs circle each of these benches are to study the specimen and make notes about it or drawings of it. After a few minutes each group of three will move to another table. The teacher points out that these specimens are of organisms already studied in previous classes. He says that the period-long test set for the following day will involve observing some of these specimens—then to be without labels—and writing an identifying paragraph on each. Mr. Robbins points out that some of the printed labels ascribe the specimen's names different from those given in the textbook. He explains that biologists often give several names to the same organism.

The class now falls to peering, writing, and quiet talking. Mr. Robbins comes over to Mark, and in whispered words asks him to carry a requisition form for science department materials to the business office. Mark, because of his "older" status, is usually chosen by Robbins for this kind of errand. Robbins gives Mark the form and a green hall pass to show any teacher who might challenge him, on his way to the office, for being out of a classroom. The errand takes Mark four minutes. Meanwhile Mark's group is hard at work but gets to only three of the specimens before the bell rings at 10:42. As the students surge out, Robbins shouts a reminder about a "double" laboratory period on Thursday.

Between classes one of the seniors asks Mark whether he plans to be a candidate for schoolwide office next year. Mark says no. He starts to explain. The 10:57 bell rings, meaning that he is late for French class.

There are fifteen students in Monsieur Bates' language class. He hands out tests taken the day before: "*C'est bien fait, Etienne … c'est mieux, Marie … Tch, tch, Robert …*" Mark notes his C+ and peeks at the A– in front of Susanna, next to him. The class has been assigned seats by M. Bates; Mark resents sitting next to prissy, brainy Susanna. Bates starts by asking a student to read question and give the correct answer. "*James, question un.*" James haltingly reads the question and gives an answer that Bates now speaking English, says is incomplete. In due course: "*Mark, question cinq.*" Mark does his bit, and the sequence goes on, the eight quiz questions and answers filling about twenty minutes of time.

"Turn to page forty-nine. *Maintenant, lisez après moi …*" and Bates reads a sentence and has the class echo it. Mark is embarrassed by this and mumbles with a barely audible sound. Others, like Susanna, keep the decibels up, so Mark can hide. This I-say-and-you-repeat drill is interrupted once by the public address system, with an announcement about a meeting for cheerleaders. Bates finishes the class, almost precisely at the bell, with a homework assignment. The students are to review these sentences for a brief quiz the following day. Mark makes note of the assignment, because he knows that tomorrow will be a busy-work day in French class. Much though he dislikes oral drills, they are better than the workbook stuff that Bates hands out. Write, write, and write, for Bates to throw away, Mark thinks.

11:36. Down to the cafeteria, talking noisily, hanging out, munching. Getting to Room 104 by 12:17: US history. The teacher is sitting cross-legged on his desk when Mark comes in, heatedly arguing with three students over the fracas that had followed the previous night's basketball game. The teacher, Mr. Suslovic, while agreeing that the spectators from their school certainly were provoked, argues that they should neither have been so obviously obscene in yelling at the opposing cheerleaders nor have allowed Coke cans to be rolled out on the floor. The three students keep saying that "it isn't fair." Apparently they and some others had been assigned "Saturday mornings" (detentions) by the principal for the ruckus.

At 12:34, the argument begins to subside. The uninvolved students, including Mark, are in their seats, chatting amiably. Mr. Suslovic climbs off his desk and starts talking "We've almost finished this unit, chapters nine and ten …" The students stop chattering among themselves and turn toward Suslovic. Several slouch down in their chairs. Some open notebooks. Most have the five-pound textbook on their desks.

Suslovic lectures on the cattle drives, from north Texas to railroads west of St. Louis. He breaks up this narrative with questions ("Why were the railroad lines laid east to west?"), directed at nobody in particular and eventually answered by Suslovic himself. Some students take notes. Mark doesn't. A student walks in the open door, hands Mr. Suslovic a list, and starts whispering with him. Suslovic turns from the class and hears out this messenger. He then asks, "Does anyone know where Maggie Sharp is?" Someone answers, "Sick at home"; someone else says, "I thought I saw her at lunch." Genial consternation. Finally Suslovic tells the messenger, "Sorry, we can't help you," and returns to the class: "Now where are we?" He goes on for some minutes. The bell rings. Suslovic forgets to give the homework assignment.

1:11 and Algebra II. There is a commotion in the hallway: someone's locker is rumored to have been opened by the assistant principal and a narcotics agent. In the five-minute passing time, Mark hears the story three times and three ways. A locker had been broken into by another student. It was Mr. Gregory and a narc. It was the cops, and they did it without Gregory's knowing. Mrs. Ames, the mathematics, teacher, has not heard anything about it. Several of the nineteen students try to tell her and start arguing among themselves. "O.K., that's enough." She hands out the day's problem, one sheet to each student. Mark sees with dismay that it is a single, complicated "word" problem about some train that, while traveling at 84 mph, due west, passes a car that was going due east at 55 mph. Mark struggles: Is it d = rt or t = rd? The class becomes quiet, writing, while Mrs. Ames writes some additional, short problems on the blackboard. "Time's up." A sigh; some students still writing. A muffled "Shit." Mrs. Ames frowns.

"Come on, now." She collects papers, but it takes four minutes for her to corral them all.

"Copy down the problems from the board." A minute passes. "William, try number one." William suggests an approach. Mrs. Ames corrects and cajoles, and William finally gets it right. Mark watches two kids to his right passing notes; he tries to read them, but the handwriting is illegible from his distance. He hopes he is not called on, and he isn't. Only three students are asked to puzzle out an answer. The bell rings at 2:00. Mrs. Ames shouts out a homework assignment over the resulting hubbub.

Mark leaves his books in his locker. He remembers that he has homework, but figures that he can do it during English class the next day. He knows that there will be an in-class presentation of one of the *Romeo and Juliet* scenes and that he will not be in it. The teacher will not notice his homework writing, or won't do anything about it if she does.

Mark passes various friends heading toward the gym, members of the basketball team. Like most students, Mark isn't an active school athlete. However, he is associated with the yearbook staff. Although he is not taking "Yearbook" for credit as an English course, he is contributing photographs. Mark takes twenty minutes checking into the yearbook's headquarters (the classroom of its faculty advisor) and getting some assignments of pictures from his boss, the senior who is the photography editor. Mark knows that if he pleases his boss and the faculty advisor, he'll take that editor's post for the next year. He'll get English credit for his work then.

After gossiping a bit with the yearbook staff, Mark will leave school by 2:35 and go home. His grocery market bagger's job is from 4:30 to 8:00, the rush hour of the store. He'll have a snack at 4:30, and his mother will save him some supper to eat at 8:30. She will ask whether he has any homework, and he'll tell her no. Tomorrow, and virtually every other tomorrow, will be the same for Mark, save for the lack of the assembly: each period will then be five minutes longer.

Most Americans have an uncomplicated vision of what secondary education should be. Their conception of high school is remarkably uniform across the country, a striking fact, given the size and diversity of the United States and the politically decentralized character of the schools. This uniformity is of several generations' standing. It has, however, two appearances, each quite different from the other, one of words and the other of practice, a political rhetoric and Mark's world.

A California high school's general goals, set out in 1979, could serve equally well most of America's high schools, public and private. The school has as its ends:

- Fundamental scholastic achievement … to acquire knowledge and share in the traditionally accepted academic fundamentals … to develop the ability to make decisions, to solve problems, to reason independently, and to accept responsibility for self-evaluation and continuing self-improvement.

- Career and economic competence …

- Citizenship and civic responsibility …

- Competence in human and social relations …

- Moral and ethical values …

- Aesthetic awareness …

- Cultural diversity …

In addition to its optimistic rhetoric, what distinguishes this list is its comprehensiveness. The high school is to touch most aspects of an adolescent's existence—mind, body, morals, values, career. No one of these areas is given especial prominence. School people arrogate to themselves an obligation to all.

An example of the wide acceptability of these goals is found in the courts. Forced to present a detailed definition of "thorough and efficient education," elementary as well as secondary, a West Virginia judge sampled the best of conventional wisdom and concluded that

> There are eight elements of a thorough and efficient system of education: (a) Literacy, (b) The ability to add, subtract, multiply, and divide numbers, (c) Knowledge of government to the extent that the child will be equipped as a citizen to make informed choices among persons and issues that affect his own governance, (d) Self-knowledge and knowledge of his or her total environment to allow the child to intelligently choose life work—to know his or her options, (e) Work-training and advanced academic training as the child may intelligently choose, (f) Interests in all creative arts, such as music, theater, literature, and the visual arts, and (h) Social ethics, both behavioral and abstract, to facilitate compatibility with others in this society.

That these eight—now powerfully part of the debate over the purpose and practice of education in West Virginia—are reminiscent of the influential list, "The Seven Cardinal Principles of Secondary Education," promulgated in 1918 by the National Education Association, is no surprise. The rhetoric of high school purpose has been uniform and consistent for decades. Americans agree on the goals of their high schools.

That agreement is convenient, but it masks the fact that virtually all the words in these goal statements beg definition. Some schools have labored long to identify specific criteria beyond them; the result has been lists of daunting pseudospecificity and numbing earnestness. However, most leave the words undefined and let the momentum of traditional practice speak for itself. That is why analyzing how Mark spends his time is important: from watching him one uncovers the important purposes of education, the ones that shape practice. Mark's day is similar to that of other high school students across the country, as similar as the rhetoric of one goal statement to others'. Of course, there are variations, but the extent of consistency in the shape of school routine for a large and diverse adolescent population is extraordinary, indicating more graphically than any rhetoric the measure of agreement in America about what one does in high school, and by implication, what it is for.

The basic organizing structures in schools are familiar. Above all, students are grouped by age (that is freshman, sophomore, junior, and senior), and all are expected to take precisely the same time—around 720 school days over four years, to be precise, to meet the requirements for a diploma. When one is out of his grade level, he can feel odd, as Mark did in his biology class. The goals are the same for all, and the means to achieve them are also similar.

Young males and females are treated remarkably alike; the schools' goals are the same for each gender. In execution, there are differences, as those pressing sex discrimination suits have made educators intensely aware. The students in metalworking classes are mostly male; those in home economics, mostly female. But it is revealing how much less sex discrimination there is in high schools than in other American institutions. For many young women, the most liberated hours of their week are in school.

School is like a job: you start in the morning and end in the afternoon, five days a week. You don't get much of a lunch hour, so you go home early, unless you are an athlete or involved in some special school or extracurricular activity. School is conceived of as the children's workplace, and it takes young people off parents' hands and out of the labor market during prime-time work hours. Not surprisingly, many students see going to school as little more than a dogged necessity. They perceive the day-to-day routine,

↵ a Minnesota study reports, as one of "boredom and lethargy." One of the students summarizes: School is "boring, restless, tiresome, puts ya to sleep, tedious, monotonous, pain in the neck."

The school schedule is a series of units of time: the clock is king. The base time block is about fifty minutes in length. Some schools, on what they call modular scheduling, split that fifty-minute block into two or three pieces. Most schools have double periods for laboratory work, especially in the sciences, or four-hour units for smaller numbers of students involved in intensive vocational or other work-study programs. The flow of all school activity arises from or is blocked by these time units. "How much time do I have with my kids" is the teacher's key question.

Because there are many claims for those 50-minute blocks, there is little time set aside for rest between them, usually no more than three to ten minutes, depending on how big the school is and, consequently, how far students and teachers have to walk from class to class. As a result, there is a frenetic quality to the school day, a sense of sustained restlessness. For the adolescents, there are frequent changes of room and fellow students, each change giving tempting opportunities for distraction, which are stoutly resisted by teachers. Some schools play soft music during these "passing times," to quiet the multitude, one principal told me.

Many teachers have a chance for a coffee break. Few students do so. In some city schools where security is a problem, students must be in class for seven consecutive periods, interrupted by a heavily monitored 20-minute lunch period for small groups, starting as early as 10:30 a.m. and running to after 1:00 p.m. A high premium is placed on punctuality and on "being where you're supposed to be." Obviously, a low premium is placed on reflection and repose. The student rushes from class to class to collect knowledge. Savoring it, it is implied, is not to be done much in school, nor is such meditation really much admired. The picture that these familiar patterns yield is that of an academic supermarket. The purpose of going to school is to pick things up, in an organized and predictable way, the faster the better.

Close Reading Questions

1. Which of Mark's classes seem most similar to your own high school experiences (or those of someone you know well)? Overall, how accurate do you think Sizer's depiction of secondary education is and why?

2. At the end of this reading, Sizer offers several critiques of secondary education. Which of his critiques of high school do you think is most or least significant and why?

3. Why is Sizer troubled by the stated goals and the actual practices of most high school?

Analytical Writing/Discussion

4. Sizer claims that the goals of education have not changed significantly over most of a century. Why does Sizer believe the stated goals of education have remained so constant? How much or how little do you think the goals of secondary education have changed in the three decades since Sizer made this analysis? (Historical Trends)

5. As this depiction of high school follows Mark, this reading suggests several other perspectives, such as those of more engaged students like Susanna, teachers, administrators, and parents. Focusing on another perspective or two beyond Mark's viewpoint, how can this school be seen much more positively? (Multiple Perspectives)

6. According to Sizer, attending high school is "like a job." With several references to Sizer's essay,
    what do you think are several ways in which the organization of the workplace influences the
    structure of school? (Cultural Influences)

Further Options

7. Synthesis, meaning the making of connections between two (or more) readings is central to
    academic writing. In the next reading, John Dewey critiques traditional education. Which of
    Dewey's criticisms do you think are most relevant to Mark's school day? Or conversely, what
    details of Mark's school day best illustrate some of Dewey's criticisms?

8. Research the goals of your former high school or current college. How similar or different are
    these goals with those presented by Sizer? Why do you think these similarities or differences
    should be considered as positive or negative?

EXPERIENCE AND EDUCATION

by John Dewey

> John Dewey was one of the first and fiercest critics of tra-
> ditional education in the United States. He helped lead the
> reform that was known as progressive education during the
> 1920s. Yet by the end of the next decade, he faulted progres-
> sive educators for basing their reform movement too much
> in opposition to traditionalism. He instead tried to rethink
> the basic concepts and the key relationships of education,
> such as educational goals and the bond between teachers
> and students. This reading is an excerpt from *Experience and
> Education*, published in 1938, after Dewey had presented
> these ideas on education in the Kappa Delta Pi Lecture Series.

The trouble with traditional education was not that educators took upon themselves the responsibility for
providing an [educational] environment. The trouble was that they did not consider the other factor in
creating an [educational] experience; namely, the powers and purposes of those taught. It was assumed
that a certain set of [information] was intrinsically desirable, apart from its ability to evoke a certain quality of response in individuals. This lack of mutual adaptation made the process of teaching and learning
accidental. Those to whom the provided [information was] suitable managed to learn. Others got on as
best they could. Responsibility for selecting [course information] carries with it, then, the responsibility
for understanding the needs and capacities of the individuals who are learning at a given time. It is not
enough that certain materials and methods have proved effective with other individuals at other times.
There must be a reason for thinking they will function in generating an experience that has educational
quality with particular individuals at a particular time.

From *Experience and Education* by John Dewey. Copyright © 1938 by Kappa Delta Pi International Honor Society in Education.
Reprinted by permission.

FIGURE 1 A Traditional Classroom

It is no reflection upon the nutritive quality of beefsteak that it is not fed to infants. It is not an invidious reflection upon trigonometry that we do not teach it in the first or fifth grade of school. It is not the subject per se that is educative or that is conducive to growth. There is no subject that is in and of itself, or without regard to the stage of growth attained by the learner, such that inherent educational value can be attributed to it. Failure to take into account adaptation to the needs and capacities of individuals was the source of the idea that certain subjects and certain methods are intrinsically cultural or intrinsically good for mental discipline. There is no such thing as educational value in the abstract. The notion that some subjects and methods and that acquaintance with certain facts and truths possess educational value in and of themselves is the reason why traditional education reduced the material of education so largely to a diet of predigested materials. According to this notion, it was enough to regulate the quantity and difficulty of the material provided, in a scheme of quantitative grading, from month to month and from year to year. Otherwise a pupil was expected to take it in doses that were prescribed from without. If the pupil left it instead of taking it, if he engaged in physical truancy or in the mental truancy of mind-wandering and finally built up an emotional revulsion against the subject, he was held to be at fault. No question was raised as to whether the trouble might not lie in the subject-matter or in the way in which it was offered. The principle of interaction makes it clear that failure of adaptation of material to needs and capacities of individuals may cause an experience to be non-educative quite as much as failure of an individual to adapt himself to the material.

The principle of continuity in its educational application means, nevertheless, that the future has to be taken into account at every stage of the educational process. This idea is easily misunderstood and is badly distorted in traditional education. Its assumption is, that by acquiring certain skills and by learning certain subjects which would be needed later (perhaps in college or perhaps in adult life) pupils are as a matter of course made ready for the needs and circumstances of the future. Now "preparation" is a treacherous idea. In a certain sense every experience should do something to prepare a person for later experiences of a deeper and more expansive quality. That is the very meaning of growth, continuity, reconstruction of experience. But it is a mistake to suppose that the mere acquisition of a certain amount of arithmetic, geography, history, etc., which is taught and studied because it may be useful at some time in the future, has this effect, and it is a mistake to suppose that acquisition of skills in reading and figuring will automatically constitute preparation for their right and effective use under conditions very unlike those in which they were acquired.

Almost everyone has had occasion to look back upon his school days and wonder what has become of the knowledge he was supposed to have amassed during his years of schooling, and why it is that the technical skills he acquired have to be learned over again in changed form in order to stand him in good stead. Indeed, he is lucky who does not find that in order to make progress, in order to go ahead intellectually, he does not have to unlearn much of what he learned in school. These questions cannot be disposed of by saying that the subjects were not actually learned for they were learned at least sufficiently to enable a pupil to pass examinations in them. One trouble is that the subject-matter in question was learned in isolation; it was put, as it were, in a water-tight compartment. When the question is asked, then, what has become of it, where has it gone to, the right answer is that it is still there in the special compartment in which it was originally stowed away. If exactly the same conditions recurred as those under which it was acquired, it would also recur and be available. But it was segregated when it was acquired and hence is so disconnected from the rest of experience that it is not available under the actual conditions of life. It is contrary to the laws of experience that learning of this kind, no matter how thoroughly engrained at the time, should give genuine preparation.

Nor does failure in preparation end at this point. Perhaps the greatest of all pedagogical fallacies is the notion that it person learns only the particular thing he is studying at the time. Collateral learning in the way of formation of enduring attitudes, of likes and dislikes, may be and often is much more important than the spelling lesson or lesson in geography or history that is learned. For these attitudes are fundamentally what count in the future. The most important attitude that can be formed is that of desire to go on learning. If impetus in this direction is weakened instead of being intensified, something much more than mere lack of preparation takes place. The pupil is actually robbed of native capacities which otherwise would enable him to cope with the circumstances that he meets in the course of his life. We often see persons who have had little schooling and in whose case the absence of set schooling proves to be a positive asset. They have at least retained their native common sense and power of judgment, and its exercise in the actual conditions of living has given them the precious gift of ability to learn from the experiences they have. What avail is it to win prescribed amounts of information about geography and history, to win ability to read and write, if in the process the individual loses his own soul: loses his appreciation of things "worthwhile," of the values to which these things are relative; if he loses desire to apply what he has learned and, above all, loses the ability to extract meaning from his future experiences as they occur?

What, then, is the true meaning of preparation in the educational scheme? In the first place, it means that a person, young or old, gets out of his present experience all that there is in it for him at the time in which he has it. When preparation is made the controlling end, then the potentialities of the present are sacrificed to a suppositious future. When this happens, the actual preparation for the future is missed or distorted. The ideal of using the present simply to get ready for the future contradicts itself. It omits, and even shuts out, the very conditions by which a person can be prepared for his future. We always live at the time we live and not at some other time, and only by extracting at each present time the full meaning of each present experience are we prepared for doing the same thing in the future. This is the only preparation which in the long run amounts to anything.

All this means that attentive care must be devoted to the conditions which give each present experience a worthwhile meaning. Instead of inferring that it doesn't make much difference what the present experience is as long as it is enjoyed, the conclusion is the exact opposite. Here is another matter where it is easy to react from one extreme to the other. Because traditional schools tended to sacrifice the present to a remote and more or less unknown future, therefore it comes to be believed that the educator has little responsibility for the kind of present experiences the young undergo. But the relation of the present and the future is not an Either-Or affair. The present affects the future anyway. The persons who should have some idea of the connection between the two are those who have achieved maturity. Accordingly, upon them devolves the responsibility for instituting the conditions for the kind of present experience which has a favorable effect upon the future. Education as growth or maturity should be an ever-present process.

Close Reading Questions

1. According to Dewey, what are two crucial factors of effective education? How does traditional education often fail to fulfill both factors?

2. What larger point do you think Dewey is trying to make using the examples of steak and trigonometry?

3. Dewey also was one of the leading philosophers of the early twentieth century so his writing often is abstract and highly theoretical. Rather than trying to comprehend of this entire reading immediately, please pick a short passage that seems very true to you and answer: why does this passage seem so significant to you? (See Chapter 1 on engaging with a text.)

Analytical Writing/Discussion

4. Why does Dewey believe that some subject matter may be learned by one student but not by another? Why do you agree or disagree that the "adaptation" of material may contribute to this educational failure as well as the efforts of an individual student? (Multiple Perspectives)

5. Why are you persuaded or not by Dewey that education focused on "preparation" for the future can be a "treacherous idea"? Using some of Dewey's detailed analysis, what do you think are the best and worst ways to focus education on preparing for the future? (Historical Trends)

6. Dewey insists that although specific information may be later forgotten, the "collateral learning" of school often persists. What do you think he means by the phrase "collateral learning"? Using yourself or a student you know well, what is a positive or negative example of this collateral learning? (Cultural Influences)

Further Options

7. In Question 1 above, you were asked to create what is known as a double-entry response to a specific passage. Now let's take this form of reading response even further: using either Freewrite 1 or the first reading by Sizer, how can you connect that text to a specific passage from this reading? In other words, how does the other text help to explain the passage by Dewey? (For more on double-entry responses, see p. 11 of Chapter 1.

8. In our explanation of multiple perspectives, we asserted that it is vital to test a viewpoint by considering an opposing opinion. Working away from your initial support or skepticism of Dewey's critique of traditional education and his advocacy of a revised form of progressive education, what are several aspects of the opposing opinion? In other words, why might someone else disagree with your initial reaction to Dewey? (For more on multiple perspectives, see pp. 12 and 13 in Chapter 1.)

SCHOOLS AND TRUST IN A DEMOCRACY

by Deborah Meier

Deborah Meier started her career in education as a kindergarten teacher in public schools in Chicago, Philadelphia, and New York City. In 1974, Meier founded and directed the alternative public Central Park East School for children from East Harlem, NYC. Meier then founded two other small public elementary schools, one named Mission Hill in Boston, participated in The Coalition of Essential Schools created by Ted Sizer, and became a leading advocate of small schools. Her books include *The Power of Ideas: Lessons from a Small School in East Harlem* (1995) and *Will Standards Save Public Schools* (2000). The following reading comes from a collection of essays, published in 2004, which she edited with George Wood, titled *Many Children Left Behind*.

The very definition of what constitutes an educated person is now dictated by federal legislation. A well-educated person is one who scores high on standardized math and reading tests. And ergo, a good school is one that either has very high test scores or is moving toward them at a prescribed rate of improvement.

All of this has implications for democracy, and not small ones. We worry about "public engagement" and "parental involvement," two new jargony phrases that were invented precisely as we eliminated all the natural ways in which families and citizens were engaged in their schools.

Bigger Is Not Better

The demise of small school districts was coincidental with the demise of small schools. The two phenomena together have led to a serious disconnect between young people and adults, between youth culture and adult culture.

There were good reasons to be concerned that small schools might be havens for parochial prejudices, racial bias, and insularity—and that larger consolidated school districts would be able to offer greater variety and economies of scale. Both played a role in the demise of small schools and districts, as well as the increasing role of the state and federal government in schools. We were preparing our youngsters for national and global citizenship; big schools and big districts were often seen as a way of enlarging young people's exposure to a wider range of options and offering them greater expertise and more specialized programs, as well as protecting the rights of minorities.

Furthermore, the increase over the past half-century of state and federal mandates created compliance problems in small and isolated districts. How could a small school offer the kind of library, science labs, sports programs, range of foreign language opportunities, or Advanced Placement options that would be possible in a large school?

Republished with permission of Beacon Press, Inc, from *Many Children Behind: How the No Child Left Behind Act is Damaging Our Children and Our Schools* edited by Deborah Meier and George Wood (2004). Permission conveyed through Copyright Clearance Center, Inc.

But we embarked on that path without considering the costs, either in how adults saw their responsibility for the education of the next generation, or in the growing disconnect between school and community and its impact on children's intellectual, social, and moral development. Citizenship requires a recognition of what it means to be a member of something—and we've forgotten that kids today have precious little experience being members of anything beyond their immediate family and their self-chosen peer group.

Parochialism certainly can stunt kids' growth and impede their sharing of larger social norms and concerns. The solution to parochialism, however, isn't to destroy all small communities and institutions in favor of large, anonymous ones. When we look closely, we see that the consolidation and centralization of school districts actually made the problems they were supposed to cure even worse. Rather than expanding young people's sense of membership in the world, consolidation seriously endangered their feeling of community. And it didn't even save money: the evidence suggests that the cost per graduate of small schools is less.

Nor did the consolidation lead to other hoped-for outcomes, such as greater ethnic, racial, and social class integration. Our progress on racial separatism has been substantial, if we look back as far as 1930, but in recent years we have been losing ground. As for social class, the big difference is that far more low-income children now attend school for longer periods of time—but rarely together with rich kids. And if they do attend the same schools, they rarely study in the same classes or belong to the same subgroups. For within the new large schools, kids have recreated their own small schools, made up of their like-minded and look-alike peers. You see them in the hallways and lunchrooms and on the playgrounds.

Now NCLB does not in itself demand the consolidation of districts and the creation of bigger schools. But as I hope to show, it creates an environment in which the purpose and value of small schools [are] not allowed to flourish. In fact, it undermines small schools' most important educational characteristic: they are places where citizens and professionals can exercise judgment and build trust.

A World Designed by Strangers

Local communities are in far less danger of parochialism today than in the past. The influence of television, computers, and other technology, and the vast youth-savvy world of mass entertainment has altered the landscape of our lives, especially for children.

Few of today's youngsters lack awareness of the larger demands of society, as job requirements and college expectations are largely national in scope. We are inescapably connected by these new technologies, and there are more of them every year. It's not the Big World that kids are cut off from; increasingly, it's the one at their doorsteps—their own communities.

Education has barely acknowledged, much less begun to address, this sea change toward a new world of universalism run amok. We are not much of a match anymore for the educational impact of the national norms established, not by schools, teachers, or churches, but by that great equalizer the mass media, with its relentless drive to turn our kids into world-class consumers.

By the time they are adolescents, our children are largely cut off from relationships with adults outside their immediate families—and stuck with one another in a world designed for them by strangers. They are all educated by the music, advertisements, and products designed to sell to an international youth market. They are carefully groomed to recognize ways to enhance their status in the race to look good, get ahead, and be the most. What they do not have are strong roots in any specific multiage community.

NCLB is not itself responsible for the divide between adults and children, for the breakdown of multiage communities. It merely locks these into place. Exactly at a time when we need educational policies that will counter these trends, we get NCLB, which instead amplifies their negative effects. It does so in specific ways.

By relying on standardized tests as the only measure of school quality, NCLB usurps the right of local communities to define the attributes of a sound education. Districts are further encouraged to limit any local alternatives by having schools limit their curriculum time to what will prepare children for tests … This will … dumb down decades of efforts to provide children with what was once offered only to the rich—a genuinely challenging and engaging program of study.

By ignoring ample evidence that the psychometric tools of testing provide limited predictions of school success, above all when it comes to children outside the mainstream (children of color, of the poor, those with handicaps or limited English proficiency), NCLB forces local districts to engage in one-size-fits-all practices that ignore the needs of these children. Districts will be encouraged to push out those so-called nonperformers in order to protect their movement toward Adequate Yearly Progress (AYP) or else risk being labeled a failing school.

By suggesting that public schools can produce equity regardless of social inequity, NCLB sets up local districts for failure. This failure will lead to calls for the ultimate limitation of local, democratic authority that is class for privatization of our public schools.

Above all, NCLB assumes that neither children, their families, their teachers, nor their communities can be trusted to make important decisions about their schools. It defines such parties as special biased self-interests, whose judgment is inferior to that of bureaucrats at the Department of Education (DOE) and various testing services.

More Trust, More Democracy

We need schools where strong cross-generational relationships can be built around matters of importance in the world. Schools cannot do it alone—kids also need other non-school communities—but creating such schools is a necessary start. These schools can exist only in communities that trust them. There is no short cut. The authority needed to do the job requires trust. Trusting our schools cannot be a long-term goal in some utopian vision. If you don't trust the babysitter, no accountability scheme will make it safe to leave your child in her hands tonight. The only alternative is to stay home.

There is no way around it. We have to work harder at making our schools and teachers trustworthy. And that, in turn, means we need schoolwork we can easily see, whose governors are folks we know well, and whose graduates' lives we can track without complex databases or academic studies.

The business world offers little guidance in this task. The ways of business hardly work for business, where "buyer beware" is the primary response to the demands of accountability.

We need to return schools to our fellow citizens—yes, ordinary citizens, with all their warts. The solution to the messiness of democracy is more of it—and more time set aside to make it work. If we want to continue our grand experiment in American democracy, we are stuck depending on the people "to exercise their control with a wholesome discretion," in Thomas Jefferson's words. And if they are not enlightened enough to do so, he said, "the remedy is not to take it from them, but to inform their discretion by education."

That's what local school boards are intended to be all about. If we can't trust local citizens with matters of local K-12 schooling, whatever can we trust them with? And why would we instead trust presidents and governors or the task forces they select to replace such judgments on matters so close to the raising of our children?

How might we go about establishing greater trust? We might start by multiplying, not reducing, the number of local boards, to return to the ratio we once enjoyed. At most, no school committee that makes decisions about teaching and learning should have authority over more than perhaps 2,500 students and at most ten small schools. Maybe each school should have its own board.

Trust in schools can't grow unless principals, parents, teachers, and kids know each other well, and their work is accessible to the larger community. Likewise, the board members that oversee them must know the schools intimately—through firsthand engagement, not printouts and manipulatable bureaucratic data.

Like the private and parochial schools that the current federal government seems to favor, Mission Hill School—although part of a larger citywide system in Boston—has its own board, made up of five parent representatives, five staff representatives, five public members chosen jointly, and two students. And while the Boston School Committee has ultimate power, "in-between" (which is most of the time) it's our own board that makes the important decisions on policy, budget, and personnel. That's part of the secret of our success. Maybe each school needs its own form of self-governance.

The state can set broad guidelines, and it can surely demand that schools make their standards explicit and the evidence of performance publicly accessible. It can insist on fairness for all citizens—and set out what such fairness requires. But each local board ought to be responsible for the details, including exactly how schools are held accountable to their constituents and what evidence will count toward the awarding of diplomas. There is precious little likelihood that a board will ignore what colleges and employers say, what Educational Testing Service and other credentialing bodies lay down as norms, or what the mass media and national politicians and public figures claim needs to be done.

The state might reasonably require that sample populations of students be tested to look at indicators across localities. And it might require schools to submit every few years to a review of their work by a panel of expert and lay outsiders, whose opinions and analysis would be made public. Otherwise, let there be both voice and, where possible, choice—close to where children live. While choice allows folks to vote with their feet, voice allows them to vote in the most democratic sense—by going to the polls. Both choice and voice strengthen the allegiance of communities to their schools. Not all people will get exactly what they want; but democracy is also all about compromises, building consensus, thinking about the other guy's needs and views, and a commitment to the larger community.

There will be acrimony, and there will be local fights. Hurrah, but not alas. It is the habits of mind necessary for practicing and resolving disagreements—the mental toughness that democracy rests on—that kids most need to learn about in school. If we all agreed about everything, we wouldn't need democracy; we wouldn't need to learn how people work out differences.

Local school boards need to look politicians, corporate boards, and foundation leaders in the eye and remind them: This is what America is all about. And it just so happens it's what a strong and rigorous education requires—even if we don't get it right at first or all the time. That too is what America is all about.

Rebuilding Trust

Our school boards need to turn their eyes to their real constituencies—not just to following the dictates of state and federal government bureaucrats.

Good school governance needs to keep its eyes on its real constituents—above all the kids and their families. Disappointing them is what such a board must worry about day and night. What it doesn't need to do is live in fear of state and federal government micromanagers. That's not easy, of course. But it will be the foundation of a powerful coalition of school people and local school boards creating trustworthy schools.

There is no way to give all kids a serious and high-quality education unless and until we make our schools worthy of trust.

Close Reading Questions

1. According to Meier, who defines what constitutes a good education, and what now is the definition of a well-educated person?

2. What does Meier believe are the respective benefits and disadvantages of small schools and of large schools?

3. According to Meier, why is trust essential in education, and how has trust been reduced by NCLB?

Analytical Writing/Discussion

4. Why do you agree or disagree with Meier that the typical high school student participates in a group of "like-minded and look-alike" peers? (Multiple Perspectives)

5. According to Meier, what effect does the mass media have on most students? To what degree do you think this effect contradicts Meier's fear of "look-alike" conformity among students in large schools? (Cultural Influences)

6. Why does Meier want to return to the 1930s level of local control of schools? Why do you think greater local control would be beneficial or not? (Historical Trends)

Further Options

7. Meier cites Thomas Jefferson on the role of education in a democracy. What do you think is the necessary relationship between education and democracy in the United States?

8. As explained in Chapter 5 on Rhetoric, a Rogerian argument seeks compromise and consensus among disputants by seeking, first, common ground (see pp. 113–116). Although Deborah Meier and Anthony Consiglio (see pp. 185–197) disagree on NCLB, on what aspects of educational reform might they agree? What consensus on improving public schools do you think is possible?

Freewrite 2: Tracking Students

The division of students into different ability levels for one subject—or "tracking" them into high, middle, and low sections—is practiced in almost all of America's public high schools today. This common practice, however, once was a topic of great debate among educators. The following excerpts are from two very influential reports on education: the Committee of Ten Report from 1893 and *the American High School Today*, a second report from 1959. After you read their positions on tracking, please discuss and/or freewrite in response using the questions below.

From the 1893 Report

On one very important question of general policy that affects profoundly the preparation of all school programs, the Committee of Ten and all the Conferences are absolutely unanimous. Among the questions suggested for discussion in each Conference were the following:

1. Should the subject be treated differently for pupils who are going to college, for those who are going to a scientific school, and for those who, presumably, are going to neither?

2. At what age should this differentiation begin, if any be recommended?

The first question is answered unanimously in the negative … [so] the second therefore needs no answer … Every subject which is taught at all in a secondary school should be taught in the same way and to the same extent to every pupil so long as he pursues it, no matter what the probable destination of the pupil may be, or at what point his education is to cease. Thus, for all pupils who study Latin, or history, or algebra, for example, the allotment of time and the method of instruction in a given school should be the same year by year. Not that all the pupils should pursue every subject for the same number of years; but so long as they do pursue it, they should all be treated alike. It has been a very general custom in American high schools and academies to make up separate courses of study for pupils of supposed different destinations … Each subject [should be] treated by the school in the same way by the year for all pupils.

From the 1959 Report

In the required subjects and those elected by students with a wide range of ability, the students should be grouped according to ability, subject by subject. For example, in English, American history, ninth-grade algebra, biology, and physical science, there should be at least three types of classes—one for the more able in the subject, another for the large group whose ability is about average, and another for the very slow readers who should be handled by special teachers. The middle group might be divided into two or three sections according to the students' abilities in the subject in question. This type of grouping is not to be confused with across the board grouping according to which a given student is placed in a particular section in all courses. Under the scheme here recommended, for example, a student may be in the top section in English but the middle section in history or ninth-grade algebra.

Answer one or more of the following questions by freewriting and/or discussion in order to react to these two reports:

- How did your high school handle tracking, and how might its grouping policy have been improved by heeding one or both of these reports?

- Rather than pick one side over another on tracking, how do you think each position can be considered a fair way to treat all students equally?

- During the 1890s, only a fraction of American adolescents attended high school (7%), but by the 1950s, a large majority of teenagers attended high school (though all did not complete four years and graduate). How do you think the different historical circumstances of these reports can be used to explain their opposing positions on differentiated instruction and ability grouping?

EDUCATIONAL EQUALITY: RENEWING NCLB

by Anthony Consiglio

After teaching in public schools in New York and Connecticut for more than a decade, Anthony Consiglio turned to the study of law. He has combined these professional pursuits by focusing on what he terms "the noble achievement and arduous challenge of expanding access to a quality education." The following essay was originally published in the *Brigham and Young University Education and Law Journal* in 2009, and the author asked his readers to maintain an "open and searching mind."

Presidential candidates called it "unconstitutional," an "unfunded mandate." Its fiercest critics charge its intent is to undermine and dismantle public education itself ... Yet the No Child Left Behind Act of 2001 (NCLB) is hardly the subversive, far-reaching, and peremptory law that these misconceptions and attacks suggest. Rather, NCLB is divisive because it has raised penetrating questions with profound implications for the future. NCLB is a major example of a federal initiative to respond to a well-documented nationwide need, and its success or failure will influence future solutions to stubborn national problems ranging from health care to oversight of the financial industries.

As Congress considers the renewal of NCLB, it has a moral and political imperative to get it right. The greatest support for NCLB continues to come from states, communities, organizations, and families who are sensitive to its central mission: improving the academic achievement and educational opportunities in the poorest-performing schools to match more closely those in high-performing schools. When it was enacted, NCLB enjoyed broad bipartisan support and recognition of its central, civil rights objectives. Much of the public has grown disenchanted, however—"educators, legislators, and even entire states are in open revolt over NCLB"—and liberal education scholars talk of "laudable goals" and "noble agenda" overrun by inherent flaws and "unintended consequences."

Where a sound and laudable premise meets flawed design and unintended consequences, however, revolt and abandonment are neither the normal nor the best response. The countless parodies and puns the name No Child Left Behind has inspired in the press and elsewhere suggest something more than a logical reaction is going on ...

The Two Main Objections

There are two elemental objections to NCLB. Although they are inextricably related, the first objection expresses a policy concern about education (what government should provide and require), while the second expresses a constitutional concern about federalism (how state and federal governments should function and within what limits of control). The two arguments can be summarized as follows:

1. Complying with NCLB cripples states and schools with a sterile education policy obsessively focused on annual student testing and other superficial, shortsighted goals.

From *BYU Education and Law Journal*, Vol 2009, No 2 (Pages 365–397) by Anthony Consiglio. Copyright © 2009 by BUY Education and Law Journal. Reprinted by permission.

2. While NCLB is in form a federal a federal spending program, participation in the program is optional for states in theory only—the threat of withholding federal education funds from states that have long relied on them unconstitutionally coerces their participation in NCLB. Furthermore, because the federal funding is inadequate for full compliance with NCLB's requirements, the law unconstitutionally directs states' education policy.

Both arguments sensibly address practical realities, and Congress should learn many essential points from them as it considers NCLB's future—especially as to the rigidity of NCLB's deadlines and benchmarks, the punitive nature of some of its sanctions, and its neglect of teaching methods.

Nonetheless, these arguments tend toward a negative and counterproductive logic that limits their usefulness. They draw attention to what is missing (time, money, and creative and flexible teaching), but avoid frankly weighing the states' role in presiding over the accretion of unmet need. They present a contradiction by decrying excessive federal interference and insufficient federal funding. They do not point the way forward to correcting the long intractable problem of inequality in educational opportunities, but insist that the flexibility and freedom schools have enjoyed for decades is still the solution.

The policy argument correctly maintains that the testing and data collection NCLB requires cannot effect meaningful reform without a concentrated focus on teaching and curriculum. But the implication that NCLB prevents true teaching reform is a straw man, however grounded it may be in current fiscal realities. Contrarily, the policy argument more often than not incorrectly implies that meaningful education reform can proceed without a basic system of rigorous testing and solid data collection in place. It also obscures the primary objective of equality behind NCLB's requirement that each state adopt uniform educational standards. A thorough system of assessment and accountability is the necessary basis … of any sound education policy and of any equality measure.

If NCLB is to succeed on its own terms, Congress will indeed have to partner with the states to support their development of programs for teaching and curriculum reform. By their nature, these programs require individualization and resist standardization. In the meantime, though, there is no convincing justification for denying the primacy of assessment and accountability. Those denials are, at worst, part of a uniquely American distaste for governmental discipline that has left us with financial, health care, energy, and other industries profoundly neglectful of sustainability.

NCLB's requirement of uniform standards across each state is a direct attack on the inequality inherent in our system of school financing from local property taxes. From the perspective of the Fourteenth Amendment and the perspective of antipoverty measures, equalizing opportunities should take precedence over individual communities' pursuit of excellence. Connecticut's efforts to escape some of NCLB's requirements provide an especially instructive example of this problem. Connecticut lobbied and sued the Department of Education (DOE) (the agency charged with administering NCLB) for waivers to avoid supplementing its pre-NCLB tests that were nationally recognized for their excellence, even while Connecticut was recognized as the state with the single biggest discrepancy in academic achievement between its high- and low-performing students. Connecticut is the only state that has lodged a full constitutional attack on NCLB in court. Congress [however] should remain committed to uniform standards [within] each state …

The federalism argument summarized above also has merit, especially in its perception that opting out of NCLB would amount to a politically disastrous forfeit of federal aid that could not be recaptured through other means, such as raising state taxes. There may ultimately be no satisfying answer for this problem—it may simply be a fiscal reality of the modern federal relationship and a function of the federal government's responsibility for equality measures under the Fourteenth Amendment.

Yet, the federalism argument obscures a fact of fundamental importance: NCLB does not determine a participating state's education standards; it merely requires the state to adopt standards of its choosing that are adequate and to document the uniform application of those standards. If the states' ability to opt out of NCLB is largely impractical and simply a formalism, the federalism argument is as much a rhetorical stance that puts Congress on the defensive as it is a demonstration of NCLB's coercive effects. It is telling that no state has opted out of NCLB since its inception seven years ago. Connecticut's constitutional challenge to NCLB was dismissed as premature, since the DOE had taken no enforcement actions or final decisions against Connecticut. Since it has not withdrawn from NCLB or refused to comply with any of its provisions, it may be said that Connecticut has not put its money where its mouth was. The other constitutional challenge to NCLB, *School District of Pontiac v. Secretary of the United States Department of Education*, was not joined or supported by any of the states in which the plaintiff school districts reside; furthermore, Pontiac principally alleges lack of notice rather than the fatal constitutional defect of coercion ...

State Control Versus National Accountability

The United States Constitution makes no provision for education. Since the Tenth Amendment reserves all unenumerated powers for state government, the federal government has no direct control over education. Early on, the federal government provided a small amount of funding for school construction, vocational and higher education, and some specialized programs like school lunch and impact aid; in 1958, it first provided some funding for academic instruction in regular primary and secondary schools. Federal funding of education began in earnest with the Elementary and Secondary Education Act of 1965 (ESEA), a product of the civil rights and antipoverty agendas of the 1960s. The overwhelming majority of ESEA funds were appropriated under Title I for raising education spending for disadvantaged students. Although not an unconditional grant like most earlier federal education spending, the intended uses of Title I funds were loosely specified.

Funding is not the only role the federal government has in education. The federal judiciary frequently supervised the desegregation of schools after 1954, when the Supreme Court held in *Brown v. Board of Education* that, under the Fourteenth Amendment, an opportunity for education, if provided by a state, was "a right which must be made available to all on equal terms." In 1973, in *San Antonio Independent School District v. Rodriguez*, the Court declined to extend that holding to strike down long-standing school financing laws whereby local property taxes largely supplement state and federal funding in local schools and whereby even state funding may be distributed unequally in favor of wealthier districts. *San Antonio* held that there is no fundamental federal right to an education or, if there is, then not to a particular quality of education beyond a minimally adequate one. Therefore, even greatly unequal local school financing is constitutionally permissible ...

NCLB requires states to adopt "challenging" and specific academic content standards in language arts, mathematics, and science and to align these with achievement standards for basic, proficient, and advanced levels. These standards must be embodied in student assessments given annually in grades 3 through 8 and once in high school. Most importantly, the standards and assessments must be uniform throughout the state. States are required to develop an accountability system that defines "adequate yearly progress" (AYP) and the methods for calculating it, together with a timeline to track annual progress toward NCLB's end goal of proficiency for all students in 2014. States must submit initial, detailed compliance plans to the DOE. The Secretary of Education has approval power over the compliance plans but is also required to utilize the assistance of a peer review process that includes parents, teachers, and state education officials. School districts and states are then required to publish annual reports of data, broken down to permit tracking of student performance by economic, racial, and other indicators. A number of remedies and sanctions are provided for schools that fail to meet AYP for any two consecutive years, ranging from offering students supplemental educational services (free tutoring) and school transfer privileges to closing and restructuring schools. Finally, NCLB requires "highly qualified teachers" in every classroom …

NCLB's lack of interest in dictating particular standards for states to adopt [is shown by] the section of the law that defines "challenging academic standards" for the states' purpose of writing the content and achievement standards for the three core content areas [language arts, math, and science] … The requirements concern administrative specificity and informational transparency, not any particular level of academic mastery, as the subjective descriptors "coherent," "rigorous," and "advanced" indicate. Similarly, the section of the law that sets forth the parameters for defining AYP concerns the state's demonstration of "valid and reliable" statistics, "continuous and substantial academic improvement for all students" and for specific subgroups of disadvantaged students, and high school graduation rates; it does not suggest any particular level or rate of progress. NCLB expressly denies the Secretary of Education "the authority to require a State, as a condition of approval of the State plan, to include in, or delete from, such plan on progress or more specific elements of the State's academic content standards or to use specific academic assessment instruments or items."

While it is true that NCLB's emphasis on annual testing, elaboration of standards, and collection and dissemination of data are unable to effect real academic improvement without a more profound reform of curriculum, teaching methods, and teacher preparation, it is equally true that education cannot be significantly improved without a solid foundation of assessment, accountability, and tracking, such as NCLB requires. This is especially true for low-performing schools, regardless of immediate negative impacts on passing rates and missed AYP.

In fact, educators have long concentrated their efforts on curriculum and teaching methods, but without concrete and rigorous systems of assessment and accountability in place, those efforts have made little, if any, lasting impact and have often changed with the winds and little other reason. Such efforts have frequently focused on engaging and nurturing students while overlooking and neglecting their actual academic achievement. NCLB's transparency and reporting requirements, however burdensome they may be, are appropriate and necessary in an open society. Students' and parents' educational choices depend on accurate information, and so does the civic purpose of our federation of states. NCLB puts academic achievement and accountability first because they are the cornerstone of any sound education policy …

Complaints that NCLB directs state education policy are inaccurate. Particularly misleading is any implication that NCLB imposes standards on states. In fact, NCLB requires states to develop their own standards, design their own student assessments, define proficiency and AYP, and determine how quickly their AYP will approach the 2014 goal of 100% proficiency. By requiring states to develop statewide standards that implement a uniform education policy, NCLB works carefully with the constitutional imperatives. It respects state control of education (as the Tenth Amendment requires), and it preserves local governments' prerogative to supplement education funding (as San Antonio requires) and hence to enrich the curriculum for local needs. Standards are, after all, only a base for teaching.

The complaint that standardized testing forces teachers to "teach to the test" and to neglect a rich curriculum has entered the commonplace. Research, it is argued, shows that "as a rule, better standardized exam results are more likely to go hand-in-hand with a shallow approach to learning than with deep understanding"; thus, "a rise in scores may be worse than meaningless: it may actually be reason for concern." But the assumption here—that preparing the most disadvantaged and struggling students to pass standardized tests saps all other time and energy for teaching and learning and precludes a rich curriculum fostering critical and imaginative thinking—is a fallacy. The prevalence of the complaint against "teaching to the test" is better interpreted as evidence of the need for radical teaching and curriculum reform. There is thus no foundation to the idea that NCLB imposes education policy on states …

Federal enforcement of equality is necessarily at times inimical to entrenched local interests, as the history of the Fourteenth Amendment, including its application to education pursuant to *Brown*, has amply demonstrated. It is perhaps inevitable that the pursuit of equality in education manifests itself temporarily (again) as a struggle over institutional power and financial resources. ESEA, after all, "was intended to be primarily a redistributive bill. NCLB executes that intention and upsets the status quo of vastly unequal opportunities and outcomes in education."

Federal Funding and Testing Costs

Congress's actual annual appropriations have never equaled the amounts authorized under NCLB; they have been between one-half and two-thirds of the amounts originally authorized. Nevertheless, the appropriations represent a significant increase in federal funding of education—in the first year of the program, federal funding increased by 26% and, by 2005, the increases in federal funding that had resulted from NCLB accounted for about 2% of the total education spending by states, a substantial increase, especially considering that federal funding of education constitutes only about 7% or 8% of total education spending. NCLB's critics distort this reality with irresponsible exaggerations and inaccuracies, such as the following: "NCLB places, without remuneration, financially and bureaucratically onerous reporting duties on states, districts, and schools …"

Total federal appropriations under NCLB have covered only approximately one-third of some states' costs of compliance. Since the amounts originally authorized were only twice or less than twice the actual appropriations, it is clear that even the authorized amounts would have been insufficient to pay for compliance without the need for states to incur costs of their own. Because states design their own assessments and determine their own rates of progress, each state controls the cost of its program, as the Connecticut example demonstrates.

Before the enactment of NCLB, Connecticut Mastery Tests (CMTs) were given in grades 4, 6, and 8 and were nationally recognized as models of high-quality, comprehensive testing. To avoid the cost of developing new CMTs for grades 3, 5, and 7, Connecticut requested a waiver of NCLB's annual summative testing requirement. It proposed substituting much less expensive tests individualized by classroom and offered sound rationale for such an education policy. The Bush administration's DOE denied the request and suggested that Connecticut use multiple choice tests in grades 3, 5, and 7 to comply with NCLB's requirements while avoiding the great cost of developing and implementing new CMTs. Connecticut viewed this advice as both unsound education policy and financially unworkable. The DOE thus rejected Connecticut's policy preferences in favor of strict compliance with NCLB. Connecticut, for its part, proceeded to develop new CMTs for grades 3, 5, and 7. This sequence of events makes it clear that Connecticut took on the extra cost of developing CMTs as a policy choice, not as a requirement of NCLB or the DOE, and that reality serves to keep in perspective NCLB's true financial effects …

Connecticut's policy preferences seek to maximize academic excellence, while NCLB seeks the more mundane (and historically elusive) goal of broadening basic academic achievement. Neither goal excludes the other, although limitations of funds may require focusing on one or the other at a given time. Coming three decades after *San Antonio*, NCLB is an entirely fair swing of the pendulum.

The charge that NCLB is shortsighted is therefore a matter of perspective. NCLB's priorities are democratizing and take a long view of achieving equality. Nevertheless, NCLB in no way impedes the continued supplemental funding of local education with local property taxes. It gives an incomplete and distorted picture to attribute reduction of academic enrichment programs to the costs of NCLB and not to local communities' fiscal priorities ...

Conclusion

This [essay] has argued that a sound education policy cannot exist without uniform standards and transparent accountability. It has also argued that historical forces and socio-economic realities make a federal role in education necessary to achieve equal opportunity. Such a federal role is appropriate from the viewpoint of the Fourteenth Amendment, and so is the resulting financial burden on states. Because local school districts retain the prerogative of supplementing state and federal funding of education with local property taxes, the charge that NCLB dilutes their curriculum is unconvincing.

If NCLB has diluted or qualified state control of education, it has also provided considerable new funding and carefully preserved states' choices in education policy. Weighing the proportionality of these factors is a difficult, perhaps impossible endeavor ... States should therefore reconcile themselves to NCLB's requirements, and Congress should work with them to reauthorize an improved version that moves beyond standards to encompass teaching reform as well.

Without a sustained effort to build on the foundation of an adequate education, NCLB will lose the high ground it has claimed. Initiatives to reform curriculum and teacher preparation will be much more expensive and difficult to implement than NCLB's current provisions. Congress, too, must put its money where its mouth is ...

It would be a shame if the most pervasive equality measure in decades were to lapse ... [because] education is generative of all our freedoms.

Close Reading Questions

1. According to Anthony Consiglio, what are the real reasons the NCLB law has been so divisive?

2. What are the two main objections to NCLB, and why does Consiglio believe these critiques are somewhat contradictory?

3. Why did the state of Connecticut sue the federal Department of Education (DOE), and what was the basis of the lawsuit?

Analytical Writing/Discussion

4. What constitutional principle controls the relationship between the federal government and state governments on school control? How has this relationship changed, and why do you consider this trend to be a positive or negative one? (Historical Trends)

5. In what ways can the NCLB's demand for accountability in education through annual assessment and transparent results be considered an unnecessary burden on school systems or an essential element of school reform? After considering both viewpoints, which one do you favor, and why? (Multiple Perspectives)

6. Using the example of local funding of schools (*State of Connecticut vs. the U.S. Department of Education*), what two goals of American education are shown? Why do you think the tensions between these two goals are inevitable or resolvable? (Cultural Influences)

Further Options

7. In "Schools and Trust in a Democracy," Deborah Meier opposes federal control of education and a standardized curriculum in America's public schools. According to Consiglio, why does NCLB avoid promoting a national curriculum, yet why do you think such standardization in education from state to state would be beneficial or not? Why do you think Meier would or would not support this uniformity within states yet variation among states?

8. As explained in Chapter 5 on Argument (see pp. 103–121), it usually is persuasive to anticipate and answer likely objections to one's position. How does Consiglio counter the criticism that NCLB controls state education policies and, in particular, forces teachers to "teach to the test"? Why are you persuaded (or not) by his counterarguments?

THE ECONOMIC COST OF THE ACHIEVEMENT GAP

by Byron G. Auguste, Bryan Hancock, and Martha Laboissière

As a leading consulting firm, McKinsey & Company advises corporations, institutions, and governments worldwide. In addition to consulting on business, marketing, and public opinion, the social sector division of McKinsey & Co. publishes reports on societal concerns, such as health care and education. The three authors of this report are McKinsey employees. The following report from 2009 focuses on the widening gap in achievement by students in the United States and other developed countries, and it stresses the financial effects on the American economy.

A persistent gap in academic achievement between children in the United States and their counterparts in other countries deprived the US economy of as much as $2.3 trillion in economic output in 2008, McKinsey research finds. Moreover, each of the long-standing achievement gaps among US students of differing ethnic origins, income levels, and school systems represents hundreds of billions of dollars in unrealized economic gains. Together, these disturbing gaps underscore the staggering economic and social cost of underutilized human potential. Yet they also create room for hope by suggesting that the widespread application of best practices could secure a better, more equitable education for the country's children—along with substantial economic gains.

How has educational achievement changed in the United States since 1983, when the publication of the seminal US government report A Nation at Risk sounded the alarm about the "rising tide of mediocrity" in American schools? To learn the answer, we interviewed leading educational researchers around

This article was originally published by McKinsey & Company, www.mckinsey.com. Copyright © 2009 McKinsey & Company. All rights reserved. Reprinted by permission.

the world, assessed the landscape of academic research and educational-achievement data, and built an economic model that allowed us to examine the relationships among educational achievement (represented by standardized test scores), the earnings potential of workers, and GDP.

We made three noteworthy assumptions: test scores are the best available measure of educational achievement; educational achievement and attainment (including milestones such as graduation rates) are key drivers in hiring and are positively correlated with earnings; and labor markets will hire available workers with higher skills and education. While these assumptions admittedly simplify the socioeconomic complexities and uncertainties, they allowed us to draw meaningful conclusions about the economic impact of educational gaps in the United States.

Four substantial achievement gaps emerged from our work. The first is the international one. As recently as the 1960s, the United States led the world in a variety of educational outcomes. Yet the Organization for Economic Co-operation and Development (OECD) found that in 2006, America ranked twenty-fifth out of 30 industrialized countries in math and twenty-fourth in science. Moreover, cross-country comparisons of US students at two different ages—nine to ten and fifteen—suggest that the closer they get to joining the labor force, the further they lag behind their international counterparts in reading, math, and science.

1. Finland	548	21. Hungary	491
Korea	547	Luxembourg	490
Netherlands	531	Norway	490
Switzerland	530	Spain	480
Canada	527	25. **United States**	474
Japan	523	Portugal	466
New Zealand	522	Italy	462
Belgium	520	Greece	459
Australia	520	Turkey	424
10. Denmark	513	Mexico	406
Czech Republic	510		
Iceland	506		
Austria	505		
Germany	504		
Sweden	502	Average Score	498
Ireland	501		
France	496		
United Kingdom	495		
Poland	495		
20. Slovak Republic	492		

FIGURE 2 Average PISA Math Scores

The gap's impact is startling: if the United States had closed it by 1998 and reached the level of the top performers, such as Finland and South Korea, the US GDP could have been $1.3 trillion to $2.3 trillion higher in 2008. To put the facts another way, the gap imposes a higher recurring annual economic cost on the US economy than the [2009] recession does. If the United States had closed educational-achievement gaps by 1998, its GDP in 2008 could have been $1.3 trillion to $2.3 trillion higher.

Next, we looked at other gaps in US educational achievement. A second one emerges among US students of different ethnic origins. As researchers have long known, black and Hispanic students score, on average, two to three years behind white students of the same age on standardized tests—a gap that persists regardless of how it is measured. These differences too represent sizable missed opportunities. If the gap had been bridged by 1998, the 2008 US GDP could have been up to $525 billion higher than it was. When we looked at the implications of the achievement gap on US earnings, we found that in aggregate they could have been up to $160 billion higher in 2008 had it been eliminated. Left unchecked, the magnitude of such disparities will rise in coming years as blacks and Hispanics account for a larger share of the US population.

The two remaining achievement gaps we studied—one between students at different income levels, the other between higher- and lower-performing school systems—also appear to exact a heavy price. We define lower-income students as those eligible for free lunch through a government program. Had the achievement gap between them and other students been bridged by 1998, a decade later US GDP might have been as much as $670 billion higher than it was. If the gap between low-performing states and the US average had been closed, the 2008 US GDP could have been up to $700 billion higher. Collectively, the economic impact of the four achievement gaps we studied is significant—comparable, in their effect on the US economy, to recessions since the 1970s.

Yet, there is cause for optimism amid the gloomy findings. The wide variation in performance among schools serving similar students suggests that the widespread application of best practices observed at the system level could close the gaps. California and Texas, for example, are two large, demographically similar states. But in educational attainment, students in Texas are, on average, one to two years ahead of California students of the same age, even though Texas has a lower per capita income and spends less per pupil than California does.

The same pattern holds true among school districts within states, among schools within districts, and among classrooms within schools. Indeed, the OECD finds that the variation within US schools in 2006 was 2.6 times greater than the variation across them, confirming research by McKinsey and others that consistent, high-quality teaching is a key factor determining student achievement. Moreover, international experience confirms that it is possible to make progress in closing these gaps: not only have two dozen countries made substantial progress in overall achievement, but 17 countries that exceed US performance levels also have a narrower gap among children of divergent socioeconomic backgrounds.

Close Reading Questions

1. What are the three key assumptions about education and the economy does the report make? Which one do you find to be easiest or hardest to accept and why?

2. Along with the international comparisons, what achievement gaps among US students do the authors document? Which one do you find to be most or least likely and why?

3. According to the authors, what are the economic costs of the various forms of the achievement gaps they analyze? Create a chart to present these costs.

Analytical Writing/Discussion

4. Although the report presents several problems, why do the authors also believe there are reasons for optimism? Why does their optimism make you believe that educational reform is possible? (Multiple Perspectives)

5. When did US education begin to deteriorate, and what social factors do you think might have contributed to this decline? (Historical Trends)

6. Although some defenders of public education may object that schools cannot be expected to overcome social problems like poverty and poor parenting, why do you find (or not) the report's evidence on closing the achievement gap? (Cultural Influences)

Further Options

7. Synthesis, meaning the making of connections between two (or more) readings is central to academic writing. At the start of this chapter, Horace Mann and the Supreme Court are quoted. Mann asserts, education is a "great equalizer" in society, and in 1954, the Supreme Court decided against "separate but equal" education. How could you use some evidence from the McKinsey report to argue that the United States has or has not made enough progress on the ideals of educational and social equality?

8. As explained in Chapter 5 on Argument (see pp. 103–121), we can be convinced using three rhetorical appeals: logic (logos), emotion (pathos), and character (ethos). Which appeal do you think is used primarily in this report, and which appeal is used primarily in Theodore Sizer's "What High School Is" (see pp. 175–181)? What kind of person do you think would be persuaded by this report, and what kind of person do you think would be more convinced by Sizer's argument and why?

LESS COLLEGE PREP, NOT MORE, IN HIGH SCHOOLS

by Russell Rumberger

Given the title of this reading, it may surprise you to learn that its author is a vice provost in the University of California administration. Rumberger is the author of a 2011 book titled *Dropping Out: Why Students Drop Out of High School and What Can be Done About It*. The following reading is taken from a related newspaper article that originally was published in the *Boston Globe* on September 20, 2011.

What is the purpose of high school? Over the past several years America seems to have arrived at a consensus: The overarching goal of high school is to prepare students for college. The current mantra is "college ready for all," which means high school students need to be focusing on academic preparation and study skills. It's a rare issue that crosses party lines — both Republicans and Democrats can win points by pushing for a tougher, more competitive high school education.

From *How College Prep is Killing High School* (November 20, 2013) by Russell W. Rumberger. Copyright © 2011 by Russell W. Rumberger. Reprinted by permission.

Driven by this notion, states and districts around the country have raised high school graduation requirements by increasing the number and rigor of required academic courses and by adding exit exams. Massachusetts doesn't let students graduate unless they can pass the MCAS exam in English, math, and one science or technology subject. Americans, anxious about their competitiveness, look around the world and worry that, if anything, we're not doing enough.

But as we push harder to create more demanding high schools that are more focused on college preparation, something is also going wrong. Emerging research in the education world suggests that a tougher approach to high school academics might leave students no better prepared for college and work, while also increasing the number of high school dropouts. The National Research Council concluded that high school exit exams have decreased high school graduation rates in the United States by two percentage points without increasing achievement. In Chicago, a 2010 study found no positive effects on student achievement from a school reform measure that ended remedial classes and required college preparatory course work for all students. High school graduation rates declined, and there was no improvement in college enrollment and retention rates among students who did graduate.

The United States clearly needs more college graduates: We currently rank ninth in the world in four-year college graduation rates for domestic students, and President Obama has set a goal for the United States to be first in the world by 2020.

But we also need something else: more high school graduates, and better-trained ones. And to do that, we need to think differently about what high school should be: not narrowly focused on classroom achievement, but broadly designed to keep more students engaged, reward more types of thinking, and leave young people better prepared, whatever they plan to do.

To college-minded parents and educators, rethinking high school in this way might sound like a scaling back of ambition. But it can also be a more broad-minded, accommodating vision of what school is, and who it's for. It's a vision with deep roots in American history, and one that gives more students a chance to lay the groundwork for their futures.

Despite the current focus on college preparedness, American students, parents, and public officials have long seen education as having broader goals. In 1818 Thomas Jefferson stated that the purpose of public education included giving citizens information for transacting business, the ability to express ideas in writing, and an understanding of duties to neighbors and country.

Support for a broad range of educational goals continues to this day. A recent survey of the general public, elected officials, and state legislators by Richard Rothstein from the Economic Policy Institute and his colleagues showed support for eight broad goals for public education, with "basic academic goals" being the highest rated, but generating no more than one-quarter of the votes. Other goals included critical thinking, social skills and work ethic, and citizenship.

The need for schools to do more than prepare students for college is supported by studies about jobs in the future economy. A 2010 report from Georgetown University forecasts that by 2018, 63% of all jobs in the United States will require a postsecondary education — but that also means that more than a quarter of all jobs will not require any postsecondary education. Indeed, the Department of Labor Statistics has projected that more than one-third of all job openings in the US economy between 2008 and 2018 will not require a college degree, and in fact will require one month or less of on-the-job experience or instruction to be fully qualified in the occupation.

So for a large number of Americans, a college degree won't matter at all. What will matter, however, is graduating from high school with a set of skills that they can use to get a job, to keep learning, to live a better life.

A number of economists, including Nobel economist James Heckman, have documented the need for noncognitive or so-called soft skills in the labor market, such as motivation, perseverance, risk aversion, self-esteem, and self-control. A 2001 report from the National Association of Manufacturers found the top skill deficiency in both current workers and job applicants was a lack of basic employability skills such as timeliness and work ethic.

Only 76% of public high school students in the United States earn a diploma within four years of entering the ninth grade, a rate lower than 40 years earlier. This translates into more than 1 million students who fail to earn a high school diploma each year. When these students drop out of high school, either from lack of interest or because they can't pass an academically rigorous exam, they're losing not only the chance at the diploma they'll need to get a job, but also any opportunity they might have to acquire those basic skills.

How can we keep those students in school — and better serve them when they stay? Research has shown that the key factor in student success is being engaged. Students who are not engaged are less likely to perform well in school, more likely to fail classes, and less likely to graduate. In the 2006 Civic Enterprises report, The Silent Epidemic, high school dropouts reported that the most frequent reason for leaving school was that classes were not interesting.

America's education system — and its students — would benefit from developing a broader measure of high school success, one that includes vocational and technical education as well as the arts and humanities.

Research demonstrates that career and technical education — courses that teach applied skills in agriculture, engineering, health science, and the like — increases attendance, raises completion rates, and improves earnings and employment prospects of high school graduates whether or not they attend college. International comparisons further reveal that countries offering more access to vocational options have higher high school completion rates as well as higher scores on international tests.

Such courses, if approached creatively, can also provide another way of teaching rigorous academic content. The University of California, where I work, is helping teachers design so-called integrated technical courses for high schools that meet entry requirements for the university. One example is an auto mechanics course that also teaches students college prep physics, already offered in one California high school.

A more balanced high school education would also offer students the chance to spend time in a workplace, not only learning career-specific skills, but also developing the "soft" skills needed for success. In such schools, graduation requirements could be redefined so students could succeed not just by passing MCAS-style tests, but by demonstrating mastery of an area that most interests them — whether it is math, physics, cooking, mechanics, or sports — while achieving acceptable proficiency in core academic and other areas.

High school, in short, should not just prepare adolescents for college and careers, but for successful lives as adults. And far from backing off modern notions of success, this approach actually embodies new understandings of what really helps people succeed: not just reading and math, but deeper life skills that aren't reflected on exit exams or college applications.

A long-term study by sociologist John Clausen tracked children born in the Great Depression for six decades and found that those whose lives turned out best — who obtained more education, had lower rates of divorce, had more orderly careers, achieved higher occupational status, and experienced fewer life crises such as unemployment — shared something he labeled "planful competence," a combination of dependability, intellectual involvement, and self-confidence. Those factors, he found, didn't necessarily correspond to higher education or test scores. "There's nothing that predicts better," he wrote, "than what they were like in high school."

Close Reading Questions

1. According to recent research cited by Rumberger, what are the purpose of the tougher graduation requirements and the results of these new standards?

2. Along with college preparation, how else might the goals of high school education be defined more broadly? With which of these additional goals offered by the author, do you agree most or last, and why?

3. What percentage of students is dropping out of high school now, and what are the long-term effects on their lives?

Analytical Writing/Discussion

4. How can the advocacy of broader educational goals be supported by historical evidence as well as current economics? Which evidence do you think would be most persuasive to school officials and why? (Historical Trends)

5. Along with the broadening of the goals of education, how could the courses offered in high schools also be altered? Why would you have liked to have taken some of the courses proposed or not? (Multiple Perspectives)

6. According to the sociologist John Clausen, what personal attributes make it more likely for adults to succeed at school, work, and home? To what degree do you think these qualities can be and should be taught in public high schools? (Cultural Influences)

Further Options

7. In "What High School Is," Theodore Sizer also examines the stated goals of high school education. In what specific ways do your think Sizer's and Rumberger's analyses of school goals are similar to or different from each other?

8. Using the double-entry notes explained in Chapter 1 (see p. 11), answer the following question: Which of the other authors of the previous readings of this chapter: Dewey, Meier, and Consiglio, do you think is more or less likely to agree with Rumberger on broadening the goals of high school education beyond college preparation? Explain why they agree or disagree using specific quotations selected from each reading and then explain their significance.

Freewrite 3: Two Classrooms

The following excerpts from two different books provide an unusual glimpse at the act of teaching because both describe the same poem being taught to high school students. After reading both excerpts, you will be asked to respond through freewriting and/or discussion.

Excerpts from *Savage Inequalities: Children in America's Schools* by Jonathan Kozol, copyright © 1991 by Jonathan Kozol. Used by permission of Crown Books, an imprint of the Crown Publishing Group, a division of Random House LLC. All rights reserved.

From *Savage Inequalities* by Jonathan Kozol:

In a sun-drenched corner room on the top floor, a female teacher and some 25 black and Hispanic children are reading a poem by Paul Laurence Dunbar. Holes in the walls and ceiling leave exposed the structural brick. The sun appears to blind the teacher. There are no shades. Sheets of torn construction paper have been taped to windowpanes, but the glare is quite relentless. The children look forlorn and sleepy.

> I know why the caged bird sings …
> It is not a carol of joy …

"This is your homework," says the teacher. "Let's get on with it."

But the children cannot seem to wake up to the words. A 15-year-old boy, wearing a floppy purple hat, white jersey, and striped baggy pants, is asked to read the lines.

> I know what the caged bird feels …
> When the wind stirs soft through the springing grass,
> And the river flows like a stream of glass …

A 15-year-old girl with curly long red hair and many freckles reads the lines. Her T-shirt hangs down almost to her knees.

> I know why the caged bird beats his wing
> Till its blood is red on the cruel bars.

A boy named Victor, sitting at my side, whispers the words: "I know why the caged bird beats his wing … is blood is red. He wants to spread his wings."

The teacher asks the children what the poet means or what the imagery conveys. There is no response at first. Then Victor lifts his hand. "The poem is about ancient days of slavery," he says. "The bird destroys himself because he can't escape the cage."

> "Why does he sing?" the teacher asks.
> "He sings out of the longing to be free."
> At the end of class the teacher tells me, "Forty, maybe 45 percent out of this group will graduate."

From *Reason to Believe* by Hephzibah Roskelly and Kate Ronald:

Bill Buczinsky teaches five classes: two honors ninth-grade classes, one "regular" ninth grade, and two "standard" ninth-grade sections. These last sections are filled with students who for one reason or another could be labeled "at risk." [These] students are more likely to be poor, to come from dangerous neighborhoods. Many—a disproportionately large number—are

Reprinted by permission from *Reason to Believe: Romanticism, Pragmatism, and the Teaching of Writing* by Hephzibah Roskelly and Kate Ronald, the State University of New York Press © 1998, State University of New York. All rights reserved.

black. Several students speak English as a second language. Two are physically handicapped, one with a leg brace and an arm brace that Bill will adjust to aid the student's writing. One student stutters noticeably with each sentence. They are students who are in danger of getting lost in a system that seems often to have despaired of helping them. It is an old classroom with large windows and seats ranged around on three sides. [The teacher Bill] never sits. He jokes as the bell rings, takes roll quickly, cues up a tape, writes on the board, answers questions, gives directions, all at once it seems. There are twenty-six students.

[A school official] is sitting in Bill's class to observe. She sits on one side of the room watching Bill, who walks among the students as he begins the class, laughing as he talks: "Guys, if you could do a favor for me here and get started. While you're preparing for class to begin I'm going to cue up something for you." "Notice what Andrew has on his head." "Yes, I see you have that notebook open. Good." He's speaking fast and moving as he talks, commanding their attention with his goodwill. He puts on a recording of some classical music, passes out copies of the poem they will read and discuss today, and asks students to begin to read it. It is Paul Lawrence Dunbar's "Sympathy." "You may know this poem," Bill says. "You may know what the poet feels like. Before we do anything else, I want you to take five minutes and think about it. Write for five minutes. Do you ever feel trapped like the guy in the poem? Do you know why the caged bird sings?"

… When everybody is finished or close enough, Bill asks students to read aloud their responses. Predictably they begin with characterizations of school as a time to feel caged. School is a prison. Bill talks about rules, about breaking them. He tells a story about a student he's seen eating lunch off campus. He tells them what he's said to the rule breaker: "You look like a kid I know who's a junior. So he wouldn't be here at Taco Bell because only seniors can do that, of course." The students all laugh. "Why the rule about going off campus?" Bill says. "Because people won't come back." "When is it OK to break a rule in the system?" Students ask this question but don't answer it. They are finding connections between what they have written about being caged and the discussion about breaking and making rules.

As students talk and respond, read or tell what they've written, Bill watches to see who is waiting to speak, who is quiet but ready. He does this casually, calmly, seeing the whole class, attentive to both speakers at the moment and listeners. A young woman from Columbia speaks about being caged in a culture where she's not allowed to wear long hair at her school, and the other students whistle. The students ask her about her hometown in Bogata. The conversation moves to several students who sit close together and begin complaining of being in prison at home with parents who don't let them set their own curfews or don't like their friends. One or two comment on being imprisoned in their jobs, where dress codes or hours keep them trapped.

One young man has been quietly following the discussion, looking down every so often at his paper to check it, offering a comment as others have spoken up. Finally, he raises his hand and Bill catches it. Ron begins to speak, but Bill stops him. "Why don't you read it?" he says. Ron reads: "It's bad when school is a prison or when your house is. When the walls around you trap you. But that's not the worst thing." Ron tells about his life at home. His grandmother won't let him go shoot baskets in the evening at the park because "just last week they held up some kids down there." And how he won't walk to the store anymore because there [have been] three drive-by [shootings] in the last month. "You should feel free when you're outside in the air. It's the worst thing when your own neighborhood, everything around you makes you feel like you're in a prison."

Bill asks someone to read "Sympathy" aloud now and then again. He looks at Ron and says, "Ron knows 'what the caged bird feels, alas.'" Ron laughs, "I wouldn't use 'alas.'" Everybody begins to talk at once, but time—alas—is up. Students gather up their books, a few pat Ron on the back as they leave.

After reading these two texts, answer some of the following questions by freewriting and/or discussion:

- Although students in each class demonstrate some understanding of the poem, why do you think one teacher can be deemed more effective and why?
- In what ways is each poetry similar to or different from the way you usually were taught to read, enjoy, and analyze literature?
- What do you think are crucial qualities of an effective teacher?
- How have those qualities of effective teaching been fulfilled or not in these readings?

Final Assignment 1: The Ends and the Means of Education

The authors of this chapter's readings examine the means and the ends of secondary education. Sizer, for instance, points out that the stated goals of some high schools do not match their actual practices.

Essay Question

What do you think are the most important goals and the best methods of high school education? How do you think these ends and means should be coordinated? For instance, should standardized tests be used to link goals and methods?

Write a formal and extended essay to answer this question. Be sure to include specific references and direct quotations from several readings in this chapter (see Chapter 4 on Academic Honesty on quoting and citing properly). Be sure to not only support your informed perspective but also to anticipate and answer the possible objections of those who do not already agree with you. Your task is to assert your opinion and persuade others to consider it carefully.

Freewrite 4: Assignment Analysis

Before you start to answer this complex question, analyze its parts. Reread the essay question above and underline several phrases that represent key parts of the larger answer you will be developing. Then pick two or three of these phrases and freewrite your immediate impressions: What do you think right now? Then, pause to look for connections, contradictions, and omissions within your first response: what else do you want to discuss, what else do you want to add, and/or what order of your ideas is developing? Finally, consider the audience of your essay: who does not agree with you already, and why might they disagree?

Reading Review

Once you have sketched some of your initial ideas, review some of the readings to find specific details and persuasive evidence to support, enrich, and possibly complicate your response. Here are some readings and postreading questions that you may want to consider:

1. Freewrite 1
2. Sizer, Close Reading Question 3

3. Dewey, Analytical Writing Question 5

4. Meier, Close Reading Question 1

5. Freewrite 2

6. Freewrite 3

7. Consiglio, Analytical Writing Question 5

8. Rumberger, Analytical Writing Question 5

Feel free to include other readings and postreading questions. You also may want to review the suggestions for writing persuasively in Chapter 5 on Argument as well as practicing the peer response described in Chapter 2 on the writing process.

Final Assignment 2: Rhetorical Analysis

For two readings of this chapter (or possibly using one of the additional readings suggested below), compare and/or contrast their arguments. As explained in Chapter 5, this rhetorical analysis will answer the following questions:

- Based on the rhetorical triangle, what is the message of this text? What does the publication source suggest about the audience of this text? How do you think these readers will react to this message and why? Finally, who is the writer, and how might the author affect the audience's response to the text? (See pp. 104 and 105 of Chapter 5.)

- How does the writer try to use each of the three rhetorical appeals: ethos, logos, and pathos, and when are they used effectively or not? (See pp. 105–109 of Chapter 5).

- Your professor may ask you to consider also the kind of argument being made, meaning a forensic, epideictic, or deliberative argument (see pp. 110–112 of Chapter 5). What kind of argument is being made, and how does it affect the audience's reaction to this persuasion?

- Finally, through comparing and contrasting the arguments of these two readings, what can you conclude about their power to persuade their intended audiences (and possibly additional readers)?

Your task is to help your readers to understand these two arguments and their efforts to persuade their audiences.

Final Assignment 3: Schools as Sites of Social Change

As an educational theorist, Dewey initially believed that better schooling would lead to the social reforms he desired, such as the furthering of democracy. Yet when he tried to implement his educational theories, Dewey found his task was much more difficult than he had considered. He discovered that schools, as social institutions, are slow to change because of the "opposition of those who ... realize [educational reform] would threaten their ability to use others for their own ends." Thus, the possibility of educational reform leading to social reform is complicated by the fact that schools share many of the same problems from which society in general suffers.

Essay Question

> To what degree do you think high schools can be used to help resolve social problems? Or do you think schools are limited because they reflect the problems of society?

Write a formal and extended essay to answer these questions. Be sure to include specific references and direct quotations from several readings in this chapter (see Chapter 4 on Academic Honesty on quoting and citing properly). Be sure to not only support your informed perspective but also to anticipate and answer the possible objections of those who do not already agree with you. Your task is to assert your opinion and persuade others to consider it carefully.

Freewrite 5: Assignment Analysis

Before you start to answer this complex question, analyze its parts. Reread the question above and underline several phrases that represent key parts of the larger answer you will be developing. Then pick two or three of these phrases and freewrite your immediate impressions: What do you think right now? Then, pause to look for connections, contradictions, and omissions within your first response: what else do you want to discuss, what else do you want to add, and/or what order of your ideas is developing? Finally, consider the audience of your essay: who does not agree with you already, and why might they disagree?

Reading Review

Once you have sketched some of your initial ideas, review some of the readings to find specific details and persuasive evidence to support, enrich, and possibly complicate your response. Here are some readings and postreading questions that you may want to consider:

1. Freewrite 1
2. Sizer, Analytical Writing Question 6
3. Dewey, Analytical Writing Question 6
4. Meier, Analytical Writing Question 4
5. Meier, Further Options Question 7
6. Consiglio, Analytical Writing Question 6
7. Auguste, Hancock, and Laboissiere, Analytical Writing Question 6
8. Rumberger, Close Reading Question 3

Feel free to include other readings and post-reading questions. You also may want to review the suggestions for writing persuasively in Chapter 5 on Argument as well as practicing the peer response described in Chapter 2 on the Writing Process.

Readings on Education in Other Chapters

For three additional readings on education, you may want to read the following texts:

1. "The Gutenberg Elegies: The Fate of Reading in an Electronic Age" by Sven Birkerts in Chapter 10 (see pp. 305–308)

2. "How Reading is Being Reimagined" by Matthew Kirschenbaum in Chapter 10 (see pp. 321–324)

3. "Online Literacy is a Lesser Kind" by Mark Bauerlein in Chapter 10 (see pp. 325–329)

Additional Sources for Chapter 7

To deepen your understanding of educational reform in America and strengthen your final assignment, you can consult some of the following sources:

1. To learn more about education from a teacher's perspective, you may want to read "How Parents Make Teachers Miserable" by Colleen Hughes. This essay addresses not only the frustrations caused by meddlesome parents but also the pressures of frequent testing in public schools.

   http://www.bostonglobe.com/magazine/2014/09/10/how-parents-make-teachers-miserable/uDcDfgqhJDoXJuPQF5sEtK/story.html

2. For more information on the new curriculum and testing program by the federal government, you may want to read (or listen to) "The Common Core Curriculum Void" by Cory Turner. This report by a National Public Radio correspondent explains how the Common Core is replacing the NCLB program for education; however, the implementation of this national curriculum has not yet been matched by curriculum materials.

   http://www.npr.org/blogs/ed/2014/06/03/318228023/the-common-core-curriculum-void

3. For further information on how public schools are rushing to fulfill the Common Core, you may want to read (or listen to) "Postcards from the Common Core." This report from National Public Radio describes the efforts by various public schools to implement the new national goals of the Common Core.

   http://www.npr.org/blogs/ed/20/08/02/334883799/postcards-from-the-common-core-classroom

4. To learn more about the history of racial segregation and the struggle to desegregate public school in the United States, you may want to read an excerpt from *Carlotta's Story: A Mighty Long Way to Go* by Carlotta Walls Lanier. In this memoir, Lanier recalls her experience in 1959 as one of the

"Little Rock Nine" who led the desegregation of public school in Arkansas and faced discrimination by many students.

https://www.alphachihonor.org/tasks/sites/default/assets/File/Publications/Recorders/Recorder_Af10.pdf

5. To examine the continuing problem of racial segregation in public schools, you may want to read "On the Anniversary of Brown v. Board, New Evidence that U.S. Schools are Resegrgating" by Emma Brown. In this news article from *The Washington Post*, Brown analyzes a government report on a troubling trend in public education in 2016.

https://www.washingtonpost.com/news/education/wp/2016/05/17/on-the-anniversary-of-brown-v-board-new-evidence-that-u-s-schools-are-resegregating/?utm_term=.1437cad2b19a

6. For more information on the economic implications of educational achievement, you may want to read and view "The Economic Impact of the Achievement Gap" by McKinsey & Company. This report on the financial consequences of undereducated students for American society can be viewed in an introductory video and read as a longer downloadable document.

http://mckinseyonsociety.com/the-economic-impact-of-the-achievement-gap-in-americas-schools/

7. For an international perspective on educational reform, you may want to view a video for Amanda Ripley's book *The Smartest Kids in the World*. This video introduces Ripley's research on the best practices of public schools in several countries, such as Finland and Poland.

http://www.youtube.com/watch?v=VSXt5bzQN-U&feature=youtu.be

Race and Identity

CHAPTER 8

We have come over a way that with tears has been watered,
We have come, treading our path through the blood of the slaughtered.

—James Weldon Johnson (1900)

An identity is questioned only when it is menaced, as when the mighty begin to fall, or when the wretched begin to rise, or when the stranger enters the gates, never, thereafter, to be a stranger.

—James Baldwin (1976)

I am an American, not an Asian-American. My rejection of hyphenation has been called race treachery, but it is really a demand that America deliver the promises of its dream to all its citizens equally.

—Bharati Mukherjee (1997)

I see Americans of every party, every background, every faith who believe that we are stronger together: black, white, Latino, Asian, Native American; young, old; gay, straight; men, women, folks with disabilities. . . That's the America I know!

—President Barack Obama (2016)

Introduction

W. E. B. Du Bois famously wrote: "The problem of the twentieth century is the problem of the color line." Surely this Harvard-educated sociologist, intellectual, and cofounder of the NAACP knew of what he spoke. Born just after the Civil War and raised amid relative integration in southern Massachusetts, Du Bois was an African American man who would see vast changes in race relations during his 95 years.

It is likely that Du Bois would not have celebrated for long had he lived long enough to see Barack Obama become the first African American president in the history of the United States. Du Bois was a proponent of higher education and during Obama's presidency, African American, Native American, and Hispanic males earned the fewest number of bachelor's degrees than any other population. Other lows that centered on race have persisted, which surely would have caused Du Bois great concern:

- Obama's first election in 2008 sparked a marked rise in racially motivated hate crimes. Again, after the 2016 Presidential election, hate crimes increased.

- Hispanic women who were paid hourly earn an average of $12 per hour, while Asian men earned twice that amount per hour.

- Integrated neighborhoods became more prevalent in the 2000s but when white families moved out of those neighborhoods they were almost always replaced by families of color, perpetuating a pattern of resegregation.

- Asian American and white students outperformed all other races in SAT critical reading, math, and writing scores.

In the final days of his presidency, Obama noted that it was "naïve and unrealistic" to believe that his election to the highest office in the nation would lead to a postracial society. Despite the activism of Du Bois and thousands of other men women, it is hard to argue that the problem of the twenty-first century is the problem of the color line.

Indeed, race matters in the United States. Sociologist Michael S. Kimmel, in his 2003 book *Privilege: A Reader*, argues that "it is a luxury that only white people have in our society not to think about race every day of their lives."

Race is a part of everyone's identity and not just people of color. Race affects friendships, romantic partners, and workplace relationships. Race affects where we live and how we worship, what we eat, and how we speak. Race affects whom we regard as attractive, intelligent, safe, worthwhile, even redeemable. Yet race need not be a bridge that cannot be crossed. In the words of poet Audre Lorde, "It is not our differences that divide us. It is our inability to recognize, accept, and celebrate those differences."

These texts, along with the reading questions, freewriting activities, and visual elements of this chapter, are designed to develop the reading and writing abilities required for academic study. The readings in this chapter include many different terms used to identify races and ethnicities. While these terms may now be unpopular or even detested by some, the inclusion of such language is in keeping with the historic and/or cultural choices made by the authors. As such, the postreading questions will often use the same terms used by the authors in their essays, articles, and short stories. This chapter cannot address every race or related aspects of identity; instead the readings strive to raise key questions that can be applied to many variations of race and identity.

After each reading, you will find a set of questions that are divided into Close Reading Questions, Analytical Writing/Discussion, and Further Options. Some questions involve the same investigation of multiple perspectives, cultural influences, and historical trends that were introduced in Chapter 1. Answering some and discussing more of the postreading questions will better prepare you to complete the final assignments options. These final writing assignments will ask you to assert your own, more informed perspective on education, equality, and outcomes. This chapter asks: **Why does the intersection of race and identity continue to be relevant in the United States in the twenty-first century?**

Freewrite 1: Initial Impressions

Before you read the perspectives of the writers in the rest of this chapter, freewrite to explore your own thoughts and experiences. Try answering some of the following questions:

- Where have you learned the most about racial identity? In school? At home? With friends?
- Do you think race is a bigger deal for your generation than for older or younger generations? Why or why not?

- Has anyone ever assumed something about you because of your race?

- Why do you think it is (or is not) difficult to talk about race?

HOW IT FEELS TO BE COLORED ME

by Zora Neale Hurston

Zora Neale Hurston was one of the most prolific writers of the cultural era known as the Harlem Renaissance. Hurston, a native of Eatonville, Florida, often called upon the recollections of her childhood to write novels like *Their Eyes Were Watching God* (1937) and *Mules and Men* (1935). Hurston briefly studied at Howard University and Barnard College. Despite gaining incredible notoriety in her day, Hurston died in poverty in 1960. Her grave was without a headstone until 1973, when writer Alice Walker spearheaded an effort to find Hurston's gravesite. The following essay was written by Hurston in 1928.

I am colored but I offer nothing in the way of extenuating circumstances except the fact that I am the only Negro in the United States whose grandfather on the mother's side was *not* an Indian chief.

I remember the very day that I became colored. Up to my thirteenth year, I lived in the little Negro town of Eatonville, Florida. It is exclusively a colored town. The only white people I knew passed through the town going to or coming from Orlando. The native whites rode dusty horses, the Northern tourists chugged down the sandy village road in automobiles. The town knew the Southerners and never stopped cane chewing when they passed. But the Northerners were something else again. They were peered at cautiously from behind the curtains by the timid. The more venturesome would come out on the porch to watch them go past and got just as much pleasure out of the tourists as the tourists got out of the village.

The front porch might seem a daring place for the rest of the town, but it was a gallery seat for me. My favorite place was atop the gatepost. Proscenium box[1] for a born first-nighter. Not only did I enjoy the show, but I didn't mind the actors knowing that I liked it. I usually spoke to them in passing. I'd wave at them and when they returned my salute, I would say something like this: "Howdy-do-well-I-thank-you-where-you-goin'?" Usually automobile or the horse paused at this, and after a queer exchange of compliments, I would probably "go a piece of the way" with them, as we say in farthest Florida. If one of my family happened to come to the front in time to see me, of course negotiations would be rudely broken off. But even so, it is clear that I was the first "welcome-to-our-state" Floridian, and I hope the Miami Chamber of Commerce will please take notice.

During this period, white people differed from colored to me only in that they rode through town and never lived there. They liked to hear me "speak pieces" and sing and wanted to see me dance the parse-me-la, and gave me generously of their small silver for doing these things, which seemed strange to me for I wanted to do them so much that I needed bribing to stop. Only they didn't know it. The colored people gave no dimes. They deplored any joyful tendencies in me, but I was their Zora nevertheless. I belonged to them, to the nearby hotels, to the county—everybody's Zora.

But changes came in the family when I was thirteen, and I was sent to school in Jacksonville. I left Eatonville, the town of the oleanders, as Zora. When I disembarked from the river-boat at Jacksonville, she was no more. It seemed that I had suffered a sea change. I was not Zora of Orange County any more, I was now a little colored girl. I found it out in certain ways. In my heart as well as in the mirror, I became a fast[2] brown—warranted not to rub nor run.

But I am not tragically colored. There is no great sorrow dammed up in my soul, nor lurking behind my eyes. I do not mind at all. I do not belong to the sobbing school of Negrohood who hold that nature somehow has given them a lowdown dirty deal and whose feelings are all hurt about it. Even in the helter-skelter skirmish that is my life, I have seen that the world is to the strong regardless of a little pigmentation more or less. No, I do not weep at the world—I am too busy sharpening my oyster knife.[3]

Someone is always at my elbow reminding me that I am the granddaughter of slaves. It fails to register depression with me. Slavery is sixty years in the past. The operation was successful and the patient is doing well, thank you. The terrible struggle that made me an American out of a potential slave said "On the line!" The Reconstruction said "Get set!"; and the generation before said "Go!" I am off to a flying start and I must not halt in the stretch to look behind and weep. Slavery is the price I paid for civilization, and the choice was not with me. It is a bully adventure and worth all that I have paid through my ancestors for it. No one on earth ever had a greater chance for glory. The world to be won and nothing to be lost. It is thrilling to think—to know that for any act of mine, I shall get twice as much praise or twice as much blame. It is quite exciting to hold the center of the national stage, with the spectators not knowing whether to laugh or to weep.

The position of my white neighbor is much more difficult. No brown specter pulls up a chair beside me when I sit down to eat. No dark ghost thrusts its leg against mine in bed. The game of keeping what one has is never so exciting as the game of getting.

I do not always feel colored. Even now I often achieve the unconscious Zora of Eatonville before the Hegira.[4] I feel most colored when I am thrown against a sharp white background.

For instance at Barnard. "Beside the waters of the Hudson" I feel my race. Among the thousand white persons, I am a dark rock surged upon, and overswept, but through it all, I remain myself. When covered by the waters, I am; and the ebb but reveals me again.

Sometimes it is the other way around. A white person is set down in our midst, but the contrast is lust as sharp for me. For instance, when I sit in the drafty basement that is The New World Cabaret[5] with a white person, my color comes. We enter chatting about any little nothing that we have in common and are seated by the jazz waiters. In the abrupt way that jazz orchestras have, this one plunges into a number. It loses no time in circumlocutions, but gets right down to business. It constricts the thorax and splits the heart with its tempo and narcotic harmonies. This orchestra grows rambunctious, rears on its hind legs and attacks the tonal veil with primitive fury, rending it, clawing it until it breaks through to the jungle beyond. I follow those heathen—follow them exultingly. I dance wildly inside myself; I yell within, I whoop; I shake my assegai[6] above my head, I hurl it true to the mark yeeeeooww! I am in the jungle and living in the jungle way. My face is painted red and yellow and my body is painted blue. My pulse is throbbing like a war drum. I want to slaughter something—give pain, give death to what, I do not know. But the piece ends. The men of the orchestra wipe their lips and rest their fingers. I creep back slowly to the veneer we call civilization with the last tone and find the white friend sitting motionless in his seat smoking calmly.

"Good music they have here," he remarks, drumming the table with his fingertips.

Music. The great blobs of purple and red emotion have not touched him. He has only heard what I felt. He is far away and I see him but dimly across the ocean and the continent that have fallen between us. He is so pale with his whiteness then and I am so colored.

At certain times I have no race, I am *me*. When I set my hat at a certain angle and saunter down Seventh Avenue, Harlem City, feeling as snooty as the lions in front of the Forty-Second Street Library,[7] for instance. So far as my feelings are concerned, Peggy Hopkins Joyce[8] on the Boule Mich[9] with her gorgeous raiment, stately carriage, knees knocking together in a most aristocratic manner, has nothing on me. The cosmic Zora emerges. I belong to no race nor time. I am the eternal feminine with its string of beads.

I have no separate feeling about being an American citizen and colored. I am merely a fragment of the Great Soul that surges within the boundaries. My country, right or wrong.

Sometimes, I feel discriminated against, but it does not make me angry. It merely astonishes me. How can any deny themselves the pleasure of my company? It's beyond me.

But in the main, I feel like a brown bag of miscellany propped against a wall. Against a wall in company with other bags, white, red, and yellow. Pour out the contents, and there is discovered a jumble of small things priceless and worthless. A first-water diamond,[10] an empty spool, bits of broken glass, lengths of string, a key to a door long since crumbled away, a rusty knife-blade, old shoes saved for a road that never was and never will be, a nail bent under the weight of things too heavy for any nail, a dried flower or two still a little fragrant. In your hand is the brown bag. On the ground before you is the jumble it held—so much like the jumble in the bags, could they be emptied, that all might be dumped in a single heap and the bags refilled without altering the content of any greatly. A bit of colored glass more or less would not matter. Perhaps that is how the Great Stuffer of Bags filled them in the first place—who knows?

Notes

[1.] Box at the very front of the auditorium, closest to the stage
[2.] Dyed colors that do not fade
[3.] An allusion to Shakespeare's *The Merry Wives of Windsor*, 2.2.3-4:'Why, then the world's mine oyster,/ Which I with sword will open."
[4.] In Islam, Mohammed's emigration from Mecca to Medina in A.D. 622; here the journey to Jacksonville.
[5.] Popular Harlem nightclub in the 1920s
[6.] A slender spear used by some South African tribes
[7.] The headquarters of the New York Public Library
[8.] A socialite and heiress, much photographed
[9.] The elegant Boulevard St. Michel in Paris, a street on the left bank of Paris running near the Sorbonne University
[10.] A high quality diamond

Close Reading Questions

1. Why was the gatepost one of Hurston's favorite places as a child?

2. Why did Hurston feel that being the descendant of slaves ". . . failed to register depression" within her? (Multiple Perspectives)

3. Although Hurston was discriminated against, why didn't it make her angry?

Analytical Writing/Discussion

4. In what ways did Hurston's hometown support her racial identity? (Cultural Influences)

5. Hurston notes that she did not always feel like a member of her race. Under what circumstances did she feel more, or less, identified as "colored?"

6. Hurston described herself as "a brown bag of miscellany." Why do you think Hurston selected this image? How does it compare to modern day ideas about diversity? (Historical Trends)

Further Options

7. Synthesis, meaning the making of connections between two (or more) readings is central to academic writing. How can you connect Hurston's essay to one of the opening quotations in this chapter? Which quotation seems to support or refute one or more of the ideas of which Hurston writes?

8. Hurston wrote that music sparked a variety of emotions within her. What kind of music or art inspires you? Have you ever had an emotional reaction to music because it reminds you of your heritage or identity?

IN SEARCH OF OUR MOTHER'S GARDENS

by Alice Walker

Alice Walker is one of the most celebrated writers of the twentieth century. Born in Georgia to sharecropping parents, she was the youngest of eight children. Walker attended Spelman College and graduated from Sarah Lawrence College. Walker's best-known work, the 1992 novel, *The Color Purple,* won the Pulitzer Prize for fiction. Walker is also the author of several novels and books of poetry, essays, non-fiction, including *Revolutionary Petunias, Now Is the Time to Open Your Heart, The Temple of My Familiar,* and *Anything We Love Can Be Saved.* The following excerpt comes from her 1983 collection of essays, *In Search of Our Mother's Gardens: Womanist Prose.*

I described her own nature and temperament. Told how they needed a larger life for their expression. . . . I pointed out that in lieu of proper channels, her emotions had overflowed into paths that dissipated them. I talked, beautifully I thought, about an art that would be born, an art that would open the way for

"In Search of our Mothers' Gardens" from *In Search of Our Mothers' Gardens: A Womanist Prose* by Alice Walker. Copyright © 1974 by Alice Walker. Reprinted by permission of Houghton Mifflin Harcourt Publishing Company. All rights reserved.

women the likes of her. I asked her to hope, and build up an
inner life against the coming of that day. . . . I sang, with a
strange quiver in my voice, a promise song.

—*"Avey," Jean Toomer,*[1] *Cane*

The poet speaking to a prostitute who falls asleep while he's talking—

When the poet Jean Toomer walked through the South in the early twenties, he discovered a curious thing: black women whose spirituality was so intense, so deep, so unconscious, that they were themselves unaware of the richness they held. They stumbled blindly through their lives: creatures so abused and mutilated in body, so dimmed and confused by pain, that they considered themselves unworthy even of hope. In the selfless abstractions, their bodies became to the men who used them, they became more than "sexual objects," more even than mere women: they became Saints. Instead of being perceived as whole persons, their bodies became shrines: what was thought to be their minds became temples suitable for worship. These crazy "Saints" stared out at the world, wildly, like lunatics—or quietly, like suicides; and the "God" that was in their gaze was as mute as a great stone.

Who were these "Saints"? These crazy, loony, pitiful women?
Some of them, without a doubt, were our mothers and grandmothers.

In the still heat of the post-Reconstruction South, this is how they seemed to Jean Toomer: exquisite butterflies trapped in an evil honey, toiling away their lives in an era, a century, that did not acknowledge them, except as "the *mule* of the world." They dreamed dreams that no one knew—not even themselves, in any coherent fashion—and saw visions no one could understand. They wandered or sat about the countryside crooning lullabies to ghosts, and drawing the mother of Christ in charcoal on courthouse walls.

They forced their minds to desert their bodies and their striving spirits sought to rise, like frail whirlwinds from the hard red clay. And when those frail whirlwinds fell, in scattered particles, upon the ground, no one mourned. Instead, men lit candies to celebrate the emptiness that remained, as people do who enter a beautiful but vacant space to resurrect a God.

Our mothers and grandmothers, some of them: moving to music not yet written. And they waited.

They waited for a day when the unknown thing that was in them would be made known; but guessed, somehow in their darkness, that on the day of their revelation they would be long dead. Therefore to Toomer they walked, and even ran, in slow motion. For they were going nowhere immediate, and the future was not yet within their grasp. And men took our mothers and grandmothers, "but got no pleasure from it." So complex was their passion and their calm.

To Toomer, they lay vacant and fallow as autumn fields with harvest time never in sight: and he saw them enter loveless marriages, without joy; and become prostitutes, without resistance; and become mothers of children, without fulfillment.

For these grandmothers and mothers of ours were not Saints, but Artists; driven to a numb and bleeding madness by the springs of creativity in them for which there was no release. They were Creators, who lived lives of spiritual waste, because they were so rich in spirituality—which is the basis of Art—-that the strain of enduring their unused and unwanted talent drove them insane. Throwing away this spirituality was their pathetic attempt to lighten the soul to a weight their work-worn, sexually abused bodies could bear.

What did it mean for a black woman to be an artist in our grandmothers' time? It is a question with an answer cruel enough to stop the blood.

Did you have a genius of a great-great-grandmother who died under some ignorant and depraved white overseer's lash? Or was she required to bake biscuits for a lazy backwater tramp, when she cried out in her soul to paint watercolors of sunsets, or the rain falling on the green and peaceful pasturelands? Or was her body broken and forced to bear children (who were more often than not sold away from her)—eight, ten, fifteen, twenty children—when her one joy was the thought of modeling heroic figures of Rebellion, in stone or clay?

How was the creativity of the black woman kept alive, year after year and century after century, when for most of the years black people have been in America, it was a punishable crime for a black person to read or write? And the freedom to paint, to sculpt, to expand the mind with action did not exist. Consider, if you can bear to imagine it, what might have been the result if singing, too, had been forbidden by law. Listen to the voices of Bessie Smith, Billie Holiday, Nina Simone, Roberta Flack, and Aretha Franklin, among others, and imagine those voices muzzled for life. Then you may begin to comprehend the lives of our "crazy," "Sainted" mothers and grandmothers. The agony of the lives of women who might have been Poets, Novelists, Essayists, and Short Story Writers, who died with their real gifts stifled within them.

And if this were the end of the story, we would have cause to cry out in my paraphrase of Okot p'Bitek's[2] great poem:

> O, my clanswomen
> Let us all cry together!
> Come,
> Let us mourn the death of our mother,
> The death of a Queen
> The ash that was produced
> By a great fire,
> O this homestead is utterly dead
> Close the gates
> With lacari thorns,
> For our mother
> The creator of the
> Stool is lost!
> And all the young women
> Have perished in the wilderness!

But this is not the end of the story, for all the young women—our mothers and grandmothers, ourselves—have not perished in the wilderness. And if we ask ourselves why, and search for and find the answer, we will know beyond all efforts to erase it from our minds, just exactly who, and of what, we black American women are.

One example, perhaps the most pathetic, most misunderstood one, can provide a backdrop: Phillis Wheatley, a slave in the 1700s.

Virginia Woolf, in her book, *A Room of One's Own*, wrote that in order for a woman to write fiction she must have two things, certainly: a room of her own (with key and lock) and enough money to support herself.

What then are we to make of Phillis Wheatley, a slave, who owned not even herself? This sickly, frail, black girl who required a servant of her own at times—her health was so precarious—and who, had she been white would have been easily considered the intellectual superior of all the women and most of the men in the society of her day.

Virginia Woolf wrote further, speaking of course not of our Phillis, that "any woman born with a great gift in the sixteenth century [insert eighteenth century, insert black woman, insert born or made a slave] would certainly have gone crazed, shot herself, or ended her days in some lonely cottage outside the village, half witch, half wizard [insert "Saint"], feared and mocked at. For, it needs little skill and psychology to be sure that a highly gifted girl who had tried to use her gift for poetry would have been so thwarted and hindered by contrary instincts [add chains, guns, the lash, the ownership of one's body by someone else, submission to an alien religion] that she must have lost her health and sanity to a certainty."

The key words, as they relate to Phillis, are "contrary instincts." For when we read the poetry of Phillis Wheatley—as when we read the novels of Nella Larsen or the oddly false-sounding autobiography of that freest of all black women writers, Zora Hurston—evidence of "contrary instincts" is everywhere. Her loyalties were completely divided, as was, without question, her mind.

But how could this be otherwise? Captured at seven, a slave of wealthy, doting whites who instilled in her the "savagery" of the Africa they "rescued" her from . . . one wonders if she was even able to remember her homeland as she had known it, or as it really was.

Yet, because she did try to use her gift for poetry in a world that made her a slave, she was "so thwarted and hindered by . . . contrary instincts, that she . . . lost her health. . . ." In the last years of her brief life, burdened not only with the need to express her gift but also with a penniless, friendless "freedom" and several small children for whom she was forced to do strenuous work to feed, she lost her health. Suffering from malnutrition and neglect and who knows what mental agonies, Phillis Wheatley died.

So torn by "contrary instincts" was black, kidnapped, enslaved Phillis that her description of "the Goddess"-as she poetically called the liberty she did not have—is ironically, cruelly humorous. And, in fact, has held Phillis up to ridicule for more than a century. It is usually read prior to hanging Phillis's memory as that of a fool. She wrote:

> The Goddess comes, she moves divinely fair,
> Olive and laurel binds her *golden* hair
> Wherever shines this native of the skies
> Unnumber'd charms and recent graces rise [My italics]

It is obvious that Phillis, the slave, combed the "Goddess's" hair every morning; prior, perhaps to bringing in the milk, or fixing her mistress's lunch. She took her imagery from the one thing she saw elevated above all others.

With the benefit of hindsight we ask "How could she?"

But at last, Phillis, we understand. No more snickering when your stiff, struggling ambivalent lines are forced on us. We know now that you were not an idiot nor a traitor; only a sickly little black girl, snatched from your home and country and made a slave; a woman who still struggled to sing the song that was your gift, although in a land of barbarians who praised you for your bewildered tongue. It is not so much what you sang, as that you kept alive, in so many of our ancestors, *the notion of song*.

Black women are called, in the folklore that so aptly identifies one's status in society, "the mule of the world," because we have been handed the burdens that everyone else—everyone else—refused to carry. We have also been called "Matriarchs," "Superwomen," and "Mean and Evil Bitches." Not to mention "Castraters" and "Sapphire's Mama." When we have pleaded for understanding, our character has been distorted; when we have asked for simple caring, we have been handed empty inspirational appellations, then stuck in a far corner. When we have asked for love, we have been given children. In short, even our plainer gifts, our labors of fidelity and love, have been knocked down our throats. To be an artist, and a black woman, even today, lowers our status in many respects, rather than raises it: and yet, artists we will be.

Therefore, we must fearlessly pull out of ourselves and look at and identify with our lives the living creativity some of our great-grandmothers knew, even without "knowing" it, the reality of their spirituality, even if they didn't recognize it beyond what happened in the singing at church—and they never had any intention of giving it up.

How they did it—those millions of black women who were not Phillis Wheatley, or Lucy Terry or Frances Harper or Zora Hurston or Nella Larsen or Bessie Smith—nor Elizabeth Catlett, nor Katherine Dunham, either—brings me to the title of this essay, "In Search of Our Mothers' Gardens," which is a personal account that is yet shared, in its theme and its meaning, by all of us. I found, while thinking about the far-reaching world of the creative black woman, that often the truest answer to a question that really matters can be found very close.

In the late 1920s, my mother ran away from home to marry my father. Marriage, if not running away, was expected of 17-year-old girls. By the time she was 20, she had two children and was pregnant with a third. Five children later, I was born. And this is how I came to know my mother: she seemed a large, soft, loving-eyed woman who was rarely impatient in our home. Her quick, violent temper was on view only a few times a year when she battled with the white landlord who had the misfortune to suggest to her that her children did not need to go to school.

She made all the clothes we wore, even my brothers' overalls. She made all the towels and sheets we used. She spent the summers canning vegetables and fruits. She spent the winter evenings making quilts enough to cover all our beds.

During the "working" day, she labored beside—not behind—my father in the fields. Her day began before sunup, and did not end until late at night. There was never a moment for her to sit down, undisturbed, to unravel her own private thoughts; never a time free from interruption—by work or the noisy inquiries of her many children. And yet, it is to my mother—and all our mothers who were not famous—that I went in search of the secret of what has fed that muzzled and often mutilated, but vibrant, creative spirit that the black woman has inherited, and that pops out in wild and unlikely places to this day.

But when, you will ask, did my overworked mother have time to know or care about feeding the creative spirit?

The answer is so simple that many of us have spent years discovering it. We have constantly looked high, when we should have looked high—and low.

For example: in the Smithsonian Institution in Washington, D.C., there hangs a quilt unlike any other in the world. In fanciful, inspired, and yet simple and identifiable figures, it portrays the story of the Crucifixion. It is considered rare, beyond price. Though it follows no known pattern of quilt-making, and though it is made of bits and pieces of worthless rags, it is obviously the work of a person of powerful imagination and deep spiritual feeling. Below this quilt, I saw a note that says it was made by "an anonymous black woman in Alabama, a hundred years ago."

If we could locate this "anonymous" black woman, she would turn out to be one of our grandmothers—an artist who left her mark in the only materials she could afford, and in the only medium her position in society allowed her to use.

As Virginia Woolf wrote further, in A Room of One's Own:

> *Yet genius of a sort must have existed among women as it must have existed among the working class. [Change this to slaves and the wives and daughters of sharecroppers.] Now and again an Emily Brontë or a Robert Burns [change this to a Zora Hurston or a Richard Wright] blazes out and proves its presence. But certainly it never got itself on to paper. When, however, one reads of a witch being ducked, of a woman possessed by devils [or Sainthood], of a wise woman selling herbs [our rootworkers], or even a very remarkable man who had a mother, then I think we are on the track of a lost novelist, a suppressed poet, of some mute and inglorious Jane Austen. . . .*

Indeed, I would venture to guess that Anon, who wrote so many poems without signing them, was often a woman. . .

And so our mothers and grandmothers have, more often than not anonymously, handed on the creative spark, the seed of the flower they themselves never hoped to see: or like a sealed letter they could not plainly read.

And so it is, certainly, with my own mother. Unlike "Ma" Rainey's songs, which retained their creator's name even while blasting forth from Bessie Smith's mouth, no song or poem will bear my mother's name. Yet so many of the stories that I write, that we all write, are my mother's stories. Only recently, did I fully realize this: that through years of listening to my mother's stories of her life, I have absorbed not only the stories themselves, but something of the manner in which she spoke, something of the urgency that involves the knowledge that her stories—like her life—must be recorded. It is probably for this reason that so much of what I have written is about characters whose counterparts in real life are so much older than I am.

But the telling of these stories, which came from my mother's lips as naturally as breathing, was not the only way my mother showed herself as an artist. For stories, too, were subject to being distracted, to dying without conclusion. Dinners must be started, and cotton must be gathered before the big rains. The artist that was and is my mother showed itself to me only after many years. This is what I finally noticed:

Like Mem, a character in *The Third Life of Grange Copeland*, my mother adorned with flowers whatever shabby house we were forced to live in. And not just your typical straggly country stand of zinnias, either. She planted ambitious gardens—and still does—with over 50 different varieties of plants that bloom profusely from early March until late November. Before she left home for the fields, she watered her flowers, chopped up the grass, and laid out new beds. When she returned from the fields she might divide clumps of bulbs, dig a cold pit, uproot and replant roses, or prune branches from her taller bushes or trees—until it was too dark to see.

Whatever she planted grew as if by magic, and her fame as a grower of flowers spread over three counties. Because of her creativity with her flowers, even my memories of poverty are seen through a screen of blooms—sunflowers, petunias, roses, dahlias, forsythia, spirea, delphiniums, verbena . . . and on and on.

And I remember people coming to my mother's yard to be given cuttings from her flowers; I hear again the praise showered on her because whatever rocky soil she landed on, she turned into a garden. A garden so brilliant with colors, so original in its design, so magnificent with life and creativity, that to this day people drive by our house in Georgia—perfect strangers and imperfect strangers—and ask to stand or walk among my mother's art.

I notice that it is only when my mother is working in her flowers that she is radiant, almost to the point of being invisible except as Creator: hand and eye. She is involved in work her soul must have. Ordering the universe in the image of her personal conception of Beauty.

Her face, as she prepares the Art that is her gift, is a legacy of respect she leaves to me, for all that illuminates and cherishes life. She had handed down respect for the possibilities—and the will to grasp them.

For her, so hindered and intruded upon in so many ways, being an artist has still been a daily part of her life. This ability to hold on, even in very simple ways, is work black women have done for a very long time.

This poem is not enough, but it is something, for the woman who literally covered the holes in our walls with sunflowers:

They were women then
My mama's generation
Husky of voice - Stout of Step
With fists as well as

Hands
How they battered down
Doors
And ironed
Starched white
Shirts
How they led
Armies
Headragged Generals
Across mined
Fields
Booby-trapped
Ditches
To discover books
Desks
A place for us
How they knew what we
Must know
Without knowing a page
Of it
Themselves.

Guided by my heritage of a love of beauty and a respect for strength—in search of my mother's garden, I found my own.

And perhaps in Africa over 200 years ago, there was just such a mother; perhaps she painted vivid and daring decorations in oranges and yellows and greens on the walls of her hut; perhaps she sang in a voice like Roberta Flack's—sweetly over the compounds of her village; perhaps she wove the most stunning mats or told the most ingenious stories of all the village storytellers. Perhaps she was herself a poet—though only her daughter's name is signed to the poems that we know.

Perhaps Phillis Wheatley's mother was also an artist.

Perhaps in more than Phillis Wheatley's biological life is her mother's signature made clear.

Notes

[1.] Jean Toomer (1894-1967), African American poet and novelist
[2.] Okot p'Bitek (1931-1982), Ugandan poet whose most famous poem, *Song of Lawino*, was the story of a Ugandan woman who fears the loss of African traditions after her husband takes another wife who has a European education.

Close Reading Questions

1. How did Walker describe black women who lived in the southern United States during Reconstruction?

2. Why did Walker insist that a black woman—particularly an artist—is the "mule of the world?" (Multiple Perspectives)

3. When was it that Walker's mother was the most "radiant?"

Analytical Writing/Discussion

4. According to Walker, what socially and/or legally sanctioned activities prevented women of her grandmother's generation from living creative lives?

5. In what ways did poverty affect the women in Walker's life? How did their poverty affect Walker's own life as a writer? (Historical Trends)

6. For what reasons does Walker offer the example of the quilt that hangs in the Smithsonian museum? (Cultural Influences)

Further Options

7. Writers take great care in naming their articles, essays, and books. Why do you think this essay is called "In Search of Our Mother's Gardens" and not "In Search of My Mother's Garden?" If you were the author of this essay, what title would you have suggested?

8. Walker notes the use of the term "contrary instincts" as they applied to poet Phillis Wheatley. How does this concept also apply to Zora Neale Hurston's "How it Feels to be Colored Me" on pp. 213–216 in this chapter?

Freewrite 2: from THE SOULS OF BLACK FOLKS

William Edward Burghardt (W. E. B.) Du Bois was the most influential black intellectual of the twentieth century. He was born in the integrated community of Great Barrington, MA in 1868 and earned his Ph.D. in from Harvard University in 1895. Du Bois was a researcher, writer, and editor before becoming a professor of sociology at Atlanta University. He was one of the founders of the National Association for the Advancement of Colored People (NAACP). Du Bois wrote extensively about race and class and believed that the future of black people in America depended on the rise of black intellectuals whom he would later call the "Talented Tenth." The following excerpt is from *The Souls of Black Folk* (1903), Du Bois' influential collection of essays. After reading the excerpt, see the freewrite questions below.

Between me and the other world, there is ever an unasked question: unasked by some through feelings of delicacy; by others through the difficulty of rightly framing it. All, nevertheless, flutter round it. They approach me in a half-hesitant sort of way, eye me curiously or compassionately, and then, instead of saying directly, How does it feel to be a problem? they say, I know an excellent colored man in my town; or, I fought at Mechanicsville; or, Do not these Southern outrages make your blood boil? At these I smile, or am interested, or reduce the boiling to a simmer, as the occasion may require. To the real question, How does it feel to be a problem? I answer seldom a word.

And yet, being a problem is a strange experience,—peculiar even for one who has never been anything else, save perhaps in babyhood and in Europe. It is in the early days of rollicking boyhood that the revelation first bursts upon one, all in a day, as it were. I remember well when the shadow swept across me. I was a little thing, away up in the hills of New England, where the dark Housatonic winds between Hoosac and Taghkanic to the sea. In a wee wooden schoolhouse, something put it into the boys' and girls' heads to buy gorgeous visiting-cards—ten cents a package—and exchange. The exchange was merry, till one girl, a tall newcomer, refused my card,—refused it peremptorily, with a glance. Then it dawned upon me with a certain suddenness that I was different from the others; or like, mayhap, in heart and life and longing, but shut out from their world by a vast veil. I had thereafter no desire to tear down that veil, to creep through; I held all beyond it in common contempt, and lived above it in a region of blue sky and great wandering shadows. That sky was bluest when I could beat my mates at examination-time, or beat them at a foot-race, or even beat their stringy heads. Alas, with the years all this fine contempt began to fade; for the words I longed for, and all their dazzling opportunities, were theirs, not mine. But they should not keep these prizes, I said; some, all, I would wrest from them. Just how I would do it I could never decide: by reading law, by healing the sick, by telling the wonderful tales that swam in my head, some way. With other black boys, the strife was not so fiercely sunny: their youth shrunk into tasteless sycophancy, or into silent hatred of the pale world about them and mocking distrust of everything white; or wasted itself in a bitter cry, Why did God make me an outcast and a stranger in mine own house? The shades of the prison-house closed round about us all: walls strait and stubborn to the whitest, but relentlessly narrow, tall, and unscalable to sons of night who must plod darkly on in resignation, or beat unavailing palms against the stone, or steadily, half hopelessly, watch the streak of blue above.

After the Egyptian and Indian, the Greek and Roman, the Teuton and Mongolian, the Negro is a sort of seventh son, born with a veil and gifted with second-sight in this American world—a world which yields him no true self-consciousness, but only lets him see himself through the revelation of the other world. It is a peculiar sensation, this double-consciousness, this sense of always looking at one's self through the eyes of others, of measuring one's soul by the tape of a world that looks on in amused contempt and pity. One ever feels his twoness, an American, a Negro; two souls, two thoughts, two unreconciled strivings; two warring ideals in one dark body, whose dogged strength alone keeps it from being torn asunder.

The history of the American Negro is the history of this strife—this longing to attain self-conscious manhood, to merge his double self into a better and truer self. In this merging, he wishes neither of the older selves to be lost. He would not Africanize America, for America has too much to teach the world and Africa. He would not bleach his Negro soul in a flood of white Americanism, for he knows that Negro blood has a message for the world. He simply wishes to make it possible for a man to be both a Negro and an American, without being cursed and spit upon by his fellows, without having the doors of Opportunity closed roughly in his face.

After reading Du Bois' excerpt, freewrite or discuss one or more of the following questions:

- Why does Du Bois say that "being a problem is a strange experience?"

- To what extent have you ever wrestled with two or more identities in the way Du Bois refers to "double consciousness?"

- In what ways does this 1903 text compare to race relations in the United States in the twenty-first century? What are the similarities and/or differences?

LOVE MEDICINE

by Louise Erdrich

Louise Erdrich was born in Little Falls, Minnesota in 1954. She incorporates Native American culture, especially her own Chippewa Indian culture, in her writing. Erdrich is also

"Love Medicine" from the book *** Love Medicine: New and Expanded Edition *** by Louise Erdrich. Copyright © 1984, 1993 by Louise Erdrich. Used by permission of Henry Holt and Company. All rights reserved.

the author of more than 14 novels and numerous books of poetry, including *The Antelope Wife, The Plague of Doves, The Round House, and LaRose*. The following excerpt is from Erdrich's 1984 debut novel, *Love Medicine*, which won the prestigious National Book Critics Circle Award. The novel focuses on a different character in each chapter. The narrator of this chapter is Lipsha Morrissey, a young Chippewa Indian.

I never really done much with my life, I suppose. I never had a television. Grandma Kashpaw had one inside her apartment at the Senior Citizens, so I used to go there and watch my favorite shows. For a while, she used to call me the biggest waste on the reservation and hark back to how she saved me from my own mother, who wanted to tie me in a potato sack and throw me in a slough. Sure, I was grateful to Grandma Kashpaw for saving me like that, for raising me, but gratitude gets old. After a while, stale. I had to stop thanking her. One day I told her I had paid her back in full by staying at her beck and call. I'd do anything for Grandma. She knew that. Besides, I took care of Grandpa like nobody else could, on account of what a handful he'd gotten to be.

But that was nothing, I know the tricks of mind and body inside out without ever having trained for it, because I got the touch. It's a thing you got to be born with. I got secrets in my hands that nobody ever knew to ask. Take Grandma Kashpaw with her tired veins all knotted up in her legs like clumps tails. I take my fingers and I snap them on the knots. The medicine flows out of me. The touch. I run my fingers up the maps of those rivers of veins or I knock very gentle above their hearts or I make a circling motion on their stomachs, and it helps them. They feel much better. Some women pay me five dollars.

I couldn't do the touch for Grandpa, though. He was a hard nut. You know, some people fall right through the hole in their lives. It's invisible, but they come to it after time, never knowing where. There is this woman here, Lulu Lamartine, who always had a thing for Grandpa. She loved him since she was a girl and always said he was a genius. Now she says that his mind got so full it exploded.

How can I doubt that? I know the feeling when your mental power builds up too far. I always used to say that's why the Indians got drunk. Even statistically we're the smartest people on the earth. Anyhow with Grandpa I couldn't believe it, because all my youth he stood out as a hero to me. When he getting toward second childhood he went through different moods. He would stand in the woods and cry at the top of his shirt. It scared me, scared everyone, Grandma worst of all.

Yet he was so smart—do you believe it?—that he *knew* he was getting foolish.

He said so. He told me that December I failed school and come back on the train to Hoopdance. I didn't have nowhere else to go. He picked me up there and he said it straight out: "I'm getting into my second childhood." And then he said something else I still remember: "I've been chosen for it. I couldn't say no." So I figure that a man so smart all his life—tribal chairman and the star of movies and even pictured in the statehouse and on cans of snuff—would know what he's doing by saying yes. I think he was called to second childhood like anybody else gets a call for the priesthood or the army or whatever. So I really did not listen too hard when the doctor said this was some kind of disease old people got eating too much sugar. You just can't tell me that a man who went to Washington and gave them bureaucrats what for could lose his mind eating too much Milky Way. No he put second childhood on himself.

Behind those songs he sings out in the middle of Mass, and back of those stories that everybody knows by heart, Grandpa is thinking hard about life. I know the feeling. Sometimes, I'll throw up a smokescreen to think behind. I'll hitch up to Winnipeg and play the Space Invaders for six hours, but all the time there and back I will be thinking some fairly deep thoughts that surprise even me, and I'm used to it. As for him, if it was just the thoughts there wouldn't be no problem. Smokescreen is what irritates the social structure, see, and Grandpa has done things that just distract people to the point they want to throw him in the cookie jar where they keep the mentally insane. He's far from that, I know for sure, but even Grandma had trouble keeping her patience once he started sneaking off to Lamartine's place. He's not supposed to have his candy, and Lulu feeds it to him. That's one of the reasons why he goes.

Grandma tried to get me to put the touch on Grandpa soon after he began stepping out. I didn't want to but before Grandma started telling me again what a bad state my bare behind was in when she first took me home, I thought I should at least pretend.

I put my hands on either side of Grandpa's head. You wouldn't look at him and say he was crazy. He's a fine figure of a man, as Lamartine would say, with all his hair and half his teeth, a beak like a hawk, and cheeks like the blades of a hatchet. They put his picture on all the tourist guides to North Dakota and even copied his face for artistic paintings. I guess you could call him a monument all of himself. He started grinning when I put my hands on his templates, and I knew right then he knew how come I touched him. I knew the smokescreen was going to fall.

"Let's pitch whoopee,[1]" he said across my shoulder to Grandma.

They don't use that expression much around here anymore, but for damn sure it must have meant something. It got her goat right quick.

She threw my hands off his head herself and stood in front of him, over-matching him pound for pound, and taller too, for she had a growth spurt in middle age while he had shrunk, so now the length and breadth of her surpassed him. She glared and spoke her piece into his face about how he was off at all hours tomcatting[2] and chasing Lamartine again and making a damn old fool of himself.

"And you got no more whoopee to pitch anymore anyhow!" she yelled at last, surprising me so my jaw just dropped, for us kids all had pretended for so long that those rustling sounds we heard from their side of the room at night never happened. She sure had pretended it, up till now, anyway. I saw that tears were in her eyes. And that's when I saw how much grief and love she felt for him. And it gave me a real shock to the system. You see I thought love got easier over the years so it didn't hurt so bad when it hurt, or feel so good when it felt good. I thought it smoothed out and old people hardly noticed it. I thought it curled up and died, I guess. Now I saw it rear up like a whip and lash.

She loved him. She was jealous. She, mourned him like the dead.

And he just smiled into the air, trapped in the seams of his mind.

So I didn't know what to do. I was in a laundry then. They was like parents to me, the way they had took me home and reared me. I could see her point for wanting to get him back the way he was so at least she could argue with him, sleep with him, not be shamed out by Lamartine. She'd always love him. That hit me like a ton of bricks. For one whole day I felt this odd feeling that cramped my hands. When you have the touch, that's where longing gets you . I never loved like that. It made me feel all inspired to see them fight, and I wanted to go out and find a woman who I would love until one of us died or went crazy. But I'm not like that really. From time to time I heal a person all up good inside, however when it comes to the long shot I doubt that I got staying power.

And you need that, staying power, going out to love somebody. I know this quality was not going to jump on me with no effort. So I turned my thoughts back to Grandma and Grandpa. I felt her side of it with my hands and my tangled guts, and I felt his side of it within the stretch of my mentality. He had gone out to lunch one day and never came back. He was fishing in the middle of Matchimanito. And there was big thoughts on his line, and he kept throwing them back for even bigger ones that would explain to him, say, the meaning of how we got here and why we have to leave so soon. All in all, I could not see myself treating Grandpa with the touch, bringing him back, when the real part of him that stayed around causing trouble, after all, and we could handle most of it without any problem.

Besides, it was hard to argue with his reasons for doing some things. Take Holy Mass.

Take Holy Mass. I used to go there just every so often, when I got frustrated mostly, because even though I know the Higher Power dwells everyplace, there's something very calming about the cool green-ish inside of our mission. Or so I thought, anyway. Grandpa was the one who stripped off my delusions in this matter, for it was he who busted right through what Father Upsala calls the sacred serenity of the place.

We filed in that time. Me and Grandpa. We sat down in our book— pews. Then the rosary got started up pre-Mass and that's when Grandpa filled up his chest and opened his mouth and belted out them words.

HAIL MARIE FULL OF GRACE.

He had a powerful set of lungs.

And he kept on like that. He did not let up. He hollered and he yelled them prayers, and I guess people was used to him by now, because they only muttered theirs and did not quit and gawk like I did. I was getting red-faced, I admit. I give him the elbow once or twice, but that wasn't nothing to him. He kept on. He shrieked to heaven and he pleaded like a movie actor and he pounded his chest like Tarzan in the Lord I Am Not Worthies. I thought he might hurt himself Then after a while I guess I got used to it, and that's when I wondered: how come?

So afterwards I out and asked him. "How come? How come you yelled?"

"God don't hear me otherwise," said Grandpa Kashpaw.

I sweat. I broke right into a little cold sweat at my hairline because I knew this was perfectly right and for years not one damn other person had noticed it. God's been going deaf Since the Old Testament, God's been deafening up on us. I read, see.

Besides the dictionary, which I'm constantly in use of, I had this Bible once. I read it. I found—there was discrepancies between then and now. It struck me. Here God used to raineth bread from clouds, smite the Phillipines, sling fire down on red-light districts where people got stabbed. He even appeared in person every once in a while.

God used to pay attention, is what I'm saying.

Now there's your God in the Old Testament and there is Chippewa Gods as well. Indian Gods, good and bad, like tricky Nanabozho or the water monster, Missepeshu, who lives over in Matchimanito. That water monster was the last God I ever heard to appear. It had a weakness for young girls and grabbed one of the Pillagers off her rowboat. She got to shore all right, but only after this monster had its way with her. She's an old lady now. Old Lady Blue. She still won't let her family fish that lake.

Our Gods aren't perfect, is what I'm saying, but at least they come around. They'll do a favor if you ask them right. You don't have to yell. But you do have to know, like I said, how to ask in the right way. That makes problems, because to ask proper was an art that was lost to the Chippewas once the Catholics gained ground. Even now, I have to wonder if Higher Power turned it back, if we got to yell, or if we just don't speak its language.

I looked around me. How else could I explain what all I had seen in my short life—King smashing his fist in things, Gordie drinking himself down to the Bismarck hospitals, or Aunt June left by a white man to wander off in the snow. How else to explain the times my touch don't work, and farther back, to the old time Indians who was swept away in the outright germ warfare and dirty-dog killing of the whites. In those times, us Indians was so much kindlier than now.

We took them in.

Oh yes, I'm bitter as an old cutworm just thinking of how they done to us and doing still.

So Grandpa Kashpaw just opened my eyes a little there. Was there any sense relying on a God whose ears was stopped? just like the government? I says then, right off, maybe we got nothing but ourselves.

And that's not much, just personally speaking. I know I don't got the cold hard potatoes it takes to understand everything.

Still, there's things I'd like to do. For instance, I'd like to help some people like my Grandpa and Grandma Kashpaw get back some happiness within the tail ends of their lives.

I told you once before I couldn't see my way clear to putting the direct touch on Grandpa's mind, and I kept my moral there, but something soon happened to make me think a little bit of mental adjustment wouldn't do him and the rest of us no harm.

It was after we saw him one afternoon in the sunshine court yard of the Senior Citizens with Lulu Lamartine. Grandpa used to like to dig there.

He had his little dandelion fork out, and he was prying up them dandelions right and left while Lamartine watched him.

"He's scratching up the dirt, all right," said Grandma, watching Lamartine watch Grandpa out the window.

Now Lamartine was about half the considerable size of Grandma, but you would never think of sizes anyway. They were different in an even more noticeable way. It was the difference between a house fixed up with paint and picky fence, and a house left to weather away into the soft earth, is what I'm saying.

Lamartine was jacked up, latticed, shuttered, and vinyl sided, while Grandma sagged and bulged on her slipped foundations and let her hair go the silver gray of rain-dried lumber. Right now, she eyed the Lamartine's pert flowery dress with such a look it despaired me. I knew what this could lead to with Grandma. Alterating tongue storms and rock-hard silences was hard on a man, even one who didn't notice, like Grandpa. So I went fetching him.

But he was gone when I popped through the little screen door that led out on the courtyard. There was nobody out there either, to point which way they went. Just the dandelion fork quibbling upright in the ground. That gave me an idea. I snookered over to the Lamartine's door and I listened in first, then knocked. But nobody. So I went walking through the lounges and around the card tables. Still nobody. Finally it was my touch that led me to the laundry room. I cracked the door. I went in. There they were, And he was really loving her up good, boy, and she was going hell for leather. Sheets was flapping on the lines above, and washcloths, pillowcases, shirts was also flying through the air for they was trying to clear out a place for themselves in a high-heaped but shallow laundry cart. The washers and dryers was all on, chock-full of quarter: shaking and moaning. I couldn't hear what Grandpa and the Lamartine was billing and cooing, and they couldn't hear me.

I didn't know what to do, so I went inside and shut the door.

The Lamartine wore a big curly light-brown wig. Looked like one of them squeaky little white-people dogs. Poodles they call them. Anyway, that wig is what saved us from the worse. For I could hardly shout and tell them I was in there, no more could I try and grab him. I was trapped where I was. There was nothing I could really do but hold the door shut. I was scared of somebody else upsetting in and really getting an eyeful. Turned out though, in the heat of the clinch, as I was trying to avert my eyes you see, the Lamartine's curly wig jumped off her head. And if you ever been in the midst of something and had a big change like that occur in the someone, you can't help know how it devastates your basic urges. Not only that, but her wig was almost with a life of its own. Grandpa's eyes were bugging at the change already, and swear to God if the thing didn't rear up and pop him in the face like it was going to start something. He scrambled up, Grandpa did, and the Lamartine jumped up after him all addled looking. They just stared at each other, huffing and puffing, with quizzical expression. The surprise seemed to drive all sense completely out of Grandpa's mind.

"The letter was what started the fire," he said. "I never would have done it."

"What letter?" said the Lamartine. She was stiff-necked now, and elegant, even bald, like some alien queen. I gave her back the wig. The Lamartine replaced it on her head, and whenever I saw her after that, I couldn't help thinking of her bald, with special powers, as if from another planet.

"That was a close call," I said to Grandpa after she had left.

But I think he had already forgot the incident. He just stood there all quiet and thoughtful. You really wouldn't think he was crazy. He looked like he was just about to say something important, explaining himself. He said something all right, but it didn't have nothing to do with anything that made sense.

He wondered where the heck he put his dandelion fork. That's when I decided about the mental adjustment.

Now what was mostly our problem was not so much that he was not all there but that what was there of him often hankered after Lamartine. If we could put a stop to that, I thought, we might be getting someplace. But here, see, my touch was of no use. For what could I snap my fingers at to make him faithful to Grandma? Like the quality of staying power, this faithfulness was invisible. I know it's something that you got to acquire, but I never known where from. Maybe there's no rhyme or reason to it, like my getting the touch, and then again maybe it's a kind of magic. . . .

Notes

1. pitch whoopee: out-of-date expression for having sex
2. tomcatting: old-fashioned expression for promiscuity

Close Reading Questions

1. Why had Grandpa Kashpaw become "a handful" for Lipsha? What was Lipsha's life like before he began to care for his grandparents? (Historical Trends)

2. When does Lipsha realize his grandmother was not just annoyed by but also loved his grandfather?

3. What images did Lipsha use to compare Lamartine to his grandmother?

Analytical Writing/Discussion

4. Lipsha states that "smokescreen is what irritates the social structure." How does this image compare to Du Bois' comments about double consciousness (see pp. 223 and 224)?

5. In what ways is Catholic church in opposition to the Native American belief in "the higher power?"

6. How is Lipsha's identity as a young Native American affected by practices and values within Chippewa culture? (Cultural Influences)

Further Options

7. Erdrich's chapter begins with Lipsha explaining that he was raised by his grandparents. What does this relationship reveal about alternative or nontraditional family structures? How is this family similar to or different than families you know? (Multiple Perspectives)

8. Using the double-entry notes explained in Chapter 1 (see p. 11), answer the following question: How is Lipsha like and or unlike Alice Walker in his role as an observer of the elders in his family? Use specific quotations selected from each reading and to support your perspective.

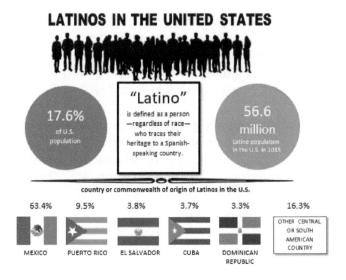

LATINOS IN THE UNITED STATES

"Latino" is defined as a person —regardless of race— who traces their heritage to a Spanish-speaking country.

17.6% of U.S. population

56.6 million Latino population in the U.S. in 2015

country or commonwealth of origin of Latinos in the U.S.

63.4%	9.5%	3.8%	3.7%	3.3%	16.3%
MEXICO	PUERTO RICO	EL SALVADOR	CUBA	DOMINICAN REPUBLIC	OTHER CENTRAL OR SOUTH AMERICAN COUNTRY

SOURCE: U.S. CENSUS BUREAU, U. S. DEPARTMENT OF COMMERCE, 2016

FIGURE 1   Latinos in the United States.

STOP DENYING ME MY BLACKNESS

by Vanessa Mártir

Vanessa Mártir is an essayist, memoirist, and educator. Born and raised in the Bushwick section of Brooklyn, New York, Mártir is a graduate of Columbia University. Her writing has appeared in numerous publications, including in the VONA anthology, *Dismantle*, *Poets & Writers*, and *Kweli Journal*. Mártir established the *Writing Our Lives* writing workshop and also teaches writing in several after-school programs in and around New York City. She is completing work on her memoir, *A Dim Capacity for Wings*. The following 2015 essay first appeared in Mártir's highly praised blog, *The Relentless Files*.

I'd been in Wellesley, [Massachusetts] for all of a few weeks when it first happened. It was the fall of 1989, my first year in boarding school. I was walking with another ABC (A Better Chance)[1] student back to our dorm on the outskirts of the Wellesley College campus. We were the "scholarship kids"—her a St. Lucian girl from Flatbush,[2] me a Boricua-Hondureña[3] from Bushwick.[4] We were walking along Washington Avenue, the main street that runs through the town, past the Town Hall that looks like a castle, and the duck pond. I don't remember what we were talking about or if we were even talking, but I remember his face, bloated and red and angry. He stuck that face out of the truck that slowed down as it passed, then he threw a lit cigarette at us, two teenage girls, her 16, me 13, and said, "Go home, niggers." We jumped away to avoid getting burnt and stared at the truck as it sped off. She started crying, a quiet, blubbering cry that shook her shoulders. I stayed quiet the rest of the walk home.

Copyright © by Vanessa Mártir. Reprinted by permission.

The following year, a black girl who was all of a shade darker than me told me I didn't know prejudice, "because you're not black." She pursed her lips and shook her head. I thought back to that lit cigarette and that bloated red face.

In the summer of 1985, my mother took us to Honduras for the first time. One morning, my brother Carlos and I were picking naranjas off the tree whose branch extended out into our family's patio. We were just kids—I was nine, Carlos was thirteen. We just wanted some oranges. Suddenly the neighbor came running out of her house screaming. She called us malditos prietos,⁵ thieves and criminals for picking fruit off her tree. She said she'd rather they rot than have us eat them. My brother pulled open an orange with his fingers, put it to his mouth and sucked on it while he stared at that woman. She sneered and called him, "un prieto sucio." My brother laughed, juice dripping down his chin, grabbed my hand and walked off. I gave her the universal fuck you sign—the middle finger.

* * * * * * * *

I didn't grow up talking about race. There was no time for that. There were other more important issues—like keeping the fridge full and making sure that crack, the drug that ravaged our neighborhoods in the late 80s and 90s, stayed outside our doors. It was hard enough keeping the family together, but I look back now and can see the ways that race influenced my life: in how my sister was always called the pretty one "con su pelo rubio"; that black girl in seventh grade who said, as my friends and I were walking by, "I hate these little Spanish bitches swearing they all that."

Sure, there were some racial tensions in the largely black and Puerto Rican neighborhood I grew up in in Brooklyn, but the pervasive issue was poverty. We were all poor. We all lived in the rubble and crack that was 1980s Bushwick.

* * * * * * * *

The summer before my senior year, I participated in the LEAD Business Program at UPenn's Wharton School of Business for three weeks. One day we were talking about who knows what when I started talking about my sister, how amazing she was, how I looked up to her, how gorgeous she was. "She has this straight blonde hair and light eyes. She's just beautiful." A black boy I had a thing with said, "You talk like she's all that because she's white, Vanessa." I didn't know what to say but I look back on that moment as a key step in my awakening to my racial consciousness and the ways that the European ideals of beauty were instilled in me.

* * * * * * * *

Years ago, my mother told me a story of when we kids were really little. She went to a "face to face" (pronounced "fay tu fay") appointment at the welfare office and brought us in tow—my sister, la gringa who then had almost-white-blonde hair; my brother, el moreno, and me, la india. The case worker stared at us then back at mom. "Those are your children?" she asked. "Seguro," mom said, without blinking. "Those are not your kids!" The woman said we didn't even look like we were related to each other, much less to her. She accused mom of trying to cheat the system, and even called security, threatening to bring her up on fraud charges. Mom said, "Yo le quería meter en la cara con las actas de naciminto de ustedes." And if I know my mom, she would have done exactly that, smack that woman upside her head with her paperwork.

* * * * * * * *

We hear so much about those latinos who straight out negate their blackness. Like my ex-boyfriend's Dominican mother who whispered with pride that Trujillo[6] was her distant cousin. I heard this woman say, "Yo soy india" several times over the six year relationship I had with her son. I remember staring at her full lips, wide nose and coarse hair, her dark skin that she took caution with, staying out of the sun, walking around with an umbrella on especially beaming days, "ay no, ese sol me va 'cer prieta y yo no soy prieta." It all made sense when I learned the history of the Dominican Republic and how Trujillo would put make up on his face and hands to lighten his skin.

* * * * * * * *

In an interview in the March 2015 VONA[7] newsletter, Mat Johnson wrote:

> *I thought the mixed race advocates were sellouts at first, just trying to run away from their own blackness. Over time, though, I began to feel that by just saying I was black I was denying half of my family and my own cultural influences. Also, I was being forced to fit into an archetype that visually I didn't fit. The constraint and struggle of that started to wear me down, so I had to reexamine my identity. Your proclaimed identity should fit you, not the other way around.*

I've been thinking a lot about race, as a Boricua-Hondureña who identifies as BOTH black and indígena,[8] because I am both and neither is mutually exclusive. Here's the thing, I'm all for conversations about blackness. They are necessary. But to have a complete conversation, we need to talk about how some people, African American and even my own Latino people, have denied me my blackness because "you don't look black," they've said. The issue is that people like me do not fit into their construct of what race is.

I'm writing this as I stare at a picture of my deceased brother and I to the left of my computer screen. When you negate my blackness, you deny him as my brother. I can't have that. I won't have it. I will respond viscerally.

I get that this essay is going to get some folk riled up and shifting uncomfortably. I'm cool with that. These conversations are necessary and long overdue. Yes, I am black. I am also indígena. It is not up to the world to decide my identity for me. Seriously, what's good with this policing of one's racial & cultural identity? To say that I have a "choice" is to say that I can "choose" to deny my black brother and my black aunt and my grandmother and my great grandmother and the long history of blackness in my blood. Not gonna happen. This construct of race is much more layered than people want or care to admit. I'm cool with dialogue. I am not cool with some cualquiera claiming dominion over my identity. You can take several seats with that pendejada. I'll open an auditorium full of seats for you, if you wish.

* * * * * * * *

I had someone, an academic, try to impose the label of "afro-latina" on me. Friends have asked me, "why don't you call yourself afro-latina?" It's an accusation. They are saying I am denying my blackness. Here's the thing: yes, I am black, but that's not all of who I am. It's problematic to impose an identity on someone. It's problematic when my blackness is denied of me because "you don't look black." Because my hair is curly and my skin is that of my Mayan ancestors, because, see, I'm not just black, tambien soy indígena. One does not negate the other. Why does it have to?

I think of my greatgrandmother Tinita, her skin brown like the frijoles she shelled in the patio for hours, her waist-length hair pulled back into a braid that hung over her shoulder. When she heard about what the neighbor had said to my brother and me, she laughed her toothless laugh and pulled us into her chest. "Si somos prietos, y que?" Then she sat us down and served us tortillas and frijoles with her specially made crema and the white cheese she soaked all day to remove some of its saltiness.

* * * * * * * *

One time, when I was in my mid-twenties, I went to a barbecue at my mom's house with my boy, an African American writer. Mom greeted him politely and showed him how to climb out the window of her first floor apartment into the backyard where the grill was already on and people were milling around eating and sipping on beer. When he was outside, mom pulled me aside and said: "Tu no estaras con un moreno, Vanessa." I gasped and said, "Ma, you know we're black, right?" She rolled her eyes and went back to seasoning the meat.

* * * * * * * *

When was eight or nine, I was playing with a black boy from around the corner named Damon. We were playing scully in the street with the bottle caps we filled with wax. My second mom Millie, a Boricua straight from the campos of Lares,[9] was sitting on the stoop of our building peeling an orange with her pocket knife. She called me over, feigning to offer me a piece. When I reached for it, she pulled me closer and whispered, "No te atrevas enamorarte de uno d'esos prietos, ¿oistes?" I ate that orange slice slowly, trying to hide my frown. When I was done, I told Damon that I had to go inside. I didn't play with him much after that.

* * * * * * * *

Race is a complex thing. It's been a unique experience for me as a Latina who looks more like her indigenous roots, but who is one of only five light-skinned people in my family, my mom, my sister and me, and our kids.

Once, when I was pregnant with my daughter, my daughter's father said some shit to me that still shocks me ten years later. We were on our way home after having dinner at my grandmother's house with the rest of my family. I was rubbing my huge belly when he looked over at me and said, "Our kid could be black, V." He sounded exasperated. An "Oh my God" lingered in the air like one of those fogs in scary movies that portends some shit is about to go down. "And?" I said, all Brooklyn attitude and what the fuck. "Nothing, I'm just saying, ma." He knew he was in trouble. "You know your mother's black, right?" I said and glared at him. He sucked his teeth and rolled his eyes. "Ay, forget it," he said. We never talked about it again, but I wondered what crossed his mind when he saw our daughter for the first time. I wonder if he said a silent prayer thanking God for her having inherited his lighter skin.

* * * * * * * *

This essay has been simmering in me for a long time but I knew I had to write it when the other day a black poet attacked VONA for not including any black alumni in the line-up of a faculty-alumni reading at an AWP[10] event entitled *Consequences: VONA/Voices Generation One*. There are multiple issues with the accusation (including an assumption of maliciousness without knowing how the alumni were selected), but this essay addresses one: the negation of my blackness and that of another Latino writer on the line-up. This woman talked about the invisibility of blacks without realizing (or perhaps, not caring) that she too was imposing invisibility on Latinos like me who have time and again been denied their blackness. I took that rage and put it into this essay.

Race is such a layered, complex thing. I won't pretend to have all the answers. I won't pretend to know fully how to confront and talk about race in ways that will make everyone happy. I understand that my views on race are complicated by my experience being one of two or three Latinas in the entire boarding school I attended, at a time where race was polarized into white and black (which is still very much is). I had too much melanin and was too Latina to fit into the white world, and I was poor to boot. I didn't have enough melanin to fit in with the black kids, so where did I belong? I didn't. I had to learn how to pave my own path. Create my own little niche, which largely meant solitude. That solitude gave this rage time to gestate.

This is what I know at almost 40:

1. I cannot and will not deny my indigenous blood to fit a construct of race that's not inclusive of the layers that make me me, especially since my appearance is clear evidence of that Mayan blood.

2. To deny a latin@ her blackness just because she doesn't "look black" or has a different experience because she's not African American, is to be ignorant of history. There were millions more Africans taken to the Caribbean and Latin America in the African slave trade. You think racism is bad in the U.S.? Go to Latin America and then we can talk. This attempt to erase my history and my blood because it doesn't fit into your construct of race is problematic on numerous levels, and must be included in these oftentimes uncomfortable conversations about race.

3. I'm done being politically correct and trying to tiptoe around these conversations because I'm often attacked or dismissed. That shit's been happening to me since I was a kid and I'm tired of it. I have my story and you have yours. A dialogue is possible, albeit probably uncomfortable, but for you to impose your view of blackness on me is a single story, and we already know what Chimamanda Ngozi Adichie[11] has to say about that: it's dangerous.

This is why I penned this here essay: because I'm tired of the divisiveness within our own communities. I counter and confront it in the way I do best: by writing about it, screaming and raging and crying on the page. Es con hablar que nos entendemos. I'm ready to talk when you are.

Notes

1. ABC (A Better Chance): a college preparatory program for low-income, academically able students of color who enroll in independent schools across the United States
2. Flatbush: a neighborhood in the center of the borough of Brooklyn, NY
3. Boricua-Hondureña; a person of Puerto Rican and Honduran descent
4. Bushwick: a neighborhood in the borough of Brooklyn, NY situated on the edge of the borough of Queens
5. Prietos: slang for someone dark-skinned; often used in a derogatory manner
6. Rafael Trujillo (1891–1961), former dictator of the Dominican Republic from 1930 until his assassination.
7. Voices of Our Nations Arts Foundation (VONA), a multi-genre writing organization for writers of color
8. Indígena: indigenous, native
9. Lares: a town in Puerto Rico

10. AWP: Association of Writers & Writing Programs
11. Chimamanda Ngozi Adichie, Nigeran-born novelist who believes that people are defined by multiple stories or perspectives, as opposed to a single story

Close Reading Questions

1. As a boarding school student, how did race impact Mártir's life? (Historical Trends)
2. How does Mártir identify herself racially and ethnically?
3. What did Mártir's daughter's father say that offended Mártir?

Analytical Writing/Discussion

4. According to Mártir, "race is such a layered, complex thing." Which arguments in the essay do you think best articulate this complexity? (Cultural Influences)
5. What do the descriptions about Mártir's family members reveal about the impact of skin color on their familial relationships? Which family members are more or less aligned with Mártir's feelings about skin color and race? (Multiple Perspectives)
6. Why do you think Mártir opposes the practice of "policing one's racial and cultural identity?"

Further Options

7. Vanessa Mártir cites numerous incidents throughout her life that impacted her racial identity. How are Mártir's experiences similar to or different than those of "Living with Racial Battle Fatigue" by Dionne Irving Bremyer on pp. 240–251 in this chapter?
8. Mártir felt compelled to write this essay in reaction to several events involving her sense of racial identity. When have you been inspired to write something after—or during—a challenging time in your life? To begin crafting your answer, use one or more of the techniques for collecting information as discussed in Chapter 2 on the Writing Process (see p. 25).

WHITE TIGERS

by Maxine Hong Kingston

Maxine Hong Kingston is an author, educator, and activist. Raised in Stockton, California, Kingston's work largely focuses on the experiences of Chinese immigrant communities in America. She is the author of a novel (*Tripmaster Monkey: His Fake Book)* and several works of nonfiction, including *The Fifth*

"White Tigers" from *The Woman Warrior: Memoirs of a Girlhood Among Ghosts* by Maxine Hong Kingston, copyright © 1975, 1976 by Maxine Hong Kingston. Used by permission of Alfred A. Knopf, an imprint of the Knopf Doubleday Publishing Group, a division of Penguin Random House LLC. All rights reserved.

Book of Peace. Kingston is a professor emeritus of creative writing at her alma mater, University of California, Berkeley. In 2013, Kingston was presented with the National Medal of Arts from President Barack Obama. The following excerpt is from her award-winning memoir, *The Woman Warrior: Memoirs of a Girlhood Among Ghosts.* First published in 1976, Kingston's stories are voiced by an unnamed female narrator who recounts the mythological tales from her mother's China ("talk stories") and the challenges of being the American-born daughter of immigrants from China.

My American life has been such a disappointment.

"I got straight A's, Mama."

"Let me tell you a true story about a girl who saved her village."

I could not figure out what was my village. And it was important I do something big and fine, or else my parents would sell me when we made our way back to China. In China there were solutions for what to do with little girls who ate up food and threw tantrums. You can't eat straight A's.

When one of my parents or the emigrant villagers said, "Feeding girls is feeding cowbirds," I would thrash on the floor and scream so hard I couldn't talk. I couldn't stop.

"What's the matter with her?"

"I don't know. Bad, I guess. You know how girls are. 'There's no profit in raising girls. Better to raise geese than girls.'"

"I would hit her if she were mine. But then there's no use wasting all that discipline on a girl. 'When you raise girls, you're raising children for strangers.'"

"Stop that crying!" my mother would yell. "I'm going to hit you if you don't stop. Bad girl! Stop! I'm going to remember never to hit or to scold my children for crying, I thought, because then they will only cry more.

"I'm not a bad girl," I would scream. "I'm not a bad girl. I'm not a bad girl." I might as well have said "I'm not a girl."

"When you were little, all you had to say was 'I'm not a bad girl,' and you could make yourself cry," my mother says, talking-story about my childhood.

I minded that the emigrant villagers shook their heads at my sister and me. "One girl—and another girl." They said, and made our parents ashamed to take us out together. The good part about my brothers being born was that people stopped saying, "All girls," but I learned new grievances. "Did you roll an egg on *my* face like that when *I* was born?" "Did you have a full-month party for *me*?" "Did you turn on all the lights'" "Did you send *my* picture to Grandmother?" "Why not? Because I'm a girl? Is that why not?" "Why didn't you teach me English?" "You like having me beaten up at school, don't you?"

"She is very mean, isn't she?" the emigrant villagers would say.

"Come, children. Hurry. Hurry. Who wants to go out with Great-Uncle?" On Saturday mornings, my great-uncle, the ex-river pirate, did the shopping. "Get your coats, whoever's coming."

"I'm coming. I'm coming. Wait for me."

When he heard girls' voices, he turned on us and roared, "No girls!" and left my sisters and me hanging our coats back up, not looking at one another. The boys came back with candy and new toys. When they walked through Chinatown, the people must have said, "A boy—and another boy—and another boy!" At my great-uncle's funeral I secretly tested out feeling glad that he was dead—the six-foot bearish masculinity of him.

I went away to college—Berkeley in the sixties—and I studied, and I marched to change the world, but I did not turn into a boy. I would have liked to bring myself back as a boy for my parents to welcome with chickens and pigs. That was for my brother, who returned alive from Vietnam.

If I went to Vietnam, I would not come back; females desert families. It was said, "There is an outward tendency in females," which meant that I was getting straight A's for the good of my future husband's family, not my own. I did not plan ever to have a husband. I would show my mother and father and the nosey emigrant villagers that girls have no outward tendency. I stopped getting straight A's.

And all the time, I was having to turn myself American-feminine, or no dates.

There is a Chinese word for the female *I*—which is "slave." Break the women with their own tongues!

I refused to cook. When I had to wash dishes, I would crack one or two. "Bad girl," my mother yelled, and sometimes that made me gloat rather than cry. Isn't a bad girl almost a boy?

"What do you want to be when you grow up, little girl?"

"A lumberjack in Oregon."

Even now, unless I'm happy, I burn the food when I cook. I do not feed people. I let the dirty dishes rot. I eat at other people's tables but won't invite them to mine, where the dishes are rotting.

If I could not eat, perhaps I could make myself a warrior like the swordswoman who drives me. I will—I must—rise and plow the fields as soon as the baby comes out.

Once I get outside the house, what bird might call me; on what horse could I ride away? Marriage and childbirth strengthen the swordswoman, who is not a maid like Joan of Arc. Do the women's work; then do more work, which will become ours too. No husband of mine will say, "I could have been a drummer, but I had to think about the wife and kids. You know how it is." Nobody supports me at the expense of his own adventure. Then I get bitter: no one supports me; I am not loved enough to be supported. That I am not a burden has to compensate for the sad envy when I look at women loved enough to be supported. Even now China wraps double binds around my feet.

When urban renewal tore down my parents' laundry and paved over our slum for a parking lot, I only made up gun and knife fantasies and did nothing useful.

From the fairy tales, I've learned exactly who the enemy are. I easily recognize them—business-suited in their modern American executive guide, each boss two feet taller than I am and impossible to meet eye to eye.

I once worked at an art supply house that sold paints to artists. "Order more that nigger yellow, will-ya?' the boss told me. "Bright, isn't it? Nigger yellow."

I don't like that word. I had to say in my bad, small-person's voice that makes no impact. The boss never deigned to answer.

I also worked at a land developer's association. The building industry was planning a banquet for contractors, real estate dealers, and real estate editors. "Did you know the restaurant you chose for the banquet is being picketed by CORE[1] and the NAACP?" I squeaked.

"Of course I know." The boss laughed. "That's why I chose it."

"I refuse to type these invitations," I whispered, voice unreliable. He leaned back in his leather chair, his bossy stomach opulent. He picked up his calendar and lowly circled a date. "You will be paid up to here," he said. "We'll mail you the check."

If I took the sword, which my hate must surely have forged out of the air, and gutted him, I would put color and wrinkles into his shirt.

It's not just the stupid racists that I have to do something about, but the tyrants who for whatever reason can deny my family food and work. My job is my own only land.

To avenge my family, I'd have to storm across China to take back our farm from the Communists; I'd have to rage across the United States to take back the laundry in New York and the one in California.

Nobody in history has conquered and united both North America and Asia. A descendant of eighty pole fighters,[2] I ought to be able to set out confidently, march straight down our street, get going right now. There's work to do, ground to cover. Surely, the eighty pole fighters, though unseen would follow me and lead me and protect me, as is the wont of ancestors.

Or it may well be that they're resting happily in China, their spirits dispersed among the real Chinese, and not nudging me at all with their poles. I mustn't feel bad that I haven't done as well as the swordswoman did; after all, no bird called me, no wise old people tutored me. I have no magic beads, or water gourd sight, no rabbit that will jump in the fire when I'm hungry. I dislike armies.

I've looked for the bird. I've seen clouds make pointed angel wings that stream past the sunset, but they shred into clouds. Once at a beach after a long hike, I saw a seagull, tiny as an insect. But when I jumped up to tell what miracle I saw, before I could get the words out I understood that the bird was insect-size because it was far away. My brain had momentarily lost its depth perception. I was that eager to find an unusual bird.

The news from China has been confusing. It also had something to do with birds. I was nine years old when the letters made my parents, who are rocks, cry. My father screamed in his sleep. My mother wept and crumpled up the letters. She set fire to them page by page in the ashtray, but new letters came almost every day. The only letters they opened without fear were the ones with red borders, the holiday letters that mustn't carry bad news. The other letters said that my uncles were made to kneel on broken glass during their trials and had confessed to being landowners. They were all executed, and the aunt whose thumbs were twisted off drowned herself. Other aunts, mothers-in-law, and cousins disappeared; some suddenly began writing to us again from communes or from Hong Kong. They kept asking for money. The ones in communes got four ounces of fat and one cup of oil a week, they said, and had to work from 4 A.M. to 9 P.M. They had to learn to do dances waving red kerchiefs; they had to sing nonsense syllables. The communists gave axes to the old ladies and said, "Go and kill yourself. You're useless." If we overseas Chinese would just send money to the Communist bank, our relatives said, they might get a percentage of it for themselves. The aunts in Hong Kong said to send money quickly; their children were begging on the sidewalks and mean people put dirt in their bowls.

When I dream that I am wire without flesh, there is a letter on blue airmail paper that floats above the night ocean between here and China. It must arrive safely or else my grandmother and I will lose each other.

My parents felt bad whether or not they sent money. Sometimes they got angry at their brothers and sisters for asking. And they would not simply ask but have to talk-story too. The revolutionaries had taken Fourth Aunt and Uncle's store, house, and lands. They attacked the house and killed the grandfather and oldest daughter. The grandmother escaped with the loose cash and did not return to help. Fourth Aunt picked up her sons, one under each arm, and hid in the pig house, where they slept that night in cotton clothes. The next day she found her husband, who had also miraculously escaped. The two of them collected twigs and yams to sell while their children begged. Each morning they tied the faggots, [which were bundles of sticks] on each other's back. Nobody bought from them. They ate the yams and some of the children's rice. Finally, Fourth Aunt saw what was wrong. "We have to shout 'Fuel for sale' and 'Yams for sale,'" she said. "We can't just walk unobtrusively up and down the street." "You're right," said my uncle, but he was shy and walked in back of her "Shout," my aunt ordered, but he could not. "They think we're carrying these sticks home for our own fire," she said. "Shout." They walked, about miserably, silently, until sundown, neither of them able to advertise themselves. Fourth Aunt, an orphan since the age of ten, mean as my mother, threw her bundle down at his feet and scolded Fourth Uncle, "Starving to death, his wife and children starving to death, and he's too damned shy to raise his voice." She left him standing by himself and afraid to return empty-handed to her. He sat under a tree to think, when he spotted a pair of nesting doves. Dumping his bag of yams, he climbed up and caught the birds. That was when the Communists trapped him in the tree. They criticized him for selfishly taking food for his own family and killed him, leaving his body in the tree as an example. They took the birds to a commune kitchen to be shared.

It is confusing that my family was not the poor to be championed. They were executed like the barons in the stories, when they were not barons. It is confusing that birds tricked us.

What fighting and killing I have seen have not been glorious but slum grubby. I fought the most during junior high school and always cried. Fights are confusing as to who has won. The corpses I've seen had been rolled and dumped, sad little dirty bodies covered with a police khaki blanket. My mother locked her children in the house so we couldn't look at dead slum people. But at news of a body, I would find a way to get out; I had to learn about dying if I wanted to become a swordswoman. Once there was an Asian man stabbed next door, words on cloth pinned to his corpse. When the police came around ask questions, my father said, "No read Japanese. Japanese words. Me Chinese."

I've also looked for old people who could be my gurus. A medium with red hair told me that a girl who died in a far country follows wherever I go. This spirit can help me if I acknowledge her, she said. Between the head line and heart line in my right palm, she said, I have the mystic cross. I could become a medium myself. I don't want to be a medium. I don't want to be a crank taking "offerings" in a wicker plate from the frightened audience, who, one after another asked the spirits how to raise rent money, how to cure their coughs and skin diseases, how to find a job. And martial arts are for unsure little boys kicking away under fluorescent lights.

I live now where there are Chinese and Japanese, but no emigrants from my own village looking at me as if I had failed them. Living among one's own emigrant villagers can give a good Chinese far from China glory and a place. "That old busboy is really a swordsman," we whisper when he goes by. "He's a swordsman who's killed fifty. He has a tong ax in his closet." But I am useless, one more girl who couldn't be sold. When I visit the family now, I wrap my American successes around me like a private shawl, I am worthy of eating the food, From afar I can believe my family loves me fundamentally. They only say, "When fishing for treasures in the flood, be careful not to pull in girls," because that is what one says about daughters. But I watched such words come out of my own mother's and father's mouths; I looked at their ink drawing of poor people snagging their neighbor's flotage with long flood hooks and pushing the girl babies on down the river. And I had to get out of hating range. I read in an anthropology book that Chinese say, "Girls are necessary, too"; I have never heard the Chinese I know make this concession. Perhaps it was a saying in another village. I refuse to shy my way anymore through our Chinatown, which tasks me with the old sayings and the stories.

The swordswoman and I are not so dissimilar. May my people understand the resemblance soon so that l can return to them. What we have in common are the words at our backs. The ideographs for revenge are "report a crime" and "report to five families." The reporting is the vengeance—not the beheading, not the gutting, but the words. And I have so many words—"chink" words and "gook" words too—that they do not fit on my skin.

Notes

[1] Congress of Racial Equality. A nonviolent student group that rose to prominence in the 1960s.
[2] Pole fighters. A centuries old technique of martial arts fighting using long pole or spears.

Close Reading Questions

1. What is the author's mother's response when she learns that Kingston earned straight As in school? What reaction do you think the younger Kingston was expecting? (Multiple Perspectives)

2. Why does Kingston say that she wants to be "a lumberjack in Oregon?"

3. What was Kingston's reaction to her parents' laundry business being torn down?

Analytical Writing/Discussion

4. According to Kingston, "nobody in history has conquered and united both North American and Asia." In what ways is this statement a commentary on the author's American and Chinese identity? (Historical Trends)

5. Kingston notes that is the swordswoman who motivates her. How does Kingston's attitude about being a swordswoman affect the traditional expectations imposed on Chinese girls?

6. Why was Kingston eager to be a boy? In what ways would that have changed her affinity for being Chinese? (Cultural Influences)

Further Options

7. Maxine Hong Kingston notes that she had hoped her life would change because she went to college. How has attending new school changed your life in unexpected ways?

8. Kingston does not always fit into the racial expectations imposed by her family. Discuss the ways in which Kingston's story mirrors the family expectations of race and gender identity in Vanessa Mártir's "Stop Denying Me My Blackness" in this chapter (see pp. 230–235).

LIVING WITH RACIAL BATTLE FATIGUE: WHY FIGHTING MICROAGRESSIONS CAN FEEL LIKE TREADING WATER

by Dionne Irving Bremyer

Dionne Irving Bremyer is a native of Mississauga, Ontario, Canada. She is a professor of English at St. Mary's College, where she teaches creative writing. Bremyer is a graduate of Florida State University, Rhode Island College, and Georgia State University. Her writing has appeared in publications like *The Missouri Review*, *Terminus Magazine*, and *New Delta Review*. The following essay was published by Literary Hub in 2016.

As long as I have been able to afford it in my adult life, I have found, whenever possible, a swimming pool. I learned to swim in Canada of all places, the only little black girl in my swimming class. I had been anxious to get in the water for as long as I could remember. My only delay was the tubes I'd had put in

Copyright © 2016 by Dionne Irving Bremyer. Reprinted by permission.

my ears at three years old. I come from island people, and my love of water happens on the prereflective level, joyfully, and with abandon. The smells of sea, of salt, of chlorine, of damp, slightly moldy bathing suits—all make me happy. My people come from Hong Kong, India, Africa, Scotland, and have ended up in Jamaica, Canada, and now the United States. I am the first who will have lived most of my life here. My family history is a collection of names and a handful of dates, most lost or faded. Like the way the ocean pounds away at the shore, our history, like the white sand of the island, slips through my fingers all the time.

Both heritage and joy bring me to the water. I swim laps, sometimes in community swimming pools or at fancy gyms with heated pools and bins thick with flutter boards. I will sometimes emerge from a stroke to see an older black person staring at me, the man or woman usually in his or her sixties or seventies. They might be a part of a water aerobics class or running in a physical therapy pool.

If I catch their eye they will say "Hello" or "Good morning" or "Good evening." Our pleasantries break them from some kind of trance. I return to my laps, turning my head usually to the right in order to take a breath. I love feeling my lungs expand and contract as I move through the water. I am aware of them for the first time all day. I marvel at my body's capacity to stay buoyant, to take in air, to propel me forward. There are no sounds but the thrum of my heart and the cadence of my breath. In these moments, I understand the human body as a beautiful construct. When I stop, out of breath and panting, those eyes are on me again, watching. . . .

When we swim, when we plunge into oceans or lakes or backyard swimming pools, we feel some mastery over water, as though it could be ours to control. In these spaces, we don't wear much clothing and are in close contact with strangers. In and around these bodies of water, we reveal our public private parts. I think about this every time I pull on a bathing suit. I look at the way each of my "flaws" becomes visible and open for judgment. As we swim together, we experience intimacy regardless of age, race, or size. Each time we enter the water in a public space, we show ourselves.

It took me a few years of living in the United States before I understood the way water is loaded for African Americans. A horrible legacy surrounds water, and the story of who has access to it is a story dominated by a violence that is intricately tied to the ongoing battle for civil rights and against racism in the United States. In a hearing regarding public swimming spaces in Baltimore in 1954, just after the decision in *Brown v. Board of Education*, city solicitor Edwin Harlan said, "There must be segregation in fields of intimate contact or else there may be trouble."

Trouble. What a wonderful word. Purposefully vague, it can suggest innumerable possibilities. Perhaps it was the kind of trouble that Harlan had in mind that resulted in a married couple's arrest. Only two hours south of Baltimore and four years later, Mildred and Richard Loving would find themselves behind bars after breaking antimiscegenation laws.[1] Trouble begets intimacy, and intimacy is always trouble for those who believe fundamentally that skin color implies basic biologic difference.

Intimacy has certainly brought me my fair share of trouble because I have a very white life. To steal and alter a line from the old platitude: Some of my best friends are white. My white life happened in the way one usually does: I grew up middle class, attended mostly white schools and a mostly white college, worked in mostly white offices, and went to mostly white graduate programs. English departments, for all their best efforts, are still primarily white spaces. I live in the Midwest, which is largely white, and where most of my coworkers and almost all of my students are white. I have compounded this racial isolation by marrying a white man, so much of my family is also white. In my life, so filled with whiteness, I avoid talking about Ferguson,[2] about Eric Garner,[3] about the movie *Selma*.[4] I don't remind people how easily I could have been that fourteen-year-old, bikinied black girl in McKinney, Texas, who was recently slammed to the ground by an overzealous police officer on the lawn outside a largely white pool.

Because I am often the only person of color in the room, these topics become loaded. I risk becoming the angry black woman in the eyes of those around me. I risk sounding like I am delivering a sermon, or instruction, or chastisement. The angry black woman is a powerful archetype. The finger-waving, head-snapping sister-girl is an image I have to work hard to combat. Not because it represents any part of my character but because it is the only lens through which many white people see a black woman's anger. It's as though any time I am angry, I am liable to "go off." My fear of this image often silences me in meetings where I might like to speak up. It makes me hesitate in moments where my temper flares; it alters my behavior in every single facet of my life; it is one of the things that contribute to my invisibility. So I have avoided conversations that could externalize the pain I've felt welling up inside me over these past few months in response to the sad state of the world.

The truth is that even intimacy cannot assure that people I love won't disappoint me. The malaise and nausea I feel when I recognize the rhetoric of racism and privilege coming out of the mouths of people whom I have confided in, brought into my life, whom I work with and respect, keeps me off the Internet and away from the papers for days; it makes me send incoming calls to voice mail. It visits me with the symptoms of a depression so deep and so all-consuming that I have, more than once, closed my office door in the middle of the day to cry. I cannot eat, cannot sleep, cannot write, and cannot think.

A friend recently sent me an article about a condition called Racial Battle Fatigue. In a study published in the *Journal of Anxiety Disorders,* the authors focused on generalized anxiety disorder and found that people of color in the United States suffer from the condition at alarming rates. Defined as more than six months of general, free-floating anxiety and worry, the disorder was present not only in black people but also in soldiers of all races who live in theaters of war. It is a condition of living in a constant state of anxiety when the perceived threat can come from those whom you are close to. I read the piece and thought, "Aha! So it isn't just me."

My friends, my extended family, are good, well-meaning people. They are loving, they are accepting, they are generous, but they are people who take their privilege for granted. They don't have to live in fear of what may happen to them or to their children at an innocent pool party.

Who has access to water and who doesn't, who is allowed to swim and when and where and how that swimming takes place, connotes a privilege. When I read about how other forms of racial discrimination began to be dismantled after World War II, I kept coming back to swimming pools as battlegrounds. In his book *Contested Waters: A Social History of Swimming Pools in America,* Jeff Wiltse explores how, as public places starting in the North became increasingly more desegregated, whites simply abandoned municipal and public swimming pools for private pools and country clubs. A 2010 study by the USA Swimming Foundation conducted by the University of Memphis found that nearly 70 percent of African American children couldn't swim. The reasons for this statistic are varied, but the result is a greater number of drowning deaths of African American children each year. Not everyone has the privilege of recreational water, something I've learned a little at a time throughout my life. Only now do I consider how I, a young black woman moving confidently through the water, might have warranted a closer look.

I was a teenager when my family moved to Florida from Canada. I didn't understand then what water meant in America, and what it continues to mean. I didn't know the way access to water could communicate the underlying issues of race, class, and privilege in the United States. Instead, what I imagined was the beach, the ocean lapping at my toes, and the soft sand. It was a scene that conjured everything that was good about the water. What a disappointment, then, when instead of being close to the beach, we were landlocked in northern Florida, nowhere near the water.

That fall I joined my high school swim team. I was the only person of color, my face little more than a smudge in the back of the yearbook photograph. We swam at the local university early in the morning.

We got to practice at 5 a.m., and were in the water for an hour and a half and then off to high school on the other side of town. In the semidarkness, the air was damp with the early morning and tinged with the chlorine I loved so much. I loved making my way down the lanes as the sun came up. It was the only time of day when I felt like me, the girl I'd been in Canada, the one who wasn't always confused and heartbroken and alone. I didn't understand Florida, and maybe I never would.

"Perfect form," my high school swim coach would call out at each practice. "But you're too slow!". . .

In the water, my teammates cheered me on, told me I would do better next time. They didn't seem to understand that I wasn't discouraged by my placement in the races or by my clear lack of athleticism. I couldn't explain to them that all I really wanted was to be in the water. I didn't want to be coached or cheered. I just wanted the connection to breath and body and self. Just as people do now, they watched me then, too, but perhaps for different reasons, staring at me from the sidelines as I made my way up and down the lanes.

During that first year in Florida, I swam mostly at home in our family swimming pool. It seemed to me the ultimate luxury as a Canadian girl, being able to swim outdoors into September and even early October. A dream, but not an altogether pleasant one. But then again, all of America was like a dream, familiar in some ways but the rest of it so unfamiliar, so confusing.

My understanding came in the form of a searing punch that connected with my jaw after I left math class on a scorching hot October afternoon. I turned when someone called my name but didn't react quickly enough to see the closed fist that connected with the right side of my jaw and sent vibrations shooting up through my face. She hadn't drawn blood, but I clutched my cheek, thick with pain. The pain floored me and made me drop to the patch of grass between two portable classrooms. I had never been hit before. The girl towered above me, her message clear: You're either with us or against us. What I wasn't clear on until later that day was who that "us" was.

"You speak too proper," a girl confided in me as she helped me press paper towels soaked in cool water onto my face. "You act too white. People don't like it when they think you think you better than them."

Too white or *too* black. It hadn't occurred to me that there was a way to "act" black or white, that one was inherently better or worse. To be "too" something implied that you needed to find a balance, or, more to the point, that your pendulum should swing toward your own race in a way that made you easy to understand for other people. That way no one would question your grooming habits or the way you spoke. At my high school, it meant you signed up for girls' basketball or track and field. It meant that if you were smart, you joined the Black Brain Bowl Team (not its white counterpart, called simply the Brain Bowl) but it certainly did *not* mean you joined the swim team and signed up to be on the yearbook staff.

I managed to wash the mud from my shorts that afternoon before my mother noticed. But my face—black and blue, swollen and puffy where the girl's fist had landed—was less easy to hide, and my mother certainly noticed.

I can't recall the details of the lie I told. Something highly improbable, I'm sure. I relied on my ability to tell a good story. Mostly, I was ashamed. Most 14-year-olds think they know everything, and I was no different. I wanted to think I understood the world implicitly and that it had order and sense. I didn't want my mother to know I had seemingly miscalculated who I was and my place in this new, bizarre world. I was ashamed that although I'd always made friends quickly and easily, I was so emotionally tone-deaf that I could not pick up on the rhythms, the strokes, and the breath of this new place.

I can still feel the lingering effects of that punch, all these years later, the way it indoctrinated me into the subtleties of racial life in America, the way I continually find myself being indoctrinated. I'm grateful that there are no longer any overt punches. Instead, a thousand microaggressions land, as painful and as visceral as that closed fist against my jaw. And in my white world, I see those around me taking language for granted. Language—the words we use and the words we choose—is a privilege, and taking things for granted is at the very heart of privilege.

* * * * * * *

I dragged my feet on where to go to college, and through a combination of apathy and chiding from my parents, I ended up at Big Southern University. In the summer before my sophomore year, I signed up for Multi-Ethnic American Literature. I had taken an American lit class the previous fall with the same professor, who had managed to crack open Ralph Ellison's *Invisible Man* for me. When the book came into focus, I felt as though something made sense, as if the book announced something I had long felt but never been able to articulate. It seemed to explore the sense memory you have in the water when you know innately when to breathe and where your body is most buoyant. I had learned when, where, and how to be invisible in America. When to talk, when to stay silent, when to make sure it felt like I wasn't there at all. In his novel, Ellison expressed the invisibility I cultivated and made sense of it, identified a purpose. As I began to understand that desire, I wanted to unpack it, to explore it. . . .

As I do now in my own college classes, the professor had us each introduce ourselves and talk about why we were taking the class. But first, he discussed the class and pushed us to consider our own identities, to consider the ways in which race and privilege might define how we considered the texts we were going to read.

Most of the introductions were generic and similar, announcing a desire to learn whatever the student could from the semester. Some students told stories about their own backgrounds. Many were first-generation college students or students who wanted to learn more about a cultural heritage that had been whitewashed. With my professor's ears, I know now that these are things students say to please the teacher. But then, I didn't pay much attention. I was terrified of speaking in public, and I waited anxiously for my turn to come, trying to figure out what I was going to say about my interest in ethnic American literature. It would destroy my invisibility if I had to explain why I needed to be invisible.

Eventually I told a story about a racial heritage spanning four continents and owing mostly to the lasting effects of colonialism, ship travel, and—of course—slavery. When I got to the end I felt relieved, ready to return to a kind of invisibility and prepared to listen to the two or three rows of students sitting behind me.

"I'm excited to take this class because it's amazing to hear about other people's backgrounds, because I'm just white."

The words caught my attention immediately. I craned my neck to see who had spoken, a girl in a long paisley-print skirt, her crop top exposing the soft expanse of belly atop the skirt's waistband, and her curly hair frizzing away from her head. She was one of the girls I had taken to avoiding in college, those who smelled of patchouli and decorated their dorm rooms with Bob Marley posters. That kind of girl tended only to be interested in the fact that my Jamaican parents might somehow be indicative of a secret stash of pot. In my Canadian upbringing, I had never heard anyone call himself or herself "just white." Greek, Romanian, Czechoslovakian, Irish; elementary school seemed to capture a wide swath of eastern bloc countries and colonial outliers. Lunch was so inclusive that one could trade a bologna sandwich for some curry chicken or exchange a Jamaican meat patty for a piece of baklava. What did this mean, "just white"? It implied that somehow, in this class of diverse backgrounds and narratives, whiteness was somehow not as exciting, as interesting, as exotic. It was the opposite of being "too white." "Just" implied a kind of blandness and homogeny in an American cultural paradigm that cultivated and elevated whiteness and simultaneously normalized it to make it less interesting or important. Whiteness, I had quickly learned in my American education, was the standard for beauty, intellect, and acceptability, but no one should admit this or discuss it, particularly not a white hippie girl in a multiethnic lit class. Was whiteness somehow not going to be valued in this class? To say "just white" seemed like treading water, not moving toward understanding the course's purpose and not able to look back and understand what came before this point in time. "Just" implied stasis, a lack of growth regarding ideas of whiteness or anything other than whiteness. "Just" was a lie. The professor chuckled a bit. "None of us are 'just white,'" he said. "Whiteness is a construct and a category like any other that we will unpack this semester."

Later that day in the water, I swam my slow freestyle up and down the middle lane. Taking my time and measuring my breath, I made sure to remember the way the girl's skirt had dragged on the floor, the ring in her nose, and the timbre of her voice: high-pitched, girlish, and loud. I gathered these details for a story as my arms glided through the water, barely making a splash on its surface, the sun hitting my goggles as I came up for air again, and again, and again.

"Just white" stuck with me for an entire year. I told the story to a group of friends in a coffee shop, to my older siblings, to my new friend Keith, who like me had parents from the Caribbean and a passion for death metal. The combined naïveté and irony of the statement was typical of so many attempts at racial parity that came out so wrongheaded at Big Southern University. There were those people who tried to convince me that they did not see race, the boy who shied away from introducing me to his parents, the classmate so stunned that I had passed college algebra on the first try. "You must be really smart!" he marveled while flipping through his basic math text.

It was at about that time that I met her again, this time at a meeting for the staff of the school newspaper. The girl, this time looking decidedly less like a relic of the 1960s introduced herself as "Alice."

"Oh, I know you," I blurted out. "You were in my ethnic American lit class last summer. You were the 'just white girl.'"

It came out without any thought. I hadn't realized that this anecdote might be less funny to the person who was the butt of the joke.

"What?" she said, confused.

She furrowed her brow, and I recounted the story to her about her shame at being "just white." She looked embarrassed, and I felt bad. This person whom I had used in an anecdote for a year had no clue what her language that day had implied. And at the time, I didn't fully understand what that privilege meant. It was a funny story to me, and I didn't see the ways in which it indicated a naïveté about the world.

"Wow," she said. "That was dumb. I don't even know why I said that. My family's Italian."

She was chastened, and in that moment of shared embarrassment, we started building a friendship. In this moment of revelation, we seemed to be able to find a kind of honesty. This ability to speak freely to each other became the cornerstone of our friendship. We had agreed to be honest with each other in a way that meant we confessed too much, but it also meant that we held onto each other's secrets.

My husband, who studies the politics, philosophies, and theories of race, tells me that authentic intimacy might be the thing that helps people move beyond issues of racial difference. He reminds me that if we truly know a person, race recedes into the background and becomes secondary to who they are. I am not his black wife but his wife. I want that to be true. I don't want to be anyone's "black" anything. I only want people to see me, not black me.

As I look through pictures online of the history of the desegregation of swimming pools, I click past images of children, black and white, still standing in groups segregated by race, not touching. The white children are in the minority. In the photos, each group looks at the other warily. I want to believe they got to know each other, that the intimacy of the shared swimming space meant they learned each other's names and lives. But the other images, the ones that show a hotel manager throwing muriatic acid into a swimming pool where whites and blacks swam together to protest the integrated space, make me believe otherwise. Intimacy, even when it is only the kind that comes from standing close to one another in bathing suits, is just as frightening when it arrives in a friendship.

* * * * * * * *

After Alice and I graduated from college and moved on to other cities, we visited each other periodically. We slipped back into the roles we knew so well from college: the girl who was "just white," who said directly, bluntly what was on her mind and in her heart regardless of whom it might offend; and I, caustic and mean, the one who collected small details and used them to make jokes at others' expense. There are other things I could say about the ways in which our friendship morphed and changed over time that might round her out, things about her wicked sense of humor, her willingness for adventure, her openness to new things. There are times we laughed so hard we cried; we shared experiences that make for excellent cocktail-party stories. There are times I cried on her shoulder or she on mine. These are all measures of our friendship, a relationship defined not by our differences but one that seemed to transcend them.

Even so, invariably over the years, we would have odd or awkward moments between us when all of a sudden the girl I'd called "the just white girl" would rear her head and I wasn't sure what to do. She introduced me to new people as her gorgeous friend, always noting my tiny waist, my ample bosom, and my skin. Only later did I understand that this seemingly flattering list was actually reducing me to my physicality, a collection of pleasing and palatable parts. Again, thinking she was being complimentary, she would reduce me further, nudging me toward whiteness by telling me she was blacker than I was when she ridiculed me for a succession of white boyfriends, when she told me she thought about dating a black man but never could because of how her parents might react.

We both got master's degrees in English; she focused on literature while I pursued creative writing. We exchanged professional materials, swapped dating stories, continued to travel together, and were in each other's weddings. Over the period that encompassed my 20s, she was one of my closest friends. As we closed out that decade of our lives, we both, suddenly and rather unexpectedly, found ourselves divorced.

I was excited at what seemed to be a fresh start for us both of us as we entered into new and promising relationships. Alice and I were living closer than we had throughout most of the previous decade, only a six-hour drive apart, and it seemed the opportune moment for a visit. I had met a wonderful new man, intelligent and kind. Less than a year later, he would become my husband in a ceremony that excluded most of the people we know. In that first blush of new love, what I wanted most of all was for him to meet the people who were important to me.

On the drive from Atlanta to Chapel Hill, the sky opened up no less than half-a-dozen times. Fat drops and steady waves of rain made it feel as though we were crawling along the freeway.

Alice lived in a former cotton and dye mill, recently converted to lofts, on the banks of a river just outside Chapel Hill. The water in the river churned a muddy brown from the pounding of the constant rain. We held sweaters over our heads and ran into the building as quickly as we could in the late-summer rain.

The floors, original to the space, had been heavily varnished, and the contractors had left the occasional textile button or staple to offer what real estate agents and home design shows will often call "character." On its website, the management company advertised the space as "rural renaissance done right." The idea of a Southern "rural renaissance" only made me think of the South's rural history, so closely linked to slavery. I could still hear the overtones of cotton culture. The idea of renaissance "done right" was a juxtaposition that embodied the contemporary South completely. It wanted to revise its past, to focus on its glories, to ignore its fundamental truth.

In the stairwell up to Alice's loft, I kissed my boyfriend. I was excited at the fun weekend ahead, the good time we were going to have. When we arrived on the top floor and knocked on her door, she pulled it open and said, "Oh, good, you got a little fat too!"

I was taken aback by her words. She was trying to make a joke—at least, I think she was. Was it a way to dissipate some tension she felt about the visit? About herself? I wasn't sure. We drank some wine. Then some more. And then we shared a bottle of sparkling wine when we got to a restaurant.

"You look happy," she remarked when we went to the bathroom midway through the meal.

"I am happy," I said.

It was true. It was the first happiness I could remember, after a protracted and grueling divorce, after several years of a bad marriage and a life I felt I had settled for.

"I am too," she said quickly as we washed our hands in the big farm-style sink. In what I thought was a celebratory gesture, she ordered more sparkling wine when we got back to the table. Instead, the mood of the evening shifted startlingly and suddenly. Alice started in with stories of our college escapades and then shifted to a series of stories that seemed intended to lay bare for this new man in my life the worst parts of me, those that would make him cringe, feel insecure, and lead to conflict.

He got quieter and quieter. By the time the evening ended, he would barely look at me. We returned to her apartment, and my boyfriend and I barely spoke. Tossing and turning on her fold-out couch, I tried to figure out where things had gone so wrong. When I finally drifted off to sleep, he got up and walked down to the river. I awoke, startled, after he had been gone a little while. The rain from the previous evening had started coming down harder and faster. The river churned dark and fast. I had no idea where he was or when he was coming back.

After several hours, he did return, cold, wet, muddy, and shivering, I was angry, relieved, and overwhelmed. I was frustrated with him, with myself, and with her. We had a frenzied exchange in the dark, whispering hoarsely, resolving nothing. Somehow, I felt I had done something wrong. There was some code of whiteness I had broken, had overstepped, or had failed to see. In that moment, I was the outsider. And as Alice woke up and the day began, it seemed that I was the one whom everyone was angry with.

Treading water is hard work. You appear still from the water's surface, as though you are levitating, yet below the surface, your lower body and arms work frantically, kicking and pounding against the water's pressure. The energy you exert just to keep your head and neck aloft will tire you out quickly enough. It is one of the best illusions in swimming: the surface doesn't indicate what is going on below.

I tried to make everything right with them both and to keep my head above water. The day went from drizzly to a downpour, the water less like droplets and more like buckets dropped from the sky. We got soaked going to lunch, and we agreed to stay in that evening. We planned to grill on the communal patio in her converted mills, a giant concrete slab with a roof. The space was lined with an array of gas and charcoal grills, one of those contemporary spaces that invite apartment dwellers to be neighborly. It was this community that had attracted Alice after her divorce, when she felt adrift in a city to which she had relocated for her ex-husband.

Still rain-drenched and cold, I felt exhausted but nevertheless relieved that as the day neared its end I had been successful on both fronts. My friend and my boyfriend both seemed more relaxed, more at ease.

We decided on kabobs and spent the early evening cutting up vegetables and meats. As Alice chattered on about the new place where she was living and her fellow tenants, the phrase "porch monkey" hissed and slid out of her mouth like a water moccasin. I was stunned to silence for a moment, and then I said, "What?"

"Oh, you know," she said, slicing up hunks of smooth, pink, raw chicken and running them through with skewers. "I mean hippie kids who come out to the porch and eat everyone's food without asking. Porch monkeys."

But I didn't know.

"Start over," I said.

She rolled her eyes. "It isn't racist," she said. Alice's tone implied that I was being overly sensitive.

I hadn't said much of anything at all, yet something in her understood how loaded her words were. How racist the phrase was. Did she think it was okay to say it because she didn't think I was "really" black? She knew she was wrong but didn't want to admit it. I wanted to give her an out, so I said, with the slightest hint of a joke in my voice, "I don't think that expression means what you think it means."

She shrugged. "That's what they are."

She was done with the subject. She had moved on to considering which vegetables to grill next, and I stood there, flummoxed.

The origins of the slur *porch monkey* are nebulous. However, the words have been used alongside *jungle bunny, yard ape, coon, nigglet,* and a host of other racial slurs that emphasize the animalistic when it comes to black people. The history of assigning the phenotypic characteristics of a monkey or ape to black people goes back even further. It is meant to dehumanize, to make a black person a beast, to ascribe qualities of the feral, the frightening, the untamed, the uncivil and brutish to our people.

I exchanged a glance with my boyfriend across the room. He, too, was incredulous. He was white, I thought. He got it. How could this woman, one of my closest friends for over a decade, be so obtuse? Or worse, so cruel?

✳ ✳ ✳ ✳ ✳ ✳ ✳ ✳

Language is tenuous and ever changing. There is nothing fixed about it. All three of us were English professors, and we understood this. Language was our livelihood, and as close examiners and interpreters of that language, to assume that words are without power? It seemed naïve; it seemed callous. This "porch monkey" thing, like a weeping wound in the middle of the meal preparations, compounded everything else that had happened that weekend. While she had been intent on first trying to use my past to subjugate me, when that hadn't worked she seemed to have gone for the last thing left, the color of my skin. But she had done it covertly, quietly, sneakily. She made my race itself the problem. And what could I do but stand there, stunned? I had two options: to reopen the turmoil bubbling beneath the surface or to let it go.

In hindsight, I made the coward's choice, the passive-aggressive choice. I stayed hurt, and I said nothing. I helped her finish making the kabobs, and we went out to the impromptu party that had assembled on the common patio. But I didn't stay long. I felt conspicuously black in this forced community setting. And when I heard her retelling the porch-monkey joke over and over again to the delighted young urban professionals, hipsters, and trust-funded hippies who had gathered to draw community from each other, I felt the beginnings of that soul-crushing sadness with which I had become so familiar.

In the days afterward, that's all I felt. On the way back to Atlanta, I tried to discuss it with my boyfriend, not having the language in that moment to articulate why these two words had bothered me so much. Why I couldn't just let it go as I had a million times before with her, with other people. A few days after our return she sent me an e-mail in which she wrote the following:

> *We swore to be honest, so I'm going to tell you what I see. I have to say these things to you because if I didn't, I would feel like I failed you as one of the few people in your life who can say*

this. I love you very much, and I want you to be happy. Here's the real problem: your boyfriend has eliminated YOUR ability to be honest.

The words stung, because there was truth in them. I hadn't been honest, but the person I hadn't been honest with was her. I couldn't tell her the way the words she used resonated in my head. That I felt like she had tried to annihilate me with that phrase, over and over. How I'd thought about it for days after, trying to figure out why she hadn't understood. But I kept coming back to myself again and again as the person who was at fault, because I hadn't been honest, I hadn't been intimate. I had closed the gates to her without giving her an opportunity to defend herself. But really, how many chances do we get? I don't have an infinite number of chances, so why must I give them?

The truth is that no matter what I accomplish, no matter what I do, no matter what I don't do, some people in the world will always see my dark skin, not me. In their eyes, I am a rare exception. Like a tap-dancing dog, I am dazzling but not indicative of what other dogs might do.

The term *racial microaggression* has been around since the 1970s and describes the overt and covert ways in which people of color receive messages about how race defines them. It is the most powerful catalyst of Racial Battle Fatigue. It is the casual use of a phrase like *porch monkey*. It is the student who said I had made her "a bit less racist" because she assumed most young black women were "pregnant, on welfare, and ill spoken." It is the professor who told me that no one wants to read stories about people of color and asked if I weren't limiting myself by writing those stories. It is the yoga instructor who told me with a pat on my upturned ass during the middle of a class, "We need to get more of your people out here doing yoga. It's good for them!" It is the friend who fingered my hair and asked if I had a weave. Any one of these things on its own dehumanizes me; the hundreds that I keep in a file on my computer exhaust me. It is enough to make someone not want to get out of bed in the morning. It is a society that devalues your personhood, a friend who makes you an object, and a stranger who turns you into a curiosity.

Like language, a soul is very tenuous. What does it mean to have one? In what way can it be hurt? Can language injure the soul? I cannot point to an injured spot on my body to show a doctor where I have been hurt by language, but the injury manifests itself in creases on my forehead, fluctuating weight loss and gain, in the defeated look in my eyes. I register it by counting the days I fail to leave my bed and eventually in the ways in which I brutalize myself emotionally. All of this. But it's that drizzly North Carolina afternoon I can't forget. A small choice of language from, as Alice put it, "one of the people who were supposed to love me," hurts me most.

The pain echoes still, because no matter how much water I treaded, no matter how much I tried to make Alice (and so many others) feel comfortable with my blackness, I never seemed to get the same in return.

* * * * * * * *

Years later and back in the water, I am eight months pregnant. My pregnancy has brought me back to my body in a way I thought only swimming could. I am acutely aware of each movement, each moment, and each breath. I feel another life, just beneath the surface of my skin, doing his own laps, making his way alongside me.

Swimming relieves the aches and pains of pregnancy, the weight of my yet-to-be-born son on my back, on my belly, in my hips. In the water I feel light. I glide through, effortlessly, forgetting the twenty-five extra pounds on me, feeling like myself in the way I only can in the water. It transforms now, as it always has, the rhythmic movements, the focus on my breath, the concentration it takes so that I slice through without much of a splash.

Swimming clears my mind, offers me a kind of meditation, a meaningful connection between my body and my mind. Between my body and my baby's. In the water, I hear my heartbeat and that of my son echoing though my ears above the din of the senior water aerobics class in the next lane.

I have already found a place for him to swim. By the time he is six months, I plan on bringing him into the water. This desire lives alongside a list of things that all parents want for their children: health, good schools, a passion for reading. I feel strongly about this. I want him to love the water the way I do. I want it to be calming. I want him not to be frightened but to be soothed by it.

He will be my first blood relative who is American. Much of the legacy and the baggage of his skin will be foisted on him before he takes his first breath. But he will also have roots in Kansas, like the president. In the middle of that state, there is a small Kansas town where he will be able to see his last name etched on the side of a building and to find his great-great-grandfather's picture on the wall of the Main Street Deli. This is one of the things my husband can offer him, that stake in American life that is inaccessible to me. All I have for him is water. Water that is murky at times, and a fluid past absent of dates, names, photographs, or specificity.

Notes

[1.] Antimiscegenation: Laws in the United States that prohibited interracial marriage. The Supreme Court deemed those laws unconstitutional in 1967 in the *Loving v. Virginia* case.

[2.] Ferguson, Missouri: where an unarmed African American man, Michael Brown, was shot and killed by a white police officer in August 2014. Protests, both violent and peaceful, began the night of the shooting and continued for three months.

[3.] Eric Garner (1970-2014), an African American man from Staten Island, NY who was killed when New York City police, in an attempt to arrest him for selling cigarettes illegally, placed him in a chokehold. Garner's death was later ruled a homicide.

[4.] *Selma*: 2014 motion picture account of the voting rights marches in 1965 from Selma to Montgomery, Alabama

Close Reading Questions

1. Why does Bremyer regard swimming as a form of intimacy?

2. What did Bremyer learn about "acceptability" after she moved to the United States?

3. Bremyer states that "treading water is hard work." How did that idiom apply to her adult life?

Analytical Writing/Discussion

4. Why do you think Bremyer begins her essay with a description of her racial and ethnic heritage? (Historical Trends)

5. According to Bremyer, why was her encounter with Alice in North Carolina a pivotal point in their friendship? To what extent do you think Alice would agree with this assessment? (Multiple Perspectives)

6. Bremyer states that some people will always view her as "a rare exception." Why do you agree or disagree with this statement?

Further Options

7. Dionne Irving Bremyer seeks to maintain her racial identity in the presence of racial micro-aggressions. In what ways does Judith Ortiz Cofer in "Don't Call Me Maria" in Chapter 1 on pp. 45–49 use similar or different responses to microaggressions in order to maintain pride in her racial heritage? (Cultural Influences)

8. Bremyer mentions the *Journal of Anxiety Disorders* article about Racial Battle Fatigue. Read that article using the strategies for reading a text in Chapter 1 on The Reading Process on pp. 8–12. Then, find specific ways that the scholarly journal applies to Irving's essay.

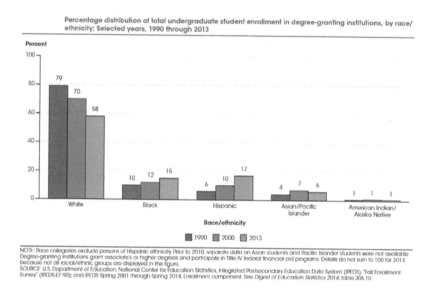

FIGURE 2   College Enrollment by race/ethnicity, 1990-2013

Freewrite 3: "Driving While Me"

The following essay by writer and educator Kerry L. Beckford provides a look at the multiple reasons that purchasing a car goes beyond economic realities. The essay was published by *Grub Street Writes* in a series about the effects of police brutality on people of color. After reading this text, you will be asked to respond through freewriting and/or discussion.

For a time, I dreamed of owning a brand-new Cadillac. How amazing it would feel to drive to work in my crimson red or champagne-colored beauty.

I wish the color of my new car was my only concern. But I am a black woman in America. When I get behind the wheel, I am Sandra Bland[1] in Texas and Philando Castile[2] in Minneapolis and every other black man and woman in America. Driving a shiny new Cadillac is too risky.

I'm a respectful driver, I've never had a car accident, and have one ticket for breezing through a stop light . . . in 1982. I brake for squirrels, geese, and wild turkeys. I don't text and drive. I keep the volume on the radio low so I can hear emergency vehicles when they approach.

Yet, when I'm driving, all anyone can see is a black woman with glasses and dreadlocks.

When I'm driving my heart is invisible, as is my compassion and creativity, my love for God, my four college degrees, and my obsession with nail polish.

I was raised to be proud of who I am. My New England roots kept my back straight and my Caribbean roots kept my chin up. I was called beautiful and smart and strong as early as I can remember.

The thing is, I'm not feeling so resilient these days. Sadness has taken root where confidence used to reside. I cannot watch the news because it feeds my anxiety yet I have to watch the news to know what I am up against.

I finally bought the car I needed: a Buick SUV. It is dark brown with 20-inch tires and a front grill that looks like a panther baring its teeth. It is a beast of a car and I feel safe in it. I have to. It is all the protection I have against the road, the world, and me.

Notes

[1.] Sandra Bland: an African American woman who arrested in Texas in 2015 after being stopped by police for a traffic violation. She was found hanged in her cell three days later.

[2.] Philando Castile: an African American man shot and killed by police in Minnesota in 2016 after being stopped for a traffic violation.

After reading this text, answer some of the following questions by freewriting and/or discussion:

- Why does Beckford discuss the reasons she is "a respectful driver?"

- In what ways does your identity—particularly race and gender—affect decisions you make, like buying a car and driving that vehicle?

- Why do you think or not think that the onus is on people of all races not to appear threatening?

Final Assignment 1: Contested Identities

The subject of race is often mired in oppression as much as it is a cause for celebration. Zora Neale Hurston delighted in being a black woman, while Dionne Irving Bremyer found that racial identity was a heavy cloak to wear.

Essay Question

In what ways do you think racial identity is a shifting, externally driven concept and/or a static, personally defined concept?

Write a formal and extended essay to answer these questions. Be sure to include specific references and direct quotations from several readings in this chapter (see Chapter 4 on Academic Honesty on quoting and citing properly). Be sure to not only support your informed perspective but also to anticipate and answer the possible objections of those who do not already agree with you. Your task is to assert your opinion and persuade others to consider it carefully.

Freewrite 4: Assignment Analysis

Before you start to answer this complex question, analyze its parts. Reread the essay question above and underline several phrases that represent key parts of the larger answer you will be developing. Then pick two or three of these phrases and freewrite your immediate impressions: What do you think right now? Then, pause to look for connections, contradictions, and omissions within your first response: what else do you want to discuss, what else do you want to add, and/or in what order are your ideas developing? Finally, consider the audience of your essay: who does not agree with you already, and why might they disagree?

Reading Review

Once you have sketched some of your initial ideas, review some of the readings to find specific details and persuasive evidence to support, enrich, and possibly complicate your response. Here are some readings and post-reading questions that you may want to consider:

1. Freewrite 1
2. Hurston, Close Reading Question 3
3. Hurston, Analytical Writing Question 5
4. Walker, Close Reading Question 2
5. Freewrite 2
6. Bremyer, Analytical Writing Question 4
7. Bremyer, Analytical Writing Question 5
8. Freewrite 3

Feel free to include other readings and post-reading questions. You also may want to review the suggestions for writing persuasively in Chapter 5 on Argument as well as practicing the peer response described in Chapter 2 on the Writing Process.

Final Assignment 2: Rhetorical Analysis

For two readings of this chapter (or possibly using one of the related or additional readings suggested below), compare and/or contrast their arguments. As explained in Chapter 5, this rhetorical analysis will answer the following questions:

- Based on the rhetorical triangle, who do you think is the writer and what is the message of this text? Who is the primary audience that the writer wanted to reach (consider the publication source)? (See pp. 104–105 of Chapter 5.)

- How does the writer try to use each of the three rhetorical appeals in this text, and when are they used effectively or not? (See pp. 105–109 of Chapter 5).

- Your professor may ask you to consider also the kind of argument being made, meaning a forensic, epideictic, or deliberative argument (see pp. 110–112 of Chapter 5). What kind of argument is being made, and why do you find it this kind to be a good choice (or not)?

- Finally, through comparing and contrasting the arguments of these two readings, what can you conclude about their power to persuade their intended audiences (and possibly additional readers)?

Your task is to help your readers to understand these two arguments and their efforts to persuade their audience.

Final Assignment 3: Family, Race, and Culture

When it comes to race, family values mold and shape racial identities based on complex ideas. In Maxine Hong Kingston's memoir, the unnamed narrator struggles to merge her Chinese and American selves. Vanessa Mártir's family is sometimes sympathetic and sometimes dismissive when it comes to matters of race.

Essay Question

In what ways can families support or dismantle one's racial identity?

Write a formal and extended essay to answer these questions. Be sure to include specific references and direct quotations from several readings in this chapter (see Chapter 4 on Academic Honesty on quoting and citing properly). Be sure to not only support your informed perspective but also to anticipate and answer the possible objections of those who do not already agree with you. Your task is to assert your opinion and persuade others to consider it carefully.

Freewrite 5: Assignment Analysis

Before you start to answer this complex question, analyze its parts. Reread the essay question above and underline several phrases that represent key parts of the larger answer you will be developing. Then pick two or three of these phrases and freewrite your immediate impressions: What do you think right now? Then, pause to look for connections, contradictions, and omissions within your first response: what else do you want to discuss, what else do you want to add, and/or in what order are your ideas developing? Finally, consider the audience of your essay: who does not agree with you already, and why might they disagree?

Reading Review

Once you have sketched some of your initial ideas, review some of the readings to find specific details and persuasive evidence to support, enrich, and possibly complicate your response. Here are some readings and post-reading questions that you may want to consider:

1. Freewrite 1
2. Walker, Analytical Writing Question 6

3. Erdrich, Close Reading Question 3

4. Mártir, Analytical Writing Question 4

5. Mártir, Further Options Question 7

6. Kingston, Close Reading Question 3

7. Kingston, Analytical Writing Question 5

8. Bremyer, Close Reading Question 1

Feel free to include other readings and post-reading questions. You also may want to review the suggestions for writing persuasively in Chapter 5 on Argument as well as practicing the peer response described in Chapter 2 on the Writing Process.

Readings on Race and Identity in Other Chapters

For four additional readings related to race and identity, you may want to read the following texts:

1. "Don't Call Me Maria" by Judith Ortiz Cofer in Chapter 3 (see pp. 45–49)

2. "Families Enslaved" by Frederick Douglass in Chapter 6 (see pp. 136–140)

3. "Finding Families for African American Children: The Challenges of Transracial Adoption" by The Evan B. Donaldson Adoption Institute in Chapter 6 (see pp. 156–160)

4. "What Makes a Family?" by Vanessa de la Torre in Chapter 6 (see pp. 163–165)

Additional Readings for Chapter 8

To deepen your understanding of race and identity and strengthen your final assignment, you can consult some of the following sources:

1. For a deeper understanding of racial categories in the United States, view the Pew Research Center interactive website, "What Census Calls Us: A Historical Timeline." This site chronicles the history of how racial categories have changed since the first census was taken in 1790.

   http://www.pewsocialtrends.org/interactives/multiracial-timeline/

2. To learn more about the landmark 1967 Supreme Court case that overturned laws preventing interracial marriage, listen to National Public Radio's conversation with author Sheryll Cashin. The link also provides a transcript of the interview:

   http://kcur.org/post/50-years-later-loving-revisits-landmark-supreme-court-ruling#stream/0

3. To read more about the racial composition of America's cities in the twenty-first century, you might want to read the editorial by Michael Bader, PhD, professor of sociology at American University. The editorial cites Bader's research into racially segregated neighborhoods.

   http://www.latimes.com/opinion/op-ed/la-oe-bader-resegregation-los-angeles-20160401-story .html

4. To read about a Filipina woman's experience with her family in Los Angeles, read "Walang Hiya, Brother" by Melissa R. Sipin. Sipin's essay chronicles the challenges she faced in adhering to expected gender roles in her family.

   http://www.kwelijournal.org/prose/2014/5/18/walang-hiya-brother-by-melissa-r-sipin

5. For more information about white racial identity in the United States, read "White Privilege: Unpacking the Invisible Knapsack" by Peggy McIntosh, founder of The National SEED Project (Seeking Educational Equity and Diversity).

   https://nationalseedproject.org/white-privilege-unpacking-the-invisible-knapsack

6. For an in-depth essay on the shooting of Florida teenager Trayvon Martin, read "How To Slowly Kill Yourself and Others in America." The essay, published in 2011, was written by novelist and professor, Kiese Laymon.

   http://gawker.com/5927452/how-to-slowly-kill-yourself-and-others-in-america-a-remembrance

7. For an examination of the effects of Mexican immigration to the United States on Mexican and non-Mexicans, you may want to read the chapter *The Souls of Anglos* from the 2014 book *Up Against the Wall: Reimagining the U. S.-Mexico Border* by Edward S. Casey and Mary Watkins. This scholarly book discusses borders and boundaries from multiple perspectives.

   http://www.esocsci.org.nz/wp-content/uploads/2017/03/Up_Against_the_Wall-Casey-Watkins-2014.pdf

8. For additional perspective on how students of color reconcile their racial and student identities, you might want to view the 2016 TEDTalk "How Students of Color Confront Imposter Syndrome." Dena Simmons, PhD, Director of Education at the Yale Center for Emotional Intelligence, offers insight about creating educational environments where students of color can thrive.

   https://www.ted.com/talks/dena_simmons_how_students_of_color_confront_impostor_syndrome

Energy and Sustainability

To waste, to destroy, our natural resources, to skin and exhaust the land instead of using it so as to increase its usefulness, will result in undermining in the days of our children the very prosperity which we ought by right to hand down to them.

—President Theodore Roosevelt (1907)

We've got to pause and ask ourselves: How much clean air do we need?"

—Lee Iacocca (1974)

Global warming has become a new religion.

—Dr. Ivar Giaever (2008)

Saving our planet, lifting people out of poverty, advancing economic growth: these are one and the same fight.

—Ban Ki-moon (2011)

Introduction

Author Barbara Kingsolver lived a comfortable life with her husband and two children in their Arizona home. However, Kingsolver was curious as to whether her family could become more mindful of their energy usage and overall impact on the planet. So, for one year, Kingsolver's family moved to rural Virginia vowing to eat food grown within 100 miles of their home—including food grown in the family garden. In her 2007 memoir, *Animal, Vegetable, Miracle,* Kingsolver admits that their journey began with hope, yet was also filled with reminders of their ties to the habits she was seeking to avoid. She writes:

> As the U.S. population made an unprecedented mad dash for the Sun Belt, one carload of us paddled against the tide, heading for the Promised Land where water falls from the sky and green stuff grows all around. We were about to begin the adventure of realigning our lives with our food chain. Naturally, our first stop was to buy junk food and fossil fuel.

So many Americans are not accustomed to the frugal and environmentally-aware lifestyle Kingsolver tried to create, for it means making a serious assessment of the energy usage contemporary lifestyles demand.

According to the 2015 Residential Energy Consumption Survey, the average household had at least two televisions. Households with people over 65 tend to have desktop computers, while much younger households have laptops, smart phones, and video game consoles. Most homes had washing machines and dryers, microwave ovens, dishwashers, and air conditioning. According to the National Household Travel Survey (NHTS), 70 percent of households in 1969 did not own a car; by 2009, that number dropped to less than 40 percent. By the end of the first decade of the twenty-first century, 91 percent of American households had at least one car and many had at least two cars. Less than 3 percent of Americans walked to work and only a few used public transit. The vast majority drove to and from work, often with one person per car. We are a nation of convenience and energy consumption.

The three historical readings of this chapter include diverse discussions about energy and sustainability. The historical readings include Brian C. Black's article, which traces the way oil and oil-based products became an integral part of American life, while James Atwater's *Saturday Evening Post* article provides a glimpse of 1960s America, when households were brimming with energy-hogging appliances. Among the three contemporary readings, David W. Orr implores a new generation of designers to consider the environment in all aspects of building design. Nicolas Loris asserts that scientists cannot agree that global warming exists, while Colin Beavan believes he can limit his family's carbon footprint while living in energy-dependent New York City. Every reading in this chapter provides perspectives on the storied history of energy usage in America and the varied attempts to create sustainable lifestyles amid an affinity for convenience and consumption.

These texts, along with the reading questions, freewriting activities, and visual elements of this chapter, are designed to develop the reading and writing abilities required for academic study. After each reading, you will find a set of questions that are divided into Close Reading Questions, Analytical Writing/ Discussion, and Further Options. Some questions involve the same investigation of multiple perspectives, cultural influences, and historical trends that were introduced in Chapters 1. Answering some and discussing more of the postreading questions will better prepare you to complete the final assignments options. These final writing assignments will ask you to assert your own, more informed perspective on energy usage in the United States. This chapter asks: **To what extent should energy sustainability be a top priority?**

Freewrite 1: Initial Impressions

Before you read the varying opinions of the other writers in the rest of this chapter, freewrite to explore your own thoughts and experiences about energy and sustainability. Try answering some of the following questions:

- To what extent do you think your daily use of energy impacts the environment?

- Why do you think the United States should or should not reduce its dependence on oil as its primary energy source?

OIL FOR LIVING

by Brian C. Black

Brian C. Black is an associate professor of history and environmental studies at Pennsylvania State University, Altoona, and is the author of several books, including *Petrolia: The Landscape of American's First Oil Boom* and *Crude Reality: Petroleum in World History*. The following excerpt is from Black's 2012 article, "Oil for Living: Petroleum and American Conspicuous Consumption," which was published in the *Journal of American History*.

Americans proudly streamed to the 1939 World's Fair in New York City as World War II flared on the other side of the Atlantic. Not yet part of the conflict, Americans used the opportunity to escape the present and wax utopian. Although the dreams on display took many forms, they were woven together by an invisible hand—more specifically, by a basic assumption—concealed within each of the fair's scenes: bountiful supplies of cheap energy. The novelist E. L. Doctorow provides one of the most revealing descriptions of one of the fair's best-known attractions:

> We rode across the Bridge of Wheels and got out, of course, at the General Motors Building. That was everyone's first stop. . . . In front of us a whole world lit up, as if we were flying over it, the most fantastic sight I had ever seen, an entire city of the future, with skyscrapers and fourteen-lane highways, real little cars moving on them at different speeds, the center for the higher speeds, the lanes on the edge for the lower. . . . This miniature world demonstrated how everything was planned. . . .It was a toy that any child in the world would want to own. You could play with it forever . . . it was a model world.

Inside General Motors' Futurama, five million visitors rode on the "Magic Motorways" exhibit, designed by Norman Bel Geddes, that led to the "Town of Tomorrow." Details of reality—such as grocery stores and gas stations—were left out of the vision, but the nation was abuzz with the futuristic marvels such as flying sedans found on the model expressways of Ford's "Road of Tomorrow."[1] Although that dream world possessed iconic aspects that resonated for generations, its greatest appeal may have been its vision of a world in which basic aspects of everyday life occurred easily—requiring neither care nor attention. With their basic needs met, humans might occupy themselves with greater challenges or endless diversion.

Even though automobiles have, for the most part, remained grounded, many other details of that futuristic landscape materialized. The remarkable accomplishments that shaped everyday American life

From "Oil for Living: Petroleum and American Conspicuous Consumption," by Brian C. Black. *The Journal of American History*, Volume 99, Issue 1, June 2012 (Pages 40–50). Used by permission of Oxford University Press.

---

[1] E. L. Doctorow, *World's Fair* (New York, 1985), 252–53. Jeffrey L. Meikle, *Twentieth Century Limited: Industrial Design in America, 1925–1939* (Philadelphia, 1979), 200–209. For more on the 1939 World's Fair in New York City, see Robert W. Rydell and Laura Burd Schiavo, eds., *Designing Tomorrow: America's World's Fairs of the 1930s* (New Haven, 2010).

after World War II have many common threads that bind them together, but perhaps none is as central as petroleum. Measured in terms of quadrillion Btus (British thermal units), which is the basis for charting energy consumption, U.S. consumption of petroleum rose from less than ten after 1945 to twenty in 1960, forty in 1975, and over forty after 2000. It was approximately 1950 when petroleum overtook coal as the nation's leading energy producer, and today the rate of petroleum consumption ranks approximately double its nearest competitors, coal and natural gas. Although the nation passed through different eras in the commodity's centrality, petroleum's ongoing predominance in American life after 1945 demands new terminology. The inculcation is so dramatic that Americans during the postwar era can be said to exist within an ecology of oil.[2]

When the French philosopher Roland Barthes sought to condemn the overconsumption and superficiality of the modern era, his symbol was the substance of many forms—plastic. Similar to the people that he condemns, Barthes overlooks the raw material that made possible the iconic plastic.[3] Before Americans could have the hula hoops and Twinkies that helped define the postwar era, there had to be a prodigious and reliable supply of crude oil. The best evidence of twentieth-century Americans' overwhelming dependence on petroleum may be that they have completely neglected to give it proper credit for enabling the nation's overall high standard of living. Even now, most Americans barely get past an elementary-level understanding of their dependence on oil. Oil does not just fuel Americans' vehicles. Oil has changed their diet, their clothes, their neighborhoods, their jobs, their fun—in fact, everything about U.S. society. Although Americans continue this profound reliance today, the nation's culture of crude has begun to shift in dramatic ways.

Taken for granted for decades, the flow of surplus crude came to a sudden halt during the 1970s when increasing imports converged with political limitations. As abundance turns to scarcity in the second decade of the twenty-first century, the American ecology of oil has come to include concepts such as resource wars, peak oil, petro-dictators, and bottom kill. This increasing appreciation of petroleum's importance and the complexity of acquiring it demands that we also revise our historical narratives—that we acknowledge the hidden hand (or nozzle) when it was most essential to American life and history.[4]

---

[2] "Figure 5. Primary Energy Consumption by Source, 1775–2009," in Annual Energy Review 2009, by U.S. Energy Information Administration (Washington, 2010), xx. Myrna I. Santiago uses the term "ecology of oil" to describe the wholesale changes that developing crude meant to the lives of native inhabitants in her work about Mexico. See Myrna I. Santiago, The Ecology of Oil: Environment, Labor, and the Mexican Revolution, 1900–1938 (Cambridge, Eng., 2006).

[3] Roland Barthes, Mythologies, trans. Annette Lavers (New York, 1972), 97–99. This book was originally published in French in 1957.

[4] On the factors relating to the 1970s oil crisis, see, for instance, Daniel Yergin, The Prize: The Epic Quest for Oil, Money, and Power (New York, 1991); Karen R. Merrill, The Oil Crisis of 1973–1974: A Brief History with Documents (New York, 2007); and Daniel Horowitz, Jimmy Carter and the Energy Crisis of the 1970s: The "Crisis of Confidence" Speech of July 15, 1979; A Brief History with Documents (New York, 2004). On American reaction to energy transition after the 1970s crisis, see David E. Nye, Consuming Power: A Social History of American Energies (Boston, 1998); Michael T. Klare, Resource Wars: The New Landscape of Global Conflict (New York, 2001); Kenneth S. Deffeyes, Hubbert's Peak: The Impending World Oil Shortage (Princeton, 2008); Paul Roberts, The End of Oil: On the Edge of a Perilous New World (New York, 2005); and Thomas L. Friedman, Hot, Flat, and Crowded: Why We Need a Green Revolution—and How It Can Renew America (New York, 2008). For efforts by historians to include energy and petroleum in the historical narrative, see Alfred W. Crosby, Children of the Sun: A History of Humanity's Unappeasable Appetite for Energy (New York, 2006); and J. R. McNeill, Something New under the Sun: An Environmental History of the Twentieth-Century World (New York, 2000). For works by journalists who have told portions of this story, see Peter Maass, Crude World: The Violent Twilight of Oil (New York, 2009); Lisa Margonelli, Oil on the Brain: Adventures from the Pump to the Pipeline (New York, 2008); and Roberts, End of Oil.

This brief essay deconstructs the trope of American mass consumption after World War II to reveal two of its primary elements functioning symbiotically: consumer passion and cheap crude. From the Big Mac to Tupperware's burping bowl, petroleum provided the raw material for much of what defined consumption in postwar America.

Conspicuously Consuming Crude

In Futurama, science fiction–like visions merged with the ideas of intellects such as Lewis Mumford to take concrete form. Modernism was no longer an artistic genre restricted to the few; now, modernist design and "the new" were the stuff of the middle class. Consumer expectations—such as those shaped by the scene of Futurama—became a primary engine behind radical shifts in patterns of American living. The transformation of living patterns after World War II was so dramatic that historians have given it a name: "mass consumption." Lizabeth Cohen and other historians have demonstrated that the motivations that drove consumers and filled out the middle class were fed by the policies and politics of the Cold War.[5] But the factor behind the scenes that enabled this dramatic change has yet to be fully appreciated by historians.

In her work, Cohen reaches back to Thorstein Veblen's *The Theory of the Leisure Class* (1899), in which he developed the idea of "conspicuous consumption," to describe the power of social emulation expressed through extravagant display, particularly in the American model of capitalist society. Consumable items, in such a paradigm, can function as symbols of affluence that spur citizens to increase their economic standing. Similar arguments were made in other well-known critiques of postwar America such as David Riesman's *The Lonely Crowd* (1950), David Potter's *People of Plenty* (1954), and John Kenneth Galbraith's *The Affluent Society* (1958). Although in each case, scholars ultimately criticized American emphasis on consumption, there was clear agreement that the overriding priority in America of this era was the freedom to purchase goods that fleshed out a life-style that today we refer to as middle class. A society with affordable products and consumers with discretionary income to spend became primary components of the "affluence" that defined the American standard of living after World War II. Despite its implication for ideas of race, gender, and youth—not to mention of home design and the overall construction of the human habitat—mass consumption became a symbol of American success in the Cold War. Although scholars such as Cohen argue that many of these details grew from basic policies, such as the G.I. Bill, we must also ascribe credit to the lifeblood of the affluent society that took shape after World War II: cheap energy, primarily petroleum. Even more important, the scope of the affluence that oil enabled made this higher standard of living the new normal, eventually making consumption no longer conspicuous.[6]

---

[5] On Lewis Mumford and other modernist intellectuals of this era, see Meikle, *Twentieth Century Limited*, 135, 180. Lewis Mumford, *Technics and Civilization* (1934; Chicago, 1963), 357–58. For general studies of modernism and consumption, see, for example, Gary Cross, *An All-Consuming Century: Why Commercialism Won in Modern America* (New York, 2000); and Terry Smith, *Making the Modern: Industry, Art, and Design in America* (Chicago,1993). Lizabeth Cohen, *A Consumers' Republic: The Politics of Mass Consumption in Postwar America* (New York, 2003), 10–12.

[6] Thorstein Veblen, *The Theory of the Leisure Class: An Economic Study of Institutions* (New York, 1899); David Riesman, *The Lonely Crowd: A Study of the Changing American Character* (New Haven, 1950); David Potter, *People of Plenty: Economic Abundance and the American Character* (Chicago, 1954); John Kenneth Galbraith, *The Affluent Society* (Boston, 1958).

In *People of Plenty*, Potter sought to analyze this society by expanding our conceptions of what is included in a society's "culture." By including everyday patterns and habits associated with America's experience with mass consumption, for instance, these details could be seen as part of larger level social patterns, including efforts to stimulate unity or, contradictorily, exclusion. As a unifier, this emerging culture helped overcome class distinctions and cleared the way for one, predominant middle class. With this pattern in mind, theorists have constructed a critique of consumption as a homogenizing force. Barthes, however, decried the loss of meaning and depth with such flexibility and, by the end of the twentieth century, other scholars had joined the fray. For instance, the sociologist George Ritzer and others railed against the McDonaldization (or Walmartization) of American life that took away distinct, individualized opportunities for consumption and replaced them with standardized, less personal options. Other scholars, alternatively, suggest that although the disposable society has many shortcomings, by making prosperity and comfort so accessible, it may also represent the most democratic culture that American society has thus far produced.[7] Regardless of its ultimate meaning for Americans, mass consumption, scholars agree, had made the U.S. standard of living after World War II a symbol of U.S. prosperity. Unseen in many of these consumer items, unrecognizable in its finished form, the alchemy of gallons upon gallons of cheap crude played a defining role.

So where does petroleum fit into the historical paradigm of post–World War II consumerism? Certainly, it was a critical cog in the engine that drove this consumptive society. Can one go one step further, in an era enabled by cheap petroleum, to argue that "black gold" has functioned as a democratizing element in American life? Big Oil has wrought mighty evils on societies all over the world and also on the natural environment; however, for the society that inculcated it more completely than any other, there is clear evidence that cheap oil empowered the middle class and helped the United States attain the world's greatest standard of living by, not least of all, helping Americans overcome very basic limits on the human condition. Our histories must accept this premise so that scholars might unravel the larger environmental, social, and cultural implications of our high-energy existence.

Petroleum Makes Consumption Less Conspicuous

As consumption became less conspicuous or exceptional after World War II, transportation became the preeminent example of the new ecology of oil. The use of human and animal power, the essential ways that humans had moved about, had remained fairly static for centuries. By the early 1900s, automated methods of transportation (powered by biofuels, gasoline, steam, or electricity) had become widely available. Fuel and vehicle prices made such options primarily available only to wealthy consumers. With few roads or conveniences, a drive in such a vehicle during the 1910s was almost purely a luxury. Local and state governments worked to make auto travel easier and more convenient, and

---

[7] "Traditionally, 'culture' had meant a collection of artifacts, actually or potentially on show in a museum," wrote David Potter. "But in very recent decades, it has come to mean a collection of customs, a series of habits." See Potter, *People of Plenty*, 35, 42. See also George Ritzer, *The McDonaldization of Society* (Thousand Oaks, 2004). Lizabeth Cohen has demonstrated that some of these developments have offered women and minority consumer groups, including African Americans, the opportunity to express and achieve social status from which they were previously excluded. Cohen, *Consumers' Republic*, 194–96.

entrepreneurs such as Henry Ford brought vehicle prices down to a level at which mass consumers became drivers. Seen as a societal good, driving became an emphasis of federal funding after World War II. Tax breaks and zoning regulations all spurred America's shift toward becoming a real-life version of Futurama. None of this mattered, though, if fuel was too costly for most consumers. Therefore, federal authority also maintained remarkably low gasoline prices—ensuring that the fuel became accessible to almost everyone. With this widespread access to modes of transportation, the landscape of consumption took shape after World War II.[8]

Suburbs, as Adam Rome portrays in *The Bulldozer in the Countryside*, were the anchors of the corridors of commerce for the new, postwar America. In those model environments, developers dropped housing tracts in outlying areas where real estate prices were low. Often, these suburbs first appeared marooned from essential services—a sort of man-made frontier when services were still predominantly located in cities (and many of these services, such as grocery stores, soda fountains, and Automat restaurants, had become quite advanced in their ability to deliver a variety of products reliably and rapidly). Recalibrating the human habitat for automobility remade the American land- scape after World War II. Between suburban homes and urban workplaces, the economic frontier of the postwar era emerged. Of one component of the new sprawl, the historian Catherine Gudis writes: "With every coming year, automobiles could be found in more and more places, thus expanding the marketing frontier and potential location of billboard spaces to areas heretofore untouched." To manage these new corridors of consumption, an industry soon took shape, led by the trade organization Outdoor Advertising Association of America (OAAA), which proclaimed in its motto: "we have changed from essentially a 'home people' to an 'automobile . . . people.'"[9]

In its various forms, petroleum enabled humans to overcome limits, particularly those of time and space. Potter discussed American expansion and restlessness in this fashion: "The man best qualified for this role was the completely mobile man, moving freely from one locality to the next, from one economic position to another, or from one social level to levels above."[10] In addition to ensuring physical movement, petroleum helped bring Americans economic and social mobility through mass consumption. Along with new information technologies and advancements in production capabilities, petroleum became a primary component in allowing producers to overcome limits of supply and production. That success then allowed for massive growth in the scale of production and, ultimately, in mass production, which brought prices down and made a whole world of products and services available to middle-class American consumers.

Possibly the longest trope in the study of American culture had been to view the push and pull of technology against agriculture and, by extension, nature. In such a paradigm, technology was a "counterforce"

---

[8] Clay McShane and Joel A. Tarr, *The Horse in the City: Living Machines in the Nineteenth Century* (Baltimore, 2007); Douglas Brinkley, *Wheels for the World: Henry Ford, His Company, and a Century of Progress, 1903–2003* (New York, 2003); David A. Kirsch, *The Electric Vehicle and the Burden of History* (New Brunswick, 2000); Edwin Black, *Internal Combustion: How Corporations and Governments Addicted the World to Oil and Derailed the Alternatives* (New York, 2006). Christopher W. Wells, "Fueling the Boom: Gasoline Taxes, Invisibility, and the Growth of the American Highway Infrastructure, 1919–1956," *Journal of American History*, 99 (June 2012), 72–81.

[9] Adam Rome, *The Bulldozer in the Countryside: Suburban Sprawl and the Rise of American Environmentalism* (New York, 2001). Owen D. Gutfreund, *Twentieth-Century Sprawl: Highways and the Reshaping of the American Landscape* (New York, 2004); Dolores Hayden, *A Field Guide to Sprawl* (New York, 2004). Catherine Gudis, *Buyways: Billboards, Automobiles, and the American Landscape* (New York, 2004), 39, 49.

[10] Potter, *People of Plenty*, 96.

against which Americans struggled to retain certain aspects of their original culture. As mass purchasers of goods and services, Americans no longer viewed such innovations and economic development as a "counterforce" in American life; instead, new technologies became inculcated into revamped life-styles. This modern sensibility of working cooperatively with technologies, such as the internal combustion engine, was captured by Lewis Mumford when he described the machine as a force that "simplifies the environment." He explained:

> As a practical instrument, the machine has enormously complicated the environment. . . . [But] without standardization, without repetition, without the neutralizing effect of habit, our mechanical environment might well, by reason of its tempo and its continuous impact, be too formidable. . . . The machine has thus, in its aesthetic manifestations, something of the same effect that a conventional code of manners has in social intercourse: it removes the strain of contact and adjustment . . . it permits intercourse between persons and groups to take place without the preliminary exploration and understanding that are requisite for an ultimate adjustment.

Mass consumption was the product of Americans internalizing the machine and domesticating it. During the Cold War era, technology was accepted as key to the nation's progress and also to keeping the Soviet Union at bay. This aesthetic was fueled by large-scale economic and social changes as well. Cohen describes this trend as the construction of a "consumer's republic" in which consumption was construed as an expression of national identity and even patriotism. She traces the emergence of "a new postwar ideal of the purchaser as citizen who simultaneously fulfilled personal desire and civic obligation by consuming."[11]

The key to this technical society—its essential element—was crude oil available at an average per-barrel price of $22–23 (in 2008 dollars) from 1869 to the present. From 1945 to 1970 the per-barrel price remained below $20, and U.S. society poured a cultural and social foundation that was, in hindsight, based on the assumption that Americans would always have a perpetual supply of petroleum at a stable price. Of course, things changed dramatically by the end of the twentieth century—by 2007–2008 the per-barrel price reached an all-time high of $145.[12] The availability of inexpensive crude persuaded American society to organize itself into an ecology of oil in which basic human needs—such as acquiring food—became reliant on crude.

Fast food is the obvious link between petroleum-powered transportation and the human need to acquire the calories that our bodies require—what scholars refer to as American foodways. This new method of foraging involved innovations such as that of Maurice McDonald and Richard McDonald when they intentionally located their McDonald's just off Route 66 in San Bernadino, California. Ray

---

[11] Mumford, *Technics and Civilization*, esp. 357–58. For discussion of these general points, see Thomas P. Hughes, *American Genesis: A Century of Invention and Technological Enthusiasm, 1870-1970* (New York, 1989). Cohen, *Consumers' Republic*, 119.

[12] For pricing data, see "Oil Price History and Analysis," WTRG *Economics*, http://www.wtrg.com/prices.htm. After the 2007–2008 peak, crude oil prices dropped dramatically. Analysts suggest this was due to the global economic difficulty in 2008–2009. In 2011 prices began to rise again and most analysts agree that they will likely return to 2007 levels as a "new reality" or baseline in crude pricing. Peter Maass, *Crude World: The Violent Twilight of Oil* (New York, 2009), 5–8; Daniel Yergin, *The Quest: Energy, Security, and the Remaking of the Modern World* (New York, 2011), 6–10. For more historical data, see "Petroleum and Other Liquids," *U.S. Energy Information Administration*, http://www.eia.gov/petroleum/.

Kroc, a milkshake-machine salesman, then expanded that form on a massive scale.[13] From White Castle to Royce Hailey's Pig Stand, burger joints, tea houses, diners, and, eventually, strip malls defined sprawl as the new American consumer environment.

Petroleum, however, was impacting Americans' food consumption through more than their reliance on automobiles; a more insidious change is symbolized by the seemingly innocent Twinkie. Although this sweet snack seems at first simple, it is actually a high-tech piece of complex chemistry, manufacturing, and distribution with no fewer than thirty-nine ingredients (most of which were also first manufactured).[14] Food production in the twentieth century, epitomized by the lusciously nutritionally void Twinkie, was characterized by efforts to simplify and streamline crop growing and processing by supplementing and embellishing those steps with the use of cheap resources such as petroleum.

Chemists played an important role in using petroleum to expand, simplify, and, at times, enhance the food that appeared in American shopping carts. Often with petroleum hydrocarbons as a basis or active ingredient, chemicals were created to control problems associated with agriculture, including managing weeds and pests (through herbicides and pesticides). Most important to the twentieth century, though, chemists also used petroleum and natural gas to create heat that manufactured and "fixed" synthetic nitrogen to enhance growing potential. The Haber-Bosch process alone increased the food production capabilities of nations throughout the world. This method for manufacturing synthetic nitrogen (as a fertilizer) has been exported to less-developed nations to enhance their ability to grow food crops. The great success of sharing this technique and other agriculture technology since 1960 is referred to as the "green revolution" and has helped avoid some famines in Africa and elsewhere.[15]

The implications of crude came in the form of the processed Twinkie as well as the seemingly organic, locally grown head of romaine lettuce. In the late twentieth century, humans (and particularly Americans) came to rely more than ever on foods acquired and prepared through the assistance of petroleum. Our histories have told many of these stories of consumption without specifically delineating the role that petroleum played in powering the autos that carried Americans to lunch or the rigs that hauled corn and other raw materials to manufacturers such as Frito-Lay. Neither have our histories clearly captured the work in chemistry laboratories that applied petroleum to an array of uses that moved innovations from the beaker to fill every shelf in local Walmart stores.[16]

---

[13] There are a number of sources that nicely capture portions of the automobile's extension into changes in American life. For one of the most useful, see James J. Flink, *The Automobile Age* (Boston, 1988).

[14] Steve Ettlinger, *Twinkie, Deconstructed: My Journey to Discover How the Ingredients Found in Processed Foods Are Grown, Mined (Yes, Mined), and Manipulated into What America Eats* (New York, 2008), xi–xii. For a general discussion of these ideas, see Michael Pollan, *Omnivore's Dilemma: A Natural History of Four Meals* (New York, 2006); and Maurice B. Green, *Eating Oil: Energy Use in Food Production* (Boulder, 1978).

[15] On the use of chemicals for military purposes, see Edmund Russell, *War and Nature: Fighting Humans and Insects with Chemicals from World War I to Silent Spring* (New York, 2001). On agricultural uses, see James McCann, *Maize and Grace: Africa's Encounter with a New World Crop, 1500–2000* (Cambridge, Mass., 2007); David R. Montgomery, *Dirt: The Erosion of Civilizations* (Berkeley, 2007); Christian Anton Smedshaug, *Feeding the World in the Twenty-First* Century: A Historical Analysis of Agriculture and Society (London, 2010); and Richard P. Tucker, *Insatiable Appetite: The United States and the Ecological Degradation of the Tropical World* (New York, 2007).

[16] See, for instance, Shane Hamilton, *Trucking Country: The Road to America's Wal-Mart Economy* (Princeton, 2008); and William Cronon, *Nature's Metropolis: Chicago and the Great West* (New York, 1991).

Chemicals and Flexible Forms Shape a New Consumer Reality

When Barthes waxed about the capabilities of plastic, his comments were stirred by the first use of a plastic replacement valve in heart surgery in the 1950s. In fact, however, he captured the germ of the method historians might use to demonstrate the scale of the transformations in American life made possible when petroleum allowed mass consumption to become inconspicuous. We must follow Barthes and move beyond gasoline-powered engines and chemically enhanced agriculture to consider products in which the petroleum content is largely unrecognizable. The symbol of such oil-based consumer products is, of course, plastics, which enabled significant cultural and social shifts in America.

The industry now known as petrochemicals is responsible for too many consumer products to list—among them, the materials that go into heart valves and Twinkie wrappers. A remarkable statistic from *Chemistry in Context*, a standard chemistry textbook, helps reveal the wide array of applications for which the petrochemical industry is responsible: "37 of the almost 45 gallons in a typical barrel of refined crude oil is simply burned for heating and transportation. The remaining 7.6 gal is used for non-fuel purposes, including only 1.25 gal set aside to serve as nonrenewable starting materials (reactants, commercially called feedstocks) to make the myriad of plastics, pharmaceuticals, fabrics, and other carbon-based industrial products so common in our society."[17] These uses of petroleum have so intrinsically altered the ways that Americans live, that as petroleum supplies dwindle, humans will likely wish they had conserved crude not to burn but to fulfill these remarkably rare capabilities in the chemistry sector.

On its way to becoming each of those useful substances, petroleum first is transformed into feedstocks, which are used to produce plastics, drugs, detergents, and synthetic fibers. For instance, almost all pharmaceuticals contain benzene rings in their chemical structure, which is refined from petroleum. In addition, such chemicals go on to serve many purposes, including refrigeration and cooling. In many of these applications, chemists initially identified alternative methods of producing the necessary compounds; petroleum entered the laboratory only later as a method for making compounds more easily and cheaply. The design historian Jeffrey Meikle describes this synthetic chemistry as, "everything and nothing."[18] As a chemical filler, petroleum was added because it cost so little, but the flexibility that it brought to chemists proved to be revolutionary.

For oil companies, the use of crude to manufacture resources for living began in the 1930s but became a corporate priority after World War II. In the case of Shell Oil, its Shell Chemical division switched from manufacturing ammonia and solvents to seeking synthetic substitutes for natural materials and then making them. Early industrial chemistry had concentrated on synthesizing molecules from coal-based feedstocks, mainly to produce chemicals such as benzene and its derivatives. With petroleum, chemists could produce such chemicals less expensively and in larger quantities while also generating more reactive hydrocarbons called olefins, including ethylene, propylene, and butylene, which became building-block chemicals of the new petrochemical industry.[19]

---

[17] American Chemistry Society, *Chemistry in Context: Applying Chemistry to Society* (New York, 2005), 45. See also Jeffrey L. Meikle, American Plastic: A Cultural History (New Brunswick, 1995).

[18] Meikle, *American Plastic*, 3. See also Gail Cooper, *Air-Conditioning America: Engineers and the Controlled Environment, 1900–1960* (Baltimore, 1998).

[19] Peter H. Spitz, *Petrochemicals: The Rise of an Industry* (New York, 1988), 63–69.

As Shell and other petroleum companies formed entire chemical divisions to research petrochemicals and apply them to everyday uses, the best known might have been synthetic glycerine. The limited supply of natural glycerine, a by-product of the soap and fatty acid industries, had become useful by the 1920s as a food preservative, a humectant for tobacco (to help retain moisture), and as a component in the manufacture of such diverse products as shaving cream, toothpaste, glue, soft drinks, mayonnaise, cosmetics, and paper. It also served as a mainstay for the paint industry and in the manufacture of cellophane. By the 1940s, Americans used over 200 million pounds of natural glycerine each year (more than a pound per person), although very few consumers realized its presence. In the late 1940s, Shell Chemical made Houston, Texas, which already served as a hub for oil shipping and refining, its focus for petrochemical development. Its $8 million synthetic glycerine plant—the world's first—went on-line at Houston Deer Park in September 1948, and by 1950 its production of synthetic glycerine equaled one-fifth of the nation's prewar output of natural glycerine.[20]

Similar developments occurred as synthetic rubber replaced natural supplies when Shell developed isoprene rubber, which duplicated the isoprene that served as the chemical building block of the natural rubber molecule. The manufacturers of automobile and truck tires began using isoprene rubber and other polymers developed from petroleum. The influence on consumer America was profound. The postwar expansion of Shell Chemical reached a high point in 1956, when chemical sales totaled a record $213 million, compared to only $24 million, ten years earlier. In terms of volume, yearly sales rose from 231,000 tons to just over 1 million tons over that period.[21] These are the type of statistics that allow conspiracy theorists to claim that the inculcation of petroleum into everyday American life through chemistry was an elaborate plan by Big Oil. And there may be some truth to such a claim; however, American consumers swept up these new, cheaper products with vigor.

"Plastics," uttered a friend of the father of Dustin Hoffman's character in *The Graduate* when asked what he foresaw as the promising future for a college graduate in the 1960s. Plastic would have thousands of applications, and some were essential to patterns of everyday human life. As one example, consider the impact of Tupperware and Saran Wrap on food preservation. Again, each innovation in this area grew from earlier resin-based materials that did not use petroleum. In large chemical companies such as DuPont, researchers worked constantly to develop any synthetic material that might prove useful. In a world filled previously only with products made of wood, clay, and a few other organic materials, by the 1930s, it became a sign of progress to insert obviously man-made objects of modernity into the most mundane areas of people's everyday lives—such as food storage.[22]

Meikle writes that these materials, known as thermoplastics, were "driven not so much by market demand as by the pressure of supply, an overabundance of chemical raw materials, waiting to be exploited." After World War II, lab experiments regularly became consumer products, such as vinyl, which quickly remade cultural genres ranging from music to automobile interiors, and nylon, the elastic threads useful in many applications. In 1939, American companies produced 213 million pounds of synthetic resins. By

---

[20] Kendall Beaton, *Enterprise in Oil: A History of Shell in the United States* (New York, 1957), 542–43, 676–77; "Shell Chemical Corporation," Shell News (April 1957), 19, cited in Tyler Priest, "The History of Shell Chemical," unpublished manuscript (in Tyler Priest's possession).

[21] "Torrance Takes an Opportunity," *Shell News*, 27 (May 1959), 1–3, cited in Priest, "History Shell of Chemical"; "Shell Chemical Corporation," 21–22.

[22] *The Graduate*, dir. Mick Nichols (Embassy, 1967). Meikle, *American Plastic*, 85. See also Alison J. Clarke, *Tupperware: The Promise of Plastic in 1950s America* (Washington, 1999).

1945, this production reached 818 million pounds, and by 1951, 2.4 billion pounds of synthetic resins were produced in the United States, partly because of the growing reliance on petroleum in the process. It was staggering growth sufficient to remake a civilization. And in the 1950s, writes Meikle, that is exactly what happened as the industry committed to such petroleum-based thermoplastics as "polyethylene that contributed to a flood of new uses—garbage pails, squeeze bottles, hula hoops—lighter, more flexible, less permanent than objects made from thermosets." The use of petroleum, in particular, allowed plastics to become "infinitely shape-shifting."[23] Infinite shapes and possibilities—a basic flexibility of form—would become a commodity in its own right if the products could fill basic human needs at extremely low cost. Throughout American consumer society, petroleum-based products fueled the ubiquity of stuff—regularizing overconsumption and making it the new normal.

Close Reading Questions

1. What made the General Motors exhibit at the 1939 World's Fair so appealing?

2. After World War II, how did transportation affect where Americans lived and worked?

3. In what ways did the abundance of crude oil impact oil companies in the 1940s and 1950s?

Analytical Writing/Discussion

4. In what ways was post-World War II affluence—especially the creation of a "middle class"—made possible by the availability of cheap sources of energy? (Multiple Perspectives)

5. To what extent do you agree or disagree with Black's assertion that petroleum changed food culture in America, particularly the development of fast food? (Historical Trends)

6. Black provides an extensive discussion of the ways chemists altered crude oil. Why is it important to understand the relationship between petrochemicals and American society? (Cultural Influences)

Further Options

7. Previewing a text is an effective way to begin to read a lengthy article or chapter (see pp. 8 and 9 in Chapter 1). Review the headings in Black's article. How do the headings help you to understand the main ideas? What reading strategies would you have used if Black's article did not have headings?

8. Black discusses the concept of "planned obsolescence," noting that Americans purchase replacements for cars and household appliances, even if those products still work well. How does this relate to James Atwater's explanation of 1960s appliances in "A Household of Helpers" in this chapter (see pp. 269–277)?

---

[23] Meikle, *American Plastic*, 176, 125–26, 176–77, esp. 82, 168.

A HOUSEFUL OF HELPERS

by James Atwater

The late 1950s and early 1960s marked a period of mass consumerism for those Americans who were eager to settle into suburban lives with televisions, cars, refrigerators, and dishwashers. The following excerpt, which appeared in the December 5, 1964 edition of the *Saturday Evening Post*, chronicles the reasons why appliance makers sought to design and sell quality products to increasingly fickle consumers.

For her birthday, she got earrings and perfume. So what she wants for Christmas is something that washes, dries, toasts, roasts, freezes, cuts, peels, percolates, or tidies up—something that may even turn a dreary household chore into an interlude of fun. She wants a new appliance, and she knows that if she doesn't get it at Christmas, she might have to wait another year.

If the appliance-craving American housewife is anxious about Christmas, the appliance manufacturer is doubly so. Depending on his line, as much as a third of his yearly sales must be made in the month of December if they are to be made at all. Will husbands buy his elegant bonnet-style hair dryer for their wives, or will they be lured away by his rival's new cordless electric slicing knife? Can his electric hedge trimmer command attention in the stores amid the crowd of equally dazzling floor waxers, electric dehumidifiers and garbage-disposal units? Worst of all, will masses of shoppers turn their backs on the Electrical Age *in toto*[1], choosing to muddle through manually? For the volatile and hotly competitive electric-appliance industry, Christmas is seldom a time of peace on earth.

Christmas, 1964, however, promises to be good to both housewives and manufacturers. Dealers' showrooms, department stores and discount palaces are aglitter with an incredible variety of ingenious devices ready to perform magic at the flip of a switch. More to the point, the industry has every expectation of selling them in a holiday splurge that will make 1964 the biggest, richest year in its history.

As histories go, this is not too long a stretch. The iceman[2] bending beneath his burden is still a vivid recollection for middle-aged Americans: in fact, the first electric refrigerator with all its parts in a single unit was introduced by Frigidaire exactly half a century ago this year. The automatic electric washing machine dates back only 27 years and the dryer only 26. There are millions of women who can remember slaving over a corrugated washboard: the wife handing out the wash and the apron-clad husband helping with the dishes are only slightly archaic stereotypes of U.S. homelife.

The New American Home

But labor conditions in the average American home have obviously undergone a profound change. Uncounted billions of woman-hours of work have been cut away by laborsaving appliances; a dishwasher

A Houseful of Helpers Awake at the Switch article © SEPS licensed by Curtis Licensing Indianapolis, IN. All rights reserved.

[1.] In toto: Latin for completely; totally; entirely

[2.] Iceman: The person who delivered ice to homes and businesses. Large blocks of ice were used to chill iceboxes, which were the precursor to the electric refrigerator.

alone, for example, reduces the average kitchen cleanup time from an hour and 13 minutes to half an hour, according to industry statisticians. Immeasurable vistas of leisure time have opened up, with social effects no statistician can really pin down. (Do housewives use their extra time to improve their minds, get jobs, enter local politics, plump pillows or find floors to wax which they wouldn't have waxed otherwise?)

Whatever the case, there is hardly an essential household task that can't be eased or eliminated by plugging in something. Americans have shown that they will buy an appliance to perform a task they had no idea needed performing until someone suggested it. Hundreds of thousands of people will buy electric can openers this month, though the job of opening cans by hand has caused no great outcry by housewives in the past. The latest, and perhaps ultimate, model switches itself on and off. Hamilton Beach is offering a power unit with five attachments called the "Gourmet Center" which permits a gourmet to open a can, sharpen a knife, toss salad, grind meat, or crush ice without expending a calorie of energy. Shoppers will also be rushing to buy electric toothbrushes, including Westinghouse's new Rocket model for children, a toothbrush shaped like an I.C.B.M.,[3] which comes with accompanying launching pad and gantry crane. They will even buy some electric swizzle sticks, a highly expendable appliance which has become a pet whipping boy for critics of the affluent society.

Competition Drives the Appliance Market

In today's competitive market, appliance makers have to expand and experiment at an unprecedented pace just to keep up. The pressure is particularly keen in the small-appliance business, where manufacturers just a few years ago had little to offer but such old reliables as the coffee maker, the toaster, and the iron. Now these markets are becoming saturated (80 percent of U.S. homes have toasters, 97 percent have irons), and while millions will still be sold as replacements, the need for new products has impelled companies like General Electric and Sunbeam to double the number of items in their lines in just the last few years. "The housewife's major chores have been automated," says Norman Langenfeld, a top G.E. official. "To survive today, you have to innovate. You have to work the fringe areas of the market."

Almost every small-appliance maker is putting out a bonnet-style hair dryer with a chic carrying case and a manicure set with power-driven nail buffers. With the rise of income, and the consequent nourishing of home entertainment, the industry is selling a whole rumpus room[4] full of new appliances designed specifically for this market—four-slice toasters, warming trays, party grills, and 20- and 30-cup coffee urns.

The newest thing in electric skillets and frying pans is Teflon, a material developed by Du Pont that keeps food from sticking to cooking surfaces and thus permits greaseless frying. New lightweight and long-life batteries are creating a whole new family of products: battery-powered shavers and clocks and mixers, rechargeable electric cigarette lighters, and even a battery-powered flour sifter. Designers are trying to hit on ideas that will make good gifts, since 30 percent of all small appliances are bought for presents. The aura of "giftability," as the trade describes it, has spurred the sales of such items as the flashy rotisserie and the electric slicing knife—appliances which easily catch the eye of the despairing husband searching for something different for his wife.

The makers of major appliances—"white goods," to the trade—do not live and die by Christmas as do small-appliance manufacturers (General Electric and Westinghouse are about the only companies

---

[3.] I.C.B.M.: Intercontinental Ballistic Missile. A missile designed to deliver nuclear warheads at ranges of more than 3,500 miles.
[4.] Rumpus room: A room in a house designed specifically for children's recreation or play.

which straddle the two divisions of the industry). But they, too, are counting on holiday business to top off their third consecutive year of rising sales. Frigidaire general manager Herman Lehman predicts that the industry's unit sales will run more than ten percent ahead of 1963, when a record 15.2 million major appliances were sold for $4.2 billion.

Less volatile, and nearly three times the size of the small-appliance market, the white-goods business tends more to majestic evolution than to rapid-fire innovation. Its fundamental statistics are majestic in themselves. Every 21 seconds a new household is formed in the U.S. with certain minimum needs for major pieces of hardware. Every three seconds a major appliance somewhere in the U.S. "outlives its useful life and needs replacements"—an industry researcher's expression, which suggests a ghastly undercurrent of domestic turmoil, but is probably deceptive. In any case, the net effect is that one new refrigerator, range, washer, freezer, dryer, dishwasher, or air conditioner is delivered to someone's home every two seconds.

The appliances themselves are changing, of course, and there have been fundamental improvements in all of them in recent year. For example, the industry has learned to control the blasts of heat that used to shrink clothes in the dryers. Dishwasher sprays are far more powerful and better diffused. Because of new and thinner insulation, a refrigerator with 12 cubic feet inside occupies no more kitchen space than a 10-cubic-foot box did a few years back. General Electric last year introduced an oven that cleans itself (with a special device that applies superhigh heat to vaporize accumulated grease); sales have soared despite a $75 premium for the feature. This year, Frigidaire is introducing a washer with a transmission that replaces troublesome belts, pulleys and gears with a compact system of rollers and wheels, for added reliability.

Appliance Sales Miss the Mark

Despite booming sales and expanding profits, however, the white-goods business is still struggling with some serious and deep-rooted problems—problems which grew out of the fierce competitive struggles of the 1950s and which have yet to be entirely resolved.

The trouble began after World War II, when a number of large and powerful companies from outside the business—companies like International Harvester and Admiral—rushed in to compete with the established manufacturers in satisfying postwar demands for appliances. The result was a tremendous spurt of overproduction and falling prices, which dropped even faster as the cut-rate discount house began to get a big share of the appliance business. Retail prices have dropped some 25 percent since 1947, eight percent in the last five years.

To make matters worse, sales did not hold up as expected. E.B. Barnes, Kelvinator's vice president for sales, points out that during the '50s there was a slight decline in the number of persons in the 18-to-34 bracket, the biggest buyers of appliances. In addition, the market was gradually becoming saturated, particularly in washers and refrigerators, the industry's two major items.

The result was a severe shakedown. International Harvester quit the business altogether. The Speed Queen washer was bought by McGraw-Edison. The Easy washer ended up under the control of the Hupp Corp., a Cleveland-based company, which also bought the Gibson refrigerator. Bendix, which put out the first automatic washer in 1937, eventually sold it to Philco, which later was bought by Ford. G.E. bought Hotpoint.

In this competitive jungle, quick reactions have been essential for survival. Whenever one company added a feature that seemed to help its appliance sales, every other company would race to copy it. In the mid-50s, for example, G.E. hit it big with the lint filter for its washer. Even Maytag, a firm which traditionally has resisted fads, joined the copycats. Maytag had been disposing of lint with a system that washed it down the drain, but it bowed to the pressures of the marketplace and added a filter it didn't need. Maytag points out, in its defense, that it really did add a feature, since it managed to incorporate the filter in a device that also dispenses the detergent. . .

Market research shows that women want versatile machines with controls that are as simple as possible. But the dealers, who have the usual male fascination with glittering dials and winking lights, believe that a flashy instrument panel is important in helping to close sales. And so the manufacturer may load on the gadgetry which the industry calls "whistles and bells."

New Year, Slightly Different Appliance

Prodded by the dealers, the manufacturers turn out a bewildering array of models to hit every possible segment of the market. One industry consultant came home recently to discover that the family washer had broken down. "I told my wife I'd drop down to a store and buy one that night," he says. "But when I got there, there were so many models with so many features that I finally went home in disgust. It was too damn confusing—and I know something about this business. The next day, I went back and bought a model of a company I admire, and that was that."

The prime example of the strong influence dealers have is the annual model change, perhaps the main source of trouble in the business, since it vastly complicates the problem of building a solid appliance and servicing it expertly.

The dealers are afraid that their sales will slip unless they can annually put on display a new product brightened by new styling and festooned with new features. Many manufacturers will admit that they don't want the annual change: it is tremendously expensive in money, time and effort. Moreover, some market research indicates that the consumer couldn't care less whether an appliance first came on the market this year or last.

In fact, there is some evidence that not even the experts can tell the difference between models put out in two consecutive years. At a meeting of the trade press Kelvinator once lined up 10 refrigerators of similar price and covered over the brand names. The display was made up of the models produced in two consecutive years by five different companies. The visitors were asked to identify the refrigerators by year and manufacturer. Half of the experts refused to take the test, and of those who tried, only 52 percent could name the brands, and only 25 percent the years.

Kelvinator abandoned the annual cycle four years ago. "We do not make changes unless they are meaningful." says sales vice president Barnes. The firm's 1964 range line, for example, is virtually identical with 1963's.

"The annual model change is senseless," says one official in the industry. "It's based on the assumption that the appliance is a status symbol, and that's just not so. You don't park your refrigerator in the driveway."

The industry's most outspoken critic of the practice of adding some chrome and changing the instrument panel to get a "new" model is Maytag, which never adopted the annual change. By stressing the reliability and long life of its washers and dryers, Maytag has prospered mightily. For the first half of 1964, its earnings were 12.8 percent of sales, far above the industry average. "We're extremely old-fashioned," says one company official. "We think it is ethically wrong to foist something on the public that is not an improvement."

The result of the annual-model flap is that the engineers are placed under impossible pressure. "You have to produce new features *and* dependability," says the director of one company's advance-engineering department. "This is what is driving the engineers nuts. The more complex a device is, the more service problems you're likely to have, no matter how well designed it is."

Skyrocketing Repair Costs

The annual model change, in fact, is the main reason that every neighborhood has its share of horror stories about the failures of refrigerators, ranges or washers that are repeated with little tingles of terror at the morning kaffeeklatsch. In Tarrytown, N.Y., for example, the neighbors talk of what happened to David and Lorraine Epstein, who installed a brand-name combination washer-dryer in their new home in 1959.

The one-year warranty had barely expired when the door began to leak. The charge was $18.85. The Epsteins now regard this bill rather wistfully, as though it were the first mild tantrum of a child who was to turn out to be incorrigible.

On July 3, 1961, the machine failed. For 28 days Lorraine Epstein improvised with the Laundromat and the neighbors' washers. When the repairs were completed, the Epsteins had a machine with a rebuilt rear end and a bill for $75. On November 6, 1961, the thing died again. This time it was out of action for 23 days, and the bill came to $54.05. Something about a bad pump and clogged vents.

Dave Epstein, an artist, is a mild and accommodating man, but this time he picked up the phone. The servicing company settled for $35. On January 26, 1962, the drying system broke down. $11.

In time, Lorraine Epstein came to know three different crews of repairmen. Each pair would utter caustic comments about the abilities of the others while peering into the stricken machine. One repairman adopted a brusquely proprietary air toward the Epsteins. Without ringing the bell, he opened the back door one morning at 8:30 and began to dismantle the machine while Lorraine was in the bedroom down the hall.

Dave eventually became something of an expert at spotting the combo's troubles. He once retrieved an ossified door gasket, as shredded and tangled as a clump of dried spaghetti, from its lodging place in the heat vent.

On September 9, 1962, the door gave way. $18.85. On December 10, 1963, the whole rear end collapsed again, the $75 collapse, "After that," recalls Dave, "we came to an agreement. Whatever happened, I was to pay for the parts, but not the labor."

On January 17, 1964, the rear end disintegrated a third time. A man came and poked at it moodily and went away. This time it was 40 days before the thing was fixed, but this time there was no bill. In four years, counting stray odds and ends, the Epsteins have spent about $300 repairing a machine that cost $420.25.

Epic disasters like this are unavoidable in any mass-production industry—they come with the territory—but the appliance manufacturers are making a sincere effort to reduce their number. The campaign had its beginnings in the late `50s when appliances began to break down at an alarming rate. Looking back, a few executives are willing to admit that one cause was that they had let their quality-control programs slip.

To make matters worse, the housewife who was stuck with a spavined dishwasher or refrigerator often had to start a great manhunt to find someone to repair it. Not only were there too few repairmen to handle the sudden avalanche of work, but many of those who were in business boggled at any job that required much more than a screwdriver and friction tape. The industry had woefully failed to train men to repair products that were getting increasingly complex.

The result was a consumer revolt that thoroughly frightened the industry. Some executives believe that the poor sales record of the early 60's was due in part to the public's growing disenchantment with appliance makers and all their works.

To improve the quality of their servicing, many companies are conducting training courses around the country that are attended free by repairmen who work for completely independent firms or for franchised dealers. G.E. alone has a force of over 100 full-time instructors and trouble-shooters.

"By running very hard (in their training program), the manufacturers are barely able to stand still," says Frederick Schlink, technical director of Consumer's Research, an independent testing service that publishes *Consumer Bulletin*. "They have trouble catching up because of the constant innovations. The poor serviceman doesn't get the parts or manuals before the appliances get in trouble. We get letters from people whose appliances are out of action for months."

Labor now accounts for 60–70 percent of most repair bills, and it is not at all unusual for a homeowner to pay $7.50 or more an hour for a service call. The best way to keep down rising service costs, of course, is to make a better product. As a whole, the industry is making a strong effort to turn out appliances that are more reliable and more easily serviced. "The service manager never used to see the product until it came off the line," says Philco's President Robert O. Fickes. "Now he's in on the creation of it from the beginning."

Quality Control for the Appliance Industry

Nearly every major manufacturer has a quality-control program that has been substantially improved in the last few years. Appliances are pulled off the line and rigorously tested at regular intervals. At Whirlpool, quality-control supervisors report directly to the president. They have the authority—the ultimate power in any manufacturing process—to shut down the line completely if their testers find a series of lemons.

This concern for a sturdy product is beginning to pay off in both small and major appliances. The Detroit Edison Co., which services 800,000 small appliances a year, is convinced that quality has improved.

Product improvement is most obvious in major appliances. "There are some indications of improved quality control in such appliances as washers and refrigerators, formerly among the worst offenders," says Morris Kaplan, technical director of Consumers Union, which publishes *Consumer Reports*. Then he adds, "but consistency of quality—what quality control tries to assure—is not necessarily equivalent to high quality. I'd like to see some manufacturer make and sell the guts and not the gleam, the stamina and not the trim. The engineer is usually required to design the product to sell at a predetermined price. He can spend a lot on fancy things like butter dishes and egg shelves and chrome and gimmicks that are supposed to sell. Or put the money into the guts of the machine."

Because quality is not as obvious as, say, a lint filter, Kaplan thinks it would have to be backed up by broad, long-term warranties patterned after those now used by the auto industry. "It would take some doing and a tremendous advertising campaign," Kaplan concludes, "but I think the appliance industry, if it wanted to, could find a way to sell quality to the public."

Here and there are scattered signs that the American public may indeed be ready to buy quality—and service—rather than going automatically for the lowest price, or falling for a cute butter compartment. Albert Sindlinger, head of the market research firm of Sindlinger & Co., thinks that consumers are tending more and more to buy appliances from dealers who emphasize good service rather than the best price deal.

The problem of servicing is one reason that product development will continue to be more evolutionary than revolutionary: appliances are complicated enough as it is. What is more, no manufacturer wants to risk losing heavily on a long shot. "This is an industry," says one executive, "in which the companies are glad when a rival tries out a new idea—and takes a chance of falling on his face."

Perhaps most important, the housewife seems to be essentially a conservative. "Unless she sees the real advantage of a product or a feature, I don't think she'll go for it" says William L. Hullsiek, vice president in charge of Admiral's appliance division. "We have to be damned down-to-earth in what we offer."

Yet, all of the major companies inevitably are experimenting with totally new and revolutionary appliances that may someday be as familiar as today's refrigerators and ranges. Some examples:

- *Sonic Cleaning.* For years the public has been hearing reports of miracle clothes and washers and dishwashers that would vibrate dirt away with bombardments of sonic waves. The principle is now used in many industries to clean metallic pans, but there are stiff problems to be overcome. Sound waves do not work too well on some soils, and in dishwashers they are blocked by the shielding effect of plates and pans. (They also have been known to clean the pattern off china, the finish off silver plate.)

- *Electronic Cooking.* The industry has been marketing small quantities of electronic ovens for some time. The oven generates microwaves that agitate the molecules of food, and the friction of the molecules produces the heat that does the actual cooking. Microwaves can bake a potato in four minutes, cook a frozen 19-pound turkey in 90 minutes, and fry an egg as soon as the oven door is closed. But the cost of this performance is high—the oven is priced at around $800. When the frozen-food business expands, as it is certain to do, the fast-action electronic oven will become more salable.

- *Home Dry Cleaning.* The popularity of coin-operated dry-cleaning machines has suggested that perhaps American homes should have their own units. Westinghouse estimates that the public might be interested in paying around $500 for a single machine that dry-cleaned as well as washed and dried clothes. So far no one in the industry has come close to reaching this figure. The main problem is finding a dry-cleaning solvent that is safe for household use, and that can be economically filtered to remove impurities.

- *Thermo-Electric Refrigeration.* For decades, engineers have known that the passage of electricity from some conductors to others produces a cooling effect. A simple device with no moving parts theoretically could replace the bulky, conventional compressor of the standard refrigerator. It could also be broken up into a series of thermoelectric drawers that could be placed around the kitchen and the house where they would be most convenient. To date the process is still far too expensive for widespread use, although several companies are marketing small thermoelectric units.

- *Clothes Washing.* "Over the years, the housewife has been satisfied with the progress in developing laundry equipment," says Whirlpool's Dr. Gale Cutler, director of research, "but it's time for a new step. It's time we got away from bleaching the dirt, or dyeing it with brighteners. And the only way we can do this is take the job out of her hands, make it completely automatic." Cutler is thinking of a washer that would only require the housewife to push a single button indicating the type of load. The machine would use uncanny electronic sensors to determine such things as the hardness of the water and the amount of dirt in the clothes, then not only add precisely the right amount of detergent, chemicals, and properly heated water, but set the spin and agitation cycles at precisely the right speeds. Whirlpool is now test-marketing what could be the forerunner of this genius washer—a unit with controls that allow the operator to choose a wide variety of agitation and spin speeds.

- *Water Purification.* As population grows, the shrinking supply of pure water will become an increasingly serious problem. The appliance industry is interested in developing a water system that would circulate household wastes through a sophisticated purifier that would make the water usable again, and so on around and around.

- *Home Computer.* G.E. believes that someday the household bookkeeping will be done instantly and automatically by a computer about the size of a desk. The computer will make up shopping lists, pay your bills, remind you of anniversaries, and even figure your income tax. Industry is now using somewhat similar electronic brains, but the price is still far too high for the kitchen.

Whatever other duties the appliances of the future will perform, they all seem bound to make money, for today's boom market is only a rumble compared to what is coming. Within the next few years millions of war babies will marry each other and buy millions of appliances to fill millions of new homes. Appliance men are also looking forward to replacing the aging appliances now in use—over 30 million homes have refrigerators, washers and ranges that are at least 10 years old.

The industry which has always called itself the housewife's best friend hopes to reaffirm that status, promising a Utopian tomorrow when every chore is reduced to the nip of a switch and every switch, almost infallibly, will work.

Close Reading Questions

1. According to Atwater, why was Christmas 1964 a critical time for appliance manufacturers? (Cultural Influences)

2. For what reasons were makers of large appliances experiencing problems that started after World War II and continued through the early 1960s?

3. Why did some appliance manufacturers resist plans to change appliance models every year while other manufacturers embraced the practice? (Multiple Perspectives)

Analytical Writing/Discussion

4. Why do you think that consumers in the 1950s and 1960s were concerned with appliances that saved time rather than energy-efficient household goods?

5. According to Atwater, manufacturers envisioned household products of the future that would appeal to the American consumer. To what extent do you think the descriptions of those imagined products reflect a desire for energy efficiency and/or symbols of continued affluence?

6. In what ways do you think the story of David and Lorraine Epstein exemplified middle-class consumption of the 1950s? What appliance do you think symbolizes America in the twenty-first century? (Historical Trends)

Further Options

7. Atwater states that William L. Hullsiek—vice-president of the appliance company, Admiral—believed that the 1960s American housewife would not continue to purchase an appliance "unless she sees the real advantage of a product or a feature." In what ways does this sentiment reflect the design considerations David Orr proposed in "Your Great Work" (pp. 285–289 in this chapter).

8. In the 1950s and 1960s, appliances like refrigerators and washers and dryers were marketed to men and women age 18–34. How is this type of marketing similar to the way cell phones and laptops are marketed to young adults today?

JUKEBOX ON WHEELS

by Raymond Loewy

Raymond Loewy was a prolific industrial designer known for such iconic designs as the Shell and Exxon logos, Studebaker and Lincoln Continental car models, and numerous household appliances, including the Sears Coldspot refrigerator. Known as "The Father of Industrial Design," Loewy was famous for his dislike of consumer goods that made life challenging for the consumer. The following article was first published by *The Atlantic Magazine* in April 1955.

In every phase of the automotive industry, certain factors have been more important than all others in relation to the way the automobile has looked. Phase One is really the Ford story.[1] Function and production were the most important considerations. The automobile was an invention, and it looked like one.

Phase Two is marked by the introduction of the steel body in mass production and appearance became a major factor for the first time. Walter Chrysler discovered that robin's-egg blue helped sales; so all other companies tried to top Chrysler in styling. It was an era of individuality and healthy competition.

By the time of World War II, the industry had reached a point where many factors had leveled out: body types, price differences, market potential, manufacturing methods, advertising, technical developments (at least, those released to the public). Independents believed that styling, with improved function, would not only sell well but create good will for the small company.

The style factors were: good visibility, compactness, lighter weights. Big companies jumped on the "style" bandwagon, but what so-called functional factor did they select? *Bulk*—a sorry choice! Bulk gets to be habit-forming, and bulk means weight. To this manufacturers added "flash." So they got into a spiral of increased weight and ornamentation. This led to the horsepower rat-race and the chrome gadget rat-race—a costly combination. As a result, standardization—a byproduct of mass production has

Raymond Loewy ™/© by Loewy Design LLC. RaymondLoewy.com

---

[1] Refers to Henry T. Ford (1963–1947), founder of the Ford Motor Company. The production of the Model T Ford revolutionized the automobile industry in the 1900s. Ford's factory was the first to employ assembly line production to mass produce an affordable car.

established as today's dreamboat a vehicle that's too big for most people, too expensive, too costly to maintain, and too gaudy.

Some might say that this apparent wastefulness is indeed a blessing—that it brings about the use of more materials, more employment, prosperity. I believe the theory would be even more valid if the industry's basic product were a model—cheaper, more economical, and therefore available to more people—within reach of the wide mass market that lies at the bottom layer of the consumers' pyramid. Instead, what have we got? The total loss of distinction among all automobiles plus the finest state of jitters in the history of the automotive industry.

Designers today are briefed to "give the public what it wants," and "what the public wants" is being translated into the flashy, the gadgety, and the spectacular. I refuse to believe that today's automobiles represent, stylewise, "what the public wants" any more than they reflect what we in the automotive industry want. But the result of this mistaken opinion is vulgarity and blatancy. Instead of the automobile's expressing advancement, the story is now one of external bric-a-brac.[2] This reflects a distorted notion of what is competitive.

I think that vulgarity is dangerous for many reasons. The American automobile has changed the habits of every member of modern society. In the past fifty years, it has become the symbol, all over the world, of American industrial genius and enterprise. It has become so potent a force that it is very nearly the symbol of American thought and morals to people who don't know us. It is more than an object to be sold for money. The automobile is an American cultural symbol.

"Some culture," one might say as one watches the sad parade of the 1955 models. The world will soon forget that under these gaudy shells are concealed masterpieces of inspired technology. What we see today looks more like an orgiastic chrome-plated brawl.

There was another great American symbol, probably exported by the GI—the jukebox. Today's jukebox moves! The automobile. This year's production includes two-tone and three-tone jukeboxes. We are probably going to have a fluorescing six-passenger jukebox before long. Seriously, aren't manufacturers doing disservice to this country if they mass-present the automobile in such misleading vulgarity? Aren't they depressing the level of American taste by saturating the market with bad taste? Is it necessary?

This point has always interested me: Big companies make two conflicting statements –"We give the public what it wants" and, also, "Whatever design we choose becomes the accepted style standard through saturation." I do not agree with this last statement. But, if it is right, isn't it the company's cultural responsibility to choose a high standard instead of a low one? I realize that I am setting myself up as an arbiter of taste, but I have helped develop a profession in this country that sells taste.

This situation in the automobile industry is the more tragic because it is so unnecessary. Without doubt, there are sufficient design taste and talent in the United States to correct the situation. But someone must demand better taste and not just better sales.

I am told that cab drivers have the highest rate of duodenal ulcers. I'll bet a chrome-plated carrot that automotive stylists have them beat. Every really creative and imaginative stylist and many engineers I know seem to be frustrated in their work today. The near-shattering pressure of their repressions is relieved in constant doodling blue-sky dreaming. They rush home and make scale models in the attic. Or they long for the weekend to go road-racing in the old red Isotta-Fraschini or the souped-up pre-war Ford.

We know that the men at the top of the industry are well aware of their economic responsibilities, of their vital roles in the nation's economy. What about their cultural responsibilities? Is it responsible to camouflage one of America's most remarkable machines as a piece of gaudy merchandise? Is it possible that they don't know the merchandise is gaudy?

[2] Bric-a-brac: decorative items, sometimes called knick-knacks, often found on mantels and shelves of American homes in the 1950s.

I don't think the automotive industry in general is showing faith in good taste today. With rare exceptions, it cannot be accused of backing design sophistication. One shocking condition is the servile copying of one company's product by the others. It seems that giants in industry are taking refuge in sameness. This is just the time when they ought to be pioneering while they have the money, the momentum, and the market. This "management by escapism" is usually a manifestation of a fearful and insecure society. Perhaps we should ask the teenagers—the consumers of tomorrow. They love automobiles—especially ones that look like automobiles. Today these kids rib what used to be the family's proudest possession. Pop buys a chrome-plated "barge" just like the one he traded in. It's a wise kid who knows his own barge.

Fixing responsibility for the present state of design and styling this year is a tricky business. It probably starts with someone's deciding that the American public really likes vulgarity. However, number of men in a company do decide to give the public what it is supposed to want, in spite of their own consciences in the matter. Hesitation and doubt then creep into the whole design-engineering-sales team. The result is just what you'd expect—safe, imitative, over-decorated chariots, with something for everyone laid over a basic formula design that is a copy of someone else's formula design. Form, which should be a clean-cut expression of mechanical excellence, has become sensuous and organic.

Progressive management may realize that it is losing contact with a segment of consumers and that, however spectacular the sales, the company is losing popularity. This unpopularity has not yet reduced sales. But I think resentment is growing. And resentment is never an asset.

The public may admire a corporation for its impressive size. Who in the United States doesn't? But when a business, however gigantic, gets smug enough to believe that it is sufficient only to match competition on trivial points instead of leading competition in valid matters, that business is becoming vulnerable to public disfavor.

If there should be any such thing as a cloud in the blue sky of bigness for bigness' sake, I believe it will be the loss of people's trust and not governmental interference or control.

I hear conversations like these: "Remove the chrome schmaltz and the name plates and you can't tell one from another." Or, "Leave a Ford and a Chevvy in the same garage overnight and nine months later you get a Plymouth!" Or vice versa! These aren't funny and loving remarks: they're cynical. Compare them with the old Ford jokes that invariably oozed love and respect for a great man and a practical car.

Isn't it a bit complacent on the part of management to feel that the public is satisfied with this situation? There will be loud shouts: Who's complacent? Don't we all have new bodies this year? If the present "all-new" bodies are all that can be eked out in a year like this one, then I think wrong decisions have been made in a lot of places.

Experts estimate that fifty years from now there will be 120 million automobiles on the roads for approximately 98 million Americans. What company will be on top then? Would anyone care to guess? You can be reasonably sure that surprises are ahead. We've had enough in the past five years to count on it. And whoever wins will win by more than the length of a chrome-plated Dagmar.[3]

Now, what are cars in the year 2005 going to look like? I'll use the same techniques we used to predict an automobile design for *Time* magazine in 1942. A few days ago, we looked at the design again and were surprised to see how many developments we had guessed correctly, including wraparound windshields, clear plastic tops, and twenty-nine other features that have since appeared in production cars.

I class the factors affecting styling as variables and constants. Among the variables are the future state of the nation's economy; the nature and cost of the available fuel; the rate and radius of decentralization of population; the development of new metals, synthetic materials, and new techniques; the development

---

[3] Dagmars referred to stylized chrome car bumpers, often in the shape of exaggerated, cone-shaped artillery shells.

of more compact power plants; the possibility of highway systems with resilient surfaces or some other quality of surface. The big variable, of course, is atomic conflict.[4]

Let's now isolate the factors that are near-certitudes and predict their probable effects:

1. Highways will be able to carry more traffic at greater average speeds. (We shall need better streamlining, smooth undercarriage, higher speeds, better deceleration.)

2. There will be more automobiles everywhere. (Automobiles must be made easier to maneuver in all directions.)

3. Automobiles will increase productivity in all industries. There will be more leisure, more family travel for longer distances. (Increased luggage space is indicated for the family car.)

4. Semiautomatic driving will become the rule. Driving will be easier—therefore more relaxing; therefore more dangerous. (Interior design must take into account that the occupants must be protected more carefully if the driver lapses in attention and dozes. Devices may become standard equipment to prevent this from happening.)

5. The standard of living will be more uniform. More people will be able to consider the possibility of owning two or more cars. (There will be a wider variety of body types made available at the low-cost level—possibly a utility car, of which no example exists, now; or a vacation car, combining advantages of the present station wagon with some of the more important facilities found in trailers: refrigerated compartments, cooking units, folding awning tents, and so forth.)

6. Finally—and by far the most effective factor—there must be greater emphasis laid on the safety factor in car design. At present, one out of every ten hospital beds is occupied by the victim of an automobile accident. In 1954, 36,000 or more people were killed. In fifty years, even if the rate of fatal accidents declines (as it does annually, based on the number of miles traveled), we may expect as many as 120,000 killed annually. Obviously, something will have to be done about this, by driver education—the biggest factor—and by the automotive industry itself. (This fact will affect appearance, because structural revisions may shift glazed areas, simplify instrument panels. Automobiles, like planes today, will need to be studied as human engineering problems. Style will follow function.)

Now let's see if we can visualize an ensemble. Our 2005 model has a compact engine that does not require a high hood. This engine can be placed anywhere, and the cooling intake, if any, will be small. The body encloses large luggage spaces. The car is correctly streamlined; the undercarriage is smooth. The body is built strongly to be safe in case of collision. Therefore, window arrangement will be changed, by the new type of structure. I believe the goldfish-bowl or greenhouse superstructure is on its way out, especially in the rear of the vehicle.

The doors—or rather the accessibility panels will be power-operated and will open so that one can get in and out without crouching. The car can move laterally for close parking.

Inside, the automobile will be quite changed. With emphasis on de-lethalization, air conditioning, and partial convertibility, all-new interiors are inevitable. Seats will probably incorporate a pneumatic network to control resiliency.

Various devices will have made driving a semiautomatic process. It is known that metabolic and neuro-electrical variations take place in the human body when one relaxes and goes to sleep. It is

---

[4] Refers to the nuclear weapon capacities of the United States and the Soviet Union and the global political, economic, and military implications of the Cold War.

conceivable that in the next fifty years means will be found to detect these fluctuations in body condition so as to stop the car automatically whenever the danger point approaches. Perhaps the driver will wear wrist electrodes. Or, the steering wheel may transmit the body impulses. That steering wheel must, by all means, be mounted on a telescoping column.

Visibility in a 360-degree-arc is assured. Inside, windows closed, the car is quiet. The roof is a light-reflecting surface that will keep the car from getting too hot inside in the sun.

The electronics industry will probably have developed a low-priced radar unit for driving in the fog. Also, I see a possibility of a return to the flat windshield, which eliminates misleading light reflections at night. The tire started tubeless, and we are now back to the tubeless tire. As to the rear window, I wouldn't be surprised if it were the type that can be opened.

But now we come back to 1955 and our automotive jukeboxes. Are we proud of them? What do you think? Nothing about the appearance of the 1955 automobiles offsets the impression that Americans must be wasteful, swaggering, insensitive people. Automotive borax offers gratuitous evidence to people everywhere that much of what they suspect about us may be true. Our values are off beat, our ostentation acute, *if* the 1955 automobile is any reflection of ourselves and our taste.

Close Reading Questions

1. After World War II, what style decisions positively impacted car design?

2. When referring to the size of 1955 car models, why did Loewy describe the size of 1995 car models as "apparent wastefulness" and "a blessing?" What changes to the automobile validates the author's use of these apparently contradictory terms?

3. What factors did Loewy believe lead to an increased resentment of the choices made by the management departments of automobile companies? Why did Loewy insist that management was "vulnerable to public disfavor?" (Multiple Perspectives)

Analytical Writing/Discussion

4. Consider the role of cars in your life in relation to the 1950s. To what extent is having a car with particular styling—like a high-end audio system—symbolic of modern American culture in the way that cars in the 1950s reflected American culture?

5. What values does Loewy connect to 1950s automobile manufacturers? What do you think is the environmentally conscious equivalent the twenty-first century? (Cultural Influences)

6. Given the 1950s view of energy conservation, which predictions of the role and structure of the car in 2005 American culture do you think came true? Why? (Historical Trends)

Further Options

7. In "Jukebox on Wheels," the author debates whether the automobile designers of the 1950s do or should fulfill public tastes for large, gaudy cars. What do you think has a greater effect on twenty-first century automobile manufactures in the United States: consumer desires for fuel-efficient cars and Congressional mandates for greater fuel efficiency or consumer desires for status objects

and advertisements creating those desires? For more information about research strategies, see pp. 86–100 in Chapter 4.

8. Owning a car and a home is, for many, a key part of the American Dream. In what ways can you imagine the American Dream being maintained as we seek a more sustainable way of living? To begin crafting your answer, review the ways you can collect ideas as described in Chapter 2: The Writing Process and Assignment Analysis.

FIGURE 1   1970s gasoline shortage, Long Island, NY

SOURCE: © Associated Press.

Freewrite 2: America's Responses to Energy Crises

> Thomas Friedman is a Pultizer Prize-winning author and a columnist for the *New York Times*. The following is from Friedman's 2008 book *Hot, Flat, & Crowded: Why We Need a Green Revolution—And How It Can Renew America*. After reading the excerpt, see the freewrite questions below.

I can think of no better example of America's lack of sustained focus to take on a big challenge than the way we have dealt with our energy crises. In the wake of the 1973–74 Arab oil embargo, the Europeans and Japanese responded by raising gasoline taxes and, in Japan's case particularly, by launching a huge drive toward energy efficiency. France invested especially heavily in nuclear energy as a state project, with the result that today, France gets 78 percent of its electricity from nuclear plants and much of the waste is reprocessed and turned into energy again. Even Brazil, a developing country, launched a national program to produce ethanol from sugarcane to make itself less dependent on imported oil. Today, between Brazil's domestic oil production and its ethanol industry, it doesn't need to import crude oil.

Excerpts from "Dumb As We Wanna Be" from *Hot, Flat, and Crowded: Why We Need a Green Revolution and How it Can Renew America* by Thomas Friedman. Copyright © 2008 by Thomas L. Friedman. Reprinted by permission of Farrar, Straus, and Giroux.

America's initial response was significant. Urged on by Presidents Gerald Ford and Jimmy Carter, the United States implemented higher fuel economy standards for American cars and trucks. In 1975, Congress passed the Energy Policy and Conservation Act, which established corporate average fuel economy (CAFE) standards that required the gradual doubling of passenger vehicle efficiency for new cars to 27.5 miles per gallon within ten years.

Not surprisingly, it all worked. Between 1975 and 1985, American passenger vehicle mileage went from around 13.5 miles per gallon to 27.5, while light truck mileage increased from 11.6 miles per gallon to 19.5—all of which helped to create a global oil glut from the mid-1980s to the mid-1990s, which not only weakened OPEC but also helped to unravel the Soviet Union, then the world's second-largest oil producer.

So what happened next? Did we keep our focus on the long term? No. After the original Congressional mandate of 27.5 miles per gallon took full effect in 1985, President Reagan, rather than continuing to increase the fuel economy standard to keep reducing our dependence on foreign oil, actually rolled it back to 26 miles per gallon in 1986. . . .In backing away from fuel economy standards, Reagan apparently thought he was giving America's then sagging domestic oil and auto industries a boost. The result: We quickly started to get readdicted to imported oil. While the Reagan administration was instrumental in bringing down the Soviet Union, it was also instrumental in building our current dependence on Saudi Arabia.

The Reagan administration was an environmental turning point too. We forget, because it was so long ago, that there was a time when Washington had a bipartisan approach to the environment. It was a Republican, Richard Nixon, who signed into law the first wave of major environmental legislation in the United States, which addressed our first generation of environmental problems—air pollution, water pollution, and toxic waste. But Reagan changed that. Reagan ran not only against government in general but against environmental regulation, in particular. He and his interior secretary, James Watt, turned environmental regulation into a much more partisan and polarizing issue than it had ever been before. . . .

In 1989, the elder Bush's administration at least moved the fuel economy standard back up to the 1985 level of 27.5 miles per gallon. It also passed substantial improvements in building standards and new appliance standards, introduced a production tax credit for renewable energy, and elevated the Solar Energy Research Institute to the status of a national institution as the National Renewable Energy Laboratory. But as soon as Bush liberated Kuwait from Saddam Hussein, and oil prices went back down, he did nothing strategic to liberate America from dependence on Middle East oil.

When the Clinton administration came into office, it looked into raising fuel economy standards further, just for light trucks. But to make sure there would be none of that, Congress, spurred on by the Michigan Congressional delegation—which is a wholly owned subsidiary of the Big Three automakers and the United Auto Workers—literally gagged and blindfolded the government when it came to improving mileage standards. Specifically, Congress inserted an appropriations rider into the fiscal year 1996–fiscal year 2001 Department of Transportation appropriations bill that expressly prohibited the use of appropriated funds for any rule-making by the National Highway Traffic Safety Administration to tighten fuel economy standards for American cars and trucks—thereby freezing the whole process. Congress effectively banned the NHTSA from taking any steps to improve mileage standards for American cars! This move blocked any mileage improvements until 2003, when the younger Bush's administration made a tiny adjustment upward in the mileage standard for light-duty trucks. . . .

Detroit introduced the sport-utility vehicle and successfully lobbied the government to label these as light trucks so they would not have to meet the 27.5 miles per gallon standard for cars, but only the light truck standard of 20.7. So, we became even more addicted to oil. When I asked Rick Wagoner, the chairman and CEO of General Motors, why his company didn't make more fuel-efficient cars, he gave me the standard answer: that GM has never succeeded in telling Americans what cars they should buy. "We build what the market wants," he said. If people want SUVs and Hummers, you have to give them what they want."

But what the Detroit executives never tell you is that one big reason the public wanted SUVs and Hummers all those years was that Detroit and the oil industry consistently lobbied Congress against raising gasoline taxes, which would have shaped public demand for something different. European governments imposed very high gasoline taxes and taxes on engine size and kept imposing them—and guess what? Europeans demanded smaller and smaller cars. America wouldn't impose more stringent gasoline and engine taxes, so American consumers kept wanting bigger and bigger cars. Big Oil and Big Auto used their leverage in Washington to shape the market so people would ask for those cars that consumed the most oil and earned their companies the most profits—and our Congress never got in the way. It was bought off for more than two decades.

These were the years the locust ate—brought to a filling station near you by a bipartisan alliance of special interests—with Democrats supporting the auto companies and their unions and Republicans supporting the oil companies, while the groups representing the broad national interest were marginalized and derided as part of some eco-fringe. That is "dumb as we wanna be." When the public is engaged, as it was after 1973, when people were waiting in lines for gasoline, it can override the entrenched interests of the auto and oil lobbies. But the minute—and I mean the minute—the public takes its eye off the ball, those special interest lobbyists barge back into the cloakrooms of Congress, passing out political donations and calling the shots according to their needs, not the nation's. What was good for General Motors was not always good for America, but few Democrats or Republicans in high office were ready to lead the country on a different path.

And so it is with America. Alas, we are not just the people we've been waiting for. We are the people we have to overcome. We have been consuming too much, saving too little, studying too laxly, and investing not nearly enough. And, our political institutions are also the institutions we have to overcome. As long as our political system and Congress and Senate seem incapable of producing the right answers to big problems, as long as our politicians can only behave like Santa Claus and give things away, and never like Abraham Lincoln and make the really hard calls, the greatness that America is capable of will elude it in this generation.

Have no doubts. The era we have entered is one of enormous social, political, and economic change—driven in part by the Market and in part by Mother Nature. If we want things to stay as they are—that is, if we want to maintain our technological, economic, and moral leadership, and a habitable planet, rich with flora and fauna, leopards and lions, and human communities that can grow in a sustainable way—things will have to change around here, and fast.

After reading Friedman's excerpt, freewrite or discuss one or more of the following questions:

- Do you think Presidents Ford, Carter, Reagan, Bush (Sr.), and Clinton acted responsibly to the energy challenges during their respective presidencies? Why or why not?

- In what ways can you support the following two positions: Detroit fulfills consumer demands for autos *and* Detroit manipulates car buyers to create the most profitable products?

- How discerning is the American public when it comes to purchasing cars? What features, including fuel efficiency, have persuaded you or someone you know to purchase a car?

- What lessons, if any, do you think can be learned from the energy policies and car manufacturing of other countries?

YOUR GREAT WORK

by David W. Orr

David W. Orr is the Paul Sears Distinguished Professor of
Environmental Studies and Politics at Oberlin College, where
he is also special advisor to the president. Orr is also a James
Marsh Professor at the University of Vermont. He is the author
of six books, including *Ecological Literacy.* Originally titled
"The Designer's Challenge," Orr delivered this speech in 2007
to the graduates of the University of Pennsylvania's School of
Design, challenging them to consider a multitude of factors
in their work as designers.

Dean Hack, distinguished faculty of the School of Design, honored guests, and most important, you the
members of the class of 2007: It is a great privilege to stand before you on your graduation day.

As a Penn alumnus, I feel a deep sense of affection for this institution and for this place. My own
interest in design was kindled here long ago by Ian McHarg, who as much as anyone was the founder of
modern landscape design and the larger field of ecological design. His book *Design with Nature* remains a
classic statement of the art of intelligent inhabitation. From its founding, the city of Philadelphia has been
home to a great deal of innovative urban design and experimentation now carried on here in the School
of Design. You are a part of a great history and have inherited a legacy of which you may be justly proud.
But the work of designers is now entering its critical and most important phase.

It is said that we are entitled to hold whatever opinions we choose, but we are not entitled to whatever
facts we wish. Whatever opinions you may have, there are four facts that will fundamentally shape the
world in which you will live and work.

The first is the fact that we spend upwards of 95 percent of our time in houses, cars, malls, and offices.
We are becoming an indoor species increasingly shut off from sky, land, forests, waters, and animals.
Nature, as a result, is becoming more and more an abstraction to us. The problem is most severe for
children who now spend up to eight hours each day before a television or computer screen and less and
less time outdoors in nature. Author Richard Louv describes the results as "nature deficit disorder"—the
loss of our sense of rootedness in place and connection to the natural world. In some future time, it is not
farfetched to think that disconnected and rootless, we would become unhinged in a fundamental way and
that is a spiritual crisis for which there is no precedent.

Second, when Benjamin Franklin walked the streets of Philadelphia there were fewer than one billion
of us on Earth. The human population is now 6.5 billion and will likely crest at 9 or 10 billion. One-and-
a-half billion live in the most abject poverty, while another billion live in considerable wealth. One billion
suffer from the afflictions of eating too much while others suffer from malnutrition. When I was a graduate student at Penn, the ratio of richest to poorest was said to be 35:1. It is now approaching 100:1 and
growing. The problem of a more crowded world is not just about what ecologists call carrying capacity of
the Earth. It also a problem of justice with more and more people competing for less and less.

A third fact has been particularly difficult for a society built on the foundation of cheap portable
fossil fuels to acknowledge. We are at or near the year of peak oil extraction, the point at which we will

From *The Designer's Challenge* by David W. Orr. Copyright © 2007 by David W. Orr. Reprinted by permission.

have consumed the easy and better half of the accessible oil. The other half is harder to refine, farther out, and deeper down, and mostly located in places where people do not like us. We are not likely to run out of oil or liquid fossil fuels from one source or another, but we are nearing the end of the era of cheap oil. We have known this for decades, but we still have no coherent or farsighted energy policy. In the meantime, the penalty for procrastination grows daily along with the risks of supply interruptions and volatile energy prices.

There is a fourth fact. When the University of Pennsylvania was founded, the level of CO_2 in the atmosphere was about 280 parts per million. But now, the level of all human-generated heat-trapping gases is 430 parts per million CO_2 equivalent. We have already warmed the Earth by .8 degrees C and are committed at least to another .6 degrees C. According to the scientists who participated in writing the Fourth Report for the Intergovernmental Panel on Climate Change we are not just warming the Earth, but destabilizing the entire planet. Climate scientist James Hansen says that we are close to making Earth a different planet and one that we will not much like.

Four facts.

- One has to do with the largeness of the human spirit and our capacity to connect to life.
- The second has to do with justice, fairness, and decency in a more crowded world.
- The third has to do with our wisdom and creativity in the face of limits to the biosphere.
- The last is about human survival on a hotter and less stable and predictable planet.

In the face of the remorseless working out of large numbers do you have reason to be optimistic? Frankly, no. Optimism is a prediction that the odds are in your favor—like being a Yankees fan with a one-run lead in the ninth inning and two outs and a two-strike count on a .200 hitter and Mariano Rivera—in his prime—on the mound. You have good reason to believe that you will win the game. That's optimism. The Red Sox fans, on the other hand, believing in the salvation of small percentages, hope for a hit to get the runner home from second base to tie the game. Optimism is a bet that the odds are in your favor; hope is the faith that things will work out whatever the odds. Hope is a verb with its sleeves rolled up. Hopeful people are actively engaged in defying the odds or changing the odds. But optimism leans back, puts its feet up, and sports a confident look knowing that the deck is stacked.

If you know enough, you cannot honestly be optimistic. But you have every reason to be hopeful and to act faithfully and competently on that hope. And what does that mean for you as designers?

My message to you is this. As designers, you hold the keys to creating a far better world than that in prospect, but only if you respond creatively, smartly, wisely, and quickly to the four facts described above. Your generation does not have a choice to solve one or two of these problems. You must solve them all—rather like solving a quadratic equation. And, you have no time to lose. As designers, you must design so artfully and carefully as to help reconnect people to nature and to their places. You must design to promote justice in a more crowded world. You must design a world powered by efficiency and sunlight. You do not have the option of maintaining the status quo—a world dependent on ancient sunlight. And since Nature is a ruthless and unforgiving bookkeeper, you must do your work in a way that balances the carbon books. How will you do such things? The answers, fortunately, are many, but the principles of design are few. Let me suggest three.

The first has to do with the scope of your work. You must see design as a large and unifying concept—quite literally the remaking of the human presence on Earth. Design in its largest sense has to do with how we provision ourselves with food, energy, materials, shelter, livelihood, transport, water, and waste cycling. It is the calibration of human intentions with how the world works as a physical system and the awareness of how the world works to inform our intentions. And good design at all times joins our five senses (and perhaps others that we suspect) with the human fabricated world. When designers get it right, they create in ways that reinforce our common humanity at the deepest level.

Ecological design is flourishing in fields as diverse as architecture, landscape architecture, biomimicry, industrial ecology, urban planning, ecological engineering, agriculture, and forestry. It is gathering momentum, driven by necessity, better technology, and economic opportunity. Designers in diverse fields are learning how to

- use nature as the standard, as Ian McHarg proposed
- power the world on current sunlight
- eliminate waste
- pay the full cost of development
- build prosperity on a durable basis

Design as a large concept means, in Wendell Berry's felicitous words, "solving for pattern," creating solutions that solve many problems. When you solve for pattern, you will also have created resilience, which is the capacity of systems to persist in a world perturbed by human error, malevolence and what we call "acts of God." And by solving for pattern, you are also likely to learn the virtues of reparability, redundancy, locality, and simplicity. . . .

As a corollary, you must see yourselves as the designers, not just of buildings, landscapes, and objects, but of the systems in which these are components. That means that you must reckon with economic, political, and social aspects of design. And the hardest but most important object for designers is the design of what Peter Senge calls learning organizations, in which designing ecologically becomes the default setting, not an aberration.

Second, you will need a standard for your work, rather like the Hippocratic Oath or a compass by which you chart a journey. For that, I propose that designers should aim to cause no ugliness, human or ecological, somewhere else or at some later time. That standard will cause you to think upstream from the particular design project or object to the wells, mines, forests, farms, and manufacturing establishments from which materials are drawn and crystallized into the particularities of design. It will cause you, as well, to look downstream to the effects of design on climate and health of people and ecosystems. If there is ugliness, human or ecological, at either end, you cannot claim success as a designer, regardless of the artfulness of what you make.

As a corollary, you, as designers, ought to think of yourselves first as place-makers, not merely form-makers. The difference is crucial. Form-making puts a premium on artistry and sometimes merely fashion. It is mostly indifferent to human and ecological costs incurred elsewhere. The first rule of place making, on the other hand, is to honor and preserve other places, however remote in space and culture. When you become accomplished designers, of course, you will have mastered the integration of both making places and making them beautiful.

Third, as designers, you will need to place your work in a larger historical context—what philosopher Thomas Berry calls, your Great Work. No generation ever asks for its Great Work. The generation of the Civil War certainly did not wish to fight and die at places like Shiloh, Antietam, Gettysburg, or the Wilderness. But their Great Work, the end of human bondage, required just that of tens of thousands of them . . . and they rose to do their Great Work. Those now passing from the scene that Tom Brokaw calls "The Greatest Generation" did not wish to fight and die in places like Iwo Jima or the battlefields of Europe. But their Great Work, the fight against Nazism, required them to do so and they rose to the challenge to do their Great Work as well. Your Great Work, however, is not one of fighting wars, but of extending and speeding a worldwide ecological enlightenment that joins human needs and purposes with the way the world works as a biophysical system.

Your Great Work will be no less demanding and no less complex than that of any previous generation. But in outline it is very simple. Your Great Work as designers is to

1. Stabilize and reduce all heat-trapping gases

2. Make a rapid transition to efficiency and renewable energy

3. Build a world secure by design for everyone . . . a world in which every child has a decent home, food, water, education, medical care

4. Preserve the best of our history and culture

5. Enable us to see our way forward to a world that is sustainable and spiritually sustaining

This challenge, your Great Work, is neither liberal nor conservative; neither Republican nor Democrat. It is, rather, the recognition that the present generation is a trustee standing midway between a distant past and the horizon of the future. As trustees, we are obligated to pass on the best of our civilization and the ecological requisites on which it depends—including a stable climate and biological diversity—to future generations. The idea that we are no more than trustees was proposed long ago by Edmund Burke, the founder of modern conservatism (1790), and by one of the founders of modern revolutionary politics, Thomas Jefferson (1789), as well. It is a perspective that unites us across our present divisions in service to our posterity.

Your Great Work is a sacred trust given only to your generation. If you do not rise to do your Great Work, it will not be done. We know enough now to say what no other generation could rightfully say: the price for that dereliction—not rising to do your Great Work—will be high and perhaps total. Your Great Work as designers is to honor wholeness, health, and the great holy mystery of life. No other generation before you ever had a greater challenge and none more reason to rise to greatness.

My charge to you is to do your work so well that those who will look back on your time —the beneficiaries of your Great Work—will know that this was indeed humankind's finest hour.

Close Reading Questions

1. Why do you think Orr compares the population of Philadelphia in 2007 to the Philadelphia of Benjamin Franklin's time?

2. Why does Orr say that "Nature is a ruthless and unforgiving bookkeeper?"

3. For what reasons does Orr deflect political labels when describing the tasks facing the design profession?

Analytical Writing/Discussion

4. Why do you agree or disagree with Orr's contention that designers face four facts "that will fundamentally shape the world in which [we] live and work"? Which fact strikes you as more or least critical? Why? (Multiple Perspectives)

5. In what ways do you think Orr's use of a sports analogy is an effective or ineffective way to illustrate the responsibilities of design professionals to create in environmentally conscious ways? (Cultural Influences)

6. How does Orr define the design graduates' "Great Work?" How does their Great Work compare to the nineteenth- and twentieth-century examples of Great Work? (Historical Trends)

Further Options

7. In the middle of his speech, Orr tells the graduates the unequivocal tasks ahead of them as newly minted designers. What would you imagine that students in other disciplines—like English, business, or education—would say is their plan for using their careers to maintain an environmentally conscious world?

8. Colin Beavan in his essay "No Impact Man," is initially certain that his personal actions damage the environment and vows to lessen his carbon footprint. How do you imagine Orr would respond to Beavan's views on an individual's ability to affect cause such damage to affect change? (Cultural Influences)

HOW THE "SCIENTIFIC CONSENSUS" ON GLOBAL WARMING AFFECTS AMERICAN BUSINESS—AND CONSUMERS

by Nicolas Loris

Nicolas Loris is a policy analyst in the Thomas A. Roe Institute for Economic Policy Studies at The Heritage Foundation, a research and educational think tank. Loris's work has also appeared in publications like *The Wall Street Journal, The Washington Times,* and *Investor's Business Daily.* The following excerpt is from a 2010 article written partly in response to the 2007 report by the United Nations about greenhouse gas emissions.

For years, businesses and the general public have been told by mainstream climatologists that the planet is warming due to human activity and that immediate action is necessary to avoid a global catastrophe. The U.S. government relied heavily on a 2007 report by the United Nations' Intergovernmental Panel on Climate Change (IPCC) to justify the need to reduce emissions of carbon dioxide (CO_2) and other greenhouse gases (GHGs) created anthropogenically.[1] Over time, Congress enacted numerous policies to increase clean energy production, such as mandates for renewable fuels, expanded tax credits for renewable energy, and new energy efficiency targets for vehicles and appliances. All of these policies had the goal of reducing America's carbon footprint. Congress is now seeking to expand and create new policies

From "How the 'Scientific Consensus' on Global Warming Affects American Business—and Consumers" (October 25, 2010) by Nicolas D. Loris. Copyright © 2010 by The Heritage Foundation. Reprinted by permission.

---

[1] created or caused by human activity

aimed at further reducing emissions by placing a national cap on carbon emissions and enforcing a fed-eral mandate for renewable energy production. Meanwhile, the Environmental Protection Agency is on its own regulatory path to decrease CO_2.

The business landscape consequently changed, and not for the better. Energy producers became vested stakeholders and lobbied for handouts to produce what Congress determined to be cleaner energy from cleaner sources, such as windmills, solar panels, and ethanol. Major oil companies invested in renewable energy technology to capitalize on subsidies and tax breaks while enhancing their image. Most businesses factored the threat of global warming into their daily operations and became cognizant of the threat of higher energy prices caused by government policies.

Despite vigorous dissension among the scientific community concerning the effects of anthropogenic warming, the climatologists who believe the warming to be a serious problem controlled the message for years. Simply put, they convinced the general public that global warming posed an imminent threat and drastic cuts in greenhouse gas emissions were necessary to prevent a catastrophe. Recent flaws discovered in the scientific assessment of climate change have shown that the scientific consensus is not as settled as the public had been led to believe. Leaked e-mails from the University of East Anglia's Climate Research Unit in the U.K. revealed conspiracy, exaggerated warming data, possibly illegal destruction and manipu-lation of data, and attempts to freeze out dissenting scientists from publishing their work in reputable journals. Furthermore, gaffes exposed in the IPCC report have only increased skepticism among busi-nesses and the public, and raised serious questions about sacrificing economic activity to reduce CO_2 emissions.

Policy should never rest on a shaky set of assumptions, particularly when it can have far-reaching implications for American businesses and everyday Americans, and could therefore fundamentally alter decisions in ways that harm America's productive system of free enterprise. While the government can pick winners and prop them up with subsidies, every winner comes at the expense of the taxpayer and discourages the innovation necessary to discover new and economically competitive sources of energy. Moreover, business uncertainty created by the government's wavering on more climate change policy is stunting America's economic recovery. With such inconclusive scientific evidence, Congress should not implement any new GHG-reduction policies, and it should prohibit the EPA from doing the same.

The Shifting Consensus

The alleged scientific consensus on climate change holds that the planet is warming at a dramatic rate. But not long ago, scientists thought that global *cooling* was a threat to the planet. As recently as 1975, *The New York Times* ran an article titled, "A Major Cooling Widely Considered to Be Inevitable." Some proposals even included covering the polar ice caps with black soot to melt them. Only six years later, climatologists predicted that global warming was inevitable, and the issue gained more traction throughout the 1980s and 1990s. The IPCC published multiple reports, the first in 1990, pronouncing that human activities, predominately fossil fuel use, were warming the planet. A supplementary report followed in 1992, the second report appeared in 1995, and the third in 2001—all presenting "newer and stronger" evidence that the planet's surface was heating due to human activity.

The message that warming was incontrovertible continually gained momentum and exploded in 2006 when former Vice President Al Gore released his book and documentary film *An Inconvenient Truth*, claiming that the planet would witness more Hurricane Katrina-like disasters and rising sea levels if humans do not drastically reduce man-made greenhouse gas emissions. The 2007 IPCC report became Al Gore's *magnum opus* on climate change and the main source for the "evidence" he relentlessly pitched to Congress. The 2007 report declared that global warming is "unequivocal," and the frequency and intensity of natural disasters is likely to increase. The report's "Summary for Policymakers" warned that carbon emissions from fossil fuel production and nitrous oxide, and methane emissions from agricultural production, are significantly contributing to global warming. Government officials in the U.S. and around the world continually use and exaggerate the IPCC report to justify the need for carbon reduction policies, creating a large disparity between hype and reality. For instance, even the IPCC projection of sea level rising over the next century is a modest 7 to 23 inches, with the lower end of that projection occurring over the past two centuries.

Is There a Scientific Consensus?

Several recent events, including revelations that forced the IPCC to retract parts of its 2007 report, have called the scientific consensus into question. Although the study puts the probability of Himalayan glaciers melting by 2035 at "very high," the authors acknowledged that they based this and other claims on speculation. Further, the IPCC's assessment of reductions in mountain ice in the Andes, Alps, and Africa came from two dubious sources. One was from a magazine that discussed anecdotal evidence from mountain climbers; the other came from a student dissertation. The IPCC also acknowledged overstating crop loss in Africa, depletion of the Amazon rain forest, sea level increases in the Netherlands, and damage from weather catastrophes.

Climate data sets are also raising questions. Hackers leaked thousands of e-mails and other documents from the University of East Anglia's Climate Research Unit that detailed how these climatologists, many with important roles in promulgating the official UN science, refused to share data, plotted to keep dissenting scientists from being published in leading journals, and discarded original data. Some have resigned and others have been investigated for breaching data laws under the Freedom of Information Act. Russian climatologists blamed the scandal-laden Climate Research Unit (CRU) for omitting cooler data points from its data set. In the U.S., computer programmer E. Michael Smith and meteorologist Joseph D'Aleo detailed how the National Climatic Data Center (NCDC) dropped thousands of data points from its climate data set—data points that were in cooler regions around the globe.

A few errors in the three-volume, almost 1,000-page IPCC report may not warrant dismissal of the entire study, but climatologists questioned the IPCC's findings before these gaffes. University of Virginia professor Fred Singer recently published an 800-page report titled, "Climate Change Reconsidered," which questions and debunks many of the IPCC conclusions and emphasizes that there is no scientific consensus on climate change. Richard Lindzen, professor of meteorology at the Massachusetts Institute of Technology, notes that the IPCC's models fail to take into account naturally occurring cycles such as El Niño, the Pacific decadal oscillation, or the Atlantic multidecadal oscillation. Other prominent scientists called political action "irresponsible and immoral" because of the lack of credible evidence. When the IPCC released its report in 2007, 400 climate experts disputed the findings; that number has since grown to more than 700 scientists, including several current and former IPCC scientists.

The profusion of scientific dissent should have been sufficient evidence for policymakers to call the alleged consensus into question, and these recent events should raise even more red flags, especially in light of the economic costs that policies to mitigate greenhouse gases carry.

Government Plans to Reduce Greenhouse Gases

Despite these revelations about scientific research on global warming, the U.S. government has aggressively pursued climate change policies to reduce carbon dioxide emissions. During the past two decades, the federal government has spent more than $79 billion on climate change policies, "including science and technology research, administration, education campaigns, foreign aid, and tax breaks." Legislation signed into law in 2005 and 2007 included more steps to transition from fossil fuels and improve energy efficiency to reduce CO_2 emissions. More recently, the Obama Administration has attempted to tip the balance in favor of renewable energy by advocating a cap-and-trade system, CO_2 regulations, renewable electricity mandates, and additional billions of dollars in government spending for government-picked "clean-energy" sources. Key legislative and regulatory steps are

2005 and 2007 Energy Bills and 2009 Green Stimulus. Over the past five years, the government implemented two key policies to support renewable energy production, and passed a stimulus bill in 2009 with billions allocated to renewable energy projects. The Energy Policy Act (EPACT) of 2005 contained loan guarantees for technologies, such as nuclear energy carbon capture, and sequestration, that would reduce greenhouse gas output by increasing the supply of carbon-free energy, as well as a host of subsidies and policies to increase renewable energy production. The act also included the first requirement that renewable fuels be mixed into the gasoline supply.

The Energy Independence and Security Act (EISA) of 2007 increased the renewable fuel mandate from 7.5 billion gallons in 2012 to 36 billion gallons by 2022, and included more tax credits for wind power, solar energy, and small irrigation power. Congress implemented a number of other energy-efficiency mandates for vehicles, buildings, and appliances to reduce energy consumption and consumers' carbon footprint. . . .

The 2009 American Recovery and Reinvestment Act included funding for renewable energy as well. Also known as the stimulus bill, the $814 billion package allocates nearly $47 billion for renewable energy sources, smart grids, and energy-efficiency programs. Congress granted an additional $20 billion to manufacturers of renewable energy technology in the form of tax credits.

The reason these sources of energy need government help is that they are too uncompetitive to reach the market otherwise. To the extent that there is a valid economic case for wind energy, solar energy, and ethanol fuel, industry will provide them even in the absence of government dictates and subsidies. Moreover, government-mandated energy-efficiency programs may sound good to consumers, but it is rarely good when Washington controls the market, since the forced energy-efficiency standards can result in decreased product performance, features, or reliability, which destroys value for the consumer. Mandatory improvements in efficiency usually raise the purchase price of appliances; sometimes the increase is more than enough to negate the energy savings.

Cap and Trade. One way to make clean energy more competitive is to tax fossil fuels to make them more expensive through a cap-and-trade system. Under cap and trade, emitters of greenhouse gases, primarily carbon dioxide derived from fossil fuel production, would be required to obtain permits (also known as allowances) for each ton of CO_2 emitted. The price of the allowances, in essence the tax on energy, is determined by supply and demand. As the carbon cuts become more stringent, the government allocates fewer permits, thus driving up the price for the energy-intensive sectors required to buy them. By taxing fossil-fuel-derived energy with artificial caps on carbon dioxide, clean energy artificially becomes more economically viable. In July 2009, the House of Representatives passed a cap-and-trade bill to reduce greenhouse gases 83 percent below 2005 levels by 2050. Since nearly 85 percent of America's energy needs come from fossil fuels, capping carbon dioxide amounts to an enormous tax on energy consumption.

EPA Regulations. With Congress unable to deliver a final cap-and-trade bill to the President, the Environmental Protection Agency (EPA) has been working on a backdoor policy to regulate greenhouse gas emissions much like cap and trade. A 2007 Supreme Court case decided that carbon dioxide and five other GHGs are pollutants and can be regulated under the Clean Air Act. The court ordered the EPA administrator to determine whether these GHG emissions were dangerous to human health and the environment and whether the scientific consensus on the effects of GHGs was settled. In April 2009, the EPA issued an endangerment finding, saying that current and future greenhouse gas emissions pose a serious threat to public health and safety. The EPA relied on the 2007 IPCC report as well as data from the NCDC to establish this finding. Thus, questionable science is guiding major changes in economic regulation. Under this approach, almost any activity that emits carbon dioxide and other greenhouse gases could be regulated under the Clean Air Act. Like cap and trade, regulating CO_2 emissions under the Clean Air Act would similarly burden the economy with higher energy costs, and would also include higher administrative compliance costs for businesses, higher bureaucratic costs for enforcing the regulations, and higher legal costs from the inevitable litigation.

Business Responds to Government

Recognizing policymakers' commitment to reducing greenhouse gases, businesses shaped their plans around government policies, despite the fact they are based on poor scientific evidence. Companies worldwide are taking climate change into consideration when making short-term and long-term business decisions. A June 2009 PricewaterhouseCoopers global survey asked 1,124 CEOs how their respective businesses were responding to climate change policies. In a series of yes or no questions, when asked about making changes to the products and services provided due to climate change policies, 46 percent said they were already making changes to day-to-day operations, and 40 percent are already changing how they manage risk.

Businesses are not just changing day-to-day operations and preparing for higher energy costs, but also how they invest for the future. Johnson & Johnson is investing in renewable energy and now uses the most hybrid vehicles of any company in America. Wal-Mart CEO Scott Lee made a pledge that each of his stores would eventually run on 100 percent renewable energy. Coca Cola's environmental initiative focuses not only on water stewardship and sustainable packaging, but also climate protection. Goldman Sachs invested $1.5 billion in wind, solar, and ethanol projects in 2006.

There is nothing wrong with these business decisions, if they are made voluntarily. But, if they are made in response to government policies favoring renewable energy over other sources, especially on questionable scientific grounds, it misallocates private resources, crowds out innovation, and wastes taxpayer money. In Spain, solar companies enjoyed lucrative subsidies for years; when the global recession forced the Spanish government to cut back its handouts, the Spanish solar market crashed.

In a free market, the private sector should bear the risk and, therefore, reap the reward or suffer the consequences of an investment decision. If the government dictates these decisions by subsidizing a portion of the project, businesses receive all rewards with minimal risk. With start-up companies and large corporations alike receiving money from the government through stimulus funds or tax credits, firms will divert investments to clean-energy technology away from other—potentially more profitable and value-creating—investments.

As the government moves more actively toward funding renewable technology, investors are waiting to determine who the government winners will be before they spend more of their own money on innovative ideas, expanding their businesses, and hiring more employees. As Darryl Siry, former head of marketing at Tesla Motors, put it, "The existence of an 800-pound gorilla putting massive capital behind select start-ups is sucking the air away from the rest of the venture-capital ecosystem. Being anointed by DOE [U.S. Department of Energy] has become everything for companies looking to move ahead."

Large corporations also flooded the halls of Congress with thousands of lobbyists to ask for preferential treatment on energy policy. In 2007, 10 of the largest companies in the U.S. formed the United States Climate Action Partnership (USCAP) urging the government to cut GHG emissions. USCAP has since grown to 28 businesses and environmental organizations. Businesses heavily ramped up lobbying efforts in the past decade. More than 1,700 firms and groups sent lobbyists to work in the area of energy in 2009, up from 1,300 the year before, and 900 in 2006. . . .

Politics governed by special interests typically worsens conditions for the consumer. Consumers are the ones who bear the costs of these government policies; meanwhile, industry receives a seemingly free windfall. The more that government becomes involved in energy decisions, the more money will be used for special interest politicking. As founding father, Ben Franklin said, "When the people find that they can vote themselves money, that will herald the end of the republic."

Congressional Action Required

Congress has spent years and billions of dollars building policy around an alleged scientific consensus and is on a path to spend billions more as well as implement policies that would significantly reduce this country's economic potential. Congress should instead focus on the following measures to prevent more unnecessary economic damage and promote sound energy policy that would create jobs and increase energy supply:

1. **Refrain from Legislating for the Purpose of Reducing GHGs.** Congress should not pursue policies, such as cap and trade, a renewable electricity standard, or subsidies for "clean energy" as long as grave scientific disputes remain. Even if a scientific consensus emerges, Congress should still refrain from taking any action unless the economic cost of climate change mitigation justifies any benefits.

2. **Prohibit EPA Regulations.** Congress should rein in the EPA's regulatory authority by amending the Clean Air Act to exclude carbon dioxide and other greenhouse gases from coming under the EPA's purview.

3. **Focus Energy Policy on Energy, not GHGs.** Instead of artificially propping up certain energy sources with subsidies and mandates based on a false scientific consensus, Congress should focus

on creating a regulatory and legal framework for all energy policies to succeed or fail on their own merit by removing subsidies and reducing regulatory red tape that prevents the development of all energy sources.

Uncertain Science, Certain Cost

If the scientific consensus behind global warming is crumbling, so, too, should the economically harmful policies that stem from it. When asked about the scientific consensus on climate change, Phil Jones, former climate-research director at the University of East Anglia, said, "I don't believe the vast majority of climate scientists think this. This is not my view. There is still much that needs to be undertaken to reduce uncertainties, not just for the future, but for the instrumental (and especially the paleoclimatic) past as well." If the vast majority of climatologists do not believe that the debate on climate change is over, politicians should not be pushing for greenhouse gas reduction policies that not only have significant economic costs, but will also deeply alter the business landscape of the United States.

Close Reading Questions

1. How did the business community initially respond to warnings about global warming? What does the business community now say about global warming? (Historical Trends)

2. According to Loris, why are consumers negatively affected by government-mandated energy programs?

3. How are some businesses planning for higher energy costs created by climate change policies?

Analytical Writing/Discussion

4. As Loris questions the validity of climate-change warnings, how do the phrases he uses to describe the science involved change and develop? What do you think this series of phrases reveals about Loris's argument?

5. Loris cites Ben Franklin on "people . . . [voting] themselves money" in order to promote free enterprise by businesses and oppose lobbying by special interests. To what degree do you think large corporations in energy or other economic sectors, such as medicine, agriculture, and national defense, should refrain from lobbying and engage in true competition? (Cultural Influences)

6. Loris states that Congress should focus on specific measures that create jobs and foster sensible energy policies. Which of the three suggestions by Loris do you believe are the most or least likely to occur, and why? (Multiple Perspectives)

Further Options

7. In James Atwater's article "A Household of Helpers," he notes that the post-World War II economy encouraged American families to purchase a variety of household appliances. In what ways would those energy-dependent purchases—and thus, the American economy—have been affected by what Loris calls "questionable science"?

8. As explained in Chapter 5 on Argument and Rhetoric, a Rogerian argument seeks compromise and consensus among disputants by seeking, first, common ground (see pp. 133–146). Loris discusses several contradictory reports of the existence of global warming, including the 1975 *New York Times* article and the 2006 documentary. What aspects of climate change do these opposing sides agree upon? How might these areas of consensus affect the perspective of writers like Loris?

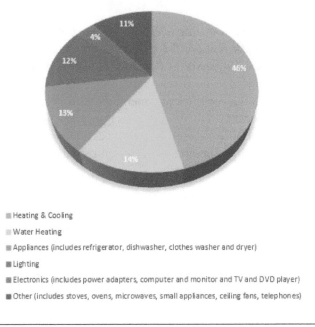

■ Heating & Cooling

■ Water Heating

■ Appliances (includes refrigerator, dishwasher, clothes washer and dryer)

■ Lighting

■ Electronics (includes power adapters, computer and monitor and TV and DVD player)

■ Other (includes stoves, ovens, microwaves, small appliances, ceiling fans, telephones)

FIGURE 2   Annual Energy Bill for a Typical Single-Family Home in the U.S.: $2,200

SOURCE: U.S. Dept. of Energy, Lawrence Berkeley National Laboratory, 2009

Freewrite 3: "Become No Impact Man"

The following is from the 2009 book *No Impact Man* by blogger and author Colin Beavan, who in 2006, decided to try to live without significantly impacting the environment. After reading this excerpt, see the freewrite questions below

For one year, my wife, baby daughter, and I, while residing in the middle of New York City, attempted to live without making any net impact on the environment. Ultimately, this meant, we did our best to create no trash (so no take-out food), cause no carbon dioxide emissions (so no driving or flying), pour no toxins in the water (so no laundry detergent), buy no produce from distant lands (so no New Zealand

Excerpts from "How a Schlub Like Me Gets Mixed Up in A Stunt Like This" and "Day One and the Whole Thing Is a Big Mistake" from *No Impact Man: The Adventures of A Guilty Liberal Who Attempts to Save the Planet, and Discovers He Makes About Himself and Our Way of Life in the Process* by Colin Beavan. Copyright © 2009 by Colin Beavan. Reprinted by permission of Farrar, Straus, and Giroux.

fruit). Not to mention: no elevators, no subway, no products in packaging, no plastics, no air conditioning, no TV, no buying anything new . . . I planned to write a book about what I was doing, and in the meantime I'd keep a blog on the Internet. I would breach the norms of our normally consumptive society inside a transparent bubble, into which, I imagined, a small number of blog readers and, later, a larger number of book readers would eventually get to look . . . .

For all my grand ideas about saving the world and figuring out a happier way of life and changing people's minds and living according to my principles and—let's face it—being way overearnest, it turns out that becoming No Impact Man does not mean running into a phone booth and coming out transformed into some sort of eco-hero with my underwear stretched over my trousers. It doesn't, in fact, feel heroic at all. What it feels like, waking up at 6:00 a.m. and hoping to get just a little more shut-eye before your eighteen-month-old greets the day by jumping up and down on your head, is enforced martyrdom of the most trivial and ridiculous kind. Because day one starts with me standing in my skivvies, looking through the purple dawn light and into the bathroom closet at a roll of paper towel (which I've always preferred to flimsy tissues), really needing to blow my nose, and suddenly realizing I'm not supposed to use the paper towel.

Today is the first day of my environmental lifestyle experiment. The one that is supposed to make me feel like I'm not contributing to the planet's destruction. The one that I have decided to ease myself into by starting with the seemingly simple first step of not making trash. The one, in other words, that means that I should not use a paper towel to blow my nose. So what do I do now that I am officially No Impact Man? Now that I have chosen a nom de guerre that makes me sound like an environmental superhero? Now that I have begun living in a self-imposed blog, book, and documentary bubble where for the next 364 days, 23 hours, and 50 frigging minutes anyone can look and judge how well I'm living up to my public declaration about making no negative environmental impact? What would anybody do? I reach for the paper towel. I tear off a piece, blow my nose, realize what an awful mess I've gotten myself into with this project, start feeling depressed before I even wake up, turn around, and shuffle back to the bedroom. I discover Isabella standing in the crib, opening and closing her hands and saying, "Uppie, Daddy, uppie." Instantly my self-recrimination begins: I'm selfish. I blew my nose on a dead tree. And now God has punished me by making the sound of my honking wake up Isabella so that she can jump up and down on my head.. . . .

No one can live without making *some* environmental impact. Even breathing creates carbon dioxide. You can turn your own lights out, but residing in a culture that provides street lighting means you still have an impact. The very fact that I had chosen to call this project No Impact went to the underlying point: I was naive and idealistic. I was not an environmentalist or an activist. I had no credentials. All I had was the knowledge that world events were freaking me out and the faith that we could do better. I knew nothing, at that stage, about environmental living or environmental choices or carbon offsets or green spin or the relative worth of individual versus political action or, for that matter, anything else relevant to the question of maintaining a safe habitat for humanity. Hell, I still didn't know the answer to the paper-or-plastic question. But that was the point. The idea was not to become an environmental expert and then apply what I'd learned. The idea was to start from scratch—with not a clue about how to deal with our planetary emergency—and stumble forward. To see what I could find out. To see how I evolved. What I learned in that moment in the yoga grocery store was that I would find no well-blazed path to follow. I would have to figure out my extreme eco-lifestyle for myself.

Lack of well-sourced information mixed with a surfeit of corporate PR resulted only in confusion. I'd hear of one study saying that the energy used washing ceramic cups damages the environment as much as the use of disposable plastic cups that won't degrade for a thousand years. I'd hear of another that said using hot water and detergent to wash cloth rags harms the planet more than cutting down trees to make paper towels. If I listened to the promulgated wisdom, it seemed that everything was as bad as everything else. The spin merchants seemed to want to convince me that trying to make any difference was futile. I might as well give up. Toss away another plastic cup. Forget about electric cars because of the deleterious effects of disposing of their worn-out batteries. Go on, guzzle, the spurious wisdom seemed to say. There *is* no right way to live lightly on the land. . . .

[T]here didn't seem to be any reliable environmental-living road map to follow. The "science" did not seem to be so much about making things clear, but more about confusing us and wearing us down so that we just carried on the way things were. "Stasis through obfuscation," my wife, Michelle, called it.

I read an article in *The New York Times* about the corporate rush to label products "green." Companies were slapping environmentally friendly labels on everything from tree-killing chainsaws that used less gas to highly toxic bug sprays. "Greenwashing" abounded, and to obsessively try to figure out which products truly harmed the planet less seemed like a fast path to an ulcer.

Then I began to wonder: Instead of driving ourselves nuts trying to find a way through the maze of product spin, might it not be simpler just to climb out of the maze? The trick to environmental living might not be in choosing *different* products. Instead—at least for profligate citizens of the United States and Western Europe—it might partly be about choosing *fewer* products. It might not just be about using different resources. It might be about using *fewer* resources.

As the ancient Chinese *Tao Te Ching* says, "The man who knows that enough is enough will always have enough."

After reading about Beavan's plans to reduce his family's impact on the environment, freewrite, or discuss one or more the following questions

- What are two or three reasons that Beavan does not feel like "some sort of eco-hero?" Which of the concerns about his project do you find the least or most convincing and why?

- Why does Beavan's No Impact project make you feel optimistic or pessimistic about being environmentally responsible?

- How do you think science experts, product manufacturers, and or the media have confused, rather than clarified, methods for living an environmentally sustainable life?

FINAL ASSIGNMENT 1: Prioritizing Energy

The American love affair with consumption has soured with rising energy costs and their environmental implications. Black suggests that the post–World War II years were the beginning of an energy-dependent lifestyle for millions of Americans. That lifestyle was at the center of Americans' need for oil during the 1973 oil embargo and continues today. While there is not always agreement about energy-related topics—as is the case with Loris and Orr, who have opposing views on the presence of climate change—scientists, environmentalists, researchers, and corporate leaders agree that it is important to continue the debates about energy use.

Essay Question

Given the rate of energy consumption in the United States, in what ways do you think that the perspectives of government, business, consumers, and science can and cannot be prepared to accept the various debates about energy usage? Your answer should include a discussion of American energy usage in the twentieth and twenty-first centuries.

Write a formal and extended essay to answer this question. Be sure to include specific references and direct quotations from several readings in this chapter (see Chapter 4 on Academic Honesty on quoting and citing properly). Be sure to not only support your informed perspective but also to anticipate and answer the possible objections of those who do not already agree with you. Your task is to assert your opinion and persuade others to consider it carefully.

Freewrite 4

Before you start to answer this complex question, analyze its parts. Reread the question above and underline several phrases that represent key parts of the larger answer you will be developing. Then pick two or three of these phrases and freewrite your immediate impressions: What do you think right now? Then, pause to look for connections, contradictions, and omissions within your first response: what else do you want to discuss, what else do you want to add, and/or what order of your ideas is developing? Finally, consider the audience of your essay: who does not agree with you already, and why might they disagree?

Reading Review

Once you have sketched some of your initial ideas, review some of the readings to find specific details and persuasive evidence to support, enrich, and possibly complicate your response. Here are some readings and post-reading questions that you may want to consider:

1. Black, Close Reading Question 3
2. Figure 9.1
3. Atwater, Analytical Writing/Discussion Question 5
4. Freewrite 2
5. Loris, Close Reading Question 2
6. Loris, Analytical Writing/Discussion Question 6
7. Orr, Close Reading Question 2
8. Freewrite 3

Feel free to include other readings and post-reading questions. You also may want to review the suggestions for writing persuasively in Chapter 5 on Argument as well as practicing the peer response described in Chapter 2 on the Writing Process.

FINAL ASSIGNMENT 2: Rhetorical Analysis

For two readings of this chapter (or possibly using one of the related or additional readings suggested below), compare and/or contrast their arguments. As explained in Chapter 5, this rhetorical analysis will answer the following questions:

- Based on the rhetorical triangle, who do you think is the writer and what is the message of this text? Who is the primary audience that the writer wanted to reach (consider the publication source)? (See pp. 104–105 of Chapter 5.)

- How does the writer try to use each of the three rhetorical appeals in this text, and when are they used effectively or not? (See pp. 105–109 of Chapter 5).

- Your professor may ask you to consider also the kind of argument being made, meaning a forensic, epideictic, or deliberative argument (see pp. 110–112 of Chapter 5). What kind of argument is being made, and why do you find it this kind to be a good choice (or not)?

- Finally, through comparing and contrasting the arguments of these two readings, what can you conclude about their power to persuade their intended audiences (and possibly additional readers)?

Your task is to help your readers to understand these two arguments and their efforts to persuade their audience.

FINAL ASSIGNMENT 3: Lessons about Sustainability

The quest to live a sustainable life in the United States can be difficult, especially because the United States has a history of producing more goods than any other nation on earth. Thomas Friedman offered a reality check of sorts in his reflection on America's addiction to cars and oil knowing that—as Brian C. Black's article stated—oil dependence permeated nearly every facet of American life. Orr and Beavan are intrigued by the idea of living a sustainable life, yet even Beavan doubts that the efforts of one person can make the planet a greener place.

Essay Question

To what degree do you think that the possibility of living a sustainable lifestyle is complicated by the perspective that sustainable efforts are only a trend and not a serious commitment on the part of some Americans? Your answer should include a discussion of the sustainability efforts in the United States during the second half of the twentieth century and the beginning of the twenty-first century.

Write a formal and extended essay to answer this question. Be sure to include specific references and direct quotations from several readings in this chapter (see Chapter 4 on Academic Honesty on quoting and citing properly). Be sure to not only support your informed perspective but also to anticipate and answer the possible objections of those who do not already agree with you. Your task is to assert your opinion and persuade others to consider it carefully.

Freewrite 5

Before you start to answer this complex question, analyze its parts. Reread the question above and underline several phrases that represent key parts of the larger answer you will be developing. Then pick two or three of these phrases and freewrite your immediate impressions: What do you think right now? Then, pause to look for connections, contradictions, and omissions within your first response: what else do you want to discuss, what else do you want to add, and/or what order of your ideas is developing? Finally, consider the audience of your essay: who does not agree with you already, and why might they disagree?

Reading Review

Once you have sketched some of your initial ideas, review some of the readings to find specific details and persuasive evidence to support, enrich, and possibly complicate your response. Here are some readings and post-reading questions that you may want to consider:

1. Black, Close Reading Question 1
2. Black, Analytical Writing/Discussion Question 4
3. Figure 1
4. Orr, Close Reading Question 3
5. Orr, Analytical Writing/Discussion Question 5
6. Loris, Close Reading Question 1
7. Loris, Analytical Writing/Discussion Question 6
8. Figure 2

Feel free to include other readings and post-reading questions. You also may want to review the suggestions for writing persuasively in Chapter 5 on Argument as well as practicing the peer response described in Chapter 2 on the Writing Process.

Readings on Energy and Sustainability in Other Chapters

For three additional readings related to energy and sustainability, you may want to read the following texts:

1. "Young and Unplugged: Digital Natives in Retreat" by Bella English in Chapter 1 (see pp. 6–8)
2. "The Nineteenth-Century Retreat: Family and Home" by Tamara K. Hareven in Chapter 6 (see pp. 127–136)
3. "The Persistence of Paper" by William Powers in Chapter 10 (see pp. 315–321)

Additional Readings for Chapter 9

To deepen your understanding of energy and sustainability and strengthen your final assignment, you can consult some of the following sources:

1. For more information about energy and sustainability, visit sustainability section of the website for Scientific American. This website, maintained by the magazine of the same name, chronicles news and feature stories about science and innovation.

   https://www.scientificamerican.com/sustainability/

2. For an examination of the reasons to live sustainably, you might want to read "Why Bother?" by Michael Pollan. This 2008 article casts doubt on the extent to which one person can make changes to save the environment.

   http://michaelpollan.com/articles-archive/why-bother/

3. For more information about electric cars, you may want to read the interview "A Claim That Electric Cars Aren't Green Fuels Firestorm" by Robin Young. In this interview, conservationist Ozzie Zelmer claims that electric cars do not contribute to a cleaner environment.

   http://hereandnow.wbur.org/2013/07/29/electric-cars-green

4. For another reading about modern energy consumption, you may want to read "Energy: What Americans Really Want" by Stephen Ansolabehere and David Konisky. This contemporary text examines what the results of a national survey about what Americans know and believe about energy resources.

   http://www.bostonglobe.com/ideas/2014/09/13/energy-what-americans-really-want/SdM914A5hoIK4rKP2rKn3O/story.html

5. For another reading on the personal factors that impact how and when we use energy, you may want to read "Fracking in the U.S.: The Story of One Man's Oil Well" by William Sargent. This article offers a look at the influence of family and culture on the oil business.

   http://www.csmonitor.com/Environment/2014/0928/Fracking-in-the-US-The-story-of-one-man-s-oil-well

6. For information about how much energy is required to operate workplace and household appliances, you might want to read "How We Use Energy: Home & Work." This 2017 article from the National Academy of Science discloses historical and contemporary data about every day energy usage in homes and commercial buildings.

   http://needtoknow.nas.edu/energy/energy-use/home-work/

7. For additional perspective on sustainability choices, you might want to view the 2014 TEDTalk "Paper Beats Plastic? How to Rethink Environmental Folklore." Leyla Acaroglu, a sustainability strategist, offers insight about the products that factor into daily sustainability choices.

   https://www.ted.com/speakers/leyla_acaroglu

8. For information about the tiny house movement, read "Resist . . . the Temptation to Hide Away in a Tiny House" by Umbra Fisk, who argues that the ability to live a sustainable lifestyle is contingent upon factors like social class, education, and economic status.

   http://grist.org/living/the-missed-opportunity-of-a-tiny-tidy-life/

Literacy and Technology

CHAPTER 10

There is no Frigate like a Book/To Take us Lands Away…
How frugal is the Chariot/That bears the Human soul.

—Emily Dickinson (1873)

Describing computer technology as either beneficial or detrimental, either good or bad … [limits] our understanding …. With such as simple [dichotomous] representation, … [we] are encouraged to take a side—for or against technology—rather than to understand the complex ways in which technology has become linked with our conception of literacy.

—Cynthia Selfe (1999)

Between 1982 and 2002, the percentage of Americans who read literature declined not only in every age group but in every generation …. We are reading less as we age, and we are reading less than people who were our age ten or twenty years ago …. [S]ome sociologists speculate that the reading books for pleasure will one day be the province of a special "reading class," much as it was before the arrival of mass literacy in the second half of the nineteenth century.

—Caleb Crain (2007)

Young people write far more than any generation before them. That's because so much socializing takes place online, and it almost always involves text …. Students [are] remarkably adept at … assessing their audience and adapting their tone and technique to best get their point across.

—Clive Owens (2009)

Introduction

When most of us consider literacy *and* technology, we probably think of computers first. Computers are a primary link between our ability to read and write and our use of technology. Computers, of course, now include an array of associated technologies and programs, such as the Internet, websites, e-readers, tablets, word processing, spell check, Facebook, Twitter, Instagram, Snapchat, and more.

It may be hard to imagine that many of the older literacy technologies we now take for granted once struck some in the past as new and threatening. For instance, in the nineteenth century, some teachers worried that attaching erasers to the then new, mass-produced pencils would ruin students' handwriting. For, if students could eliminate their penmanship errors with a quick rub of an eraser, how would they ever learn to write neatly? Now very few people consider the eraser to be a dangerous development or even to be a literacy technology.

The history of literacy includes many technological developments that we never stop to consider:

- Clay tablets
- Papyrus paper
- Wood pulp paper
- Quill pens and inkwells
- The printing press
- The fountain pen
- The pencil
- The typewriter
- Carbon copy paper
- The disposable plastic pen
- The "Xerox" copier

In their time, some of these developments were just as controversial as a pencil with an eraser. For example, in 1874, Samuel Clemens (Mark Twain) wrote that he was struggling "to get the hang of this new fangled writing machine," but he marveled, that it "piles an awful stack of words on one page … [without scattering] ink blots around." This now obsolete technology altered the office work of nineteenth-century companies because they could keep detailed records much more easily (especially with the additional invention of carbon paper). Typewriters also allowed authors like Clemens to draft and deliver their manuscripts with greater efficiency. But as one critic of new literacy technologies named Nicholas Carr reports, the technology of the typewriter may also have affected not only how a text was written but also what was written. For example, another early user of the typewriter, the German writer Frederick Nietzsche, felt that his writing became more direct and more compact when he changed from handwriting to typing. Now, Carr poses a similar question about computer technologies: Does how we read affect what we can (and cannot) comprehend?

Those who are very comfortable with the latest literacy technologies may be tempted to dismiss those critics as elders unable to embrace the new and afraid of change. However, even one of the inventors of the virtual reality of the Internet, Jaron Lanier, now worries that the social networks of the more interactive Web 2.0 promote shallow thinking and stifle individual creativity. This chapter consists of current readings on literacy and technology, such as Nick Bilton's defense of digital literacy, and historical ones like William Powers' analysis of centuries-old paper. These texts, along with reading questions, freewriting activities, and visual elements, are designed to develop the reading and writing abilities required for academic study. After each reading, you will find a set of questions that are divided into Close Reading Questions, Analytical Writing/Discussion, and Further Options. Some questions involve the same investigation of multiple perspectives, cultural influences, and historical trends that were introduced in Chapters 1. Answering some and discussing more of the post-reading questions will prepare you to complete the final assignment options. These final writing assignments will ask you to assert your own, more informed perspective on this topic. This chapter asks: **What do you think are the effects of computer technologies on our literacy practices?**

Freewrite 1: Initial Impressions

Before you read the conflicting and often vehement opinions of the writers in the rest of this chapter, freewrite to explore your own thoughts and experiences. Try answering some of the following questions:

- How often do you rely on the computer and its associated technologies, such as web pages and word processing, when you read and write?

- What are some of your most and least favorite various ways to use new media technologies when you read and write?

- When and why do you rely on paper and print sources when you write and read?

- What effects, if any, do you think new technologies have had on your literacy? In other words, how might your reading and writing practices be different if you did not use these newer technologies?

THE GUTENBERG ELEGIES: THE FATE OF READING IN AN ELECTRONIC AGE

by Sven Birkerts

As computers became household items during the 1980s and the Internet became widely used in the 1990s, concerns about their effect on our reading practices developed. Sven Birkerts captured this cautious spirit in his highly regarded book *The Gutenberg Elegies: The Fate of Reading in an Electronic Age*. As an essayist, a professor, and a literary critic, Birkerts has continued to express the joys of literature as well as his concerns about our reading habits in such works as *Reading Life: Books for the Ages* (2007) and "Resisting the Kindle" (2009). This excerpt is taken from *The Gutenberg Elegies,* published in 1994.

In the fall of 1992, I taught a course called "The American Short Story" to undergraduates at a local college. I assembled a set of readings that I thought would appeal to the tastes of the average undergraduate and felt relatively confident. We would begin with Washington Irving, then move on quickly to Hawthorne, Poe, James, and Jewett, before connecting with the progressively more accessible works of our century. I had expected that my students would enjoy "The Legend of Sleepy Hollow," be amused by its caricatures and ghost-story element. Nothing of the kind. Without exception they found the story over long, verbose, a chore. I wrote their reactions off to the fact that it was the first assignment and that most students would not have hit their reading stride yet. When we got to Hawthorne and Poe, I had the illusion that things were going better.

But then came Henry James' "Brooksmith" and I was completely derailed. I began the class, as I always do, by soliciting casual responses of the "I liked it" and "I hated it" sort. My students could barely muster the energy for a thumbs-up-or-down. It was as though some pneumatic pump had sucked out the last dregs of their spirits. "Bad day, huh?" I ventured. Persistent questioning revealed that it was the

For better formatting of text below, SEE pp. 343–46 of 1e

reading that had undone them. But why? What was the problem? I had to get to the bottom of their stupefaction before this relatively—I thought—available tale.

I asked: Was it a difficulty with the language, the style of writing? Nods all around. Well, let's be more specific. Was it vocabulary, sentence length, syntax? "Yeah, sort of," said one student, "but it was more just the whole thing." Hmmmmm. Well then, I said, we should consider this. I questioned whether they understood the basic plot. Sure, they said. A butler's master dies and the butler can't find another place as good. He loses one job after another—usually because he quits—then falls into despair and disappears, probably to end it all. "You don't find this moving?" One or two students conceded the pathos of the situation, but then the complaints resurfaced, with the original complainer chiming in again that it was not the story so much as "the whole thing."

The whole thing. What whole thing? My tone must have reflected my agitation, my impatience with their imprecision. But then, after endless going around, it stood revealed: These students were entirely defeated by James's prose—the medium of it—as well as by the assumptions that underlie it. It was not the vocabulary, for they could make out most of the words; and not altogether the syntax, although they admitted to discomfort, the occasional abandoned sentences. What they really could not abide was what the vocabulary, the syntax, the ironic indirection, and so forth, were communicating. *They didn't get it*, and their not getting it angered them, and they expressed their anger by drawing around themselves a cowl of ill-tempered apathy. Students whom I knew to be quick and resourceful in other situations suddenly retreated into glum illiteracy. "I dunno," said the spokesman. "the whole thing just bugged me—I couldn't get into it."

Disastrous though the class had been, I drove home in an excited mood. What had happened, I started to realize, was that I had encountered a conceptual ledge, one that may mark a break in historical continuity. This was more than just a bad class—it was a corroboration of something I had been on the verge of grasping for years. You could have drawn a lightbulb over my head and turned it on.

What is this ledge, and what does it have to do with the topic I have embarked upon? To answer the second question: Everything. As I wrote before: the world we have known, the world of our myths and references and shared assumptions, is being changed by powerful forces. We are living in the midst of a momentous paradigm shift. My classroom experience, which in fact represents hundreds of classroom experiences, can be approached diagnostically.

This is not a simple case of students versus Henry James. We are not concerned with an isolated clash of sensibilities, his and theirs. Rather we are standing in one spot along a ledge—or, better, a fault line—dividing one order from another. In place of James we could as easily put Joyce or Woolf or Shakespeare or Ralph Ellison. It would be the same. The point is that the collective experience of these students, most of whom were born in the early 1970s, has rendered a vast portion of our cultural heritage utterly alien. *That* is the breaking point: it describes where their understandings and aptitudes give out. What is at issue is not diction, not syntax, but everything that diction and syntax serve. Which is to say, an entire system of beliefs, values, and cultural aspirations.

In Henry James are distilled many of the elements I would discuss. He is inward and subtle, a master of ironies and indirections; his work manifests a care for the range of moral distinctions. And one cannot "get" him without paying heed to the twist and turn of the language. James's world, and the dramas that take place in that world, are predicated on the idea of individuals in an organic relationship with their societies. In his universe, each one of those individuals are still surrounded by an aura of importance; their actions and decisions are felt to count for something.

I know that the society of James's day was also repressive to many, and was, further, invested in certain now-discredited assumptions of empire. I am not going to argue for its return, certainly not in that form. But this was not the point, at least not in the discussions I pursued with my students. For we did, after our disastrous James session, begin to question not only our various readings, but also the reading act itself and their relation to it. And what emerged was this: that they were not, with a few exceptions, readers—never had been; that they had always occupied themselves with music, TV, and videos; that they had difficulty slowing down enough to concentrate on prose of any density; that they had problems with what they thought of as archaic diction, with allusions, with vocabulary that seemed "pretentious"; that they were especially uncomfortable with indirect or interior passages, indeed with any deviations from straight plot; and that they were put off by ironic tone because it flaunted superiority and made them feel that they were missing something. The list is partial.

All of this confirmed my longstanding suspicion that, having grown up in an electronic culture, my students would naturally exhibit certain aptitudes and lack others. But the implications, as I began to realize, were rather staggering, especially if one thinks of this not as a temporary generational disability, but rather a permanent turn. If this were true of my twenty-five undergraduates, I reasoned, many of them from relatively advantaged backgrounds, then it was probably true for most of their generation. And not only theirs, but for generations on either side of them as well. What this meant was not, narrowly, that a large sector of our population would not be able to enjoy certain works of literature, but that a much more serious situation was developing. For, in fact, our entire collective subjective history—the soul of our societal body—is encoded in print. Is encoded, and has for countless generations been passed along by way of the word, mainly through books. I'm not talking about facts and information here, but the somewhat more elusive soft data, the expressions that tell us who we are and who we have been, that are the record of individuals living in different epochs—that are, in effect, the cumulative speculations of the species. If a person turns from print—finding it too slow, too hard, irrelevant to the excitements of the present—then what happens to that person's sense of culture and continuity?

These issues are too large for mere analysis; they are over-determined. There is no way to fish one strand and think it through. Yet think we must, even if we have to be clumsy and obvious at times. We are living in a society and culture that is in dissolution. Pack this paragraph with your headlines about crime, eroded values, educational decline, what have you. There are many causes, many explanations. But behind them all, vague and menacing, is this recognition: that the understandings and assumptions that were formerly operative in society no longer feel valid. Things have shifted; they keep shifting. We all feel a desire for connection, for meaning, but we don't seem to know what to connect with what, and we are utterly at sea about our places as individuals in the world at large. The maps no longer describe the terrain we inhabit. There is no clear path to the future. We trust that the species will blunder on, and we don't know where to. We feel imprisoned in a momentum that is not of our own making.

I am not about to suggest that all of this comes of not reading Henry James. But I will say that of all this comes not being *able* to read James or any other emissary from that recent but rapidly vanishing world. Our historically sudden transition into the electronic culture has thrust us into a place of unknowing. We have been stripped not only of familiar habits and ways, but of familiar points of moral and psychological reference. Looking at our society, we see no real leaders, no real figures of wisdom. Not a brave new world at all, but a fearful one.

Close Reading Questions

1. Beyond representing an admittedly "disastrous" class, what larger concerns does Birkerts think this classroom example represents? In other words, what do you think is the thesis of this reading?

2. Using annotated comments or double-entry notes (for more, see pp. 10–12 in Chapter 1 on Reading), what are two or three assertions by Birkerts with which you strongly agree or disagree?

3. Birkerts concludes this excerpt with a claim for which he provides little evidence. What examples can you provide for his conclusion that we live in a "fearful" world, and how can you connect these supports to his concern about the reading habits of his students?

Analytical Writing/Discussion

4. Birkerts admits that his students, who grew up in an electronic culture of televisions and computers, "exhibit certain aptitudes and lack others." What abilities does he think they specifically lack, and what positive aptitudes do you think they might possess? (Multiple Perspectives)

5. As an excerpt from the first chapter of Birkerts' book, this reading includes several strong assertions about major cultural changes. Pick one of Birkerts' statements about these changes, and why do you think this "permanent turn" is or is not underway? (Cultural Influences)

6. In Chapter 1 on Reading, a brief history of literacy standards is presented (see p. 17). How do you think that history, and the graph of rising standards in particular, can be used to support or challenge Birkerts? (Historical Trends)

Further Options

7. In Chapter 5 on Rhetoric, the three appeals by ethos (character), pathos (emotions), and logos (reason) are explained (see pp. 105–106). Which of these three appeals do you think Birkerts uses most or least effectively, and why?

8. Writing in 1994, Birkerts could not consider the increased access to books, and great literature in particular, created by e-reading devices, such as the Kindle. However, later in 2009, he wrote in opposition of e-readers, fearing the "page-to-screen transfer." Research his article titled "Resisting the Kindle" (*The Atlantic* 3/2/09). Why do you find his more recent argument to be convincing or not?

FROM PENCILS TO PIXELS: THE STAGES OF LITERACY TECHNOLOGY

by Dennis Baron

> As a professor who has studied digital technologies and regularly writes a blog on this topic, Baron is a highly regarded expert in this field. As his title suggests, Baron traces the development of such literacy technologies as pencils and the pixel-filled screens of computer monitors. Baron has expanded this article from 2000 into a book titled *A Better Pencil: Readers, Writers, and the Digital Revolution* (2009).

The computer, the latest development in writing technology, promises, or threatens, to change literacy practices for better or worse, depending on your point of view. For many of us, the computer revolution came long ago, and it has left its mark on the way we do things with words. We take word processing as a given. We don't have typewriters in our offices anymore ....

I will not join in the hyperbole of predictions about what the computer will or will not do for literacy, though I will be the first to praise computers, to acknowledge the importance of the computer in the last fifteen years of my own career as a writer and to predict that in the future the computer will be put to communications uses we cannot now even begin to imagine ....

The Stages of Literacy Technologies

Each new literacy technology begins with a restricted communications function and is available only to a small number of initiates. Because of the high cost of the technology and general ignorance about it, practitioners keep it to themselves at first—either on purpose or because nobody else has any use for it—and then, gradually, they begin to mediate the technology for the general public. The technology expands beyond this "priestly" class when it is adapted to familiar functions often associated with an older, accepted form of communication. As costs decrease and the technology becomes better able to mimic more ordinary or familiar communications, a new literacy spreads across a population. Only then does the technology come into its own, no longer imitating the previous forms given us by the earlier communications technology but creating new forms and new possibilities for communication ... [Most literacy] technologies, including writing itself, were initially met with suspicion as well as enthusiasm.

The pencil may be old, but like the computer today ..., it is an indisputable example of a communications technology ... [As Bill Henderson explains, Henry David] Thoreau's father founded "the first quality pencil [factory] in America." In Thoreau's day, a good pencil was hard to find, and until Thoreau's father and uncle began making pencils in the New World, the best ones were imported from Europe. The family fortune was built on the earnings of the Thoreau Pencil Company, and Thoreau not only supported his sojourn at Walden Pond and his trip to the Maine woods with pencil profits, he himself perfected some of the techniques of pencil-making that made Thoreau pencils so desirable.

The pencil may seem a simple device in contrast to the computer, but although it has fewer parts, it too is an advanced technology. The engineer Henry Petroski (1990) portrays the development of the wood-cased pencil as a paradigm of the engineering process, hinging on the solution of two essential problems: finding the correct blend of graphite and clay so that the "lead" is not too soft or too brittle; and getting the lead into the cedar wood case so that it doesn't break when the point is sharpened or when pressure is applied during use. Pencil technologies involve advanced design techniques, the preparation and purification of graphite, the mixing of graphite with various clays, the baking and curing of the lead mixture, its extrusion into leads, and the preparation and finishing of the wood casings. Petroski observes that pencil-making also involves a knowledge of dyes, shellacs, resins, clamps, solvents, paints, woods, rubber, glue, printing ink, waxes, lacquer, cotton, drying equipment, impregnating processes, high-temperature furnaces, abrasives, and mixing (Petroski, 12). These are no simple matters. A hobbyist cannot decide to make a wood-cased pencil at home and go out to the craft shop for a set of instructions. Pencil-making processes were from the outset proprietary secrets as closely guarded as any Macintosh code.

The development of the pencil is also a paradigm of the development of literacy. In the two hundred fifty years between its invention, in the 1560s, and its perfection at John Thoreau and Company, as well as in the factories of Conte in France, and Staedtler and Faber in Germany, the humble wood pencil

Republished with permission of Utah State University Press, from *Passions, Pedagogies, and 21st Century Technologies* edited by Gail E Hawisher and Cynthia L Selfe (1999). Permission conveyed through Copyright Clearance Center, Inc.

underwent several changes in form, greatly expanded its functions, and developed from a curiosity of use to cabinet-makers, artists, and note-takers into a tool so universally employed for writing that we seldom give it any thought.

The Technology of Writing

Of course, the first writing technology was writing itself. Just like … the computer, writing itself was once an innovation strongly resisted by traditionalists because it was unnatural and untrustworthy. Plato was one leading thinker who spoke out strongly against writing, fearing that it would weaken our memories. Pessimistic complaints about new literacy technologies, like those made by Plato, by Bill Henderson, and by Henderson's idol, Henry David Thoreau, are balanced by inflated predictions of how technologies will change our lives for the better. According to one school of anthropology, the invention of writing triggered a cognitive revolution in human development (for a critique of this so-called Great Divide theory of writing, see Street 1984). Historians of print are fond of pointing to the invention of the printing press in Europe as the second great cognitive revolution (Eisenstein 1979). The spread of electric power, the invention of radio, and later television, all promised similar bio-cultural progress. Now, the influence of computers on more and more aspects of our existence has led futurologists to proclaim that another technological threshold is at hand. Computer gurus offer us a brave new world of communications where we will experience cognitive changes of a magnitude never before known. Of course, [some] … think otherwise.

Both the supporters and the critics of new communication technologies like to compare them to the good, or bad, old days. Jay Bolter disparages the typewriter as nothing more than a machine for duplicating text, and as such, he argues, it has not changed writing at all. In contrast, Bolter characterizes the computer as offering a paradigm shift not seen since the invention of the printing press, or for that matter, since the invention of writing itself. But, when the typewriter first began to sweep across America's offices, it too promised to change writing radically, in ways never before imagined. So threatening was the typewriter to the traditional literacies that in 1938, the *New York Times* editorialized against the machine that depersonalized writing, usurping the place of "writing with one's own hand."

The development of writing itself illustrates the stages of technological spread. We normally assume that writing was invented to transcribe speech, but that is not strictly correct. The earliest Sumerian inscriptions, dating from ca. 3500 BCE, record not conversations, incantations, or other sorts of oral utterances, but land sales, business transactions, and tax accounts (Crystal 1987). Clay tokens bearing similar marks appear for several thousand years before these first inscriptions. It is often difficult to tell when we are dealing with writing and when with art (the recent discovery of 10,000-year-old stone carvings in Syria has been touted as a possible missing link in the art-to-writing chain), but the tokens seem to have been used as a system of accounting from at least the 9th millennium BCE [9000 BCE]. They are often regarded as the first examples of writing, and it is clear that they are only distantly related to actual speech …. So far as we know, writing itself begins not as speech transcription but as a relatively restricted and obscure record-keeping shorthand.

As innovative uses for the literacy technology are tried out, practitioners may also adapt it to older, more familiar forms in order to gain acceptance from a wider group. Although writing began as a tool of the bean counters, it eventually added a second, magical/religious function, also restricted and obscure as a tool of priests. For writing to spread into a more general population in the ancient world, it had first to gain acceptance by approximating spoken language. Once writers—in a more "modern" sense of the word—discovered what writing could do, there was no turning back …. Of course, writing never spread very greatly in the ancient world. William Harris (1989) argues convincingly that no more than 10 percent of the classical Greek or Roman populations could have been literate. One reason for this must be that writing technology remained both cumbersome and expensive: writing instruments, paints, and inks had to be handmade, and writing surfaces like clay tablets, wax tablets, and papyrus had to be laboriously prepared. Writing, therefore, remained exclusive, until cheap paper became available, and the printing press made mass production of written texts more affordable and less labor-intensive ....

The Pencil as Technology

Just as writing was not designed initially as a way of recording speech, the pencil was not invented to be a writing device. The ancient lead-pointed stylus was used to scribe lines—the lead made a faint pencil-like mark on a surface, suitable for marking off measurements but not for writing. The modern pencil, which holds not lead but a piece of graphite encased in a wooden handle, doesn't come on the scene until the 1560s ....

The sixteenth-century pencil consists of a piece of graphite snapped or shaved from a larger block, then fastened to a handle for ease of use. The first pencils were made by joiners, woodworkers specializing in making furniture, to scribe measurements in wood. Unlike the traditional metal-pointed scribing tools, pencils didn't leave a permanent dent in the wood. By the time Gesner observed the pencil, it had been adopted as a tool by note-takers, natural scientists, or others who needed to write, sketch, or take measurements in the field. Carrying pens and ink pots outdoors was cumbersome. Early pencils had knobs at one end so that they could be fastened with string or chain to a notebook, creating the precursor to the laptop computer.

Pencils were also of use to artists. In fact, the word pencil means "little tail" and refers not only to the modern wood-cased pencil but to the artist's brush. Ink and paint are difficult to erase: they must be scraped off a surface with a knife or painted over. But, graphite pencil marks were more easily erased by using bread crumbs, and of course later by erasers made of rubber—in fact the eraser substance (caoutchouc, the milky juice of tropical plants such as ficus) was called *rubber* because it was used to rub out pencil marks ....

Thoreau set about to improve his father's pencil. According to Petroski, Thoreau began his research in the Harvard Library. But then, as now, there was little written on pencil manufacture. Somehow, Thoreau learned to grind graphite more finely than had been done before and to mix it with clay in just the right proportion .... [H]is improvements on the pencil-making process, combined with the high import duty imposed on British pencils after the War of 1812, led to great demand for Thoreau pencils .... His pencils sold for seventy-five cents a dozen, higher than other brands ....

The Computer and the Pattern of Literacy Technology

Writing was not initially speech transcription, and pencils were first made for woodworkers, not writers. Similarly, the mainframe computer when it was introduced was intended to perform numerical calculations too tedious or complex to do by hand. Personal computers were not initially meant for word-processing either, though that has since become one of their primary functions.

Mainframe line editors were so cumbersome that even computer programmers preferred to write their code with pencil and paper. Computer operators actually scorned the thought of using their powerful number-crunchers to process mere words. Those who braved the clumsy technology to type text were condemned to using a system that seemed diabolically designed to slow a writer down well below anything that could be done on an IBM [electric typewriter] or even with a pencil ....

Early word-processing software for personal computers did little to improve the situation. At last, in the early 1980s, programs like WordStar began to produce text that looked more like the typing that many writers had become used to. Even so, writers had to put up with screens cluttered with formatting characters .... [P]aragraphs had to be reformatted every time they were revised. Furthermore, printed versions of text seldom matched what was on the computer screen, turning page design into a laborious trial-and-error session. Adding to the writer's problems was the fact that the screen itself looked nothing like the piece of paper the text would ultimately be printed on. The first PC screens were grayish-black with green phosphor letters, displaying considerably less than a full page of text.... Today we expect displays not only with black on white, just like real paper, and high resolution text characters, but also with color, which takes us a step beyond what we could do with ordinary typing paper.

If the initial technical obstacles to word processing on a PC weren't enough to keep writers away from the new technology, they still had to come up with the requisite $5,000 or more ... for an entry-level personal computer. Only die-hards and visionaries considered computer word processing worth pursuing, and even they held on to their [electric typewriters] and their Bic [pens] just in case .... The next generation of word processors gave us WYSIWYG: "what you see is what you get" and that helped less-adventurous writers make the jump to computers. Only when Macintosh and Windows operating systems allowed users to create on-screen documents that looked and felt like the old, familiar documents they were used to creating on electric typewriters did word-processing really become popular. At the same time, start-up costs decreased significantly and with new, affordable hardware, computer writing technology quickly moved from the imitation of typing to the inclusion of graphics.

Of course that, too, was not an innovation in text production. We've been pasting up text and graphics for ages. The decorated medieval charters of eleventh-century England are a perfect parallel to our computerized graphics a millennium later. But just as writing in the middle ages was able to move beyond earlier limitations, computer word processing has now moved beyond the texts made possible by earlier technologies by adding not just graphics, but animation, video, and sound to documents. In addition, Hypertext and HTML allow us to create links between documents or paths within them, both of which offer restructured alternatives to linear reading ....

Conclusion

As the old technologies become automatic and invisible, we find ourselves more concerned with fighting or embracing what's new. Ten years ago, math teachers worried that if students were allowed to use calculators, they wouldn't learn their arithmetic tables. Regardless of the value parents and teachers still place on knowing math facts, calculators are now indispensable in math class. When we began to use computers in university writing classes, instructors didn't tell students about the spell-check programs on their word processors, fearing the students would forget how to spell. The hackers found the spelling checkers anyway, and now teachers complain if their students don't run the spell check before they turn their papers in.

Even the pencil itself didn't escape the wrath of educators. One of the major technological advances in pencil-making occurred in the early twentieth century, when manufacturers learned to attach rubber tips to inexpensive wood pencils by means of a brass clamp. But American schools allowed no crossing out. Teachers preferred pencils without erasers, arguing that students would do better, more premeditated work if they didn't have the option of revising. The students won this one, too: eraserless pencils are now extremely rare. Artists use them, because artists need special erasers in their work; golfers use pencils without erasers, too, perhaps to keep themselves honest. As for the no-crossing-out rule, writing teachers now routinely warn students that writers never get it right the first time, and we expect them to revise their work endlessly, until it is polished to perfection.

The computer has indeed changed the ways some of us do things with words, and the rapid changes in technological development suggest that it will continue to do so in ways we cannot yet foresee .... [R]esearchers tend to look at the cutting edge when they examine how technology affects literacy. But, technology has a trailing edge as well as a down side, and studying how computers are put to use raises serious issues in the politics of work and the mechanisms of social control. Andrew Sledd pessimistically views the computer as actually reducing the amount of literacy needed for the low end of the workplace: "As for ordinary kids, they will get jobs ... dragging computerized Cheerios boxes across computerized check-out counters."

Despite Sledd's legitimate fear that in the information age computers will increase the gap between active text production and routine, alienating, assembly-line text processing, in the United States we live in an environment that is increasingly surrounded by text .... The simplest one-word Web search returns pages of documents, which themselves link to the expanding universe of text in cyberspace ....

We have a way of getting so used to writing technologies that we come to think of them as natural rather than technological. We assume that pencils are a natural way to write because they are old—or at least because we have come to think of them as being old .... Whether the computer will one day be as taken-for-granted as the pencil is an intriguing question. One thing is clear: were Thoreau alive today he would not be writing with a pencil of his own manufacture .... More likely, he would be keyboarding his complaints about the information superhighway on a personal computer that he assembled from spare parts in his garage.

References

Crystal, David. 1987. *The Cambridge Encyclopedia of Language*. Cambridge: Cambridge Univ. Press, p. 196.
Eisenstein, Elizabeth L. 1979. *The Printing Press as an Agent of Change*. Cambridge: Cambridge Univ. Press.
Harris, William V. 1989. *Ancient Literacy*. Cambridge: Harvard Univ. Press.
Henderson, Bill. 1994. "No E-Mail from Walden." *New York Times* (March 16), p. A15.
Petroski, Henry. 1990. *The Pencil: A History of Design and Circumstance*. New York: Alfred A. Knopf.
Sledd, Andrew. 1988. Readin' not Riotin': The Politics of Literacy. *College English* 50: 495–507.
Street, Brian V. 1984. *Literacy in Theory and Practice*. Cambridge: Cambridge Univ. Press.

Close Reading Questions

1. Baron explains that we tend to become "so used to writing technologies that we come to think of them as natural." What is one detail about writing itself and another on the pencil that surprised you?

2. To understand the pencil as a writing technology, consider its manufacture. According to Baron, what are several of the distinct steps required in the making of a pencil?

3. Neither the pencil nor the computer are being used now primarily for their original purpose. What were the original purposes of the pencil and the computer? Why do you think the later, innovative use led to the widespread acceptance of each technology? (Historical Trends)

Analytical Writing/Discussion

4. Pick a quotation from Baron that either describes or contradicts your experiences with the computer. Then present this quotation using a signal phrase, such as "According to Dennis Baron, …" Cite it properly and elaborate on its meaning (see pp. 81–83 of Chapter 4 for more on Quotations and Citation). In what ways does this quotation describe or contradict your experiences?

5. Each new literacy technology is considered by its critics to be a negative influence. What do you think were some of the most or least significant criticisms of writing and later the computer? Why do you think each technology has been met with criticism from some skeptics? (Cultural Influences)

6. How can you use the pattern of technological resistance to support or oppose the detractors of computers and the Internet, such as Birkerts? (Multiple Perspectives)

Further Options

7. In an argument, the writer's character and tone are crucial to his or her ability to be persuasive (see p. 106 on "ethos" in Chapter 5). In what ways, if any, do you think the tone of the arguments by Baron and Birkerts differs? Why do you think (or not) that one of these arguments is more persuasive?

8. Baron, along with many others concerned about computers, worry that a "digital divide" exists between those that have easy access to computers and those that do not. Using some of the strategies presented in Chapter 4, research the development and distribution of inexpensive computers to less privileged people both in the United States and other countries. To what degree do you think the digital divide can and should be overcome by further technological and political developments?

FIGURE 10.1   The Technological Advances of Paper and Pencil

THE PERSISTENCE OF PAPER

by William Powers

As part of the Discussion Paper Series at Harvard University, William Powers wrote an extended essay of 75 pages titled "Hamlet's Blackberry: Why Paper Is Eternal." The essay from 2007 was received so well that Powers, a media critic for the *National Journal*, has written a related book: *Hamlet's BlackBerry: A Practical Philosophy for Building a Good Life in the Digital Age* (2010). In the following excerpt from the original essay, Powers helps his audience take a second look at paper, a literacy technology that most of us never stop to consider, and he argues that some of the apparent limitations of paper actually constitute its strengths for readers.

The condition of American journalism in the first decade of the twenty-first century can be expressed in a single unhappy word: crisis. Whether it's a plagiarism scandal at a leading newspaper, the fall from grace of a network anchorman, or a reporter behind bars, the news about the news seems to be one emergency after another. But the crisis that has the greatest potential to undermine what the craft does best is a quiet one that rarely draws the big headlines: the crisis of paper. Paper's long career as a medium of human communication, and in particular as a purveyor of news, may be ending ....

There is a sense in the culture, inchoate but unmistakable, that all print media, including magazines and books, are careening toward obsolescence. This is hardly a new idea. Since the advent of the computer in the mid-twentieth century, futurists have been foretelling the death of paper-based communication. So far, the obituaries have all been wrong or at least premature. Time and again, advances in computer technology that were supposed to make hard-copy media obsolete failed to do so. Paper lived on.

But with the rise of the Internet, the popularity of online media outlets, and the proliferation of devices to conveniently access those outlets—personal computers, cell phones, personal digital assistants, e-books, etc.—a paperless media world often seems not just possible or likely but inevitable. After all, in countless other ways, paper already has either surrendered to the newer media or is in rapid retreat. Most financial transactions .... can now be done online. The personal letter, which handily survived the advent of the telephone, has been largely done in by e-mail. Even libraries, those seeming bastions of paper culture, are conspirators in paper's demise. Most public and university libraries long ago traded their card catalogs for electronic databases .... And the content of the libraries themselves has been moving online, too, as librarians rush, often with outside partners, such as Google, to create digital doppelgangers of their holdings ....

In short, paper is an increasingly subordinate medium. Like a brain-dead patient on life support, it lives because other technologies allow it to live. The only question, it seems, is when we will put paper out of its misery .... [P]aper's days are most certainly numbered.

Or are they? We live in an age obsessed with new technologies. The sophisticated modern consumer knows the fine points of all the latest media devices. Comparisons between competing technologies—PC versus Mac, plasma versus LCD, Blackberry versus iPhone, satellite versus terrestrial radio—are a staple

From HAMLET'S BLACKBERRY: WHY PAPER IS ETERNAL by WILLIAM POWERS. Copyright © 2010 by William Powers. Reprinted by permission.

of consumer culture. There are countless popular magazines dedicated to helping us stay abreast of our media devices, and they cover every imaginable kind of technology except the one on which the magazines themselves are printed. Paper is the most successful communications innovation of the last 2000 years, the one that has lasted the longest and had the profoundest effect on civilization. One can easily make the case that without the technology that is paper, there would be no civilization. Yet most of the time, we don't even think of paper as a technology. And so, we don't ask the questions we routinely ask about other technologies: How does it work? What are its strengths and weaknesses? Is it easy and enjoyable to use?

Taking a Second Look at Paper

Paper doesn't seem to require much consideration because it's so simple: a thin, flexible material that reflects light, crisply displaying any marks you make on it. What more is there to say? It has no circuits or chips, no ports, touchpad, speakers, or screen. It doesn't link to any networks or "sync" with other devices. It won't download files, burn CDs, or play movies. It just sits there, mute and passive, like a dog that knows one trick, waiting to perform it again ....

Although paper appears to be a relatively "dumb" medium, it too performs tasks that require special abilities. And many of paper's tricks, the useful purposes it serves, are similarly products of its long relationship with people. There are cognitive, cultural, and social dimensions to the human–paper dynamic that come into play every time any kind of paper, from a tiny Post-it note to a groaning Sunday newspaper, is used to convey, retrieve, or store information. Paper does these jobs in a way that pleases us, which is why, for centuries we have liked having it around. It's also why we will never give it up as a medium, not completely. For some of the roles paper currently fulfills in our media lives, there is no better alternative currently available. And the most promising candidates are technologies that are striving to be more, not less, like paper ....

From the end of World War II through 1990—a period that coincides exactly with the rise of the computer—U.S. consumption of paper grew dramatically. Even in the last fifteen years, as the Internet has made the networking of computers seamless, and e-mail and electronic documents have proliferated, consumption of paper for communications (writing and printing) has not declined. One late twentieth-century study found that when offices began using e-mail, paper consumption increased by an average of 40 percent. "The World Wide Web, far from decreasing paper consumption, served to increase the amount of printing done at home and in the office," wrote Abigail J. Sellen and Richard H. R. Harper in their 2002 book, *The Myth of the Paperless Office.* "With the Web, people could access more information more easily than before, but though they used digital means to find and retrieve information, they still preferred to print it out on paper when they wanted to read it." ....

The persistence of paper flies in the face of a widely held popular assumption about technology, propagated over the years by breathless futurists and science-fiction writers. This is the notion that newer, more advanced devices inevitably kill off older ones, as the automobile famously did to the buggy whip. Paul Duguid of the University of California at Berkeley calls this concept "supersession," meaning "the idea that each new technological type vanquishes or subsumes its predecessors." ... Obviously, some technologies do supersede others. Paper itself is a case in point. When it first appeared about 2,000 years ago, it was an astonishing new gizmo, the iPod of its day. Tradition credits the invention to a Chinese official named Cai Lun, a eunuch of the imperial court. Hoping to improve on the silk-based tissuey medium that the Chinese then used for writing, he experimented with various fibrous materials including tree bark, hemp, old rags, and fish nets. These were macerated to a pulp, which was then mixed with water and drained through some kind of screen. When the resulting soggy mat dried, it was paper.

Cai Lun introduced his innovation to the court in 105 A.D and the Chinese became the first great papermaking culture. But, the new technology did not immediately race across the world and triumph over existing media. It spread slowly, first to Korea and Japan, then west across Central Asia. In the year 751 A.D., the Chinese lost a battle in Turkestan. Some of the Chinese soldiers who were taken prisoner knew how to make paper and turned over the secret to their Turkish captors, and soon papermaking was underway in Samarkand. From there, the technology moved around the Middle East and finally, at some point around 1,000 A.D., it reached Western Europe. The oldest known example of Western paper is *The Missal of Silos*, a church manuscript from the eleventh century preserved in a Benedictine abbey in central Spain.

When paper arrived in a given society, rather than wiping out the existing communications media—which were, principally, papyrus and parchment—it moved in beside them. It was accepted and embraced to varying degrees, and over different stretches of time, depending on social, cultural, and political circumstances. In Egypt, for instance, it appears that paper was quickly recognized as an improvement over the relatively inflexible and less durable parchment ....

Even as paper thrived in the Middle East, Europeans received it tepidly. "The early paper of Europe was regarded with disfavour," writes historian Dard Hunter, "as not only was it higher in price and more fragile than parchment, which had been used for bookmaking, but it was distrusted on account of its introduction by Jews and Arabs." In 1221, the Holy Roman Emperor Frederick II issued a decree forbidding the use of paper for public documents. The suspect medium eventually caught on in Europe, of course, and ultimately superseded the older media that were there when it arrived. But that happened over many hundreds of years. By the middle of the fifteenth century, when Johannes Gutenberg invented the movable-type printing press, paper had been in use on the Continent for more than four centuries. Yet of the 180 bibles Gutenberg is thought to have printed, about one-quarter had pages made of vellum, a parchment made of animal skin that was still preferred for important documents because of its beauty and durability.

In With the New

In the literature of media studies, there is a determinist school, which holds that technologies shape society. Whether it's the printing press, the telegraph, or the cell phone, the new device sets the tune and people basically dance along. This is an appealingly facile way of organizing history, but in practice things are far more complicated. New technologies do not come out of nowhere. They are human creations in the first place, and they succeed, or not, to the extent that they meet human needs. In other words, as much as communications media influence the way people of a particular time and place live, the reverse is also true: People have tremendous influence over how technologies evolve. Why do we still listen to the radio when television offers both sound and images? Why did the Apple Newton fail miserably, while the Palm Pilot succeeded? When it comes to communication, we are a finicky, eccentric species. As a result, information media evolve unpredictably, not in a straight line but a wild zigzag.

For instance, Gutenberg's printing press famously changed the course of history, setting the stage for the Reformation and countless other social, political, and cultural shifts. What's less well known is that the arrival of print set off a tremendous explosion in writing itself—the old-fashioned kind of writing, by hand. The handwritten books of the pre-Gutenberg era were time consuming and costly to produce, and the class of people that was exposed to such things on a regular basis was a relatively small elite. The press made printed matter widely available, which in turn popularized and democratized the idea of written expression itself. Manuscripts were still produced in great numbers. And important new inventions for writing by hand, including graphite pencils and fountain pens, appeared .... In short, even as the world-changing new technology was taking hold—and in some ways because it was taking hold—the older one gained new life ....

From One Function to Another

When a book is open on a reader's lap it is communicating; when it's sitting on a library shelf, it is storing the contents of its pages until the next reader comes along. In the last thirty years, computers and other digital devices have taken over much of the storage work that used to be paper's job .... In 1992, futurist Paul Saffo described how paper was giving up its storage role and becoming mainly an "interface." In his insightful essay, "The Electronic Piñata," Saffo wrote: "Paper today has become an increasingly volatile, disposable medium for viewing information on demand. We are solidly on our way to a future where we create and store information electronically, reducing it to paper only when we're ready to read it." ....

Why does this functional change matter? Because, it points to a fallacy in the popular "container" theory of newspapers and other paper media. As I mentioned earlier, this theory holds that it doesn't matter what vehicle is used to deliver information, as long as the information reaches its intended recipient. Of course, the main purpose of a container is storage. A Tupperware container stores last night's leftovers, and a newspaper stores news for the journey it must make between the printing plant and the reader's doorstep. But, the argument that hard-copy newspapers are just containers implies that of the two roles paper performs, only one has value: the storage role. Since that happens to be the role paper is losing over time, it's no wonder that, by the lights of the container school, paper appears doomed. Although paper's work has been shifting away from storage and toward communication, for some reason we seldom think or talk about what exactly happens when paper communicates. This is because media communication appears to be a form of transportation: Like UPS trucks, information technologies simply move the product from one place to another. However, there is one important way in which they are not like trucks at all. After information arrives at its destination, something else has to happen for the communication to be complete: The individual must interact with the medium, using his or her senses and cognitive abilities to understand the content. In the case of paper, this is the moment when we pick up a sheet, or dozens of sheets joined together to form a newspaper, magazine, or book, and begin reading. If we could get to the bottom of that moment—which we take for granted, although it's a profound, almost magical event—we might be able to say why paper has endured this far into the age of electronic media ....

What is paper? A thin, flexible, opaque material that's very good at reflecting light. We think of it as coming from trees, but it actually can be made of many different things .... [T]he essence of paper resides not in how it's made or what it's made from, but what it does. And this is where things get interesting. Like any tool, paper does some jobs well and some not so well. And our perception of its "talents" has changed over time. When paper first appeared, it was valued for its lightness and portability, as well as the efficient way it stored information. But relative to electronic media, paper is heavy and slow, and, as discussed earlier, it is no longer the default choice for information storage. In a digital world, paper actually has quite a few limitations: (1) It takes up physical space; (2) It can only be in one place at a time (virtual media can be accessed from anywhere); (3) It is difficult to alter or edit; (4) It does not play moving images or sound; and (5) It cannot network or connect to other media. The mystery is why a medium with so many disadvantages is still all around us ....

Conventional wisdom says paper lingers out of habit. The medium has been with us for more than 2,000 years, and we are having trouble letting go. In this view, paper effectively is what child psychologists call a "transitional object," a security blanket we carry around to help us feel better during the rocky passage to a more advanced, "grown-up" media future. The flaw in this thinking is the assumption that paper is inherently inferior to newer technologies … A wiser approach is to make no assumption whatsoever about paper's worth, relative status, or future, and focus instead on how it does its job, right now in the real world.

Why Paper Persists

In the last decade or so, a handful of researchers have looked at what happens when people interact with paper and, in some cases, compared that dynamic to human interactions with other media. Their findings suggest that paper has intrinsic properties that (1) make it easy and enjoyable to work with, (2) help us make sense of information, and (3) are conducive to certain kinds of reading and thinking ….

In the mid-1990s, Abigail J. Sellen and Richard H. R. Harper … conducted a study of how employees of the International Monetary Fund in Washington, D.C., managed the flow of information in their daily work. The IMF was chosen because it is a "knowledge-centered" organization that uses a lot of documents and because it had invested heavily in technology …. The study found that paper has inherent characteristics that make it useful. These are called "affordances" because they afford particular tasks. As it happens, many of paper's affordances are rooted in its limitations—its physicality, the fact that it can only be in one place, etc. In other words, its weaknesses are also its strengths. The IMF employees liked holding documents in their hands as they worked with them. They said that marking up and editing their work was easier and clearer on paper than on a screen. When working in face-to-face meetings with colleagues, they liked the way that paper documents could be conveniently passed around and discussed, something that's harder to do with a computer screen, even the smallest, lightest kind. They even appreciated the fact that paper takes up space, explaining that the clutter of paper in their offices was not as random as it appeared. Rather, the stacks and piles helped in the "thinking and planning" department by forming "a temporary holding pattern … that serves as a way of keeping available the inputs and ideas they might have use for in their current projects. This clutter also provides important contextual clues to remind them of where they were in their space of ideas." That is, the paper served as a physical representation of what was going on in their minds, giving abstract thoughts and plans "a persistent presence" in their lives.

Among the comments the IMF workers gave the researchers, the most striking one came from an employee whose job it was to review other people's written reports. This person explained why paper was better suited to that task than a computer screen. "You've got to print it out to do it properly. You have to settle down behind your desk and get into it." Those phrases, "settle down" and "get into it" suggest a state of mind associated with a particular kind of reading—the full-immersion, deep-dive kind that occurs when a reader is able to shut out the world and truly focus. Does reading on paper somehow help create that state? In a different study that looked at how people in various professions read, Sellen and Harper found that paper has four affordances that specifically assist reading:

Tangibility: This refers to the way that we navigate a paper document or book using our eyes and hands together. "When a document is on paper, we can see how long it is, we can flick through the pages … we can bend over a corner while searching for a section elsewhere. In other words, paper helps us work our way through documents."

Spatial Flexibility: When working with multiple paper texts, they can be spread out around a large area or reduced to fit a smaller space, depending on our needs.

Tailorability. With paper it's easy to underline, scribble in the margins, and otherwise annotate the text we are reading.

Manipulability. Because paper can be moved around, one can shuffle effectively among different paper sources, for example, putting one page aside in order to concentrate on another.

Newspapers got some of their best qualities from the paper they were printed on, [and] the good news is the medium itself is not going anywhere. Paper is all around us, quietly doing the same work it's been doing for centuries.

Close Reading Questions

1. What surprises you about the acceptance of paper by different cultures? How do some of these surprises support Powers' assertion that "People have a tremendous influence over how technologies evolve"? (Multiple Perspectives)

2. How does the effect of the printing press on handwriting disprove the concept of supersession?

3. According to Powers, what are some of the apparent weaknesses of paper in comparison to digital texts? Then why are these flaws actually some of the strengths of paper?

Analytical Writing/Discussion

4. According to Powers, we err if we consider paper only in terms of its function as a container to store information. Why do you agree or disagree that we also should consider the value of paper as based on its function of communication with readers? (Cultural Influences)

5. Although Powers joins Birkerts in promoting print literacy, in what ways does his argument strike you as different from the one made by Birkerts?

6. As part of his advocacy of paper, Powers ends with four of its special qualities or affordances. Which of the four affordances of reading a paper text seem most or least important to you and why?

Further Options

7. Like Powers, Baron invites his readers to consider the history of two other literacy technologies: the pencil as well as the computer (see "From Pencils to Pixels" in this chapter). In what ways do you think Powers' history of paper parallels Baron's analyses of the pencil and the computer? For example, what do you think is each writer's purpose as he presents this complex and sometimes quirky history? (Historical Trends)

8. Powers challenges the "determinist" thinking that "technology shapes society" but not the reverse: society influences technology. He asserts instead that society and technology influence each other. In what ways could you use his anti-determinist thinking to challenge Birkerts' negative assumptions about digital literacy?

NOTE: For further reading related to this chapter on print and digital literacy, see more on William Powers and his book, *Hamlet's Blackberry*, in Chapter 1 (see pp. 14–15).

Freewrite 2: Using Technology

Using one or more of your experiences with a literacy technology, such as a pencil, a pen, a paper, or a computer, try thinking about it more critically by employing the forms introduced in the first chapter.

Historical Trends

Using some of your knowledge gained from Bauerlein, Baron, and Kirschenbaum, how can you place your use of this literacy technology in a historical context? How has your use of this technology changed from or remained the same with its use by others in the past?

Once you have completed this freewrite, you may want to expand this rough writing into a more formal paper with some direct quotations from some of the historical texts by Bauerlein, Baron, and Kirschenbaum.

Cultural Influences

We often fail to recognize the cultural conditions that support the rise of and the continued use of literacy technologies. Pick a literacy technology, such as a pencil, a pen, a paper, or a computer, and use some of your knowledge gained from Birkerts, Baron, and Powers to freewrite a response to one or more of the following questions:

- What cultural conditions do you think supported the rise of this technology?
- What cultural influences do you think support its continued use?
- What change in cultural conditions do you think might lead to an increase or a decrease in its use?

Once you have completed this freewrite, you may want to expand this rough writing into a more formal paper with some direct quotations from some of the historical texts by Birkerts, Baron, and Powers.

HOW READING IS BEING REIMAGINED

by Matthew Kirschenbaum

As a graduate student pursuing a Ph.D., Kirschenbaum wrote one of the first electronic dissertations in the nation. Now a professor specializing in the use of digital technologies in English studies, he helps direct the Maryland Institute for Technology in the Humanities. The following article originally appeared in the *Chronicle of Higher Education* (2007). Kirschenbaum examines some of the history of book reading as well as the current controversy over its future.

From *How Reading is Being Reimagined* (December 7, 2007) by Matthew Kirschenbaum. Copyright © 2007 by Matthew Kirschenbaum. Reprinted by permission.

There is no doubt that it is time for a serious conversation about reading, not least because books themselves are changing.

Google, in cooperation with several dozen research libraries worldwide, is digitizing books at the rate of 3,000 a day. The noncommercial Open Content Alliance is scanning at a more modest pace but gaining ground, especially among institutions who chafe at some of the restrictions imposed by Google and its competitors. LibraryThing, an online book catalog that allows readers to list their books and find other readers with (sometimes uncannily) similar tastes, has almost 300,000 users who have collectively tagged some 20 million books. Newsweek ran a cover story on "The Future of Reading" in their November 26 issue. And on Monday, the same day that the National Endowment for the Arts released *To Read or Not to Read: A Question of National Consequence*, the follow-up to its controversial 2004 *Reading at Risk: A Survey of Literary Reading in America* report, Amazon.com launched Kindle, an e-book reader device that the *Newsweek* story describes as the "iPod of reading."

My purpose is not to debunk the NEA's most recent report, which synthesizes a number of studies to conclude that Americans—especially younger ones—are reading less, that they are reading "less well," and that these trends have disturbing implications for culture, civics, and even the national economy. The data are significant to anyone who cares about reading and its place in a 21st-century society, and deserve to be treated seriously. But clearly the report comes to us at a moment when reading and conversations about reading are in a state of flux. It's worth taking a moment to account for this broader context. High-profile projects like Google's and new devices like Kindle suggest what I call the remaking of reading, meaning that reading is being both reimagined and re-engineered, made over creatively as well as technologically.

Historically, we've placed very different values on different kinds of reading. The reading of novels and other "literary" works—precisely the core concern of the earlier NEA report—has not always enjoyed the pride of place it has in the current cultural canon. When Cervantes sent poor, mad Don Quixote on his delirious adventures at the beginning of the 17th century, there existed a popular prejudice surrounding the reading of chivalric romances. Until well into the 19th century, novel-reading was regarded in Europe as a pastime fit mostly for women and the indolent—and a potentially dangerous one, since women, especially, could not be trusted to distinguish fiction from reality. But both the 2004 and the current report are curiously devoid of historical awareness, as though there is but a single, idealized model of reading from which we have strayed.

To Read or Not to Read deploys its own self-consistent iconography to tell us what reading is. In the pages of the report we find images of an adolescent male bent over a book, a female student sitting alone reading against a row of school lockers, and a white-collar worker studying a form. These still lives of the literate represent reading as self-evident—we know it when we see it. Yet they fail to acknowledge that such images have coexisted for centuries with other kinds of reading that have their own iconography and accouterments: Medieval and early modern portraits of scholars and scribes at work at their desks show them adorned with many books (not just one), some of them bound and splayed on exotic devices for keeping them open and in view; Thomas Jefferson famously designed a lazy susan to rotate books in and out of his visual field. That kind of reading values comparison and cross-checking as much as focus and immersion—lateral reading as much as reading for depth.

That is the model of reading that seems compatible with the Web and other new electronic media. Yet it also raises fundamental questions about what it means to read, and what it means to have read something. When can we claim a book to have been read? What is the dividing line between reading and skimming? Must we consume a book in its entirety—start to finish, cover to cover—to say we have read it?

Pierre Bayard, a literature professor in France, recently made a stir with a naughty little volume called *How to Talk About Books You Haven't Read*. When I read it (well, most of it), the book provoked the most intense author envy I have ever felt—not because I too secretly enjoy perpetuating literary frauds, but because Bayard speaks to a dilemma that will be familiar to every literate person: namely, that there are far more books in the world (50 million or 60 million by the estimates I've seen) than any of us will ever have time to read. Reading, Bayard says, is as much about mastering a system of relationships among texts and ideas as it is about reading any one text in great depth. He quotes the extreme case of the fictional librarian in Robert Musil's *The Man Without Qualities* (a book Bayard admits to having only skimmed): The librarian resolutely reads no books whatsoever for fear that undue attention to any one of them will compromise the integrity of his relation to them all.

The structure of *To Read or Not to Read* presents itself as tacit acknowledgment that not all of its own text will likely be read by any one reader, since it is clearly designed to be "not read" in at least some of the ways that accord with Bayard's observations. The report is accompanied by an Executive Summary, a condensed version of the major findings. Its internal organization is carefully laid out, with summary points at the head of each chapter, topic sentences, extensive notes, sidebars, and sections labeled as conclusions.

The authors of the report would doubtlessly insist that the kind of person who reads (or doesn't read) books by French intellectuals writing about books they haven't read (or have only skimmed) is not the kind of reader who has them much worried. It's the people, especially the young ones, who are simply not reading at all that are cause for alarm. But the new report also places extreme emphasis on what it repeatedly terms "voluntary" reading. Reading that one does for work or for school doesn't "count" in this regard. While one can appreciate the motivations here—the NEA is interested in people who read because they choose to, not because they have to—it seems oddly retrograde. How many of us who count ourselves as avid readers are able to maintain clear boundaries between work and leisure anymore?

Likewise, while the authors of the report repeatedly emphasize that they include online reading in their data, the report sounds most clumsy and out of touch when referring to new media. The authors of the report tend to homogenize "the computer" without acknowledging the diversity of activity—and the diversity of reading—that takes place on its screen. Our screens are spaces where new forms like blogs and e-mail and chats commingle with remediations of older forms, like newspapers and magazines—or even poems, stories, and novels. Reading your friend's blog is not likely a replacement for reading Proust, but some blogs have been a venue for extraordinary writing, and we are not going to talk responsibly or well about what it means to read online until we stop conflating genre with value.

The report also fails to acknowledge the extent to which reading and writing have become commingled in electronic venues. The staccato rhythms of a real-time chat session are emblematic in this regard: Reading and writing all but collapse into a single unified activity. But there is a spectrum of writing online, just as there is a spectrum of reading, and more and more applications blur the line between the two. Many electronic book interfaces allow users to annotate their texts, for example; some allow users to share those notes and annotations with others (CommentPress, from the Institute for the Future of the Book, is exemplary in this regard, as is Zotero, from the Center for History and New Media at George Mason University). Alph, a project directed by Nancy Kaplan at the University of Baltimore, is developing new online reading interfaces for children; the ability to leave notes and marks behind for these young readers' peers is a signature design feature. Book Glutton, a Web service still in beta mode, provides adult users with a shared electronic library; readers write notes for other readers in the margins of the books, and this virtual marginalia persists over time, accreting in Talmudic fashion. Moreover, readers can choose to chat in real time with other readers perusing the same chapter that is on their screens.

What kind of activity is taking place here? What are the new metrics of screen literacy? I don't have that data, it's not my field, but anecdotally my instinct is that computer users are capable of projecting the same aura of deep concentration and immersion as the stereotypical bookworm. Walk into your favorite coffee shop and watch the people in front of their screens. Rather than bug-eyed, frenzied jittering, you are more likely to see calm, meditative engagement—and hear the occasional click of fingers on keyboards as the readers write.

Close Reading Questions

1. Why does the date November 26, 2007 represent the current debate over digital literacy? What event do you think a supporter or a critic of digital literacy would emphasize and why?

2. In what ways can the lateral and rapid reading associated with today's "new" Web pages actually be considered quite "old"? In other words, what historical parallels exist between today's digital reading patterns and older reading practices? (Historical Trends)

3. What do you think Kirschenbaum means when he asserts, "We are not going to talk responsibly … about what it means to read online until we stop conflating genre with value?" (If needed, please consult a dictionary, such as on the meaning of genre.) Why do you agree or disagree with Kirschenbaum's assertion?

Analytical Writing/Discussion

4. What historical information on literary reading does Kirschenbaum provide that would complicate Bauerlein's argument (see pp. 321–322)? Why do you think this historical information is enough (or not) to counter Bauerlein's pessimism? (Multiple Perspectives)

5. Kirschenbaum describes several "electronic book interfaces" for text annotation and reader interaction. Why do you agree or disagree that these programs can maintain and reinforce some of the best practices of print literacy? (Cultural Influences)

6. Reread the final paragraphs of Kirschenbaum's and Bauerlein's texts (see pp. 321–222). How can their conclusions be used as part of the larger debate over print and digital literacy?

Further Options

7. Please reread the three opening paragraphs of Kirschenbaum's essay with some of the principles of argument in mind (see pp. 321–324). How does Kirschenbaum use a concession as well as a rebuttal to engage readers who are skeptical of digital literacy?

8. Kirschenbaum warns against the assumption of a "single, idealized model of reading from which we have strayed." Looking back at the first two readings of this chapter by Birkerts and Baron, which writer do you think has best heeded or most failed to heed Kirschenbaum's warning? And why?

ONLINE LITERACY IS A LESSER KIND

by Mark Bauerlein

With a book titled *The Dumbest Generation: How the Digital Age Stupefies Young Americans* (2008), Bauerlein is not afraid to create controversy. He is a blunt critic of digital literacy, who has argued that because the typical teenager sends more than 2,000 text messages a month, he or she is less prepared to engage in face-to-face social interactions. In this article, Bauerlein examines the habits of people as they read Web pages and the effects these habits have on education today. This article from 2008 originally appeared in the *Chronicle of Higher Education*, which is read by college professors and administrators.

When Jakob Nielsen, a Web researcher, tested 232 people for how they read pages on screens, a curious disposition emerged. Dubbed by *The New York Times* "the guru of Web page 'usability,'" Nielsen has gauged user habits and screen experiences for years, charting people's online navigations and aims, using eye-tracking tools to map how vision moves and rests. In this study, he found that people took in hundreds of pages "in a pattern that's very different from what you learned in school." It looks like a capital letter F. At the top, users read all the way across, but as they proceed their descent quickens and horizontal sight contracts, with a slowdown around the middle of the page. Near the bottom, eyes move almost vertically, the lower-right corner of the page largely ignored. It happens quickly, too. "F for fast," Nielsen wrote in a column. "That's how users read your precious content."

The F-pattern isn't the only odd feature of online reading that Nielsen has uncovered in studies conducted through the consulting business Nielsen Norman Group (Donald A. Norman is a cognitive scientist who came from Apple; Nielsen was at Sun Microsystems). A decade ago, he issued an "alert" entitled "How Users Read on the Web." It opened bluntly: "They don't."

In the eye-tracking test, only one in six subjects read Web pages linearly, sentence by sentence. The rest jumped around chasing keywords, bullet points, visuals, and color and typeface variations. In another experiment on how people read e-newsletters, informational e-mail messages, and news feeds, Nielsen exclaimed, "'Reading' is not even the right word." The subjects usually read only the first two words in headlines, and they ignored the introductory sections. They wanted the "nut" and nothing else. A 2003 Nielsen warning asserted that a PDF file strikes users as a "content blob," and they won't read it unless they print it out. A "booklike" page on screen, it seems, turns them off and sends them away. Another Nielsen test found that teenagers skip through the Web even faster than adults do, but with a lower success rate for completing tasks online (55 percent compared to 66 percent). Nielsen writes: "Teens have a short attention span and want to be stimulated. That's also why they leave sites that are difficult to figure out." For them, the Web isn't a place for reading and study and knowledge. It spells the opposite. "Teenagers don't like to read a lot on the Web. They get enough of that at school."

From *Online Literacy is a Lesser Kind* (September 19, 2008) by Mark Bauerlein. Copyright © 2008 by Mark Bauerlein. Reprinted by permission.

Computers in Schools

Those and other trials by Nielsen amount to an important research project that helps explain one of the great disappointments of education in our time. I mean the huge investment schools have made in technology, and the meager returns such funds have earned. Ever since the Telecommunications Act of 1996, money has poured into public-school classrooms. At the same time, colleges have raced to out-technologize one another. But while enthusiasm swells, e-bills are passed, smart classrooms multiply, and students cheer—the results keep coming back negative. When the Texas Education Agency evaluated its Technology Immersion Pilot, a $14-million program to install wireless tools in middle schools, the conclusion was unequivocal: "There were no statistically significant effects of immersion in the first year on either reading or mathematics achievement." When University of Chicago economists evaluated California schools before and after federal technology subsidies (the E-Rate program) had granted 30 percent more schools in the state Internet access, they determined that "the additional investments in technology generated by E-Rate had no immediate impact on measured student outcomes." In March 2007, the National Center for Education Evaluation and Regional Assistance evaluated 16 award-winning education technologies and found that "test scores were not significantly higher in classrooms using selected reading and mathematics software products." Last spring a New York State school district decided to drop its laptop program after years of offering it. The school-board president announced why: "After seven years, there was literally no evidence it had any impact on student achievement—none."

Those conclusions apply to middle-school and high-school programs, not to higher education (which has yet to produce any similarly large-scale evaluations). Nevertheless, the results bear consideration by those pushing for more e-learning on campuses.

Backers, providers, and fans of new technology explain the disappointing measures as a matter of circumstance. Teachers didn't get enough training, they say, or schoolwide coordination was spotty, parents not sufficiently involved. Maybe so, to some extent, but Nielsen's studies indicate another source. Digitized classrooms don't come through for an off-campus reason, a factor largely overlooked by educators. When they add laptops to classes and equip kids with on-campus digital tools, they add something else, too: the reading habits kids have developed after thousands of hours with those same tools in leisure time.

To teachers and professors, a row of glistening new laptops in their classroom after a dozen years with nothing but chalk and blackboard, or a podium that has been transformed from a wooden stand into a multimedia console, can appear a stunning conversion. But to the average freshman walking through the door and finding a seat, it's nothing new. Our students have worked and played with computers for years. The Horatio Alger Association found that students in high school use the Internet four and a half hours per week for help with homework (*The State of Our Nation's Youth*, 2008–2009), while the National School Boards Association measures social networking at nine hours per week, much of it spent on homework help. The gap between viewpoints is huge. Educators envision a whole new pedagogy with the tools, but students see only the chance to extend long-established postures toward the screen. If digitized classrooms did pose strong, novel intellectual challenges to students, we should see some pushback on their part, but few of them complain about having to learn in new ways.

Student Reading Practices

Once again, this is not so much about the content students prefer—Facebook, YouTube, etc.—or whether they use the Web for homework or not. It is about the reading styles they employ. They race across the surface, dicing language and ideas into bullets and graphics, seeking what they already want and shunning the rest. They convert history, philosophy, literature, civics, and fine art into information, material to retrieve and pass along.

That's the drift of screen reading. Yes, it's a kind of literacy, but it breaks down in the face of a dense argument, a Modernist poem, a long political tract, and other texts that require steady focus and linear attention—in a word, slow reading. Fast scanning doesn't foster flexible minds that can adapt to all kinds of texts, and it doesn't translate into academic reading. If it did, then in a 2006 *Chronicle* survey of college professors, fully 41 percent wouldn't have labeled students "not well prepared" in reading (48 percent rated them "somewhat well prepared"). We would not find that the percentage of college graduates who reached "proficiency" literacy in 1992 was 40 percent, while in 2003 only 31 percent scored "proficient." We would see reading scores inching upward, instead of seeing, for instance, that the percentage of high-school students who reached proficiency dropped from 40 percent to 35 percent from 1992 to 2005.

And we wouldn't see even the better students struggling with "slow reading" tasks. In an "Introduction to Poetry" class awhile back, when I asked students to memorize 20 lines of verse and recite them to the others at the next meeting, a voice blurted, "Why?" The student wasn't being impudent or sullen. She just didn't see any purpose or value in the task. Canny and quick, she judged the plodding process of recording others' words a primitive exercise. Besides, if you can call up the verse any time with a click, why remember it? Last year when I required students in a literature survey course to obtain obituaries of famous writers without using the Internet, they stared in confusion. Checking a reference book, asking a librarian, and finding a microfiche didn't occur to them. So many free deliveries through the screen had sapped that initiative.

This is to say that advocates of e-learning in higher education pursue a risky policy, striving to unite liberal-arts learning with the very devices of acceleration that hinder it. Professors think they can help students adjust to using tools in a more sophisticated way than scattershot e-reading, but it's a lopsided battle. To repeat, college students have spent thousands of hours online acquiring faster and faster eyes and fingers before they even enter college, and they like the pace. It is unrealistic to expect 19-year-olds to perch before a screen and brake the headlong flight, even if it is the Declaration of Independence in hypertext coming through, not a buddy's message.

Some educators spot the momentum and shrug their shoulders, elevating screen scanning to equal status with slow reading. A notable instance occurred last year, when in an essay in *The New York Times*, Leah Price, a professor of English at Harvard University, criticized a report from the National Endowment for the Arts—"To Read or Not to Read" (to which I contributed)—precisely for downgrading digital scanning. Her article contained some errors of fact, such as that the 2004 NEA report "Reading at Risk" excluded nonfiction, but correctly singled out the NEA distinction between screen reading and print reading. To Price, it's a false one: "Bafflingly, the NEA's time-use charts classify 'e-mailing' and 'surfing Web sites' as competitors to reading, not subsets of it." Indeed, she said, to do so smacks of guile: "It takes some gerrymandering to make a generation logging ever more years in school, and ever more hours on the BlackBerry, look like nonreaders." (In truth, high-school students do no more in-class reading today than they did 20 years ago, according to a 2004 Department of Education report.)

Resisting a Lesser Kind of Reading

What we are seeing is a strange flattening of the act of reading. It equates handheld screens with *Madame Bovary*, as if they made the same cognitive demands and inculcated the same habits of attention. It casts peeking at a text message and plowing through *Middlemarch* as subsets of one general activity. And it treats those quick bursts of words and icons as fully sufficient to sustain the reading culture. The long book may go, Price concluded, but reading will carry on just as it did before: "The file, the list, the label, the memo: These are the genres that will keep reading alive."

The step not taken here is a crucial one, namely to determine the relative effects of reading different "genres." We need an approach that doesn't let teachers and professors so cavalierly violate their charge as stewards of literacy. We must recognize that screen scanning is but one kind of reading, a lesser one, and that it conspires against certain intellectual habits requisite to liberal-arts learning. The inclination to read a huge Victorian novel, the capacity to untangle a metaphor in a line of verse, the desire to study and emulate a distant historical figure, the urge to ponder a concept such as Heidegger's ontic-ontological difference over and over and around and around until it breaks through as a transformative insight—those dispositions melt away with every 100 hours of browsing, blogging, IMing, Twittering, and Facebooking. The shape and tempo of online texts differ so much from academic texts that e-learning initiatives in college classrooms can't bridge them. Screen reading is a mind-set, and we should accept its variance from academic thinking. Nielsen concisely outlines the difference: "I continue to believe in the linear, author-driven narrative for educational purposes. I just don't believe the Web is optimal for delivering this experience. Instead, let's praise old narrative forms like books and sitting around a flickering campfire—or its modern-day counterpart, the PowerPoint projector," he says. "We should accept that the Web is too fast-paced for big-picture learning. No problem; we have other media, and each has its strengths. At the same time, the Web is perfect for narrow, just-in-time learning of information nuggets—so long as the learner already has the conceptual framework in place to make sense of the facts."

So let's restrain the digitizing of all liberal-arts classrooms. More than that, given the tidal wave of technology in young people's lives, let's frame a number of classrooms and courses as slow-reading (and slow-writing) spaces. Digital technology has become an imperial force, and it should meet more antagonists. Educators must keep a portion of the undergraduate experience disconnected, unplugged, and logged off. Pencils, blackboards, and books are no longer the primary instruments of learning, true, but they still play a critical role in the formation of intelligence, as countermeasures to information-age mores. That is a new mission for educators parallel to the mad rush to digitize learning, one that may seem reactionary and retrograde, but in fact strives to keep students' minds open and literacy broad. Students need to decelerate, and they can't do it by themselves, especially if every inch of the campus is on the grid.

Close Reading Questions

1. Bauerlein cites Jakob Nielsen's studies of online literacy. In your own words, what exactly is the F-pattern of reading Web pages, and why does Nielsen state "F [is] for fast"?

2. According to several studies, what have been the short- and long-term results of computer technologies on student learning in middle and high schools? (Cultural Influences)

3. Bauerlein asserts that for teenagers, "the Web isn't a place for reading and study and knowledge." He believes that it instead is a site for social networking, such as by Facebook, and viewing entertainment, such as on YouTube. To what degree do your experiences and those of your friends match his assertions about adolescents' use of the Web?

Analytical Writing/Discussion

4. Bauerlein refers to the "flattening ... of reading," and he uses many other compelling phrases like "dicing language and ideas into bullets and graphics," "sapped that initiative," "violate their charge

as stewards of literacy," and "conspire against certain intellectual habits." Why do you think these phrases strengthen or weaken his argument for a reader still undecided on this topic?

5. Bauerlein distinguishes academic print literacy from leisurely digital reading. How does he then use this distinction to explain the failure of computer technologies to improve student learning in schools? Why do you find his explanation to be convincing or not?

6. Bauerlein relies heavily on Neilsen's research in order to insist that digital reading or "screen scanning is but one kind of reading, a lesser one." Neilsen, however, asserts that for various media, such as print and Web pages, "each has its strengths." As explained by Neilsen, what are the strengths of each one, and why do you believe (or not) that differences between print and digital literacies necessarily mean that one is "a lesser kind" than the other? (Multiple Perspectives)

Further Options

7. Neilsen reports that a book-like PDF file strikes many digital readers as a "content blob," and they have to print out this text in order to read it thoroughly. According to Powers (see pp. 315–316 in this chapter), what are some of the advantages of reading a difficult text in print? Why do you agree or disagree that these traits of paper promote better reading comprehension?

8. In this chapter, Kirschenbaum cautions that we should not define reading based on one particular historical model of reading (see pp. 321–323). He explains that the slow, linear comprehension of literary reading once was distrusted. How can you use this historical information to complicate the significant drop of college graduates that demonstrate proficient literacy (from 40% in 1992 to 31% in 2003)? (Historical Trends)

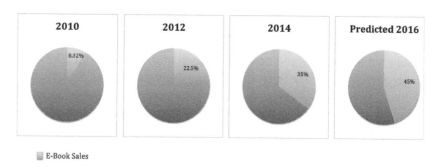

E-Book Sales

FIGURE 10.2   The Increasing Sales of e-Books

DON'T FEAR THE FUTURE … AGAIN

by Nick Bilton

Nick Bilton is a technology writer and blogger for the *New York Times;* he has been a key contributor to the paper's efforts to deliver the news online. The following excerpt comes from his book *I Live in the Future and Here's How it Works* (2011), and Bilton addresses the fears of those who doubt digital literacy. He relies on historical precedents and recent scientific

> investigations to counter some of the concerns of critics like
> Matthew Bauerlein and Nicholas Carr.

In the summer of 2008, Nicholas Carr, an author and writer for *The Atlantic* magazine, felt his brain slipping ever so slightly from its moorings. In the past, he wrote, "Immersing myself in a book or lengthy article used to be easy."

Not anymore. "Now my concentration often starts to drift after two or three pages. I get fidgety, lose the thread, begin looking for something else to do," he said. "I feel as if I'm always dragging my wayward brain back to the text."

The problem, he concluded, was the Internet generally and Google quite specifically. In a piece titled "Is Google Making Us Stupid?" and later in the book *The Shallows: What the Internet is Doing to Our Brains*, he frets that having snippets of massive amounts of information right at our fingertips may be eroding our ability to concentrate and contemplate.

Déjà vu all over again, don't you think?

In fairness, Carr recognizes that the printing press caused similar hand-wringing. And even though some of the predictions came true—the press actually did undermine religious authority, for instance— the many advantages of printing far outweighed the concerns. So he admits that he may be wrong and "a golden age of intellectual discovery and universal wisdom" may emerge from the text, tweets, bytes, and snacks of today's online world. But he still worries that deep thinking and serious reflection will be forever lost in the date stream of information the Web affords.

Although Carr is fatalistic about the future, his balanced, well-researched article offers a thoughtful perspective. Most of those who are skeptical about the shift aren't so reflective. In a *San Francisco Chronicle* article headlined "Attention Loss Feared as High-Tech Rewires Brain," the author, Benny Evangelista, citing some mental health experts, saw interpersonal relationships breaking down and attention deficit disorder increasing as more people found themselves unable to separate from email, Facebook, and Twitter.

How bad is the attention loss? The inability to detach oneself from electronic updates has spread from the office to the restaurant to the car—and now has reached into the bedroom. The story quotes a survey that found that 36 percent of people age thirty-five or younger used Facebook or Twitter after having sex. "Men," the story noted, "were twice as likely [as women] to tweet or post status updates after sex."

Said an executive who commissioned the survey: "It's the new cigarette."

Other news stories and books drip with angst over how new technologies may be destroying us, ruining our intellect, quashing our ability to converse face-to-face, and fundamentally changing relationships for both kids and adults. "Anti-social Networking?" a *New York Times* story asked, questioning whether time online diminishes intimacy and destroys the natural give-and-take of relationships. "Scientists warn of Twitter dangers," said CNN.com, stating that researches had found "social-networking tools such as Twitter could numb our sense of morality and make us indifferent to human suffering. A number of books, such as *The Dumbest Generation: How the Digital Age Stupefies Young Americans and Jeopardizes Our Future,* and the previously mentioned *Distracted: The Erosion of Attention and the Coming Dark Age*, add fuel to the fire.

But it doesn't stop there: There's a recent, oft-quoted study, "Emails 'Hurt IQ More than Pot.'" A survey of more than a thousand Britons found that the IQ of those trying to juggle messages and work fell ten points, more than double the drop seen after smoking pot.

Excerpt(s) from *I Live in the Future & Here's How It Works: Why Your World, Work, and Brain are Being Creatively Disrupted* by Nick Bilton, copyright © by Nick Bilton. Used by permission of Crown Business, an imprint of Crown Publishing Group, a division of Random House LLC. All rights reserved.

Over and over at speeches and conferences, I hear the same kinds of fears and anxieties that new technologies and developments have generated for decades: Our brains weren't wired for all this fast-paced stuff. We're too distracted to do meaningful and thorough work. At the same time, our entertainment is also dangerous and damaging, people tell me. Video games will destroy our children's brains and their relationships—if Twitter and Facebook don't do so first. We cannot effectively multitask or jump from email to writing to video, and we never will be able to.

There may be some truth to some of this; we may well be fundamentally different when this is all over. But for the most part, I believe it's bunk. Just as well-meaning scientists and consumers feared that trains and comic books and television would rot our brains and spoil our minds, I believe many of the skeptics and worrywarts today are missing the bigger picture, the greater value that access to new and faster information is bringing us. For the most past, our brains will adapt in a constructive way to this new online world, just as we formed communities to help us sort information.

Why do I believe this? Because we've learned how to do so many things already, including learning how to read.

Learning to Read

Some argue that our brains aren't designed to consume information on screens, or play video games, or consume real-time information. But the same argument holds true for the words you're reading now. It's true: Your brain wasn't built to read. Several thousand years ago, someone created symbols, which ultimately became an alphabet. That alphabet formed into a written language with its own set of unique rules. As a result, the organization of the human brain changed dramatically. But the human brain doesn't come automatically equipped with the ability to read these symbols. It's something that has to be rewired in the circuitry every time it happens. Our brains are designed to communicate and to tell stories with language. But reading letters and words is essentially man-made, just like video games and screens.

Even today, when children learn their letters and form them into words and sentences and big, powerful ideas, their brains still have to re-form and readapt to make the information fall into place.

Stanislas Dehaene, chair of Experimental Cognitive Neurology at the Collège de France, has spent most of his career in neuroscience exploring how our brains learn to read and calculate numbers. He explains that human brains are better wired to communicate by speaking. In the first year of life, babies begin to pick up words and sounds simply from hearing them. Sure, they need some help identifying that a cup is a cup and Mommy is Mommy. But by two years old, most children are talking and applying labels to objects without any special lessons or drills.

This is not the case with reading. Most children, even if they share books with their parents and hear stories every single day, won't pick up reading on their own. Instead, they must learn to recognize letters one by one and put them together into sounds or words before recognizing whole sentences and thoughts. They must learn to decode the symbols.

Some research suggests that in doing this, children and even adults actually develop a new area within the brain. Manuel Carreiras at the Basque Center on Cognition, Brain and Language has taken research on language into other complex areas. Carreiras's work over the years has been focused on the neural processes of human language and the way humans comprehend differently when reading and when interpreting sign language. When he wanted a better understanding of how people learn to read, he decided he needed to find illiterate adults to see how their brains adapt before and after learning how to read words.

At first, Carreiras had trouble finding a group of adults who really didn't have any reading skill, but finally, he recruited forty-two veterans of the Colombian guerrilla wars. Twenty of the ex-fights had recently completed a Spanish literacy training program to teach them to read. The other ex-fighters still needed to take the course and were for the most part illiterate. The former fighters were tested, taught to read, and then tested again. In the process, areas of the brain actually grew and formed connections that had not existed earlier. The brain had rewired itself while the guerrillas learned how to read.

Carreiras found that the brain changes its structure when someone properly learns to read, particularly in the white matter, which creates connections and helps information move between different areas of the brain. He explained, "We found that the literate members of our group have more white matter in the splenium ... a structure that connects the brain's left and right hemispheres—than did the illiterate members." As the former guerrillas learned to read, the scientists used imaging techniques to measure what was happening. They saw that reading triggered brain functions in the same areas that had grown over the course of the study. In other words, even adults were able to create new neural pathways as they learned a difficult new skill.

The Brain's Adaptability

What's significant in this example is that our brains are something like a muscle, which can grow stronger and more powerful with practice and work. Today, technology is building new connections as our brains interpret content and receive stimulation. There's a constant and simplistic iterative adaptation taking place in our brains as we use our computers, mobile phones, and e-readers. Our brains are learning how to navigate these gadgets, just as they do when we learn how to read.

There's one piece of this puzzle that's important to point out. With the use of computers and digital technologies, our brains are not evolving. Human beings evolve at much slower pace than do new communication mechanisms and the technologies we invent and create. Neuroscientists I spoke with explained that a brain from five hundred years ago or even ten thousand years ago would look pretty much the way it does today, just as humans look pretty much the way they did a few thousand years ago.

To illustrate this point, let's hypothetically travel back two thousand years and find a newborn baby. Imagine taking that baby and transporting him through our time machine forward to today. This child would be raised in our technology-rich society, growing up in a world of iPods, video games, the Internet, mobile phones, GPS, robotic Elmo toys, banner ads, and more. I asked several neuroscientists if this baby born two thousand years ago, would likely grow up differently than a child born today. The resounding answer was "no." A newborn's brain from two thousand years ago, I was told, would likely look and work exactly like the same as a brain does today.

But if you took an adult—let's say a thirty-year-old man from two thousand years ago—and dropped him in the middle of Times Square. He might well experience a panic attack from all the crowds, cars, flashing lights, and stimulation. But, neuroscientists said, his brain would begin to adapt. He might never get to a point where he could talk and simultaneously send text messages, but numerous research studies show that our brains are capable of substantial adaptation in about two weeks and in some instances seven days. Our two-thousand-year-old man would be just fine. His adaptation to society and the new stimuli would just take brain training, and not as much as you might think.

What Research Studies Show

How do our magnificent minds adapt? In 2008, a group of neuroscience researchers from UCLA's Semel Institute studied the brain activity of twenty-four volunteers when the subjects were reading a book or surfing the Web to see if the Web was rewiring the way our brains function.

The volunteers were divided on the basis of how much experiences they had using computers and the Internet. Twelve of the participants were labeled "Net Naive" because they used the Internet or computers once a month at most. Asked to rate their tech savvy, they gave themselves a rating of minimal to none. The other twelve participants were labeled "Net Savvy." Those in this group used a computer at least once a day, and most of them were online numerous times throughout the day. The members of this group considered themselves moderate to expert on computers and the Internet.

The researchers showed volunteers different types of content while monitoring them using functional magnetic resonance imaging (fMRI) scanners, special machines that allow the research subjects to watch screens or perform certain tasks while the scanner records the blood flow in their brains and how the brain handles its processing.

First, volunteers were shown a table of contents from a book and given fifteen seconds to pick the chapter they wanted to read. Then they had just under thirty seconds to read a page of the book. Next, the same participants were shown a search page from Google and asked to decide on a search and enter a word in the search box within fifteen seconds. The display took them to a website that corresponded with their search, and they were asked to read the page for an additional thirty seconds. To make sure they were paying attention, the participants were told they would be tested on their reading of both the print and digital versions.

When reading the printed page, the Net Naïve and Net Savvy brains reacted the same way. Those brains were slightly stimulated, although there was a little less activity in the brains of the Net Savvy while reading the printed text. But during the online searching and reading tests, the Net Savvy brains were much more active. In fact, the Net Savvy group showed almost twice as much activity while online compared with reading a book. The reading task stimulated parts of their brain used for language and reading, memory, and visual abilities. In comparison, the Web surfing task activated the same areas of the brain as reading, but in addition, the brain was involved in decision-making, complex reasoning, and vision detection.

Even more interesting, the volunteers weren't a bunch of young kids with malleable brains. Rather, the group consisted of people between fifty-five and seventy-six years old, all of them digital immigrants with varying degrees of success in adapting to the online world. The Internet wasn't even around in a meaningful way until they were in their late thirties or early forties to mid-fifties, yet the brains of the Net Savvy rewired and sprang into action to work with this new stimulation.

What was happening with those brains is a process called neuroplasticity, a theory that our brains' 100 billion neurons, or nerve cells, can re-form, or create new cells and new connections, as we learn and grow.

Many new activities we engage in on a daily basis can make this happen, from touching something hot for the first time to using the Internet or even juggling, as Bogdan Draganski and a group of scientists from the department of neurology at the University of Regensburg, Germany, discovered.

Draganski, with previous brain research as a foundation, developed a hypothesis that our brains must act differently when they learn something new. After watching a group of kids text messaging on their mobile phones at dramatic speeds, he wondered if sending hundreds of messages made the thumbs work differently. He theorized that the brain correlations that operate these functions should look differently from what they look like in people who rarely text.

To explore this theory further, Draganski told me in a phone interview, he got permission to scan the brains of a small group of young people. The initial results showed that the heavy texters had a large area of mass in the portion of the brain that controls the right hand, but that other areas were similar to the normal brains he had studied earlier. Draganski believed that this larger area most likely signified heightened use of the right hand used for texting. His original goal was to understand if brain growth would become more obvious over time as more kids learned to text. But, he said in an interview, with so many people already familiar with texting, he decided to switch to a different task that involved a clear and steep learning curve: juggling.

Draganski and his researchers took a group of participants who had never juggled before and measured the gray matter, the neurons, in each of their brains as they gradually learned to juggle with three and then four balls. As Draganski predicted, he saw significant areas of growth in gray matter in certain areas. The motor areas of the brain actually grew over a three-month period of learning. When the participants stopped juggling, however, their gray matter began to recede and return to its previous size and shape.

Another group of researchers in a different study found that when a completely new task is learned, changes in brain shape are visible after a mere seven days of practice.

When these theories were tested in a later study by the UCLA researchers in late 2009, it was found that Net Naïve Web surfers could catch up to the Net Savvy. When the Net Naïve repeatedly used the Internet over a one-week period, the brain scans showed that they, too, started to adapt and respond to the online experience in a very similar fashion to the Net Savvy. Their brains also began to show twice as much stimulation from reading a Web page as from reading a printed page.

Gary Small, director of UCLA's Semel Institute for Neuroscience & Human Behavior and one of the nation's leading experts on memory and aging, was one of the key researchers in this study. He said the brains were learning, benefiting from practice and experience. In theory, Small said, as we learn, the brain should show less activity. For example, when we get a new phone, it takes a while to figure out where all the functions are hidden. "At first I'll show a lot of activity in my brain," he said, but then, once he gets used to the experience and better at navigating the device, the activity should slow down. At that point, he said, the brain's "synapses … will grow, become strengthened, and then become efficient," and less activity should be required.

But that isn't what happened when he watched people become experienced digital surfers. Instead, his research found, our brains work completely differently while reading online than while reading a printed page, making numerous decisions based on the many options, menus, photos, text, and links on each page. In fact, the first study concluded, "Internet searching appears much more stimulating than reading."

Close Reading Questions

1. According to Bilton, what are some of the fears about digital literacy? What concerns do you think are most or least valid? (Cultural Influences)

2. Why does Bilton believe our brains are not designed to learn how to read?

3. What does Bilton state would happen if a newborn or an adult from 2000 years ago somehow were to be transported to Times Square in New York City? What is the significance of these hypothetical examples? (Historical Trends)

Analytical Writing/Discussion

4. Why do you think Bilton mentions Carr's concern in particular and then adds many other examples? Is he trying to commend and/or dismiss Carr's viewpoint?

5. How does Bilton use learning to talk versus learning to read to create a new perspective on reading? Why do you find this perspective on reading the printed page to be compelling or not? (Multiple Perspectives)

6. Which of the studies cited on brain adaptation do you find to be most or least persuasive and why?

Further Options

7. Synthesis, meaning the making of connections between two (or more) readings, is central to academic writing. Select a quotation from Bilton and another by a critic like Bauerlein. Then present each quotation using a signal phrase (as explained in Chapter 4 on pp. 81–82) and elaborate on each writer's perspective. How exactly do you think these writers disagree?

8. As defined by Aristotle, rhetoric is "the discovery of the available means of persuasion" (see p. 104 of Chapter 5). Both Bilton and Powers refer to fears of whatever technology is considered to be "new," such as the Internet or paper. How does each writer use these fears to support of his perspective? Which author's argument do you find to be more persuasive and why?

Freewrite 3

See Figure 10.2 on p. 329, then freewrite to answer some of the following questions:

- What first strikes you about these visuals?
- When you consider the progression of these visuals, what do you think is shown?
- What information do you think those who defend digital literacy, like Kirchenbaum, and those who oppose it, Bauerlein, would emphasize from these charts?

Final Assignment 1: Evidence of a Problem and Its Implications

As explained in Chapter 5, an argument is supported by evidence, and this evidence can come in many forms. A crucial first step of seeking a solution is to provide compelling evidence of a problem.

Essay Question

The authors of this chapter's readings offer various kinds of evidence ranging from personal experiences and observations to historical analysis and research studies. What do you think is some of the most persuasive evidence of a literacy problem in this chapter? Then, what do you think is the best response to this problem: a retreat from digital texts, a rush to adopt them, the appropriate use of both print and digital texts, or some other option? Why?

Write a formal and extended essay to answer these questions. Be sure to include specific references and direct quotations from several readings in this chapter (see Chapter 4 on Academic Honesty on quoting and citing properly). Be sure to not only support your informed perspective but also anticipate and answer the possible objections of those who do not already agree with you. Your task is to assert your opinion and persuade others to consider it carefully.

Freewrite 4

Before you start to answer this complex question, analyze its parts. Reread the questions above and underline several phrases that represent key parts of the larger answer you will be developing. Then pick two or three of these phrases and freewrite your immediate impressions: What do you think right now? Then, pause to look for connections, contradictions, and omissions within your first response: What else do you want to discuss, what else do you want to add, and/or what order of your ideas is developing? Finally, consider the audience of your essay: Who does not agree with you already, and why might they disagree?

Reading Review

Once you have sketched some of your initial ideas, review some of the readings to find specific details and persuasive evidence to support, enrich, and possibly complicate your response. Here are some readings and post-reading questions that you may want to consider:

1. Birkerts, Close Reading Question 1
2. Baron, Analytical Writing Question 6
3. Powers, Analytical Writing Question 5
4. Kirschenbaum, Close Reading Question 2
5. Kirschenbaum, Further Options Question 7
6. Bauerlein, Close Reading Question 2
7. Bauerlein, Close Reading Question 3
8. Bilton, Further Options Question 8

Feel free to include other readings and post-reading questions. You also may want to review the suggestions for writing persuasively in Chapter 5 on Argument as well as practice the peer response described in Chapter 2 on the Writing Process.

Final Assignment 2: Rhetorical Analysis

For two readings of this chapter (or possibly using one of the additional readings suggested below), compare and/or contrast their arguments. As explained in Chapter 5, this rhetorical analysis will answer the following questions:

- Based on the rhetorical triangle, what is the message of this text? What does the publication source suggest about the audience of this text? How do you think these readers will react to this message and why? Finally, who is the writer, and how might the author affect the audience's response to the text? (See pp. 104–105 of Chapter 5.)

- How does the writer try to use each of the three rhetorical appeals: ethos, logos, and pathos, and when are they used effectively or not? (See pp. 105–109 of Chapter 5.)

- Your professor may ask you to consider also the kind of argument being made, meaning a forensic, epideictic, or deliberative argument (see pp. 110–112 of Chapter 5). What kind of argument is being made, and how does it affect the audience's reaction to this persuasion?

- Finally, through comparing and contrasting the arguments of these two readings, what can you conclude about their power to persuade their intended audiences (and possibly additional readers)?

Your task is to help your readers to understand these two arguments and their efforts to persuade their audiences.

Final Assignment 3: Using the Best of Both

Sven Birkerts was one of the first critics to warn that reading is being "changed by powerful forces. We are living in the midst of a momentous paradigm shift." Kirschenbaum too acknowledges that reading is being "reimagined and re-engineered," but he also asserts that various kinds of reading "have coexisted for centuries." He believes that readers are not facing some "momentous … shift," instead they can continue to enjoy the best of print and digital literacies.

Essay Question

Instead of framing this issue as an either/or choice, the debate over print and digital literacy can be considered a strategic alternation: Sometimes, it is more appropriate to rely on print literacy, and at others, it is better to use digital texts. What do you think are the best uses of print and digital texts? Why do you think it is better to use each literacy in certain circumstances?

Write a formal and extended essay to answer this question. Be sure to include specific references and direct quotations from several readings in this chapter (see Chapter 4 on Academic Honesty on quoting and citing properly). Be sure to not only support your informed perspective but also anticipate and answer the possible objections of those who do not already agree with you. Your task is to assert your opinion and persuade others to consider it carefully.

Freewrite 5

Before you start to answer this complex question, analyze its parts. Reread the question above and underline several phrases that represent key parts of the larger answer you will be developing. Then pick two or three of these phrases and freewrite your immediate impressions: What do you think right now? Then, pause to look for connections, contradictions, and omissions within your first response: What else do you want to discuss, what else do you want to add, and/or what order of your ideas is developing? Finally, consider the audience of your essay: Who does not agree with you already, and why might they disagree?

Reading Review

Once you have sketched some of your initial ideas, review some of the readings to find specific details and persuasive evidence to support, enrich, and possibly complicate your response. Here are some readings and post-reading questions that you may want to consider:

1. Freewrite 1
2. Birkerts, Analytical Writing Question 4
3. Baron, Close Reading Question 2
4. Powers, Analytical Writing Question 6
5. Kirschenbaum, Analytical Writing Question 6
6. Bauerlein, Analytical Writing Question 6
7. Bilton, Close Reading Question 1
8. Bilton, Analytical Writing Question 6

Feel free to include other readings and post-reading questions. You also may want to review the suggestions for writing persuasively in Chapter 5 on Argument as well as practice the peer response described in Chapter 2 on the Writing Process.

Readings on Technology in Other Chapters

For three additional readings on education, you may want to read the following texts:

1. "Young and Unplugged" by Bella English in Chapter 1 (see pp. 6–8)
2. "Hamlet's Blackberry" by William Powers in Chapter 1 (see pp. 14–15)

Additional Sources for Chapter 10

To deepen your understanding of print as well as digital literacy and strengthen your final assignment for chapter fourteen, you can consult some of the following sources:

1. When Nicholas Carr published "Is Google Making Us Stupid?" in 2008, he renewed interest in the debate that Sven Birkerts helped to start with his 1994 book titled *The Gutenberg Elegies: The Fate of Reading in an Electronic Age*. You may want to read this controversial essay in which Carr uses personal anecdotes, pop culture references, and scientific studies to question the effects of online technologies.

   http://www.theatlantic.com/magazine/archive/2008/07/is-google-making-us-stupid/306868/

2. For a further critique of reading texts on a screen, you may want to read "Resisting the Kindle," which is another argument by Sven Birkerts. Published in 2009 after *The Gutenberg Elegies*, this essay continues the author's opposition to digital texts.

   http://www.theatlantic.com/magazine/archive/2009/03/resisting-the-kindle/307345/

3. For another argument by Nick Bilton in favor of reading and writing online, you may want to read "Fare Thee Well, My Pen: The Demise of the Pen." In this essay, Bilton examines the trend of writing on screens and the debate over whether taking notes with pen and paper is better than with a digital device.

   http://www.nytimes.com/2014/07/24/fashion/the-demise-of-the-pen.html?_r=0

4. For a provocative essay on print magazines and their future, you may want to read "The Future of Reading" *by* Josh Quittner. This reading ends with questions answered by several experts on digital literacy, such as Marc Andresson of the Web 2.0 and Kevin Kelly of *Wired* magazine.

   http://archive.fortune.com/2010/02/09/technology/tablet_ebooks_media.fortune/index.htm

5. For an argument that refuses to privilege one form of reading or another, you may want to read "*Publishing Magazines For An 'Ambidextrous' Generation*" by the National Public Radio staff. This report explains how print- and online-versions of a magazine both can appeal to readers today.

   http://www.npr.org/2013/11/16/245638811/publishing-magazines-for-an-ambidextrous-generation

6. For an update on concerns about the negative effects of digital sources on our reading habits, you may want to read this essay by Michael Agresta. It originally appeared in *The Texas Observer* (Oct. 2014) and was republished in *The Utne Reader* (spring 2015).

   http://www.utne.com/sicence-and-technology/negative-effects-of-online-reading-zm0z15szsau.aspx

7. For an update on William Powers' analysis of the persistent use of paper, you may want to read or hear two National Public Radio reports. The first, by Eric Weiner from May 26, 2015, presents contradictory evidence on the much-anticipated demise of paper. The second, from May 25, 2015, asserts that taking notes on paper is still more effective method of learning for most students.

   http://www.npr.org/2015/05/26/408794149/dont-write-off-paper-just-yet

   http://www.npr.org/2015/05/27/408794237/in-a-digital-chapter-paper-notebooks-are-as-relevant-as-ever

8. For an argument for reading deeply both in print and online, you may want to read "The Importance of Deep Reading" by Maryanne Wolf and Mirit Barzillai. Rather than pit print against digital texts, these authors seek the best of both.

   https://www.mbaea.org/documents/resources/Educational_Leadership_Article_The__D87FE2BC4E7AD.pdf

INDEX